"How I wish I could have read this book forty-five years ago. Phil Newton offers p[...] [...]p pastors young and old. It will be a special encouragement to pastors just starting out in the ministry. These forty questions cover the full range of questions pastors face. Dr. Newton offers tested wisdom that is both biblical and practical. I hope you will buy two copies—one to read and one to give to a young pastor. Outstanding!"

—Dr. Ray Pritchard
President, Keep Believing Ministries

"Imagine being able to sit down and talk to a friend who has faithfully pastored for over forty years, and in a series of sessions, you have the chance to hear him share from Scripture and personal experience what he has learned along the way. Phil Newton is a friend and a mentor in ministry, so I can hear his voice as I read these pages. In this book, Phil comes alongside pastors to talk about everything from navigating your first year, to handling opposition, to tending your own soul, to planning a sermon series, to evaluating when it may be time to leave a church. I trust this resource will be a means of great encouragement to fellow pastors!"

—Matt Mason
Senior Pastor, The Church at Brookhills, Birmingham, AL

"With more than forty years of experience, Phil Newton is well prepared by God to pose and answer these forty questions. Each answer is biblically grounded and theologically framed, rich in examples of those who pastored before us and flowing out of his own extensive and even painful experiences. Perhaps most important, he reminds us that 'love is a mark of pastoral ministry'—something none of us can afford to forget as we serve the bride of Christ. Throughout his book, Newton reveals that he is always aware of the hope of the church—Jesus Christ; and the mission of the church—making disciples. Very much worth reading and keeping as a resource near at hand."

—Richard A. Shenk, Ph.D.
Director, Non-Traditional Degree Programs, Assistant Professor of Theology
Bethlehem College & Seminary

"You hold in your hands one of the most important books on the practicality of pastoral ministry I have ever read. Additionally, I don't know of a better, wiser, more experienced pastor to write a book as this than Phil Newton. He has lived the content of this book for four decades of faithful ministry and has become a model to others pastors in the process. *40 Questions About Pastoral Ministry* is easily accessible, thoroughly biblical, and immensely practical. It needs to be read and re-read by every new pastor as well as the most seasoned pastor who needs a clear and compelling reminder of God's call, plan, and design for his undershepherds. I heartily commend this book and the man who wrote it."

—Brian Croft
Senior Pastor, Auburndale Baptist Church
Founder, Practical Shepherding
Senior Fellow, Church Revitalization Center, SBTS

"Combining rich insights from years of pastoral experience with a theologically-shaped and biblically-informed approach to ministry, Phil Newton has provided readers with a welcomed addition to Kregel's 40 Questions series. Ministers need not agree with Newton's theological and ecclesiological convictions to profit from reading this thoughtful and applicable handbook on pastoral ministry. *40 Questions About Pastoral Ministry* will serve as a valuable resource and helpful guide for pastors at various stages of their ministries. I am delighted to recommend this fine work."

—David S. Dockery
President, International Alliance for Christian Education
Distinguished Professor of Theology, Southwestern Seminary

"Whether one is an experienced pastor or one just starting in ministry, having a ministry coach is extremely helpful—someone to whom we might ask questions, gain insight, and find a way forward in tricky ministry situations. In picking up *40 Questions About Pastoral Ministry*, you have the voice of an experienced pastor-coach: someone who has followed Jesus in the midst of the challenges of ministry and someone who offers wise counsel to the most common questions we might have. Phil Newton has produced a goldmine of pastoral wisdom that should be a go-to book for pastors in every stage of ministry. I know that I will be pulling it off my shelf time and again to hear from my ministry coach!"

—Dr. Sean Michael Lucas
Senior Pastor, Independent Presbyterian Church (PCA), Memphis, TN
Chancellor's Professor of Church History, Reformed Theological Seminary

"It's one thing for Christian leaders to be admired from afar. It's another thing for one's fellow elders and a host of pastors of other congregations in one's own city to regard a man as a living example of what a biblically faithful pastor is supposed to look like. By God's grace, Dr. Phil Newton is such a man. In *40 Questions About Pastoral Ministry* you will read with great profit what I and many other pastors have experienced first-hand from Phil's life and ministry. This brother is a pastoral ninja.

"Over the past 20 years Phil and I have become dear friends. When I spend time with him, I walk away knowing he loves Jesus, loves me, and loves local churches. In this volume he imparts to fellow pastors not only the gospel of God but also his own life as well (1 Thess. 2:8).

"Pastors, *for Christ's sake* I double-dog-dare-you to prayerfully digest this abundantly wise counsel from a seasoned soul-physician whose eyes, for decades, have been fixed on the Wonderful Counselor."

—Jordan Thomas
Pastor, Grace Church, Memphis

"Since I began in pastoral ministry, Phil Newton has generously shared his extensive wisdom with me and encouraged me along the way. With *40 Questions About Pastoral Ministry*, I rejoice that his biblical knowledge and wisdom is now readily available to many others. This book is a treasure trove of doctrinally sound wisdom and insight formed as the result of Phil's careful study and faithfulness through the challenges and joys over the long haul of pastoral ministry. If you are a pastor, desire to be a pastor, or simply want to better understand what the Scriptures teach about this biblical office, read this book. And, when you finish, keep it handy as you will want to come back to the wisdom in this book for years to come."

—Josh Manley
Senior Pastor, RAK Evangelical Church, Ras al Khaimah, United Arab Emirates

"Pastoring seems to be getting harder not easier. Consequently, it's a necessity now more than ever for pastors to have more experienced collogues in ministry they can turn to with questions. Phil Newton, a humble, experienced pastor with a long-term ministry in one church, has written *40 Questions About Pastoral Ministry* to help answer some of those questions. Whether you're a young or old pastor, a new or experienced pastor, or alone or one of many pastors, you will benefit from hearing Phil answer your questions. So, pick up this book, and let Pastor Newton encourage you."

—Juan R. Sanchez
Senior Pastor, High Pointe Baptist Church, Austin, TX
Author of *The Leadership Formula: Develop the Next Generation of Leaders in the Church*

"Pastors are called by God to serve the people of God. Pastors are formed into faithful and effective servants that God desires them to be through the process of understanding the very responsibilities that their calling assigns to them. Crucial to their development is being mentored by a seasoned pastor who joyfully accepts his assignment. Phil Newton uses his pen in this volume to mentor pastors as he raises forty essential questions about pastoral ministry and seeks to answer them biblically, theologically, and practically. His wise and winsome answers have been formed from more thirty-five years of serving as a pastor. I have admired his ministry for more than twenty years. Phil does not just know how to be a shepherd; he walks with the Chief Shepherd. I can't think of a better person to mentor those who are called to pastoral ministry whether they are early in their development or have been serving as a pastor for years. They all will benefit from *40 Questions About Pastoral Ministry*."

—Keith Whitfield
Provost Southeastern Baptist Theological Seminary and
Associate Professor of Theology, Wake Forest, NC

"There is something for pastors at every stage of ministry in this book. For the future pastor, there is a roadmap to show him what lies ahead. For the young pastor, there's wisdom to help when the curves grow hard to navigate. For the veteran pastor, there's help to know which road to take next. This will be required reading for all my pastoral interns from now on. My longtime friend Phil Newton is a trusted voice who knows every pothole in pastoral ministry because he's had to drive through every single one on the way to decades of faithful local church leadership."

—Jeff Robinson
Lead Pastor, Christ Fellowship Baptist Church, Louisville, KY

"As I began to read Phil Newton's book, *40 Questions About Pastoral Ministry*, I put my highlighter down. I gazed at the fluorescent yellow manuscript pages on the desk before me and came to the realization that highlighting everything is highlighting nothing. However, when I read this book, I also quickly became aware that it was penned with a quill dipped in the author's own blood. It was authored from wisdom of four decades of faithful pastoral ministry and walking intimately with Christ. Like a typical Phil Newton expository sermon, every word in this book matters. You cannot compose a work like *40 Questions About Pastoral Ministry* as the byproduct of a research project. Writing this particular memoir and manual of biblical shepherding, takes a lifetime. In these pages, Phil keenly unfolds what Scripture teaches regarding ministry, including the foundational considerations of the pastorate, pastoral development and health, and pastoral practices. Each of these categories is fleshed out by biblical, historical, and personal examples that demonstrate the timeless biblical and theological principles outlined. Very few resources of this sort strike the right balance of grace and truth, and of admonition and encouragement. While maintaining the high bar that Scripture gives for pastoral ministry, Phil likewise expresses God's promises of grace and provision for those whom he calls.

"In the mold of such classics as Richard Baxter's *Reformed Pastor* and C. H. Spurgeon's *Lectures to My Students*, many generations have someone to assume the responsibility for writing a timeless, biblical pastoral manifesto. I praise the Lord that Phil Newton is among those who have assumed this burden for our generation and the generations to come, if the Lord tarries. Fellow pastors, do not just skim through this book. Live with it and allow it to guide you to depend more deeply on the perfect Chief Shepherd, who needs no manual of instruction."

—Brad Walker, Senior Pastor
First Baptist Church of Sparta, TN

40 QUESTIONS ABOUT
Pastoral Ministry

Phil A. Newton

Benjamin L. Merkle, Series Editor

40 QUESTIONS SERIES

40 Questions About Angels, Demons, and Spiritual Warfare
John R. Gilhooly

40 Questions About Baptism and the Lord's Supper
John S. Hammett

40 Questions About Biblical Theology
Jason S. DeRouchie, Oren R. Martin, and Andrew David Naselli

40 Questions About Calvinism
Shawn D. Wright

40 Questions About Christians and Biblical Law
Thomas R. Schreiner

40 Questions About Church Membership and Discipline
Jeremy M. Kimble

40 Questions About Creation and Evolution
Kenneth D. Keathley and Mark F. Rooker

40 Questions About Elders and Deacons
Benjamin L. Merkle

40 Questions About Heaven and Hell
Alan W. Gomes

40 Questions About Interpreting the Bible
Robert L. Plummer

40 Questions About Islam
Matthew Aaron Bennett

40 Questions About Pastoral Ministry
Phil A. Newton

40 Questions About Salvation
Matthew Barrett

40 Questions About the End Times
Eckhard Schnabel

40 Questions About the Great Commission
Daniel L. Akin, Benjamin L. Merkle, and George G. Robinson

40 Questions About the Historical Jesus
C. Marvin Pate

40 Questions About Typology and Allegory
Mitchell L. Chase

40 Questions About Pastoral Ministry
© 2021 Phil A. Newton

Published by Kregel Academic, an imprint of Kregel Publications, 2450 Oak Industrial Dr. NE, Grand Rapids, MI 49505-6020.

This book is a title in the 40 Questions Series edited by Benjamin L. Merkle.

All Scripture quotations, unless otherwise indicated, are taken from the New American Standard Bible® (NASB), Copyright © 1960, 1962, 1963, 1968, 1971, 1972, 1973, 1975, 1977, 1995 by The Lockman Foundation. Used by permission. www.Lockman.org.

The Greek font, GraecaU, is available from www.linguistsoftware.com/lgku.htm, +1-425-775-1130.

ISBN 978-0-8254-4656-6

Printed in the United States of America

21 22 23 24 25 / 5 4 3 2 1

To
Kelly
Andrew
John
Lizzy
Stephen
"Behold, children are a gift of the Lord."

Contents

Part 5: The Church and Pastoral Ministry

Foreword

by Matt McCullough

When I was a college student, just an eighteen-year-old kid with little knowledge and even less experience, Phil Newton and the members of South Woods Baptist Church opened their lives to me. It's not overstating things to say that those two summers changed my life. As an intern I got backstage access to the workings of a healthy local church. And I got a long look at the life and ministry of a faithful pastor who loves his people, who loves God's Word, and whose joy in life is bridging the two, in public and in private.

I did a lot of watching over those two summers. I got some practice, too, muddling my way through a few of my first sermons. Along the way I asked lots of questions. Lots and lots of questions. The answers Phil gave then continue to shape my ministry today. And what I love about this book is that it gives you the same chance that I had to learn from this faithful brother. Reading this book felt a bit like a walk back in time.

There are many reasons this book will be a helpful addition to your pastoral library. Like the other titles in the 40 Questions series, this book is a tool to be used. The structure and format make the content accessible quickly and easily. The questions themselves are well chosen and well framed. They're real questions, in other words, that sooner or later will resonate with what you're going through. And the answers are consistently helpful and concise.

But the main reason I believe this book will be useful to you is that in it you get to learn ministry from Phil Newton. You'll find here the same three things I appreciated most from my time as his intern and that I've appreciated in his friendship ever since.

First, you'll find a tremendous pastoral bibliography. Phil has spent his career poring over the riches of the Reformed pastoral tradition. In these answers you'll see what he's found. And I think you'll grow to love these teachers as he does.

Second, you'll find careful study of what the Bible says about pastoral ministry. Phil knows better than to stand on his own wisdom. Our only hope for fruitfulness in the work God has given us depends on following the guidance God has given us in his Word. In every answer to every question you'll find Phil taking you back to the Scriptures. And along the way this book will help you build a robust biblical theology of ministry.

Finally, you'll find the benefit of a lifetime of pastoral experience. I've said Phil stands on God's Word, not his own wisdom, but there's plenty of hard-earned wisdom in these pages too. For four decades he has tested the advice of all those pastoral books. For four decades he has trusted the guidance of God's Word. And he's done it all in the daily and weekly rhythms—dare I say grind?—of a pastoral ministry just like yours and mine. You will be able to tell. Phil is a guide who has been there.

So, whether you're a young pastor needing an ally, or a pastor looking for resources to help you train others, this is a book you can use. I certainly will.

Introduction

Most of my life has been spent in pastoring four churches from 1978 to the present. All were very different. Each needed faithful pastoral ministry. Sometimes I had no idea how to handle opposition, reform worship, preach pastorally, develop leaders, face discouragement, or change polity, among dozens of other matters. Seasoned pastors often came to my aid in answering questions (I had more than forty!). Other times, a good pastoral biography brought light—for example, Edwards, Spurgeon, Lloyd-Jones. On still other occasions, God's Word and prayer led me from quandary to settled joy. Throughout, I've sensed God's faithfulness and my weakness while learning what it means to shepherd the flock.

For years, I've been fielding questions from pastors about a variety of issues faced in life and ministry. Just as with this book, a combination of biblical exegesis, pastoral theology, and experience formed my responses. Pastoral ministry has its foundation in God's Word, works out in theological reflection, and is applied in the contextual experience of pastor and congregation. Consequently, to probe pastoral ministry, this book works through Scripture, considers theological implications, and illustrates from personal experience. Forty questions cannot exhaust pastoral work, of course, but they do provide a framework for issues facing pastors.

The book's five sections give readers a means to narrow answers about pastoral ministry. First, *foundational considerations* look at what it means to be a pastor, with attention to the character and necessary qualities for spiritual work. Second, *pastoral development and health* keep the long view in mind, steering pastors to ways that give attention to personal walk, marriage, family, relationships, and practices for endurance. Third, *pastoral practices* identify how a pastor should *pastor* the flock, handle opposition, and train leaders. Fourth, *pastoral preaching*, as the heart of pastoral ministry, centers corporate gatherings in the gospel. Fifth, *the church and pastoral ministry* starts with the nature of the church then moves to developing healthy church practices. Each question helps pastors navigate the challenges of ministry.

In my study of passages referring to and alluding to pastoral ministry, I'm convinced the pastoral office is given to men by the Lord of the church. While certainly not excluding areas of ministry for the many faithful, godly women who serve in myriad ways in the church, my conviction in this volume focuses on men holding pastoral responsibility. I'm grateful for many women who have served Christ in multiple ways in churches I've been part of. Their influence and insights in my pastoral labors is a special gift of God to me, and the other pastors serving with me.

I wrote most of this book during medical leave, as I required isolation for chemotherapy. In many ways, it served as a balm for my mental and spiritual life while my body got pounded. I'm grateful for the congregation and elders at South Woods Baptist Church in Memphis for their love and support throughout my ministry, but especially during these more challenging days. They've modeled care for their pastor.

As I finished each question, I passed it along to Matt Sliger, Chris Spano, Raymond Johnson, and Tom Tollett, who graciously read through rough drafts, offering corrections, making suggestions, and prodding me forward. While the remaining deficiencies are mine, their investment and pastoral insight improved what you will read. Thank you, brothers! Several local pastors initiated opportunities to field-test much of the book's material, including Jordan Thomas, Jeremy Wright, Ben Williams, and Nathan Sawyer. My deep thanks go to Matt Gentry and Joey Newton for help with editing. Debbie Jones assisted in countless ways. Through lots of discussion, my fellow elders and pastoral interns honed many of the ideas presented.

I've long appreciated Ben Merkle's scholarship and writing contributions for the church. I'm grateful to work with him as the 40 Questions series editor. This book represents my fourth time working with Kregel Publications. Dennis Hillman got things rolling with this book, then retired and passed it into the very capable hands of Laura Bartlett. Robert Hand and Bethany Murphy added their eyes toward editorial improvements. I'm thankful for their professionalism, dependable communication, and friendship.

Karen, my wife, has listened to my musings on various questions, encouraged me when I felt too fatigued to write, and supported me throughout this book. I would not have gotten far in pastoral ministry without her constant love and faithful endurance.

As with Karen, my children have lived the contents of this book with me. They've journeyed in pastoral ministry's ups and downs, joys and sorrows, triumphs and losses from the vantage point of pastor's kids. Throughout, they've continued to love and encourage me. During this hard season of life, they've been a ballast to keep me from sinking. Thanks Kelly, Andrew, John, Lizzy, and Stephen! I hope the journey has left wonderful memories and a faithful example to follow Christ in all things. This book is dedicated to you.

Abbreviations

ANF	Alexander Roberts, James Donaldson, eds. *Ante-Nicene Fathers: The Apostolic Fathers with Justin Martyr and Irenaeus*. American Edition. A. Cleveland Coxe, editor. Peabody, MA: Hendrickson Publishers, 2004 from 1885 original.
BECNT	Baker Exegetical Commentary on the New Testament
BDAG	Frederick W. Danker. *A Greek-English Lexicon of the New Testament and Other Early Christian Literature*. 3rd ed. Chicago: University of Chicago Press, 2000.
BDB	F. Brown, S. Driver, and C. Briggs. *The Brown-Driver-Briggs Hebrew and English Lexicon*. 1906. Peabody, MA: Hendrickson, 2018.
BST	The Bible Speaks Today
BTCP	Biblical Theology and Christian Proclamation
Calvin	John Calvin. *Institutes of the Christian Religion*. 2 vols. Edited by John T. McNeill. Translated by Ford Lewis Battles. Philadelphia: Westminster, 1960.
CSB	Christian Standard Bible
EDT	Walter A. Elwell, ed. *Evangelical Dictionary of Theology*. 2nd ed. Grand Rapids: Baker Academic, 2001.
ESV	English Standard Version.
GNT	Good News Translation
HCSB	Holman Christian Standard Bible
JETS	*Journal of the Evangelical Theological Society*.
LEKGNT	Cleon L. Rogers Jr. and Cleon L. Rogers III. *The New Linguistic and Exegetical Key to the Greek New Testament*. Grand Rapids: Zondervan, 1998.
LNTS	Library of New Testament Studies
NASB	New American Standard Bible
NICNT	New International Commentary on the New Testament
NIDNTTE	Moisés Silva. *New International Dictionary of New Testament Theology and Exegesis*. 5 vols. Rev. ed. Grand Rapids: Zondervan, 2014.

NIDOTTE	Willem A. VanGemeren, ed. *New International Dictionary of Old Testament Theology and Exegesis*. 5 vols. Grand Rapids: Zondervan, 2012.
NIGTC	New International Greek Testament Commentary
NIV	New International Version
NKJV	New King James Version
NSBT	New Studies in Biblical Theology
NT	New Testament
NTC	New Testament Commentary
OT	Old Testament
PNTC	Pillar New Testament Commentary
PTW	Preach the Word
REC	Reformed Expository Commentary
RSV	Revised Standard Version
SBL	Studies in Biblical Literature
SSBT	Short Studies in Biblical Theology
TDNT	G. Kittel and G. Friedrich, eds. *Theological Dictionary of the New Testament*. Translated by Geoffrey W. Bromiley. 10 vols. Grand Rapids: Eerdmans, 1964.
TWOT	R. Harris, G. Archer Jr., and B. Waltke, eds. *Theological Wordbook of the Old Testament*. 2 vols. Chicago: Moody, 1980.
WBC	Word Biblical Commentary.

PART 1

Foundational Considerations

What Is a Pastor?

As a college junior, my heart burned to pastor God's flock. Having sensed his call to ministry five years earlier, this calling began to narrow. At the time, I served on a church staff discipling young adults and teenagers. By doing pastoral work, my calling became clearer. Although seeing only the edges of pastoral ministry, my spirit leaped at the chance to shepherd members of our church toward spiritual health.

Had you pinned me down to ask, "What is a pastor?" I would likely have said, "A shepherd." Of course, that's correct since the English term "pastor," derived from the Old French *pastor*, and the Latin *pastorem*, means *shepherd*.[1] When referring to a leadership office in the church, we use the term metaphorically (we do not mean the actual herding of sheep). Through the centuries, governments and religious groups have used *shepherd* to refer to one ruling, leading, or caring for them. The Bible also uses the term metaphorically. How does it speak to the question, "What is a *pastor*?"

Shepherd as a Metaphor

The ancient Near Eastern culture and Holy Scripture regularly use *shepherd* metaphorically.[2] When considering shepherd as a metaphor, Timothy Laniak explains, we drag "a collection of inter-related associations from the source domain into the target domain as *prospects* for comparison."[3] In other words, we take up the original concept of shepherding sheep, mull the various implications involved in that work, and *then* consider how it is used metaphorically in various biblical contexts. From this process, we begin to derive an understanding of *shepherd/pastor*. Answering the question, "What is a

---

1. "Pastor," *Online Etymology Dictionary*, www.etymonline.com.
2. See Timothy Laniak, *Shepherds after My Own Heart: Pastoral Traditions and Leadership in the Bible*, NSBT 20, ed. D. A. Carson (Downers Grove, IL: IVP Academic, 2006), 31–74.
3. Laniak, *Shepherds*, 33 (emphasis original).

pastor?" by merely saying, "a shepherd" proves inadequate until we arrive at its meaning in the original metaphor as developed in Scripture.

The noun *shepherd* (Greek: *poimēn*) is used eighteen times in the NT, but translated only once as *pastor* (Eph. 4:11).[4] The remaining uses of *poimēn* shed light on the nominal and verbal meanings when referring to the office of pastor/elder.[5] Moisés Silva explains that Greek literature used *poimēn* literally and figuratively, even for "the divine shepherd." Metaphorically, it expressed guidance and cherishing. While often describing the actual practice of herding sheep, the biblical term also finds prominent imagery for Yahweh shepherding his people Israel.[6] Likewise, we find the NT picking up the shepherding imagery of Yahweh and applying it to the Good Shepherd in John 10. Jesus saw the distressed and dispirited multitudes "like sheep without a shepherd" (Matt. 9:36). Paralleling the OT picture of Yahweh, the Gospels fill out the work of Jesus *shepherding*, as he sought to draw near, protect, provide, and guide the shepherdless crowds.[7] But the Good Shepherd goes one step further: he lays down his life for the sheep (John 10:11–18), as prophesied by Zechariah (Zech. 13:7).[8] From the OT use of *Shepherd* in reference to Yahweh to its NT use in Jesus the Good *Shepherd*, we begin to see the metaphor's background for the NT office of pastor/shepherd.

Pastors as Reflections of a Model

Neglecting the OT use of Yahweh as Shepherd when thinking of the church office of pastor/elder/overseer impoverishes the term. As the patriarch Israel blessed Joseph's sons, he called Yahweh "the God who has been my shepherd all my life to this day" (Gen. 48:15). He expressed Yahweh's care, guidance, and protection. Similarly, the psalmist describes the Lord's power in delivering Israel from Egypt: "But He led forth His own people like sheep and guided

---

4. *NIDNTTE*, 4:84. The following translate ποιμήν (*poimēn*) as *pastor*: NASB, NKJV, HCSB, GNT, RSV, NIV, while the ESV retains *shepherd*.

5. When using *pastor* as an office, I do so with the understanding of its synonymous use with *elder* and *overseer*, both found more frequently in the NT, representing one church office, with deacon being the other office. Both offices are always referred to in plurality. For the synonymous use of the terms for the one office in the church, see Benjamin L. Merkle, *The Elder and Overseer: One Office in the Early Church*, SBL 57, ed. Hemchand Gossai (New York: Peter Lang, 2003); Benjamin L. Merkle, *Forty Questions About Elders and Deacons* (Grand Rapids: Kregel Academic, 2008), 54–56; Phil A. Newton and Matt Schmucker, *Elders in the Life of the Church: Rediscovering the Biblical Model for Church Leadership* (Grand Rapids: Kregel Ministry, 2014), 45–57. The use of one article in Ephesians 4:11 for pastors and teachers indicates a better translation as "pastor-teacher." See Merkle, *Forty Questions About Elders and Deacons*, 55–56.

6. *NIDNTTE*, 81–83; mostly "in Jeremiah (19x), Ezekiel (17x), Genesis (13x), and Zechariah (9x)." Family members were the primary shepherds in common OT usage. The Septuagint used the term eighty times.

7. Laniak, *Shepherds*, 78–84 (see Exod. 15:13; 33:15–16; Deut. 23:14; Pss. 78:19; 105:40–41).

8. *NIDNTTE*, 4:85.

them in the wilderness like a flock" (Ps. 78:52). Psalm 80:1 sounds the same note on leadership. "Oh, give ear, Shepherd of Israel, You who lead Joseph like a flock." No wonder there's great comfort in Psalm 100:3, "We are His people and the sheep of His pasture." The Lord leads, protects, comforts, and provides for his flock (Ps. 23). This divine leadership occasionally took place through human instruments. "You led Your people like a flock by the hand of Moses and Aaron" (Ps. 77:20), giving hint toward the NT use of *shepherd*.

The biblical narratives utilize shepherd language to describe David's kingship. In the ancient Near East, shepherding language "is attached most often to the institution of Kingship (both divine and human)."[9] First, David is introduced as a literal shepherd (1 Sam. 16:11; 17:28, 34). Significantly, when David joined the tribes of Israel at Hebron on the occasion of anointing him as king, the leaders identified him as a shepherd/king. "And the Lord said to you, 'You will shepherd My people Israel, and you will be a ruler over Israel'" (2 Sam. 5:1–2). Here, *shepherd* "originated with reference to middle-level shepherd contractors," writes Laniak, showing the connection of the newly appointed king under the Lord God's authority. "Israel received its desired king, but only on the condition that it understood his [the king's] role as derivative from and dependent upon the rule of YWHW, the flock's true Owner."[10] As the true Shepherd, the Lord gave Israel's king responsibilities as an undershepherd in care, rule, and protection.

Four of the prophets—Isaiah, Jeremiah, Ezekiel, and Zechariah—make extensive use of pastoral language (a) to describe the Lord God (Isa. 40:11; Jer. 31:10; Ezek. 34:11–15; Zech. 9:16); (b) to rebuke unfaithful civil and religious leaders (Jer. 10:21; 23:1–2; Ezek. 34:1–10; Zech. 10:2–3); (c) to anticipate the Good Shepherd (Ezek. 34:23–24; Zech. 13:7–9); and (d) to assure that he would appoint faithful shepherds for his people (Jer. 3:15; 23:3–4). The future pastoral office remained clearly in view throughout the OT.

The emphasis on the Lord God as Shepherd communicates his presence, care, nurture, comfort, protection, guidance, leadership, and provision. *Any future use of the shepherding metaphor for those serving his flock must connect these characteristics to pastoral ministry*. With the NT pastoral office in view, Yahweh's appointed "shepherds were not expected simply to tend a flock; they were serving its Owner."[11] Pastors, consequently, must reflect the model of the Lord God as Shepherd over his flock.

Pastors as Promised Servants

Israel grew accustomed to kings who *neglected* defending the weak, judging impartially, leading in the ways of the Lord, and keeping personal

---

9. Laniak, *Shepherds*, 94.
10. Laniak, *Shepherds*, 102.
11. Laniak, *Shepherds*, 152.

desires in check. Likewise, the priestly religious leaders disregarded those they should have shepherded toward faithful dependence upon the Lord. Consequently, the Lord took action.

First, he proclaimed that he would rescue his flock. He took initiative to deliver his people from bondage, implying future salvific peace in the Lord's presence (Ezek. 34:11–16). This promise lays groundwork for the NT use of the church as God's flock (John 10:1–30; Heb. 13:20–21).

Second, he promised to send faithful shepherds to care for, protect, guide, and provide for his flock (Jer. 3:15). "I will also raise up shepherds over them and they will tend them" (Jer. 23:4). In this eschatological passage, Jeremiah points to Jesus, the coming Messianic King, giving assurance that God would "raise up for David a righteous Branch; and He will reign as king and act wisely and do justice and righteousness in the land" (Jer. 23:5). The flock that the future shepherds would tend belongs to the promised Messiah. His promised shepherds find fulfillment in the church's pastoral office (elder/overseer). Kings and priests failed to shepherd God's flock. However, the new covenant foresaw a different dimension of shepherds who cared for the flock. Laniak observes, "It illustrates what we will call a 'divine preference for human agency.' Appointment by God implies calling, stewardship and accountability."[12] He calls forth the promised shepherds to faithfully tend his flock.

The divine promise of faithful shepherds for God's flock adds weightiness to pastors serving local congregations. God's promise of faithful shepherds came in connection with the promised Davidic Messiah (Jer. 23:5–6). No wonder Paul used such striking language to remind the Ephesian elders that they didn't merely have a job, but were shepherding people purchased at the cost of Jesus's bloody death: "Be on guard for yourselves and for all the flock, among which the Holy Spirit has made you overseers, to shepherd the church of God which He purchased with His own blood" (Acts 20:28). These men, along with countless pastors through the centuries, answered the prophetic promise to shepherd the blood-bought church of God.

Pastors as Appointed Instruments

"What does the exalted Christ give to the Church?" asks Andrew Lincoln, referring to Ephesians 4:11: "He gives people, these particular people who proclaim the word and lead."[13] The apostolic and prophetic gifts served in the earliest days of the church, but they did not continue in the same manner beyond that period. Apostles and prophets laid the foundation of the church in every age, particularly by the special inspiration through which they gave us God's Word.[14] This seems to have clearly been Paul's position (Eph. 2:19–

---

12. Laniak, *Shepherds*, 21–22.
13. Andrew T. Lincoln, *Ephesians*, WBC 42 (Dallas: Word, 1990), 249.
14. Louis Berkhof, *Systematic Theology* (Grand Rapids: Eerdmans, 1993), 585.

22; 3:1–10). Once their work of laying the foundation of the gospel in the church took place, as Thomas Schreiner notes, "such authoritative apostles and prophets are superfluous."[15] Likewise, evangelists served to extend the gospel where the church had not been planted. The remaining gift (or gifts), "teaching shepherds," continues in the pastoral office of elder/overseer.[16] Paul and Peter get at the heart of what it means to shepherd God's flock. Elders must demonstrate an aptitude to teach in order to exhort in sound doctrine. This explains what it means to be "teaching shepherds" (Acts 20:28; 1 Peter 5:1–2; 1 Tim. 3:2; Titus 1:9). "The functional talk about eldership," Derek Tidball rightly states, "is cast in the metaphor of shepherding."[17] Shepherds teach the flock.

The phrase "He gave gifts to men" followed by "And He gave some . . . as pastors and teachers" indicates the pastoral office as the divinely appointed instrument to serve the church throughout the ages (Eph. 4:8, 11). Paul places pastors in the context of God's gifts to mature and care for the church. He considered the necessity of pastoral leaders when we see him *appointing* elders in the new churches on his first missionary journey (Acts 14:23). He reconfirmed the responsibility of elders to shepherd the Ephesian church (Acts 20:28). Then he left Titus in Crete to appoint elders in communities where churches had been established (Titus 1:5). Since the Lord of the church appointed pastors to care for the flock, Paul insisted on pastoral care for churches he planted.

Pastors as Undershepherds to the Chief Shepherd

Before the ascension, Jesus called for Simon Peter to care for his flock (John 21:15–17). Jesus asked three times if he loved him. With each probing question, Peter affirmed his love for the Lord Jesus Christ. With each affirmation, Jesus followed with the call to shepherd the church: "Tend My lambs. . . . Shepherd My sheep. . . . Tend My sheep." The first term, *tend* (*boske*), was the activity of herdsmen feeding and tending their sheep. *Shepherd* (*poimaine*), similarly, means to tend or give care to the flock.[18] "Tend My *sheep*" (*boske*) reinforces the feeding, shepherding, and nurturing Jesus called Peter to regularly engage in with the church.

Thirty or more years later, as a seasoned church leader and apostle, Peter humbly wrote the elders of the scattered churches (1 Peter 5:1–5). He called himself a "fellow elder," thus identifying with the shepherding and leadership

---

15. Thomas R. Schreiner, *New Testament Theology: Magnifying God in Christ* (Grand Rapids: Baker, 2008), 723–24.
16. Merkle, *Forty Questions About Elders and Deacons*, 46–53.
17. Derek Tidball, *Ministry by the Book: New Testament Patterns for Pastoral Leadership* (Downers Grove, IL: IVP Academic, 2008), 189.
18. BDAG, βόσκω, 181; *NIDNTTE*, ποιμαίνω, 4:81–87. Each verb is a present active imperative.

responsibilities of those caring for churches throughout ancient Asia Minor (1 Peter 1:1). With this identity, he also looked *back* as a "witness of the sufferings of Christ" and *ahead* as "a partaker of the glory that is to be revealed." In doing so, he anchored his exhortations for pastoring in the cross, resurrection, reign, return, and hope of Christ, modeling the same anchor for these pastors as they served the church. He spoke to them eye to eye as fellow shepherds of the purchased flock.

How were these elders to see their responsibilities? They were to actively shepherd the flock. Peter had no need to list every shepherding detail. These early elders understood Jesus was their model for shepherding: pursuing wandering sheep, showing compassion, teaching the Scriptures, feeding and providing for the needy, healing the broken, nurturing the lambs with tenderness, calling his own by name, and laying down his life for the sheep. Yahweh provided the same kind of protection, provision, compassion, guidance, and nurturing for Israel.

In contrast to Israel's wicked shepherds, the elders were to exercise oversight "not under compulsion, but voluntarily, according to the will of God; and not for sordid gain, but with eagerness, nor yet as lording it over those allotted to your charge, but proving to be examples to the flock" (1 Peter 5:2–3). Peter pictures men eager to humbly serve God's flock, not mistaking it for *their own flock* that they could do with as they pleased, but exercising oversight "according to God." As Laniak puts it, "Humility is the distinguishing mark of their service (1 Pet. 5:5–6)."[19] They could only be examples (*tupoi*) if they were fellow members of the flock, participating fully in the life of the local church. Laniak wisely reminds us, "He is a follower *before* he is a leader. He is a leader *because* he is a follower."[20] These elders came face to face with the reality that they were pastors only as they sought to care for the flock in the way Jesus modeled shepherding. They, and all faithful pastors with them, recognize that undershepherds join the Chief Shepherd in caring for his flock (1 Cor. 3:5–9).

Summary

What is a *pastor*? A shepherd of God's flock, certainly, but the Bible freights the metaphor with meaning by how it uses the term.

(1) Pastors are those who *reflect* the model the Lord God gave in shepherding Israel: namely, prioritizing living among the flock, protecting spiritually, providing rich food from God's Word, and leading toward holiness, maturity, and unity.

---

19. Laniak, *Shepherds*, 234.
20. Laniak, *Shepherds*, 22 (emphasis original). He adds, "Israel's kings had to understand that being a member of the flock of God was more fundamental than being an appointed shepherd over the flock" (114).

(2) Pastors are those whom the Lord *promised* through the prophets he would raise up to care for his people—the church—in contrast to the many bad shepherds in Israel.

(3) Pastors are those *appointed* by the Lord Jesus as instruments to serve his church in equipping, building up, teaching sound doctrine, speaking the truth in love, and leading toward unity and maturity.

(4) Pastors are those recognized as *undershepherds* with responsibility to faithfully carry out shepherding responsibilities, conscious that they will give an account to the Chief Shepherd.

REFLECTION QUESTIONS

1. How does the OT model of the Lord as Shepherd inform and shape understanding of the question, "What is a pastor?"

2. How does the rebuke and judgment leveled against false, unfaithful shepherds in Israel (civil and religious) affect your thinking about God's call to shepherd his flock?

3. In what way is the office of pastor (elder) an appointed instrument of Christ for the church?

4. How did Peter's experience in John 21:15–17 transform his future view of pastoring?

5. In what ways does seeing oneself as being a member of a church *first* affect the way a man should view his office as pastor?

What Is Meant by Pastoral Ministry?

My first venture into pastoral ministry brought more questions than answers. As a nineteen-year-old ministry student, a small church asked me to lead their music. I agreed, if they would allow me to work with their students. The pastor never explained anything about ministry in general or in particular with that very unhealthy church. He just wanted me to show up, select a few hymns, and leave. He never asked how the students were responding to my Bible studies or discipling. He just didn't seem to care about anything that had to do with pastoral ministry. There I ascertained what *not* to do in pastoral ministry, even if I'd not yet learned what to do.

What is pastoral ministry? Simply, it's the work of pastors/elders. Yet that leaves us guessing about specifics. If we think of the pastor as a shepherd, we'll find the picture colored in a bit: pastoral ministry involves care, protection, provision, and nearness to the flock.

Sixteenth-century Strasbourg pastor Martin Bucer, John Calvin's mentor, saw pastoral ministry in a broad sweep before narrowing it: "The ministers of the church are to provide for Christ's lambs everything the Lord has promised to them in his office as shepherd."[1] Bucer follows after Jesus's way of shepherding his flock, along with what he promised in the gospel, as foundational for the breadth of pastoral ministry. He adds, ministers should see "that they [the flock] are deprived of nothing which contributes to their continual growth and increase in godliness."[2] Pastoral ministry focuses, then, on growth in godliness.

Timothy Laniak adds another layer to Bucer's thought: "A good shepherd is one who does what is required by each circumstance, in each context."[3] In

---

1. Martin Bucer, *Concerning the True Care of Souls*, trans. Peter Beale (1538; Edinburgh: Banner of Truth Trust, 2009), 69.
2. Bucer, *Care of Souls*, 69.
3. Timothy Laniak, *Shepherds after My Own Heart: Pastoral Traditions and Leadership in the Bible*, NSBT 20, ed. D. A. Carson (Downers Grove, IL: IVP Academic, 2006), 40.

other words, while pastoral ministry has biblical similarities from one people group to another, the way pastoral practices work out in real life settings must not be thought of as monolithic. How I do pastoral ministry in Memphis may differ slightly from my friend pastoring in Nairobi. Some of the circumstances he faces—syncretism, extreme poverty, challenged meeting spaces, lack of male leadership—means he will emphasize some things differently than I do with my work. We'll still build around the basics, but our contexts will require putting weight on various aspects of ministry.

Why does the Lord choose pastors to do ministry? The Genevan reformer John Calvin explained that with the Lord of the church not visibly dwelling among us, he chose pastoral work by ministers "as sort of delegated work, not by transferring to them his right and honor, but only that through their mouths he may do his own work—just as a workman uses a tool to do his work."[4] Delegated work through *chosen tools* captures the idea of pastoral ministry. But what does it involve? We'll consider pastoral ministry through exploring one word that encapsulates it, five spiritual tasks it entails, and four specifics for pastoral ministry.

Pastoral Ministry in a Word

When Laniak describes the tireless work of shepherds in the ancient world with its implications for modern pastors, he writes, "Watching . . . is a comprehensive summary of shepherding tasks."[5] Andrew Davis agrees: "Essential to the work of a pastor is the laborious watchfulness as an undershepherd of the spiritual state of the flock."[6] In the midst of being "laborious," *watchfulness* is never easy. It costs time, energy, tears, and discipline from the pastor who would be faithful to the Chief Shepherd in discharging his responsibilities for the flock's vitality (1 Peter 5:1–4).

The writer of Hebrews identifies watchfulness as an apt summary for pastoral work. "Obey your leaders and submit to them, *for they keep watch over your souls as those who will give an account. Let them do this with joy and not with grief, for this would be unprofitable for you*" (Heb. 13:17, emphasis added). Charging the church to obey (*peithō*) or to follow and to submit to (*hupeikō*) or yield to the delegated authority[7] of those leading them would be most natural *if* these spiritual leaders kept watch over their souls. To keep watch (*agrupneō*) meant to stay awake and alert, to sacrifice sleep and comfort

---

4. *Calvin*, 4.3.1.
5. Laniak, *Shepherds*, 233.
6. Andrew Davis, "Those Who Must Give an Account: A Pastoral Reflection," in *Those Who Must Give an Account: A Study of Church Membership and Church Discipline*, eds. John S. Hammett and Benjamin L. Merkle (Nashville: B&H Academic, 2012), 208–9. The balance of Davis's essay provides a sobering look at the pastor's accountability before the Chief Shepherd for his responsibilities.
7. BDAG, πείθω, 791–92, ὑπείκω, 1030.

for the purpose of vigilance.[8] Faithful shepherds keep watch over the spiritual lives of their flocks.

Pastors can only keep watch over those whom they *observe*. They can only observe the changes, ups and downs, struggles, and progress for those whom they *know*. They can only know those in whom they *invest* their lives, labors, and prayers.[9]

Davis breaks down watchfulness into three areas. First, pastors watch over "the identity of the flock." He writes, "Specifically, we must know the people the Lord has entrusted to us." This kind of watchfulness means relationships built through personal contact. It's difficult to shepherd strangers. Second, pastors watch over "the physical condition of the flock." Davis writes that we need to know what's happening in their lives, what challenges or trials they face, what's happening in their family relationships, how they get along with others, and so on. These issues will affect their spiritual lives. Third, pastors watch over "the spiritual condition of the flock." He breaks this into negative and positive sides. "Negatively, a pastor must be aware of the overpowering tendency every member of his flock has for drifting away from Christ through the deceitfulness of sin" (Heb. 3:12–13). We mustn't check our anthropology at the door of pastoral work. "Positively, a pastor must shepherd each member of the flock to be full of love and good deeds, developing fully the spiritual gifts Christ has entrusted to them" (Heb. 10:24–25). We must have aims with preaching, discipling, personal work, communication, and pastoral details that result in aiding the flock's spiritual growth.[10] That's watchfulness over the flock.

Five Spiritual Tasks Entailed in Pastoral Ministry

Pastors can get easily sidetracked in pastoral ministry while dealing with administrative and organizational tasks. They can even forget *why* they're organizing an event or ministry. *Pastoral ministry is about people.* Ironically, people sometimes get brushed behind paperwork, phone calls, emails, web details, podcasts, and pulls in a dozen directions. Bucer's five main tasks, which he couples with five categories of people, are helpful for the spiritual lives of church members.

1. Do the Work of Evangelism: Lead to Faith in Christ the Lost Sheep Who've Not Recognized Christ as Lord

Bucer functioned out of a parish context that cemented together infant baptism and citizenship. Despite that practice, he recognized that many, including those baptized into the church as infants, had not come to faith in Christ. He

---

8. *NIDNTTE*, ἀγρυπνέω, 1:141–42.
9. For a classic example, see Richard Baxter, *The Reformed Pastor* (1656; Edinburgh: Banner of Truth Trust, 1974).
10. Davis, "Pastoral Reflection," 211–12 (emphasis original).

calls on pastors to go after God's elect by going after those alienated from Christ (Matt. 22:1–14; Luke 14:16–24).[11] Here the pastor does the work of an evangelist, as Paul exhorted Timothy (2 Tim. 4:5), building relationships with unbelievers while looking for opportunity to speak the good news to them.

2. Do the Work of Formative Discipline: Restore Those Who've Fallen out of Fellowship with the Church Due to the Allurements of the Flesh or False Doctrine[12]

Pastoral ministry involves *watchfulness*. Particularly, pastors need to keep watch on those who have given way to sinful practices or false teaching, causing them to leave the fellowship and covenant of the church. This means firmly but lovingly confronting their sin—speaking the truth in love (Eph. 4:15). The pastor leads out in discipline, whether *formative* (discipling), helping restore one who has lapsed into sin; or *formal* (corrective), following the pattern of Matthew 18:15–20 that aims to restore a wandering sheep and maintain the church's testimony.[13] Some fall prey to false teaching, and so must be humbly, boldly confronted with the truth of God's Word (1 Tim. 4:1–6; 2 Tim. 2:14–19).

3. Do the Work of Exhorting and Admonishing: "Assist in the True Reformation" of Those in the Church Who Have Given Way to Grievous Sin, and Yet Remain in the Church[14]

This category may include those distancing themselves from hearing the truth or from fellowship in the body. It incorporates those that have damaged relationships with others in the church due to temper, wrong attitudes, bitterness, or a contrary spirit. Those engaged in immoral behavior, living unholy lives entrapped by the world, need reforming (repentance) in their behavior. If indeed true believers, Christ needs to be formed in them (Gal. 4:19). Bucer distinguishes this category from the former since they've remained in some part of the church without total abandonment or alienation. Yet their continuance in the church disrupts the unity and purity that should characterize the body of Christ (Eph. 4:13–5:14). Pastoral ministry directs them toward repentance and personal discipline as followers of Christ (2 Tim. 4:2).

4. Do the Work of Gentle Healing: Reestablish to Christian Strength and Health Those Persevering Yet Still Somewhat Spiritually Sick

Bucer includes in this category those fainthearted when facing difficulties, those slow to serve others, those who've grown careless in spiritual

11. Bucer, *Care of Souls*, 70–71.
12. Bucer, *Care of Souls*, 71.
13. See Andrew Davis, "The Practical Issues of Church Discipline," in Hammett and Merkle, *Those Who Must Give an Account*, 157–85. See Question 33 for more on church discipline.
14. Bucer, *Care of Souls*, 70–72.

disciplines, and "those who err in right understanding."[15] They've remained in the church, participated in the gatherings, made some effort toward perseverance, but they still remain spiritually unhealthy. Coming alongside them, partnering them with more mature believers, holding them accountable, providing them with good resources, and regularly encouraging them helps to reestablish these believers to spiritual health. Our churches have plenty fitting this category. They're believers who love the church but need shepherding toward health and vitality. We can become frustrated as pastors, hoping they will do better. Some lack the constitution to respond as well as others. So, we must patiently labor with them until we see them, in turn, serving to help others walk with Christ.

5. *Do the Work of Guarding the Flock: "Protect from All Offense and Falling Away and Continually Encourage in All Good Things Those Who Stay with the Flock in Christ's Sheep-Pen without Grievously Sinning or Becoming Weak and Sick in This Christian Walk"*[16]

These faithful members of the body press on in their spiritual walks, serve one another, participate in gospel work in the community and beyond, volunteer to assist with the work of ministry, and encourage their pastors in their work. Bucer reminds us that shepherds do not need to presume these members of the flock will manage their spiritual walks without the need of pastoral oversight. They must be watched, protected, and encouraged as much as the others. They need pastoral care, too.

The goal for pastoral ministry is to lead the congregation to fear God, believe the gospel, stay faithful to the body, and show diligence and keenness in living holy lives that give glory to Jesus Christ in all things.[17]

Four Specifics for Pastoral Ministry

"Pastors are generalists," notes Laniak.[18] They cover a broad range of responsibilities when exercising pastoral ministry. This sweep of responsibilities can frustrate pastors as they seek to shepherd the flock. Pastors sometimes feel stressed by their weakness in one area of ministry, or the ministry where they appear least competent seems to vie for more energy and time. Such is pastoral ministry. Laniak writes, "The task of shepherds is determined daily by the changing needs of the flock under their care."[19] Inevitably, pastors have strengths in some areas and weaknesses in others. That's why we must follow

---

15. Bucer, *Care of Souls*, 72–73.
16. Bucer, *Care of Souls*, 70.
17. Bucer, *Care of Souls*, 176–81.
18. Laniak, *Shepherds*, 247.
19. Laniak, *Shepherds*, 247.

the pattern of plurality found in the NT church. With plurality, one's weakness will be compensated by the strength of a fellow elder/pastor.

We might offer numerous lists of specific responsibilities in pastoral ministry. However, four categories need to be operative in every pastor's work: feeding the Word, leading the flock, watching out for the body, and setting an example for others to follow.

1. Feed the Word

Teaching and preaching God's Word remains most basic *and* essential to the work of pastoral ministry. Generations come and go, but the need for hearing the exposition of God's Word never changes. Historically, great periods of spiritual awakening always come on the heels of renewed fervency for proclaiming God's Word.[20] Martyn Lloyd-Jones, whose twentieth-century pastoral ministry still impacts the evangelical world, wrote, "I would say without hesitation that the most urgent need in the Christian Church today is true preaching; and as it is the greatest and the most urgent need in the Church, it is obviously the greatest need of the world also."[21] The reason for the urgency of preaching, of course, has nothing to do with the need for more gifted speakers. We have plenty of them. Rather, we always live with the necessity of hearing God's Word.

Mark Dever and Paul Alexander agree: "The pastor's first responsibility is to feed the sheep on the Word of God (John 21:15–17; 2 Tim. 4:2). A shepherd simply cannot be faithful to his task if he doesn't feed his flock well (Ezek. 34:2–3, 13–14; 1 Tim. 3:2; Titus 1:9)."[22] We find the pattern of biblical proclamation throughout the book of Acts wherever the apostles and early members of the church went. Peter and John preached around the temple area and were arrested for their proclamation (Acts 3–4). Stephen became the church's first martyr after preaching to religious opponents, including Saul of Tarsus (Acts 7:1–8:3). Philip left Jerusalem due to persecution and ended up preaching the gospel from Samaria to Caesarea (Acts 8:4–40). Peter preached the gospel to Cornelius (Acts 10). Paul and Barnabas preached the gospel throughout ancient Asia Minor, and continued with new preaching partners into the next round of missionary expansion (Acts 13–14; 16–21). Paul regularly reinforced the centrality of the Word to the early churches (Rom. 1:1–17; 1 Cor. 1:18–2:5; Eph. 4:11–16; Col. 4:17; 2 Thess. 2:13).

---

20. That's illustrated, for example, in the preaching of the early fathers Augustine and Chrysostom; Luther, Calvin, Bucer, Knox, and Tyndale in the Great Reformation; and the Wesley brothers, Whitefield, and Edwards in the First Great Awakening.
21. D. Martyn Lloyd-Jones, *Preaching and Preachers*, 40th anniv. ed. (Grand Rapids: Zondervan, 2011), 17.
22. Mark Dever and Paul Alexander, *The Deliberate Church: Building Your Ministry on the Gospel* (Wheaton, IL: Crossway, 2005), 94.

Some appear to think the church needs more pop wisdom, personal motivation, and inspiration instead of the hard work of laboring in the Word week after week. Dever and Alexander respond: "A man may have a charismatic personality; he may be a gifted administrator and a silken orator; he may be armed with an impressive program; he may even have the people skills of a politician and the empathic listening skills of a counselor; but he will starve the sheep if he cannot feed the people of God on the Word of God."[23]

What kind of preaching is needed? John Stott insisted, if preaching "is to be authentically Christian it must be expository."[24] In nineteenth-century Cambridge, Charles Simeon's expositions affected an entire generation. His conviction on expository preaching expressed his pastoral aim: "My endeavor is to bring out of Scripture what is there, and not to thrust in what I think might be there. I have a great jealousy on this head; never to speak more or less than I believe to be the mind of the Spirit in the passage I am expounding."[25] With Simeon's conviction, effective pastoral ministry gives primary focus to feeding the flock God's Word.

2. Lead the Flock

We don't find elders as an office used in Hebrews,[26] but we do find that biblical writer implying the shepherding work of elders with the phrase "those leading you" (*hegeomai*, Heb. 13:7, 17, my trans.). The leaders are accountable to the Chief Shepherd and must lead the flock in a way that profits the flock's spiritual lives and guards them from spiritual dangers. Pastors lead the flock into spiritual maturity, unity in the faith, doctrinal stability, and faithful life in the body (Eph. 4:11–16). As the Good Shepherd does, they lead the flock into green pastures and still waters for the feeding, meditating, and refreshing experience of God's Word (Ps. 23). They lead the church in worship, service, and organizing for mission (1 Tim. 4:13; Rom. 12:9–13; Matt. 28:18–20).

Churches gather to worship, then scatter to serve and do mission. But who will lead them in that effort? Those in covenant with one another in the local church multiply their ministries as they serve together under the leadership of thoughtful pastors. Leadership includes participation, setting an example for others to follow.

---

23. Dever and Alexander, *Deliberate Church*, 94.

24. John Stott, *Between Two Worlds: The Art of Preaching in the Twentieth Century* (Grand Rapids: Eerdmans, 1982), 135.

25. H. C. G. Moule, *Charles Simeon* (London: Methuen, 1892), 97, quoted by David Helm, *Expositional Preaching: How We Speak God's Word Today*, 9Marks Building Healthy Churches (Wheaton, IL: Crossway, 2014), 12.

26. The same word translated as elders in 1 Timothy 3:17 and Titus 1:5, πρεσβύτερος, is used in Hebrews 11:2, not for a church office but for "men of old" (NASB).

3. Protect the Body

Pastors guard their flocks from false teaching; divisive people; subtleties of novel but unbiblical ideas; patterns of sin, laziness, and neglect; and subversive, ungodly leaders (Acts 20:28; 1 Tim. 4:1–8, 16; 2 Tim. 2:14–19, 23–26; 4:14–15; Titus 3:9–11; 1 Peter 2:11–12; 2 John 7–11; 3 John 9–10).

Dever and Alexander explain that most of those seeking to subvert do so by twisting the truth of Scripture (Acts 20:28–31): "Sometimes we must be the ones who know how to defuse a potentially divisive situation. Other times we are called to engage in doctrinal battle over significant issues—those that affect the Gospel and the security of the church in it."[27] On those occasions, action must be taken to protect the flock.

Many years ago, a man visited our church, appearing to be very knowledgeable in God's Word. But the more some of our elders and I listened to him, the more we realized he held aberrant, unorthodox views on the person of Christ. Together, we immediately took action to confront and deny him any public access to spread his views in the church. He soon left to look for easier prey, hoping to find elders who were not guarding the flock.

4. Set an Example

Pastors must guard their spiritual walks, marriages, finances, and all areas that might threaten their integrity to lead God's people. Paul told Timothy, "Let no one look down on your youthfulness, but rather in speech, conduct, love, faith and purity, show yourself an example of those who believe. . . . Pay close attention to yourself and to your teaching" (1 Tim. 4:12, 16). Look out for the details in your life and doctrine. Look at the way you talk, live, care for others, and exemplify a holy life. The word translated "pay close attention to" (*epechō*) is the same word Luke used of the man at the Beautiful Gate of the temple who "fixed his attention" on Peter and John.[28] That expresses the idea well. An unexamined, unwatched life will not stand for long in the face of inward temptation and external assaults.

Recognizing inherent weaknesses that lure us into sin, lack of discipline, distractions, and self-centeredness, pastors must daily confess sin, live in the fullness and power of the Spirit, live at the cross in dying to sin, and grow in trust and confidence in the Lord (Luke 9:23; Rom. 6:1–19; 2 Cor. 5:6–10; Eph. 4:17–5:14; 5:15–18; 1 John 1:9). Pastors must discern whether they're serving others in the body or just hiding behind ministerial life (Gal. 6:1–2).

Pastors must seek to "learn what is pleasing to the Lord," walking in faithfulness and being exemplary in conduct, love, service, generosity, and devotedness to Christ and his body (Eph. 5:10).

---

27. Dever and Alexander, *Deliberate Church*, 94–95.
28. BDAG, ἐπέχω, 362.

Summary

While trying to provide everything for Christ's lambs, as Bucer exhorted in his description of pastoral ministry, we realize how important plurality in pastoral work will be to faithfully teach, lead, guard, and set an example for the flock. Our responsibilities involve evangelizing the unbelieving, seeking to restore the lapsed and fallen, and faithfully shepherding those regularly involved with the body. Just as no two churches are alike, so too will the areas of focus and emphasis in pastoral ministry differ from church to church. Yet those same four areas of service—Word, leadership, protection, and example—must be evident in every church's pastoral ministry.

REFLECTION QUESTIONS

1. What does Laniak mean by stating, "Pastors are generalists"?

2. How does the word "watchfulness" encapsulate the whole of pastoral ministry?

3. What five main tasks did Bucer identify in pastoral ministry?

4. Why must *feeding the flock* be primary in pastoral ministry?

5. What must pastors be on guard against on behalf of the body?

What Essential Qualities Must Be Present in a Christian Pastor?

Without exaggerating, character is everything when it comes to the pastor/elder. It's not that gifts, abilities, training, and experience play no part in the work of the Christian pastor. Rather, without godly character, all gifts and abilities mean nothing. Without evidence of the character described in 1 Timothy 3:1–7 and Titus 1:5–9, a pastor exercises his ministry as a hypocrite, causing far more harm than good for the body of Christ.

Amazingly, aside from the requirement to teach and the restriction on being a new convert (1 Tim. 3:2, 6; Titus 1:9), Paul does not ask for anything that shouldn't be present in any Christian. Above reproach, temperate, prudent, hospitable, gentle, peaceable—all of these characteristics picture the regenerate person walking with the Lord, serving others, and demonstrating the effects of the gospel. Faithfulness to the marriage vows, good home management, self-control, eschewing addictions, and not bullying others ought to be the norm for followers of Christ. As D. A. Carson states, "The most remarkable thing about these characteristics is that there is nothing remarkable about them."[1]

So why does Paul detail the kind of character needed in elders/pastors? First, pastors need to live like those redeemed by Christ. They are Christians before they are pastors. No amount of oratorical, leadership, or administrative skills can compensate for a lack of godly character. Second, they must be models for other believers to follow. Peter wrote that elders need "to be examples to the flock" (1 Peter 5:3). One can imagine that new Christians, living without any previous example of a godly Christian life, particularly needed

---

1. D. A. Carson, at a joint Sunday school gathering, Capitol Hill Baptist Church, Washington, DC, as reported to me in a conversation with Mark Dever and Matt Schmucker, who were present.

the model of faithful elders living before them as "an example of those who believe" (1 Tim. 4:12). Today, believers who are confused by the messages of a post-Christian world still need pastoral examples to follow. Therefore, focusing on godly character precedes shepherding responsibilities.

To consider the essential qualities of pastors, we will look at Paul's prescriptive outline to Titus for elders' character (Titus 1:5–9), interspersed with some of the similar qualities listed in 1 Timothy 3:1–7.

The character qualities Paul lists to Timothy and Titus overlap, with a few exceptions,[2] most notably, the Titus list says nothing about the elder not being a new convert (1 Tim. 3:7). Presumably, with most Cretan converts as new believers, Paul did not include the same requirement he made with Timothy at the longer established Ephesian church.[3] We will follow Paul's list to Titus, breaking it into four categories to think on necessary character qualities for pastors: examples at home, examples in personal conduct, examples in relationships, and examples in corporate life.

First-generation Cretan Christians had little idea of what it meant to live like Christians. They had "liars, evil beasts, lazy gluttons" as examples (Titus 1:12). So how would these believers understand how to treat families, employers, employees, slaves, masters, and fellow believers? Paul offered the key for elders living as examples of Christ's disciples: the pastors must have a godly home life.

Examples at Home

The statement "the husband of one wife" or, better, "a one-woman man" (*mias gynaikos anēr*, Titus 1:6) shows the pastor's singular devotedness to his wife. Debates on whether Paul meant the elder (a) must be married, (b) cannot be divorced and remarried, or (c) cannot be a polygamist miss the major point that the pastor/elder must be "a one-woman man."[4] His faithfulness to love his wife as Christ loves the church, treating her with gentleness, kindness, and sacrificial love, proclaims the power of the gospel in the marriage relationship (Eph. 5:22–33).

---

2. For a helpful chart comparing Timothy and Titus, see Benjamin L. Merkle, *Forty Questions About Elders and Deacons* (Grand Rapids: Kregel Academic, 2008), 110.

3. For more consideration on why Paul left off the "not a new convert" requirement with Titus, with implications in developing pastoral leaders in hard places, see Phil A. Newton and Matt Schmucker, *Elders in the Life of the Church: Rediscovering the Biblical Model for Church Leadership* (Grand Rapids: Kregel Ministry, 2014), 233–40; see also Benjamin L. Merkle, "Ecclesiology in the Pastoral Epistles," in *Entrusted with the Gospel: Paul's Theology in the Pastoral Epistles*, eds. Andreas Köstenberger and Terry Wilder (Nashville: B&H Academic, 2010), 185.

4. See Merkle, *Forty Questions About Elders and Deacons*, 124–29. If a pastor/elder shows unfaithfulness to his wife, then he faces immediate disqualification in his office since the marriage relationship is to model Christ and the church, as described in Ephesians 5:22–33. See a similar position in John. S. Hammett, *Biblical Foundations for Baptist Churches: A Contemporary Ecclesiology*, 2nd ed. (Grand Rapids: Kregel Academic, 2019), 195–97.

He's devoted to his children as well. His children recognize his faith in Christ as he lives out the gospel in his home (Titus 1:6). There's debate on the meaning of the adjective modifying "children," that is, "children who believe" (*tekna echōn pista*). The Pastoral Epistles, most naturally and prominently, use it as "faithful" ("having faithful children," lit.). Andreas Köstenberger explains *faithful* "probably means 'obedient and submissive to their father's orders' (cf. 1 Tim. 3:11; 2 Tim. 2:2, 13)."[5] John Piper concurs: "So the idea seems to be of children who are well bred, orderly, generally obedient, responsible, and reliable."[6] Brian Chapell notes, "We are not necessarily looking at the beliefs and actions of one child but at the character of the family as a whole." The translation of *faithful* rather than *believing* "better communicates the intended meaning that our assessment is to be based on observations of children's conduct and convictions made over time, not on isolated statements or actions."[7]

This interpretation finds further confirmation in Paul's explanatory note, "not accused of dissipation or rebellion" (Titus 1:6). Köstenberger remarks, "Paul isn't referring to occasional disobedience but deep-seated rebellion against parental authority."[8] In other words, they are not out of control. Their father exercises judicious oversight, carrying out teaching, training, instruction, and, as necessary, corrective discipline. Their faithfulness is shown by the way they respond to his fatherly leadership.

Examples in Personal Conduct

"Above reproach" is the umbrella characteristic of an elder (Titus 1:6; 1 Tim. 3:2). It controls the whole of his life. Paul does not call for perfection, or else no one could ever serve as an elder. But he does mean that pastors will be conscientious about the way they conduct their lives. They seek to make sure they have no dangling areas to dishonor Christ or detract from the gospel. They have no reason to constantly cover up or lie about their behavior. What you see in them at church will be the same at home, at work, in the community, and even when no one watches them. Elders lead by demonstrating Christian character, becoming an example for all the church (Heb. 13:7).

What does it look like to be "above reproach"? Paul fills this out by providing some examples.

---

5. Andreas J. Köstenberger, *Commentary on 1–2 Timothy and Titus*, BTCP (Nashville: Holman Reference, 2017), 314.

6. John Piper, "Biblical Eldership: Shepherd the Flock of God among You," *Desiring God* (website), Sermons, May 1, 1999, sec. 8, https://www.desiringgod.org/messages/biblical-eldership-session-1#Qualifications.

7. R. Kent Hughes and Brian Chapell, *1 and 2 Timothy and Titus: To Guard the Deposit*, PTW (Wheaton, IL: Crossway, 2000), 296–97.

8. Köstenberger, *1–2 Timothy and Titus*, 314.

(a) "Not self-willed" (Titus 1:7): The pastor is not obstinate and arrogant in the way he acts, refusing to live as though the world revolves around him. He avoids the unteachable spirit of one using rather than serving others and refuses to trample over others to achieve his own desires.

(b) "Not quick-tempered" (Titus 1:7): The pastor is not hotheaded or short-fused. Relationships matter to him, so he demonstrates patience and longsuffering with others.

(c) "Not addicted to wine" (Titus 1:7; 1 Tim. 3:3): On the island of Crete, the prominent Dionysian cult included drunkenness as part of its worship. These Christian leaders were never to be mistaken for leaders in the Dionysus cult. Self-control and restraint in their appetites distinguishes them.

(d) "Not pugnacious" (Titus 1:7; 1 Tim. 3:3): Pastors are not to be bullies or given to fighting or heavy-handedness. Their self-control does not quickly seek to defend self, or battle to get the last word in a tense conversation. Here we see the example of Christ: "while being reviled, He did not revile in return" (1 Peter 2:23).

(e) "Not fond of sordid gain" (Titus 1:7; cf. "free from the love of money," 1 Tim. 3:3; 1 Peter 5:2): Pastors must guard themselves in the areas of covetousness and greed. They demonstrate a strong work ethic yet refuse to gain things indiscreetly or dishonestly or through crass manipulation.

Examples in Relationships

In one sense, everything in Titus 1:7–8 has to do with both personal behavior and relationships. But the characteristics of Titus 1:8 particularly exemplify faithful relationships.

(a) "Hospitable" (Titus 1:8; 1 Tim. 3:2): Rather than being a bully or using people for selfish gain, the pastor practices hospitality. The word literally means "love for strangers" or "love for foreigners." He willingly opens his home to others. Two of the elders at my church have the reputation for opening their homes so often that we've thought of putting "Bed & Breakfast" signs at their doors. Hospitality befits Christian character (Rom. 12:13).

(b) "Loving what is good" (Titus 1:8): Some translate this phrase as loving those who are good or loving good things. More pointedly, elders must have an affinity for good rather than dark, evil, or questionable things. That should be evident in what they read or watch or discuss. It "denotes devotion to all that is best."[9] That also involves how they spend their time and resources, as well as what they seek in relationships with others.

(c) "Sensible" (Titus 1:8): The pastor keeps his head about him; that is, he disciplines his life with an aim toward wisdom. The NASB translates the same word in 1 Timothy 3:2 as "prudent" (*sōphrona*), which we think of as "acting wisely." Paul uses the word in Titus 2:2, 5, and 6 to imply one engaging his mind, thinking soberly with a heart of wisdom, and seeking to speak or act wisely.

(d) "Just" (Titus 1:8): The pastor has a keen sensitivity to upholding right standards of conduct and honoring God's laws. He values integrity. He treats all in the same conscientious way, regardless of a person's status in life, level of involvement in the church, or contribution to the overall ministry.

(e) "Devout" (Titus 1:8): Pastors take seriously personal piety. While sometimes construed negatively, it simply means one is concerned to live a holy, devoted life to Christ as his Lord in all things. Holiness means something to him (1 Peter 1:13–16).

(f) "Self-controlled" (Titus 1:8): As a word meaning living under "divine restraint," or living a disciplined life, it gives a clear picture of a life that dies to self or *mortifies* the flesh (Luke 9:23; Rom. 6:6). No careless word or act confuses his testimony as a follower of Christ. It means "having one's emotions, impulses, or desires under control."[10] Rather than giving way to folly, foolish living, sensual desires, or thoughtless language, pastors must rein in the natural impulses of the flesh.

Examples in Corporate Life

The primary distinguishing mark between elders and deacons is that the former must be "able to teach" (1 Tim. 3:2).[11] While two of the deacon prototypes,[12] Stephen and Philip, gave clear evidence of teaching and preaching gifts (Acts 6–8), Paul lays no mandate on deacons for teaching (1 Tim. 3:8–13). They must hold "to the mystery of the faith with a clear conscience." Mounce explains, "and as that gospel works its way out in their lives, their consciences should not condemn them of sin."[13]

---

9. *LEKGNT*, 508.
10. BDAG, ἐγκρατής, 274.
11. The distinction "able to teach" does not require elders to preach, although some do (e.g., 1 Tim. 5:17).
12. Merkle, *Forty Questions About Elders and Deacons*, 227–29.
13. William D. Mounce, *Pastoral Epistles*, WBC 46 (Waco, TX: Nelson, 2000), 199.

But pastors hold the distinct priority of proclaiming God's Word. The primary place the congregation sees a pastor will be in the ministry of teaching and preaching. In the corporate setting, the congregation finds a critical, threefold example shown by faithful pastors.

(1) Pastors demonstrate to the congregation what it means to be diligent students of God's Word, who give careful attention to properly interpreting and applying it. Their example spills over into the way that the congregation learns to read, study, interpret, and apply God's Word. The ability to teach (1 Tim. 3:2) and to exhort in sound doctrine (Titus 1:9), models the appropriate way of reading and applying the Word in daily life. Rather than church members thinking it permissible to read their own interpretations and applications into the Word, faithful pastors, week after week, expose the congregation to sound interpretations leading to healthy applications of biblical doctrine.

(2) Pastors committed to teaching sound doctrine instill a love of good doctrine in the members of their congregations (Titus 1:9). Failing to grow up hearing sound doctrine taught from the pulpit left me jaundiced. Thank God, that changed as I began to study God's Word, realizing it is a lively doctrinal book (2 Tim. 4:1–4). When pastors regularly expound God's Word and explain the doctrines in the biblical text, then the church starts to grasp the importance of doctrine as foundational to the whole of the Christian life. They begin to see that any talk of the person and work of Christ, sin, salvation, judgment, heaven, the Holy Spirit, and the church requires consideration of biblical doctrine. When they witness their pastors' excitement in preaching sound doctrine, it becomes wonderfully contagious in the congregation, as they see the bigger picture of God's Word and how doctrine connects every detail.

(3) Pastors' ability to defend the faith and "refute those who contradict" God's Word (Titus 1:9) will challenge and inspire members of the congregation to better understand their Bibles. It happens regularly that as church members face false teaching and receive help from their pastors in being able to give a faithful answer, they grow in hungering to know and apply the Word. Pastors modeling clarity in biblical interpretation, appropriately responding to those trying to contradict the faith, will likely have members asking the pastors to teach them how to do the same. It provides a wonderful opportunity to disciple the body in properly handling God's Word, not as a tool to win wars but as the message of truth that changes lives.

Summary

The apostle made clear, as apostolic delegates Timothy and Titus led congregations toward elder plurality, that they were to give attention to character above all else in candidates for the office. With the modern tendency of some churches just to look for a nice man or pleasant mannerisms or a loaded ministry résumé, Paul would have nothing of that. Character stands tall when considering those shepherding Christ's flock.

Yet in the character qualities, other than teaching and not being a new convert, Paul simply called for pastors to live like true disciples of Jesus Christ. If pastors remember they are first Christians and church members it will keep them focused on living holy lives, building relationships, and setting an example for the church as believers. Apart from this kind of intentional faithfulness as disciples, men have no warrant to serve as pastors of Christian churches.

REFLECTION QUESTIONS

1. Why should pastors pay attention to character in their lives?

2. What kind of character issues does Paul raise about marriage and family in Titus 1?

3. How does "above reproach" serve as an *umbrella* term in personal conduct for pastors?

4. What does Paul mean when calling for elders to exercise "self-control"?

5. How does the preaching and teaching of pastors affect the members of their congregations?

How Does Jesus's Life and Ministry Mark the Pastor?

We could answer this question quite simply: *with everything*. We would not go wrong with that response. Paul told the Corinthians, "Be imitators of me, just as I also am of Christ" (1 Cor. 11:1). Likewise, to the Ephesians, "Therefore be imitators of God, as beloved children; and walk in love, just as Christ also loved you and gave Himself up for us, an offering and a sacrifice to God as a fragrant aroma" (Eph. 5:1–2). Whether in word or deed, we're to find in Jesus our model for how to live, love, and serve.

So, any consideration of a few characteristics of Jesus's life and ministry must not be construed as picking some as necessary while disregarding others. We're to look to Jesus Christ every day. We're to pray, discipline ourselves, study and learn, die to self, meditate on Scripture, and rely upon the Lord until Christ is formed in us (Gal. 4:19). The Father predestined those whom he foreknew "to become conformed to the image of His Son, so that He would be the firstborn among many brethren" (Rom. 8:29). We're to seek, by God's grace, to be like Christ in life and ministry. But how do we get our heads around the massive life of Christ?

While the qualities in 1 Timothy 3 and Titus 1 help picture the Christian life lived out in faithfulness, three essential characteristics found in Jesus's life and ministry must mark the pastor as well: humility, service, and love. We see them together in the remarkable narrative of John 13, as Jesus gathered with his disciples for the Last Supper.

Humility Must Mark Pastoral Ministry

John's introduction of Jesus's act of washing the disciples' feet as a servant sets the stage for understanding how the Lord Jesus approached relationships within their circle of fellowship. The apostle emphasizes the self-consciousness of Jesus as he approached the Last Supper (John 13:1–3). He twice used "knowing" (*oida*), expressing *understanding* or *perception*, from a root word meaning *seeing*.[1] He knew he would soon return to the eternal glory that belonged to him before the incarnation (John 17:5). He knew that in hours, Judas Iscariot would betray him into the hands of the religious leaders. They would hand him over to the Romans for crucifixion (John 13:2). John writes, "Jesus, knowing that the Father had given all things into His hands, and that He had come forth from God and was going back to God, got up from supper, and laid aside His garments; and taking a towel, He girded Himself. Then He poured water into the basin and began to wash the disciples' feet and to wipe them with the towel with which He was girded" (John 13:3–5).

Jesus took the position of a servant, gladly embracing a task given to the lowest member of the household. Humility marked his entire ministry. Of course, in the incarnation itself, we find humility surrounding the entry of the Son of God into the world (Luke 2:1–7). When the disciples argued over who was greatest among them, Jesus declared, "For the one who is least among all of you this is the one who is great" (Luke 9:46–48). Jesus took the place of the least as he washed the disciples' feet. He had no desire to impress his followers or even the religious leaders in order to gain their favor. He had no reservations of being "the guest of a man who is a sinner" when he entered the home of Zacchaeus to dine with him and declare the tax collector to be a new man of faith (Luke 19:1–10). When Jesus called for all the weary and burdened to come to him for rest, he said, "Take My yoke upon you and learn from Me, for I am gentle and humble in heart, and you will find rest for your souls" (Matt. 11:28–29). Puritan pastor Richard Sibbes vividly applied this to ministers: "The ambassadors of so gentle a Saviour should not be overbearing, setting up themselves in the hearts of people where Christ alone should sit as in his own temple."[2] Throughout his ministry we find his gentleness and humility, so should these characteristics not also be clearly evident in those representing him with his people?

The most significant moment of humility for Jesus was the cross. Paul captures it in memorable language, prefacing to put into practice the same kind of thinking and attitude as that of Jesus.

> Have this mind among yourselves, which is yours in Christ Jesus, who, though he was in the form of God, did not count equality with God a thing to be grasped, but emptied himself, by taking the form of a servant, being born in the likeness of men. And being found in human form, he humbled himself by becoming obedient to the point of death, even death on a cross. (Phil. 2:5–8 ESV)

---

1. *NIDNTTE*, οἶδα, 3:460–62.
2. Richard Sibbes, *The Bruised Reed*, Puritan Paperbacks (1630; Edinburgh: Banner of Truth Trust, 1998), 26.

The same way of thinking (*phroneite*) or disposition[3] so evident in Jesus heading to the cross should shape those whom he has given the charge of shepherding his flock. That kind of humility cannot be worked up by acts of self-flagellation or morose introspection. It happens when we take a regular look at our Lord Jesus Christ in his substitutionary death. The more we grasp our sin and the more clearly we see the price paid for our sins, the more we find ourselves humbled at the sight of the crucified Son of God.

C. John Miller commented on the humility of nineteenth-century Anglican evangelist Brownlow North: "He self-consciously labored to speak from a heart knowledge that he was chief of sinners."[4] Pastors need the same position when entering the pulpit, starting a counseling session, leading an elders' meeting, or discipling one on one. Unless we see ourselves as great sinners in desperate need of a greater Savior, we'll fall prey to the lure of pride. Miller warns, "My own conviction is that the flesh is still so strong in the Christian leader that each of us needs a healthy fear of our own capacity for ruining the work of God with our *unconscious* pride."[5]

Fittingly, right after Peter's instruction to his fellow elders, he wrote, "You younger men, likewise, be subject to your elders; *and all of you* [younger men and elders], clothe yourselves with humility toward one another, for God is opposed to the proud, but gives grace to the humble" (1 Peter 5:5, emphasis added). Humility must mark our lives and ministries as it did our Lord's.

Service Must Mark Pastoral Ministry

When the disciples grew indignant with James and John jockeying for lordly places in the heavenly kingdom, Jesus corrected all of them (Mark 10:35–45). Then he peeled back the curtain for them to see the way he viewed his mission, so that, repenting of their pride, they might embrace the same attitude: "For even the Son of Man did not come to be served, but to serve, and to give His life a ransom for many" (Mark 10:45). Contemplate that for a moment. The eternal Son, sent by the Father to redeem a people through his bloody death at the cross, who would be raised from the dead by the glory of the Father and ascend back to the eternal glory he had forever known, consciously saw his mission as *serving others*. Jesus poignantly set the record straight for the disciples. If one would follow him, one must learn to serve others.

In the same context as John 13, another dispute arose when the disciples debated who among them was the greatest. Jesus said their talk sounded like the unbelieving. Then the one that had just washed their feet corrected their dispositions: "For who is greater, the one who reclines at the table or the one

---

3. BDAG, φρονέω, 1065–66.
4. C. John Miller, *The Heart of a Servant Leader*, ed. Barbara Miller Juliani (Phillipsburg, NJ: P&R, 2004), 69 (emphasis original).
5. Miller, *Servant Leader*, 86 (emphasis original).

who serves? Is it not the one who reclines at the table? But I am among you as the one who serves" (Luke 22:24–27). Even after the resurrection, we find Jesus serving by preparing breakfast for the disciples that had gone fishing in the night (John 21:9–13). Throughout his ministry, Jesus served his followers, the multitudes, and the alienated individuals.

Jesus left the table to lay aside his garments; take a towel, a pitcher of water, and a basin; and then wash the dirty feet of the disciples (John 13:1–5). Yet in that humbling act of service Jesus simply visualized what he had been doing among them, and what he would do at the cross. Jesus came to serve others.

If the Lord of the church served so faithfully, his selfless, sacrificial, and loving service must mark pastoral ministry. If pastors fail to serve their people throughout the week by loving them, showing deference to them, looking for ways to meet their needs, seeking to know them better, speaking words of counsel and encouragement, joining them in mission and service projects, they lose power in serving them from the pulpit. Jesus did not limit service to his teaching. He healed, delivered, raised the dead, fed the hungry, engaged in relationships, calmed fears, forgave, declared hope, and laid down his life for others. That's the model given to pastors charged with shepherding the flock.

Charles Haddon Spurgeon practiced this same kind of servant heart found in the Lord Jesus. Spurgeon personally knew the members of his large, nineteenth-century congregation. He saw the needy in London and acted by initiating ministries to serve the uneducated, poor, orphans, widows, jobless, and many others. He personally responded to hundreds of letters he received each month, offering counsel, gospel truth, and encouragement. Often he served others when in great physical pain. Remarkably, this man, who became the best-known preacher in that era, regularly gave himself in service to his congregation and the people of his city. But he simply followed what he saw in Jesus.[6]

The prophet Isaiah called the Messiah to come "the Servant." He predicts this servant-hearted mission, beautifully rendered in Alec Motyer's translation of Isaiah 42:1–4.

> Behold!
> My Servant, whom I uphold,
> my Chosen One whom my soul accepts with favour.
> I have bestowed My Spirit on him;
> judgment to the nations he will bring out.
> He will not shriek out, nor raise,
> nor make people hear his voice out of doors.
> A bruised reed he will not break,
> and a smoldering wick he will not snuff out;

---

6. Arnold A. Dallimore, *Spurgeon: A New Biography* (Edinburgh: Banner of Truth Trust, 1985).

in accordance with truth he will bring out judgment.
He will not smolder, nor will he bruise,
until he sets up judgment in the earth.
And for his teaching the wide world waits in hope.[7]

The gentleness of Jesus, his concern for the nations, his tenderness with the broken and disheartened, and his patience with those needing him express his servant heart—that's the model for pastors. Be servants to your congregations in the same gentle, sacrificial, and faithful way that Jesus serves us.

Love Must Mark Pastoral Ministry

John tells of Jesus's deep love for his followers even as he approached the cross: "Having loved His own who were in the world, He loved them to the end" (John 13:1). Take a good look at the group whose feet Jesus washed. Complaint, denial, cowardice, doubt, and boasting seemed to mark them more than humility, love, and service. Yet Jesus loved them to the end. He did not allow their flaws to deflate his love. This kind of love is personable, conscious of neediness, and intent on seeking their good.

Paul gives a good picture of what this love looks like in practice: "The Lord's bond-servant must not be quarrelsome, but kind to all, able to teach, patient when wronged, with gentleness correcting those who are in opposition, if perhaps God may grant them repentance leading to the knowledge of the truth, and they may come to their senses and escape from the snare of the devil, having been held captive by him to do his will" (2 Tim. 2:24–26). Notice the aim of Christlike love: to see God's mercy awaken and deliver those trapped by the snare of the devil. What posture must those serving Christ take in trying to reach people so blinded? We might think thundering away at them will turn them from their sin. But Paul counsels love through gentleness instead of running over them; kindness instead of speaking our mind in a quarrelsome way; teaching them with patience, even forgiving their harsh words and recalcitrance.

Love will be evident in our gentleness, service, and sacrificial care for others more than in flowery claims of love. The kind of love Jesus displays acts on behalf of others, taking no regard for oneself, willingly sacrificing for the other's good, and caring more for that person's condition before the Lord God than personal convenience, schedule, or cost. Jesus drew the connection between his display of love and how the same kind of love must live through his followers, when he said, "By this all men will know that you are My disciples, if you have love for one another" (John 13:35). With that being true for

---

7. Alec Motyer, *Isaiah by the Day: A New Devotional Translation* (Fearn, Tain, Ross-shire, Scotland: Christian Focus, 2011), 201.

all followers of Jesus, how much more is it true for those he entrusts to care for the lambs he has gathered by his sacrificial love at the cross.

Summary

Can we read and meditate on John 13 enough as pastors? Here we find the humility, service, and love of Jesus compressed into a single narrative that shouts to us the way to live as undershepherds of Christ's flock. We must not relegate this narrative to an occasional dusting off to remember the hours before the crucifixion. Instead, the model of Jesus humbly, lovingly serving his disciples gives pastors the template for doing the same with Christ's church.[8] Yet we'll not do so without the help of the Spirit, just as Jesus taught his disciples (John 14–16). Miller poignantly brings this together: "It's now clear to me that my zeal for making Christ known must be tempered by a humble willingness to recognize my limits as a weak person who constantly falls into the temptation of thinking that he can do the work of the Holy Spirit."[9] Humble, loving service is Holy Spirit work. It's not natural to the flesh. The call to follow Christ's model for ministry also calls us to depend upon Jesus, the Vine (John 15:1–11), apart from whom we can do nothing, and the Spirit who guides us into the truth of glorifying Christ in our ministries (John 16:12–15).

REFLECTION QUESTIONS

1. Describe the implications of John's description of Jesus's self-consciousness as he prepared to wash the disciples' feet.

2. How might we grow in humility as we serve the people of God?

3. What tangible ways may pastors regularly serve their congregations?

4. How might Paul's idea of love in action (2 Tim. 2:24–26) unfold in your ministry setting?

5. What has God given to enable us to humbly and lovingly serve others around us?

---

8. While the Pastoral Epistles guide our practice in pastoral ministry, the Gospels *must* shape the way we live and serve in pastoral ministry, as we follow the model of the Good Shepherd.

9. Miller, *Servant Leader*, 69.

Why Is Pastoral Plurality Better for the Church's Health Than Single Pastors?

In my early days of ministry, I served as a solo pastor. The churches had no elders, only deacons, so all the pastoral ministry responsibilities fell on my shoulders. Dealing with church conflict, counseling broken marriages, organizing church ministries, administrating church plans, overseeing the office, visiting hospitals, comforting the bereaved, leading worship services, preaching, and leading midweek services were all my responsibilities—alone. Occasionally, a deacon might join me in a hospital or bereavement visit, but otherwise I had to juggle these pastoral concerns while preparing to preach and teach multiple times.

Did I succeed in all these areas? Certainly not: too much time spent planning, organizing, and administrating cut into sermon preparation. Wrestling with church conflict—sometimes multiple issues happening simultaneously—spared little mental energy to think creatively on how to unpack a biblical text. The area that tended to suffer most should have been where I spent most of my time: preparing to feed the flock.[1] A single pastor model leaves much to be desired if the church will be shepherded in a healthy way.

The New Testament consistently shows a pattern of plurality for those serving as pastors/elders/overseers.[2] As theologian John Hammett explains, "When one looks at the verses containing the words *elder*, *overseer*, and

---

1. "The pastor's first responsibility is to feed the sheep on the Word of God (John 21:15–17; 2 Tim. 4:2)" (Mark Dever and Paul Alexander, *The Deliberate Church: Building Your Ministry on the Gospel* [Wheaton, IL: Crossway, 2005], 94).
2. As noted in Question 1, these terms are used interchangeably for the same biblical office. See Phil A. Newton and Matt Schmucker, *Elders in the Life of the Church: Rediscovering the Biblical Model for Church Leadership* (Grand Rapids: Kregel Ministry, 2014), 45–57. For a thorough academic study of this subject, see Benjamin L. Merkle, *The Elder and Overseer: One Office in the Early Church*, SBL 57, ed. Hemchand Gossai (New York: Peter Lang, 2003).

pastor, a consistent pattern of plurality emerges."[3] It may be that a church has only one man qualified, according to 1 Timothy 3 and Titus 1, to serve as pastor/elder. Yet that pastor, along with the congregation, should seek to add another pastor to come alongside the solo pastor as soon as possible, preferably by raising up a faithful man within the congregation to serve as a fellow elder.[4] That's the New Testament pattern.

Why does a plurality of pastors/elders best lead a local congregation? We'll investigate this question by first surveying the biblical pattern for pastors/elders. Then we'll look at ten facets found in the wisdom of plural pastors.

The Biblical Pattern

Jesus established his band of disciples, to whom he would eventually hand off his ministry, as a plurality (Luke 6:12–16; Acts 1:1–8). The post-ascension upper room discussion added Matthias to their number to reach the full complement of twelve apostles—a plurality that bore testimony to the resurrection of Jesus Christ (Acts 1:12–26; 1 Cor. 15:5). As the church began its growing pains, the complaints arising from the Hellenistic widows led to appointing seven men—a plurality—to serve alongside the apostles in caring for widows (Acts 6:1–7). The first mention of elder plurality in the church came up rather incidentally, as Luke told of the new Antioch church sending a gift for famine relief through Barnabas and Saul "to the elders" in Jerusalem (Acts 11:30). Elders appeared so normal among them, following the Jewish community's leadership structure adjusted to the local church, that Luke saw no reason to call special attention by announcing the emergence of elders.

When Paul and Barnabas established churches in Lystra, Iconium, and Derbe, they backtracked on their journey to appoint "elders for them in every church" (Acts 14:23). Note that "elders"—plural—were appointed "in every church"—singular. The pattern of multiple elders in every congregation identified the way Paul and Barnabas believed churches needed to be shepherded and led. Luke identified elders in the Jerusalem church with the apostles as leaders of that congregation (Acts 15:2). The elders and apostles listened to Paul and Barnabas's opponents debate the validity of Gentile conversion apart from circumcision and Jewish rituals. The elders' engagement in theological

---

3. John S. Hammett, *Biblical Foundations for Baptist Churches: A Contemporary Ecclesiology*, 2nd ed. (Grand Rapids: Kregel Academic, 2019), 208.

4. "In a church where more than one [elder] cannot be obtained, that one may be appointed upon the principle, that as soon as another can be procured there shall be a plurality," wrote nineteenth-century Baptist leader W. B. Johnson, *The Gospel Developed through the Government and Order of the Churches of Jesus Christ* (Richmond, VA: H. K. Ellyson, 1846), in *Polity: Biblical Arguments on How to Conduct Church Life—A Collection of Historic Baptist Documents*, ed. Mark Dever (Washington, DC: Center for Church Reform, 2001), 194. Another elder may not be financially compensated but serve as non-staff.

discussion led to a clarified doctrinal position and a critical decision affecting gospel witness for the church (Acts 15:1–29).

Without calling special attention to elder plurality, Luke does record Paul's message to Ephesus, asking "the elders of the church" (plural elders, singular church) to meet him in Miletus (Acts 20:17). In his discussion, he also calls them "overseers" (*episkopoi*—plural) who were "to shepherd [*poimainein*—the verbal form of pastor/shepherd] the church of God which He purchased with His blood" (Acts 20:28). Paul's Jerusalem visit to give James his missionary report also included "all the elders" of the Jerusalem church (Acts 21:18).

Paul refers to Timothy being set apart by the elders ("presbytery" in NASB; "council of elders" in ESV; "body of elders" in NIV) in his home congregation (1 Tim. 4:14; Acts 16:1–3). He identifies elders as "the office of overseer" in 1 Timothy 3:2,[5] while calling them "elders" in 1 Timothy 5:17. The latter passage identifies the elders having responsibility to "rule well" and to preach and teach—with the obvious use of plural language, for example, "*those* who work hard at preaching and teaching."[6] That implies a distribution of responsibilities within the plurality of elders. Titus 1:5 refers to appointing "elders in every city"—again, *plural* elders in *singular* city. In Philippians 1:1, as Paul identifies the recipients of his epistle, he mentions "the overseers and deacons," both offices in plurality.

Peter exhorted "the elders among" the scattered churches to shepherd the flock of God (1 Peter 5:1). Benjamin Merkle refers to 1 Corinthians 16:15–16 ("be in subjection to such men and to everyone who helps in the work and labors") and 1 Thessalonians 5:12 ("those who diligently labor among you, and have charge over you in the Lord and give you instruction") as additional leaders in the church "performing elderlike functions" with the plural use.[7] "Leaders" in Hebrews 13:17, literally, "those leading you," refers to the elders/overseers/pastors of the congregation. Even the reflective exhortation "those who led you," with plural reference, likely to former pastors, left a mark on the church to continue to "imitate their faith" (Heb. 13:7).

After Hammett surveys the NT use of elder plurality, he concludes, "There is no verse describing anyone as *the* elder of a church."[8] Merkle states, "The

---

5. This is one of the few instances of the singular use of overseer or elder, and on each occasion, the biblical writer singles one elder out of others (e.g., 1 Peter 1:1; 2 John 1; 3 John 1).
6. I have argued that separating elders into "ruling elders" and "teaching elders" interpreted from this passage creates an artificial distinction not intended in the text. All elders rule and all elders teach, while some due to gifting and temperament excel in one area or the other. See Newton and Schmucker, *Elders in the Life of the Church*, 71, 206–7. For a different view, see David Dickson, *The Elder and His Work*, eds. George McFarland and Philip G. Ryken (Phillipsburg, NJ: P&R, 2004).
7. Benjamin L. Merkle, "The Biblical Role of Elders," in *Baptist Foundations: Church Government for an Anti-Institutional Age*, eds. Mark Dever and Jonathan Leeman (Nashville: B&H Academic, 2015), 285.
8. Hammett, *Biblical Foundations*, 208 (emphasis original).

New Testament evidence indicates that every church had a plurality of elders. There is no example in the New Testament of one elder or pastor leading a congregation as the sole or primary leader."[9] The New Testament clearly models plurality for those shepherding the flock. But why is plurality with pastors so important? We'll look at the wisdom of plurality in light of ten facets that demonstrate why every local church should strive to have a plurality of elders/pastors leading them.

The Wisdom in Plurality

Having served as a pastor for over forty years, I've found that twenty-five years of elder plurality has done more to strengthen my pastoral ministry, better utilize my gifts, and more effectively serve my congregation than those years as a solo pastor. While not exhaustive, the ten facets in the wisdom of plurality demonstrate a sound rationale of why congregations should never settle for a solo pastor attempting to shepherd the flock, and why a pastor should persist until he has plural leadership joining him in pastoral ministry.

1. Plurality Shares the Shepherding Load

Whether large or small, the needs in a congregation require more than one set of eyes to see and one set of feet to move into action to serve. The energy and time needed to feed the flock, counsel and encourage, offer direction to the struggling, disciple new believers, check on the sick and afflicted, and help the struggling can sap the life out of one person charged to handle it all. But when multiple elders join to serve one flock, these responsibilities can be parceled out in such a way that the congregation will not be neglected and the pastor/elder will be able to accomplish the work where his gifts best serve the church.

2. Plurality Utilizes Multiple Gifts to Serve the Body

W. B. Johnson called this "a division of labor among them [the elders]." He further pointed out regarding 1 Timothy 5:17 that while the same qualifications were identified in each one, "some labored in word and doctrine, and others did not, the distinction between them was not in rank, but in the character of their service."[10] With plurality maintained, by "character of their service" he indicates that elders applied their gifts and strengths effectively and differently to the church. Not all elders have the same gifts. While all engage, to some degree, in ruling, leading, and teaching, some have stronger teaching gifts, and so must be released to exercise those gifts for the sake of the body. Others have keener gifts in leadership, organization, and administration. They need to focus their gifts on these areas, releasing those with stronger preaching and teaching gifts to instruct and train the congregation. In plurality, the elders work together

---

9. Merkle, "Biblical Role," 285.
10. Johnson, *Gospel Developed*, in Dever, *Polity*, 191.

without considering one more important than the other—the church needs all the gifts faithfully utilized within the elder body.

3. Plurality Compensates for a Single Pastor's Weaknesses by Multiple Strengths

Any pastor honestly evaluating his abilities recognizes he has weaknesses. That's normal, and he should have no shame in such an admission. Paul makes clear that the Holy Spirit distributes gifts sovereignly. It has nothing to do with the individual, but rather divine pleasure determines how the individual will serve the rest of the church (1 Cor. 12:4–7). He not only has weaknesses in areas of ministry, but he also has personal weaknesses—areas in which he wrestles to grow and solidify. If he faces the challenge of shepherding a church alone, his weaknesses will become glaring. But in plurality, multiple pastors/elders combine their strengths to compensate for one another's weaknesses, so that no one falls through the cracks in pastoral ministry and care.

4. Plurality Builds Accountability

Every believer needs accountability so that in the face of temptation, struggles with discipline, times of despondency, and wrestling with endurance, he or she might be encouraged and admonished by others in the body. Elders do that for each other. Banding together to pursue holiness, discipline, integrity, and doctrinal purity, each man within the pastoral team spurs the other toward faithfulness. We pray for one another, candidly share our struggles, discuss the Word with each other, encourage and build up, and fill the gap in what each needs to walk as men of God.

5. Plurality Curtails Authoritarianism

The aged apostle John called a church's attention to the authoritarian Diotrephes who exalted himself above others, refused apostolic counsel, spread false words about the apostle, and tried to shut others out from leading the church (3 John 9–10). Due to the reality of some with overbearing personalities, coupled with arrogant attempts to be a virtual dictator over a church, a strong elder/pastoral team curtails one man attempting to wrangle control of a congregation. Andrew Clarke is right about how to avoid this kind of spirit: "The authority of elders is exercised collectively," not individually.[11] Johnson, years earlier, agreed: "All [are] equal in rank and authority, no one having preeminence over the rest."[12] Maintaining equality among elders curtails authoritarians.

---

11. Andrew D. Clarke, *A Pauline Theology of Church Leadership*, LNTS 362, ed. Mark Goodacre (London: T&T Clark, 2008), 56. While Clarke holds overseers and elders as distinct offices—a concept that follows more second-century Ignatius's influence rather than the scriptural evidence—he's right on the matter of authority among elders.
12. Johnson, *Gospel Developed*, in Dever, *Polity*, 190.

6. Plurality Is Essential When Dealing with Disciplinary Issues

If a single pastor has attempted to lead his church to exercise discipline on a member, he has likely wished for other leaders to partner with him in the effort. I've known of some attempting this alone who then had the tables turned the other way. We need the wisdom, unity, and clarity of plurality to help with these serious matters of following the Matthew 18:15–20 steps of discipline. I've been grateful that when facing those situations, I've not had to do so alone but with the united voice and strong shoulders of fellow elders/pastors.

7. Plurality Models Maturity and Unity for the Church

The congregation watches the elders. They should, for elders are to model for them how to live as Christians (1 Peter 5:3; Heb. 13:7). The same challenge confronting the congregation—learning how to live with one another in love and unity—faces the different personalities, interests, gifts, and abilities among a team of pastors/elders. As elders demonstrate faithful growth together in maturity and unity, they serve as models for the rest of the body to do the same.

8. Plurality Provides Consistency in Leadership Decisions

Clarke refers to elders "who act in chorus, making decisions as a combined group," rather than one individual attempting to lead without consulting the others.[13] The combined wisdom, congregational insight, experience, and discernment joined together in a team of pastors will give the congregation far more consistency in leadership than a single man left to his narrow insight.

9. Plurality Multiplies Ability to Train and Mentor Future Church Leaders

Pastors/elders don't simply have meetings. They're engaged in shepherding the flock. Part of the shepherding involves proactively training up future leaders that will serve their congregation and potentially serve others. Rather than leaving mentoring to one man in the church, the wealth of spiritual maturity and pastoral insight in a team of pastors multiplies the impact on training future leaders.[14]

10. Plurality Cultivates Stable Leadership for the Church

As I write this chapter, I'm on a four-month pastoral leave for chemotherapy treatment. My isolation from public involvement, while causing me angst, has not threatened the health of our congregation due to the way that we've cultivated a steady, consistent team of pastors/elders to shepherd the church. If a single pastor leaves or has an extended illness or dies while

---

13. Clarke, *Pauline Theology*, 58.
14. See Phil A. Newton, *The Mentoring Church: How Pastors and Congregations Cultivate Leaders* (Grand Rapids: Kregel Ministry, 2017).

serving, it can leave a church shepherdless for a period of time, causing them to suffer spiritual loss. But elders/pastors serving in plurality, recognizing and utilizing one another's gifts for the body, fill the gaps left by a missing pastor. This helps the congregation learn to live in more dependence upon the Lord than upon one man serving as *the* pastor.

No doubt, others can add to the various facets of plurality in pastoral ministry, but this list should suffice to show how critical it is for congregations to maintain a healthy plurality of pastors/elders leading them week by week.

Summary

The NT evidence of the regular practice of plural pastoral ministry cannot be sidestepped. Even one writer holding to a single pastor authority for local churches admits, "It is true that whenever the term *elder* or *bishop* is used in the New Testament it is used in the plural, which would mean that the general practice of the churches in New Testament times was to have at least two elders."[15] For the health of the local church, plurality in pastoral ministry proves essential.

I can testify to the benefits of these ten facets of the wisdom in a plurality model over that of a single pastor. Each facet has benefitted me personally, as well as our congregation. It has also extended my pastoral longevity by sharing the load with a team of faithful pastors/elders.

REFLECTION QUESTIONS

1. What is the New Testament evidence of pastoral plurality?

2. How does Paul's practice of elder plurality with churches that he planted offer a model to present-day congregations?

3. Are any of the ten facets of wisdom in plurality missing in your pastoral ministry?

4. Which facet of plurality seems most important in your pastoral context?

5. How does the apostle John's conflict with Diotrephes in 3 John urge pastoral plurality for maintaining a healthy church?

---

15. Gerald Cowen, *Who Rules the Church? Examining Congregational Leadership and Church Government* (Nashville: B&H, 2003), 14 (emphasis original).

PART 2

Pastoral Development and Health

Can Pastors Remain Spiritually Healthy throughout Their Ministries?

Aside from a few years during part of college and seminary, I've served in some capacity of pastoral ministry since 1973. My walk with Christ grew stronger with the years, but that didn't mean that no struggles arose. They did. Throughout that time, I've had to learn to deal with my sin, areas where I lacked discipline, inconsistencies, coldness of heart, bitterness toward church members, dissatisfaction with life and ministry, and other heart issues. God has been gracious to sustain me through these years. With all the remaining deficiencies, I concur with the apostle Paul, "But by the grace of God I am what I am" (1 Cor. 15:10). While the Lord has carried me through many difficulties, he did not call me to idleness in my spiritual health. Rather, spiritual health is a daily pursuit by the grace of God.

With that pursuit in mind, let's consider ten areas needing attention to remain spiritually healthy throughout ministry.

1. Cultivate a Strong, Consistent Devotional Life

Nothing replaces time alone each day with God in the Word and prayer. Busyness with ministry and soul care of others must never get in the way of personal soul care. A pastor can easily spend every waking moment preparing, visiting, counseling, administrating, and doing a thousand other tasks related to ministry. But he must set aside time at the start of each day to draw near to God to meditate, reflect, confess sins, give thanks, worship, pray, and express love to Christ.[1] As the saintly Scottish pastor Robert Murray M'Cheyne said,

---

1. See Question 7 for more details on how to develop a consistent devotional life.

"I feel it is far better to begin with God—to see His face first, to get my soul near Him before it is near another."[2]

In addition to devotional time, sermon preparation should be a time of increased devotion, prayer, meditation, joy, confession, thankfulness, and glory in the Lord. Study hard, do the difficult work of exegesis, biblical theology, systematic theology, and homiletics, all the while being keen that you are studying *God's Word*. Be sensitive to the Holy Spirit exposing sins to confess, areas for renewed obedience, and new vistas for worship and praise.

2. Take a Daily Spiritual Inventory

Through the Word and the work of the Holy Spirit, open yourself to the gaze of God that exposes hidden and unrepented sins. Pray with the psalmist, "Search me, O God, and know my heart; try me and know my anxious thoughts; and see if there be any hurtful way in me, and lead me in the everlasting way" (Ps. 139:23–24). Confess your sins and believe the gospel's promise for cleansing from sin and renewing fellowship with Christ (1 John 1:5–2:2). Put sin to death (Rom. 6:1–14; Gal. 5:24; Eph. 4:17–5:21). The great Puritan theologian John Owen warned, "Thoughts are the great purveyors of the soul to bring in provision to satisfy its affections; and if sin remain unmortified [put to death] in the heart, they must ever and anon [again] be making provision for the flesh, to fulfill the lusts thereof."[3]

3. Never Let Wounds Fester

Anyone having served in ministry for even a short period of time understands what I mean by "wounds." Someone speaks a harsh, critical word to you or behind your back. Someone else starts a rumor about you in an effort to ruin your ministry. Another disrupts a congregational meeting in an attempt to make you look bad. The ones who promised you a raise three years before have still not come through, showing no signs of concern for your welfare. A staff member attempts to undermine your leadership. A power group works behind your back to get you fired. On we could go. Ministry will have great times of joy but also times when your heart gets saturated with bitterness, anger, thoughts of retaliation, and resentment.

Yet, if you're not living in the good news, you will have no good news to preach. Paul told the Ephesians, "Do not grieve the Holy Spirit of God, by whom you were sealed for the day of redemption. Let all bitterness and wrath and anger and clamor and slander be put away from you, along with all malice" (Eph. 4:30–31). While we gladly preach that to our congregation,

---

2. S. F. Smith, *The Christian Review*, Vol. 13 (Classic Reprint) (Boston: Gould, Kendall & Lincoln, 1948), 601.

3. John Owen, *Overcoming Sin and Temptation*, eds. Kelly M. Kapic and Justin Taylor (1656; Wheaton, IL: Crossway, 2006), 65.

do we preach that to ourselves? How can we put these embittering sins aside? "Be kind to one another, tender-hearted, forgiving each other, just as God in Christ has also forgiven you" (Eph. 4:32). Probably no passage has redirected me more often when wounds festered than this exhortation. Pastors: as forgiven people, we must forgive and show kindness in the same way Christ has shown to us. That calls for living at the cross with the consciousness of Jesus forgiving us. Unless we do, wounds will fester and destroy us.

4. Take Regular Time Off

Early in ministry I didn't take a day off. *I had too much to do.* Or so I thought. But that never changes. Pastors always have too much to do. Yet neglecting time off to burn the proverbial candle at both ends will shorten ministry. The weekly Sabbath rhythm where we stop what we normally do with work to rest, Jesus said, was meant for people rather than people for the Sabbath (Mark 2:27). That change of pace, withdrawing from the normal demands of work to find a point of rest and refreshment, is essential to the pastor's spiritual life. Laying aside the weight of ministry for a day off each week can recharge the spiritual batteries and invigorate the pastor to head back into the demands of ministry. Taking *all* of the vacation time allowed is critical for the pastor and his family. Even if you simply putter around the house or take the kids to the zoo or go on a family picnic, that kind of attentiveness to the family without the demands of ministry will strengthen family life while putting more miles into future ministry. Churches should figure a sabbatical period into the pastor's benefits. If your church doesn't have a sabbatical set into your schedule, then work toward it.[4]

5. Build Strong Pastoral Relationships in the Body

The worst advice that I received during my ordination council was "don't get close to your people." My inner alarm went off, knowing that pastor had bad relationships with his congregation and would never see them improve. On the contrary, you will find strength in the long journey of pastoral ministry by knowing your congregation, observing and learning their bents and life patterns, praying for them by name each week, standing with them in times of need, encouraging them in their struggles, loving them through their foibles, looking into their eyes to speak truth to them at the weekly gatherings, sending them notes of encouragement, and feeling the weight of their souls. When you love your people deeply, you want to keep pressing on even when things get difficult. You want to give attention to your soul so that you might serve them more effectively.

---

4. For help toward establishing a pastoral sabbatical, see Matt Schmucker, "Caring for the Pastor: The Sabbatical," *9Marks*, February 26, 2010, https://www.9marks.org/article/caring-pastor-sabbatical.

6. Allow Yourself to Be Pastored

Pastors tend to be the last to be pastored. But that's why the Lord established plural eldership for the local church. Elders are to pastor each other so that each is encouraged to press on in faithfulness to Christ. That requires a few things from the pastor. (1) Humbly submit to those appointed by the church to watch out for your soul. (2) Hold the attitude that you've not arrived (Phil. 3:12–16), and value God's means of grace for the journey, including other pastors pastoring you. (3) Maintain that God did not save you to go alone. Journey with your fellow elders and the body, receiving their support, encouragement, example, exhortations, forgiveness, admonitions, and multiplied contributions to your spiritual walk. (4) Regularly check your teachability so that you are learning from others whom God has put into your life (Heb. 13:17).[5] (5) Consider those with whom you will spend eternity by giving attention to growth, relationships, obedience, unity, and joy (Eph. 4:11–16).

7. Work on Your Marriage

Don't presume on your marriage. Learn to love your wife as Christ loves the church (Eph. 5:22–33). That means learning to deepen your love and service toward your wife. Watch the way you talk with her so that you build her up rather than crush with harsh words (1 Peter 3:7). Open your life to her. Keep the fires of romance ablaze. Make sure she knows by your time, energy, and focus that she has priority over your children. Never speak ill of her in public or private. Too many pastors fail to give attention to their wives so that the wives think their husbands are married to the church. Guard against presumption by enjoying God's gift of a wife.[6]

8. Invest in Building Good Leadership around You

Building leadership means learning to live life *together* in Christ. It calls for setting an example of a believer to those you lead (1 Tim. 4:12). As you lead, you set the pace in pastoral ministry by demonstrating patience with those that seem slow in catching on, gently correcting those that need your admonition, commending and encouraging people as often as you can, and turning over responsibilities to others as you steer, hone, and sharpen them. Those you lead need the example of a humble, holy, and servant-hearted pastor. You cannot live with a sense of feeling threatened by a rising leader's popularity and ability. Trust the Lord with what he will do in raising up a team

---

5. For instance, do you speak before taking time to listen? Do you try to defend yourself before listening and applying what others speak into your life? Do you recognize that God uses others in your ongoing sanctification?

6. Good encouragement in this area can be found in Paul David Tripp, *What Did You Expect? Redeeming the Realities of Marriage* (Wheaton, IL: Crossway, 2010); and Timothy Keller, *The Meaning of Marriage: Facing the Complexities of Commitment with the Wisdom of God* (New York: Dutton, 2011).

around you that will speak into your life and serve with you, and whom you will faithfully lead. That way you realize *all pastoral ministry* does not sit on your shoulders but also on those gathered around following your leadership.[7]

9. Read Good Books

Work on building a strong biblical and theological library that will serve as a tool for life and ministry.[8] Include commentaries,[9] various branches of theology—biblical, systematic, historical, practical, pastoral—biographies, hermeneutics, original languages, church history, ecclesiology, missions, devotionals, applied theology, and the broad realm of practical ministry. Also read beyond preparing for Sunday sermons. Read for your soul's encouragement. Read for pleasure. Read to learn. Do not limit your reading to only Christian books. Read good novels, world history, autobiographies, and other fields of interest. With my father having served in World War II, I happen to enjoy reading about that war, including particular battles, and the leaders during that generation. This genre of reading relaxes me while giving insights on leadership and human behavior. I usually have several books going in different genres so I can pick up what I need for the moment as sermon preparation, encouragement, devotion, or pleasure.

10. Annually Attend a Good Conference or Retreat

A pastor's time is precious. So is his need to be rekindled by biblical preaching, theological discussion, ministry interaction, and Christian fellowship. Conferences abound in our day, but time and money limit which to attend. Try to budget yearly for a conference or pastors' retreat that will help you spiritually and stir you toward greater faithfulness in pastoral work. Several seminaries offer short conferences on particular topics of interest for pastors. Local churches also provide biblical and thematic conferences that might be easy on the budget but strong on encouragement. If you are the only person that you listen to preaching, then you will likely grow stale. Be refreshed by the way others teach and preach God's Word in a conference or retreat setting. Be encouraged to persevere in ministry as you gather with other pastors walking through similar ministry demands.

---

7. See my book for details on training and mentoring leaders: *The Mentoring Church: How Pastors and Congregations Cultivate Leaders* (Grand Rapids: Kregel Ministry, 2017).
8. See Danny Akin, "Building a Theological Library," *Danny Akin* (blog), December 3, 2013, https://www.danielakin.com/building-a-theological-library-2013-update.
9. See Tremper Longman III, *Old Testament Commentary Survey*, 5th ed. (Grand Rapids: Baker Academic, 2013); and D. A. Carson, *New Testament Commentary Survey*, 7th ed. (Grand Rapids: Baker Academic, 2013).

Summary

Staying spiritually healthy throughout ministry is not complicated. But it does require discipline and consistency in the areas that spur faithfulness to Christ and ministry. Evaluate the ten areas identified in this chapter and see where you need to strengthen or make changes. Faithfulness to Christ throughout a long ministry leaves a mark on the congregation watching your life and labors. The congregation will be encouraged to persevere in the faith by observing the model you set for them. And you will have the joy of an enduring pastoral ministry.

REFLECTION QUESTIONS

1. In what areas do you need to strengthen your devotional life?

2. How might a pastor deal with the wounds that have accumulated with the strains in ministry?

3. What does it mean for a pastor to be pastored?

4. What are some ways that a pastor can work on his marriage?

5. How does building a leadership team assist in strengthening the pastor's spiritual health?

How Can a Pastor Care for His Spiritual Life?

Dangers lurk in pastoral ministry. We've heard the warnings, rightly, against greed, lust, power, and pride. Perhaps another poses greater danger due to its innocuous appearance: *presumption*. Since we study the Word, preach sermons, lead in worship, offer public prayers, pray with the sick and dying, do biblical counseling, talk about spiritual matters, and explain the gospel to others, we can think our spiritual lives to be well. Against the facade of an effective pastoral ministry, our souls dry up and decay. We wonder why we feel burned out, why the next visit irritates us, why sermon preparation has grown academic, and why we can't wait to finish on Sundays and escape the communion of the saints. While leading others spiritually, we've not given attention to our souls.

Longtime pastor Lewis Allen writes that ministry can become one of the greatest opponents to living with true joy in Christ. He confesses, "At times in my own ministry, my heart has felt like a wind tunnel, with prayers and sermon prep all focused on the needs of others rushing through it, while I was struggling to give enough time to ministering to my own spiritual needs." In such times, "Jesus ceases to be the light we're knowing and commending to others and becomes the one whose sweetness has faded."[1]

We regularly care for others' souls, but do we care for our own? Without consistent attention to our spiritual lives, we ultimately have little to offer those we're charged to shepherd. The most important focus of pastoral ministry must be the pastor's care for his own soul. With it he multiplies his pastoral effectiveness. We will look at the patterns and practices that need to be woven into the warp and woof of the pastor's spiritual life.

---

1. Lewis Allen, *The Preacher's Catechism* (Wheaton, IL: Crossway, 2018), 33.

Go Deep in Your Devotional Life

A devotional life does not mean a devotional book, although it may include one. Instead, it has to do with the ongoing deepening of communion with God. Set time apart for nothing else than knowing, enjoying, and fellowshipping with God. Through his Word we behold God. Puritan George Swinnock explained, "Those who have never seen the sun are amazed at a candle. Likewise, those who have never known the blessed God are fond of pitiful things on earth. But the whole world becomes a dunghill when we behold the incomparable God."[2]

At such a time of communing with him, everything else pales. We withdraw, following the sixteenth-century Scottish pastor Samuel Rutherford's counsel, "that ye come out and leave the multitude, and let Christ have your company."[3] Put simply, we meet God alone with open Bible to seek his presence, know his ways, and enjoy his company. We've not stopped to do more sermon work or create a new Bible study. We've come "to taste, and to want to taste more."[4] Paul Tripp narrows it: "We don't seek satisfaction, hoping that God will deliver it. No, we seek God, and the result is satisfaction of heart."[5] Consider three keys.

1. Daily Habits

I'm in a habit of talking with my wife in the mornings, kissing her on the way to the office, calling her at an appointed time late in the morning, and returning to discuss our days together. Just habits. But these habits and more have cultivated a deep love and passion for each other.

A healthy devotional life cannot develop without daily habits. As Rutherford reminds us, "Every day we may see some new thing in Christ. His love hath neither brim nor bottom."[6] Each day we seek to find our joy and confidence in Christ alone. We mustn't treat this as a job that we dutifully go to five days then rush for the weekend. It's more like a marriage that grows in love, devotion, and delight through daily engagement.

2. Focus on Communion with God

We're not simply practicing good devotional habits like other excellent duties engaging us. We're seeking communion with God centered in Jesus Christ, what Rutherford calls "a nearer communion with Christ and a growing

---

2. George Swinnock, *The Blessed and Boundless God*, ed. J. Stephen Yuille (1672; Grand Rapids: Reformation Heritage Books, 2014), 143.
3. Samuel Rutherford, *The Loveliness of Christ: Extracts from the Letters of Samuel Rutherford*, ed. Ellen S. Lister (1909; Edinburgh: Banner of Truth Trust, 2007), 56.
4. Allen, *Preacher's Catechism*, 32.
5. Paul David Tripp, *New Morning Mercies: A Daily Gospel Devotional* (Wheaton, IL: Crossway, 2014), May 24th selection.
6. Rutherford, *Loveliness of Christ*, 13.

communion."[7] Two things happen in communion. Puritan pastor John Flavel explains, "Communion with God, properly and strictly taken, consists in two things, viz., God's manifestation of Himself to the soul, and the soul's answerable returns to God."[8] The Lord shows himself to us in the Word. We respond to him in meditation, worship, delight, joy, prayer, thanksgiving, confession, and praise.

Communion engages us, not in some mystical way, but in a real, experiential knowledge of God particularly rooted in the gospel (Eph. 1:15–23; Col. 2:1–3). In the hidden part of the heart (Ps. 51:6; 1 Kings 8:39) the Lord meets us. "It is such a knowledge," wrote Swinnock, "that affects the heart with love for Him, fear of Him, and hatred for whatever is contrary to Him."[9] In other words, as we see the Lord more and more as he has revealed himself in Scripture, we respond with love and fear, affection and holy reverence. That leads to detachment from the world and detesting the old patterns of sin that yet remain.

3. Aim to Be Unhurried

We do have daily schedules that bear our attention, so we must plan to give ourselves unhurried time with the Lord each morning. Lingering marks deep love and affection, and allows for delighting in each moment together and anticipating the next time of aloneness to express joy together. Allen adds, "We do need to give our hearts time and space, and bring them, distraction free, back to the gospel. We need a fresh discovery of just how loved we are in Christ. In life's busyness we need to fight for time to listen to God's Word. If we don't, the thistles and thorns of work, ministry, and worry will choke our souls."[10]

Develop Healthy Patterns in the Devotional Life

Just as daily, unhurried communion marks our devotional time, growth only happens when we establish healthy patterns in the Word and prayer, along with other aspects of the devotional life.

1. Primary Elements in the Devotional Life

We establish healthy *patterns* by using means that God has provided to grow in devotedness to him. The Word, prayer, worship, meditation, memorization, and journaling all prove useful, some absolutely essential, if we're to

---

7. Rutherford, *Loveliness of Christ*, 16. D. A. Carson writes, "Spirituality must be thought of in connection with the Gospel" ("When Is Spirituality Spiritual? Reflections on Some Problems of Definition," *JETS* 37 [1994]: 387, quoted by A. J. Köstenberger, *Excellence: The Character of God and the Pursuit of Scholarly Virtue* [Wheaton, IL: Crossway, 2011], 68).

8. John Flavel, *The Mystery of Providence*, Puritan Paperbacks (1678; Edinburgh: Banner of Truth Trust, 1963), 144.

9. Swinnock, *Blessed and Boundless God*, 140.

10. Allen, *Preacher's Catechism*, 33. That "distraction free" works best without phones and social media.

commune with God.[11] The *Word of God* in a good, readable translation is the foundation of devotional life.[12] Devotions must be Word-driven or one drifts into unhealthy mysticism.[13] *Prayer* engages our response to the Word in confession, praise, thanksgiving, wonder, intercession, and petition. *Meditation* takes us beyond a quick reading through Scripture into a thoughtful reflection and slow meandering on its meaning in context with multiple applications to the soul (Josh. 1:8; Ps. 119:97, 103, 148). *Memorization* hides the Word in the heart for ready use throughout the day (Ps. 119:11; Eph. 6:17). An added element that many, including myself, have found helpful is *journaling*. If we're having thoughtful meditation on the Word, journaling provides a tool to write our reflections, including prayers, expressions of praise, and considerations of the many ways the Lord works in our lives.

Rutherford's quaint Scottish wording helps us understand what happens in private devotion: "There is much in our Lord's pantry as will satisfy all his bairns [children], and as much wine in his cellar as will quench all their thirst. Hunger on; for there is meat in hunger for Christ; go never from him, but fash [trouble; annoy] him (who yet is pleased with the importunity of hungry souls) with a dishful of hungry desires, till he fill you; and if he delay yet not ye away, albeit ye should fall a-swoon [faint] at his feet."[14]

2. Utilize a Reading Plan

As a young believer I, unfortunately, had no Bible reading plan. I just serendipitously plopped open a page and started reading. That didn't work. Only when I started working through books of the Bible, seeing the daily reading within context, and continuing the next day building on the previous reading did my growth in Christ take off.

How shall the pastor conduct an ongoing Bible reading? I recommend pastors read through the entire Bible yearly. We need the fresh look at obscure portions instead of just enjoying our favorite sections in Scripture. Some may do that outside their devotional time. Others frame their devotional reading in the yearly focus. I prefer the latter approach. Finding a plan that you want to use at the start of the New Year and sticking with it will encourage your

---

11. I'm not including corporate worship, since the focus is on personal devotions; both are necessary for the care of our souls.
12. I've found it a good practice to alternate translations from year to year.
13. "This 'Spirituality of the Word' must be the standard by which any spiritual discipline is measured, because study of, and obedience to, Scripture is the preeminent spiritual discipline taught in Scripture" (Köstenberger, *Excellence*, 77).
14. Rutherford, *Loveliness of Christ*, 4.

spiritual disciplines throughout the year.[15] Just remember, the pastor's own heart work "is the preacher's first responsibility, and not an optional extra."[16]

3. Prayer

Reading and meditating on the Word will affect prayer. It spurs impetus toward confession of sin, repentance, thanksgiving for God's acts, praise for God's revelation of himself, worship that may include reading or singing a hymn, joy and rejoicing, lament, petitions for God to act on his promises, intercession for those on your heart as you ponder the Word, and so on.[17] I love the way that John Piper collapses the myriad expressions on prayer: "Prayer is the translation into a thousand different words of a single sentence: 'Apart from me [Christ] you can do nothing' (John 15:5)."[18]

Just like a plan for reading the Word, a plan may be faithfully used for intercessory work that flows out of the devotional time. Prayer for family and church leaders make the everyday list. Praying for members of the congregation each day so that one prays through the membership at least monthly (preferably weekly depending on your congregation's size) becomes part of that daily list. Dividing the week into praying foci each day may include fellow pastors, local congregations, governing officials, ministry friends, extended family, missionary work, workers sent out from your church, and unbelieving friends and family.

4. Meditation and Memorization

At the start of Joshua's succession to Moses, the Lord commanded him to daily meditate on his law (Josh. 1:8). Psalm 119 is filled with exhortations and descriptions of meditation upon the Word. Peter's sermon at Pentecost gives evidence of rich meditation and memorization of God's Word and its Christ-centered focus (Acts 2). Paul's sermon at Mars Hill reflects his deep meditation upon the treasury of the Word (Acts 17:22–31). If one would wield "the sword of the Spirit" in daily battle against temptation and sin, then one must meditate upon and memorize God's Word, being ready for any situation (Eph.

---

15. Here are a few of many plans. The Robert Murray M'Cheyne Plan, developed by the nineteenth-century Scottish pastor, goes through the OT once and NT and Psalms twice: https://bibleplan.org/plans/mcheyne. The "Fifty-Two-Week Bible Reading Plan" has a reading from a different biblical genre for each day; http://www.bible-reading.com/bible-plan-nasb.html. George Guthrie, *CSB Day-By-Day Chronological Bible* (Nashville: Holman, 2018) takes you through chronologically. We've used the National Association of Evangelicals *Thru the Bible Reading Guide* for many years as an option for our congregation, https://www.nae.net/reading-the-bible-in-one-year. It also goes through the entire Bible in fifty-two weeks.
16. Allen, *Preacher's Catechism*, 34.
17. See Donald S. Whitney, *Praying the Bible* (Wheaton, IL: Crossway, 2015).
18. John Piper, *Brothers, We Are Not Professionals: A Plea to Pastors for Radical Ministry* (Nashville: B&H, 2002), 55.

6:10–20). Jesus's own battle with Satan showed his practice of memorizing Scripture and applying it contextually (Matt. 4:1–11). We need the ready recall of God's Word for life's daily challenges.[19]

Don Whitney, in his classic work *Spiritual Disciplines for the Christian Life*, defines "*meditation* as deep thinking on the truths and spiritual realities revealed in Scripture, or upon life from a scriptural perspective, for the purposes of understanding, application, and prayer." He compares it to the difference between simply dipping a tea bag in hot water instead of allowing it to steep. "Meditation on Scripture is letting the Bible brew in the brain."[20]

Within the scope of reading through the Bible, include time daily to meditate on particular portions to "brew in the brain" and work deeply into the heart. Out of this meditation, memorizing portions of the Word will be natural, leading to further meditation and application in one's life.

5. Journaling

Journaling doesn't have to be complicated. A spiral notebook will do to jot down meditations on the Word, prayers spurred by reading and reflecting on the Word, praises and thanksgiving recalled while praying and meditating, and gospel promises reiterated through reading the Word. It may happen daily or several times a week. You're not writing for public consumption but for personal edification. The time taken to journal helps the mind to better absorb what has been considered in the Word.[21]

A Personal Practice as an Example

Over the years I've varied my devotional practices. At one period I slowly read through one book, journaling meditations, and praying through a long prayer list. At another, I expanded my reading to include several chapters each day but not necessarily through the entire Bible, with my praying beyond family divided into different categories each day. For the past two decades I've committed to reading through the Bible yearly during my devotional times. I've found this to be the most fulfilling in more than fifty years as a Christian. Here's my daily routine.

---

19. See Andrew Davis, *An Approach to Extended Memorization of Scripture* (Ambassador International, 2014), available free on Kindle. For additional help in meditation and memorization, see Donald S. Whitney, *Spiritual Disciplines for the Christian Life*, rev. ed. (Colorado Springs: NavPress, 2014).
20. Whitney, *Spiritual Disciplines*, 46–47 (emphasis original).
21. See Whitney on the "value of journaling," in *Spiritual Disciplines*, 252–66: journaling helps in self-understanding and evaluation, in meditation, in expressing thoughts and feelings to the Lord, in remembering the Lord's works, in creating and preserving a spiritual heritage, in clarifying and articulating insights, in monitoring goals and priorities, and in maintaining other spiritual disciplines.

I utilize the same Bible, so I calculated how much I needed to read daily to go through the OT approximately twice, NT three times, and Psalms–Song of Solomon four to five times. I begin with reading three or more pages in the OT, followed by reading two or more pages in the Psalms–Song of Solomon, and that follows by reading a little over two pages in the NT. I generally read a chapter, as well, from the expositional series I'm doing on Sundays. During the reading, I'm reflecting. I'll pause to meditate on something that strikes me, reflect on a promise that refreshes me, or worship at an insight on the character of God. At times I'll stop to journal. Other times I wait until I've completed my reading and backtrack to journal. Or I may not journal that day, giving more attention to memorization or meditation. Something that I'm reading may spur me to pray for a friend's need or a situation we're facing at our church. Or a passage outside my normal scope for memorization grabs me, so I linger to hide it in my heart. Or some portion deeply convicts me of sin, so there's no going forward until I deal with that sin in confession and repentance. On some occasions I may read more than my day's allotment because of the flow of the text or the way that it's serving my heart. In other words, I don't hesitate to vary my practice from one day to another, although I'm still working within the framework of my reading plan. *The aim to commune with God remains primary*, so if my template gets in the way, I don't hesitate to change what I'm doing. I want my heart warmed before the Lord, sensing his presence to direct my steps for the day.

My prayer time focuses daily on my wife, children, children's spouses, grandchildren, mother, brother and his wife, my wife's siblings and their spouses, our church's elders and deacons, and our pastoral interns. We utilize a church prayer card that has family names broken into six days of the week, so I pray for the families for that day. On Saturday and Sunday, I pray for other brothers' preaching, Mondays as a catch-up day, Tuesdays for extended family, Wednesdays for government, Thursdays for close friends, Fridays for missionaries, and Saturdays for those we've sent into pastoral or missionary work. Current needs make it into the daily routine of prayer. My goal is to alternate between journaling and memorization every other day.

If something happens to disrupt a day's plan (e.g., as when going through chemotherapy when my fatigue level allowed only reading a chapter or two and mumbling a short prayer), then I don't get under bondage. The Lord knows my heart's desire to seek him and be with him in that lingering time of devotion. As soon as the disruption ends, I'm back into the routine. Staying in the routine, even if it varies from time to time, is critical to maintain momentum and get the most out of whatever devotional plan you choose.

Summary

Daily time seeking the Lord must never be an add-on to a busy life of pastoral work. Instead, it's foundational to all that we do in pastoral ministry.

As Allen reminds us, "It is the preacher's first responsibility, not an optional extra."[22] Pastors need to develop a devotional plan that fits their lives and schedules, then be consistent in practicing it daily. One may vary and improve upon it as he goes along, but consistent practice with the aim to commune with God must be his daily pursuit.

REFLECTION QUESTIONS

1. Why is a consistent devotional life critical for the pastor?

2. What elements compose the devotional life?

3. Why is a Word-centered approach to the devotional life essential?

4. What happens when meditating on the Word?

5. What aim must the pastor keep in mind with each day's devotional time?

---

22. Allen, *Preacher's Catechism*, 34.

How Can Pastors Strengthen Their Marriages?

Busy lives can strain marriages. While not every pastor is married, many are. Those who are may quickly recognize this strain. The nature of pastoral work tends toward busyness. In the midst of it, if a pastor fails to intentionally strengthen his marriage, he will likely slip into a pattern of marital apathy. That doesn't mean he's thought of casting aside his marriage vows. He loves his wife and remains fully committed to her. But with ministry pressing from all sides, he can presume his marriage will blossom without devoted attention.

When this happens, church ministry becomes an unwanted mistress, claiming time and attention that needs to be devoted to his wife. Since the marital relationship best mirrors the relationship of Jesus Christ to his bride, the church, a pastor must not allow ministry to take the place intended for his wife (Eph. 5:22–33). He must learn from Christ, and from the way Christ loves and cares for his bride.

What can pastors do to strengthen their marriages? Three focal points will help strengthen marriage.

Build Your Relationship on the Gospel

We must start with the gospel. The good news of Jesus Christ giving himself in a substitutionary death at the cross and then rising from the dead calls us to keep believing and living in the realities of the gospel. Paul explains that the justifying peace we have through the Lord Jesus Christ—the gospel—received by faith, continues to be the "grace in which we stand" (Rom. 5:1–2). We're told to keep walking in relationship to Jesus just as we received him—which we did in the gospel (Col. 2:6–7; present tense, "walk"). The gospel maintains, informs, and directs our walk with Jesus. We walk daily in the revelation of the gospel, with its effects continuing to work into every area of our lives until the day of Christ (Phil. 1:6; 2:12–13; Titus 2:11–14).[1]

That's good news for marriage! Dave Harvey rightly notes, "The gospel is an endless fountain of God's grace in your marriage."[2] As the pastor and his wife know the gospel well, and out of that experiential knowledge discuss and apply it in the normal routine of life, they learn to live in the gospel. Dealing with the kinds of issues every pastor and wife face (e.g., fears, anxieties, disruptions, discouragement, and opposition), the gospel brings comfort, peace, power, strength, and a new perspective on handling these things. The gospel assures joy amid the bombardments that unsettle marriage.

But if the husband and wife neglect this ongoing fellowship in the gospel and how it continues to work out in their lives, they fail to encourage each other to rest in the sufficiency of Christ. They will inevitably lean on other things that will not suffice. Their marital foundation will be in self-effort, emotional reactions, and advice from friends rather than standing upon the redemptive work of Christ. We must not shortchange our marriages in this way. How does a gospel foundation work out in practical ways?

1. A Gospel Foundation Demonstrates the Desire to Live to the Glory of God[3]

With this gospel foundation, the pastor and his wife order their priorities around life in Christ. That affects the way they relate to one another, the decisions they make, their conversations, the training of their children, and their connections with the congregation.[4] If they aim for God's glory in all things as those transformed by the gospel and living daily in gospel light, the pettiness of bickering over little things gets laid aside. They have higher aims than yielding their time arguing or manipulating or selfishly claiming

---

1. Note Paul's pattern in his epistles working through the truths of the gospel, *then* moving on to applying that gospel to the whole of life (e.g., Romans, Ephesians, and Colossians). How Christians live out the Christian life is rooted in an ongoing understanding, experience, and delight in the gospel. Otherwise, we fall into a legalistic way of living, rooted in personal ability and perceived spirituality, rather than in what Jesus has accomplished.
2. Dave Harvey, *When Sinners Say 'I Do': Discover the Power of the Gospel for Marriage* (Wapwallopen, PA: Shepherd, 2007).
3. Harvey, "I Do," 25–28.
4. For instance, in the corporate, marital, and family relationships of Ephesians 5:15–6:9, we find they flow out of the way that Paul builds everything on the gospel (note the gospel saturation of chapters 1–3 laying the groundwork). You love, care for, and forgive one another corporately in light of the love and substitutionary sacrifice of Christ (4:32–5:2, which he's already explained in 1:3–8; 2:1–10). The sanctifying, cleansing work of Christ in the gospel weaves its way in the instructions for husbands and wives in marriage (5:32–33). Parents guarding against provoking their children to anger will have its roots in the forgiveness of Christ (6:5 continues to apply how we behave toward one another—including our children—due to Christ's gospel work [e.g., 4:32; 5:2]).

personal rights. God's glory in Christ, centered in the gospel, redirects the details of life.

2. A Gospel Foundation Centers the Marriage Relationship in the Picture of Christ and the Church

Ephesians 5:22–33 provides the model for the way husbands and wives relate to each other. Too often, this gospel centrality gets sidestepped in the rush to emphasize submission and headship. But submission and headship must not be separated from the selfless, loving, giving, and honoring relational framework between Christ and the church set forth in this passage. When not seen in this light, those Christ-ordained roles get twisted and distorted. This gospel picture, however, brings husband and wife into accountability to resist selfishness or pride or perceived rights. It clarifies roles entrusted to each by the Lord, including how those roles work out in dependence on Christ. The husband, then, sees his role of leading his wife in light of the redemptive work of Christ in his life. As a new creature in Christ, forgiven and loved by Christ, he leads his wife with the kind of selfless, sacrificial love that Christ has shown him in the gospel.

3. A Gospel Foundation Changes the Way That Two Sinners Living Together in Marriage Respond to Each Other

The fall's effects continue to expose a husband's and wife's sinfulness (Gen. 3). Daily battling temptation and sin doesn't mean offenses never happen. They do. But the centrality of the gospel in the relationship presses toward practicing forgiveness, even as Christ has forgiven us (Eph. 4:31–32). Allowing a grudge to gain a foothold or bitterness to worm its way into the heart *cannot* last long when husband and wife continue to return to the foundation of the gospel each day.

4. A Gospel Foundation Urges Service and Love in Marriage

Jesus came into the world not to be served but to serve, giving his life as a ransom for many (Matt. 20:28). Throughout his ministry, Jesus served his disciples (John 13), the poor and needy (John 6:1–14), the sick and infirmed (John 9), the bereaved (Luke 8:49–56), and the demonized (Luke 8:26–39). He continues to serve the church by nourishing and cherishing it until presented in spotless glory in his presence (Eph. 5:25–29). That example, especially in the model for marriage in Ephesians 5, makes lovingly serving each other the norm for a healthy marriage. When counseling couples, I tell them the most important thing they can do for each other is to serve the other as Christ serves us: sacrificially, lovingly, and generously. This kind of service works out into daily living in light of Jesus serving us. Jesus's act of service in the gospel makes serving each other natural as we follow Christ. Husbands must lead the way in serving their wives, just as Jesus does with the church (Eph. 5:25–29).

Husbands, Be Intentional in Nurturing Your Wives Spiritually and Emotionally

The terms used in Ephesians 5:29 for Christ nourishing and cherishing[5] the church provide an intentional approach to a husband nurturing his wife. As terms of tenderness and endearment, they convey the idea of feeding, clothing, and caring for another. While we may take them literally, it seems better to figuratively express the intimate care the husband has for his wife, just as Jesus does for the church. Rather than wait for the church to arrive at a particularly suitable state before nourishing and cherishing, Jesus so loves the church that nothing will stop him from providing what the church needs to grow into greater enjoyment of relationship with him and to her potential as his bride. Jesus as *head* "does not crush the church," wrote John Stott. "Rather he sacrificed himself to serve her in order that she might become everything he longs for her to be, namely herself in the fullness of her glory." In the same way, a husband "will give himself for her [his wife], in order that she may develop her full potential under God and so become more completely herself."[6] The husband, then, does not use an excuse that his wife has flaws here or there keeping him from nurturing her (that attitude means he's overlooking his own flaws). Rather, as Christ pursues his bride in love, the husband does so with his wife. How does this work out in the everyday relationship?

(1) *Pay attention to your wife.* Don't get home in the evening and pick up the smartphone or start surfing the Internet or begin doing a project. Stop and focus on your wife even while the children clamor for attention. They need to see that your wife has priority in family relationships.[7] Look for opportunities during the day to give her a call, meet for lunch, or send a text. Let her in on your day while listening with interest to her recounting her day. Make good eye contact. Show warmth (the original use of "cherish" was "to make warm"). See how you can serve and care for her.

(2) *Observe your wife in detail in order to lovingly serve her.* That's what Peter had in mind: "You husbands in the same way, live with your wives in an understanding way, as with someone weaker, since she is a woman; and show her honor as a fellow heir of the grace of life, so that your prayers will not be

---

5. "Nourishing" (ἐκτρέφω) carries the idea of providing food to nourish, so acting to give the most basic needs for sustaining life (BDAG, 311); "cherishing" (θάλπω) originally meant to "make warm," which figuratively expresses to cherish or to comfort or to give care for (BDAG, 442).

6. John R. W. Stott, *The Message of Ephesians*, BST (Downers Grove, IL: InterVarsity, 1979), 229.

7. Children are temporary residents in our homes. We must nurture the husband and wife relationship, giving it priority even when we still have children in the home, modeling for our children what it means to love and serve each other as husband and wife. If, instead, the home is child-centered, then children miss this example to carry into their marriages.

hindered" (1 Peter 3:7). Peter had not the slightest thought of male superiority with his comment, since he clarified, the wife must be honored as "a fellow heir of the grace of life." His use of the comparative "weaker," means "physical weakness relative to men's strength," as Karen Jobes notes, while also inferring to guard against misuse of authority in the social structure of his era that denied women equality.[8] Rather, he insists that husbands realize their wives are women, with differences from men in most areas of life.[9] Notice the differences and delight in them, even as Adam did when God presented Eve to him (Gen. 2:23). The husband needs to see the wife's differences complementing him in every way. Living in an *understanding way* implies taking the time to comprehend the differences in the wife compared to the husband, not for the purpose of changing her but for treating her as his equal, enjoying life with her, and finding ways he might better serve her. He maintains a keen eye to see how she might be encouraged spiritually and emotionally.

Often, men tend to be dull in paying attention to details with their wives. Peter's exhortation corrects this flaw, and points to the need of regularly looking for ways the wife needs care, comfort, and cherishing. It may be as simple as commenting on how lovely she looks or seeing that her automobile needs fuel and filling the tank for her. He does not call husbands to move mountains but to know their wives so well that they understand just what they need at any time during the day. And when for some reason he can't figure it out, he asks so he won't miss a thing.

(3) *Establish a devotional routine with your wife.* While the pastor remains busy feeding the flock, taking the time to read God's Word together or working through a devotional book and praying with his wife will reinforce the intention to put her before his work.[10] Be creative. Find a pattern that works well. Here, as "a fellow heir of the grace of life," they meet the Lord together for a few minutes, lifting up their burdens and mutual prayer concerns, and trusting the Lord together. That time involves gospel communication with each other.

---

8. Karen H. Jobes, *1 Peter*, BECNT (Grand Rapids: Baker Academic, 2005), 209.
9. While that should be obvious to a man, it seems that Peter hints at the male tendency to fail to notice the little details about his wife. There may even be a bit of humor or rebuke intended: "Husband, notice that your wife is a woman, so quit treating her like you would a man."
10. This time of devotion may be with the whole family, utilizing Scripture, singing hymns, reading a devotional book, using a catechism, or reading Bunyan's *Pilgrim's Progress*, etc. In such cases, I'd suggest not just applications aimed for the children but also for each other as a married couple. If you find that devotional focus on the children is not satisfying your need as a married couple, then fold in a short devotional time as a couple. If time seems too squeezed, consider alternating days for devotions with the whole family and devotions as a couple.

Keep Working on Communicating with Each Other

R. C. Sproul explains, "Communication is, above all, a means of knowing. . . . The goal of communication is knowledge—not abstract, theoretical, impersonal knowledge but personal knowledge, the knowledge of intimacy."[11] We do want information when we communicate. But in marriage, communication takes on a different focus. It builds a relationship that grows in intimacy. Communication, in Sproul's explanation, encompasses the whole process of romance in marriage.

Since pride, arrogance, and impatience regularly intrude upon healthy communication, husbands and wives must learn to talk with each other in gentleness and humility. As spouses learn to talk with each other, giving undivided attention to what the other is saying, and listening with an aim to understand what's being communicated instead of just getting a word or two while focusing on a smartphone, they really do get to know each other. They live with each other in an understanding way. Mutual care, respect, tenderness, and attentiveness create a framework for healthy marriages. This kind of intimacy in communication preludes joyful, God-designed intimacy in the bedroom (Gen. 2:24–25; Heb. 13:4). A healthy sex life not only guards the marriage from infidelity (Prov. 5:15–23; 1 Cor. 7:1–5;[12] 1 Thess. 4:3–8) but builds the relationship as God purposed through the gift of sexual intimacy. The regular enjoyment of sexual intimacy reinforces and strengthens the marriage covenant "characterized by permanence, sacredness, intimacy, mutuality, and exclusiveness."[13]

How can husbands and wives improve communication? First, make time to be alone. That doesn't mean when you're too tired to talk and so collapse, alone, into your bed. Rather go out to dinner, go for a walk, take a short trip (we've found that even an overnighter is refreshing), or go for a drive. Just be together. You don't have to talk nonstop to communicate. Much of it is done nonverbally by eye contact, touching, holding hands, and facial expressions.

Second, talk about life: your dreams, struggles, conflicts, future, present challenges, and ways you might better know and serve each other. Talk about what the Lord has been teaching you together. Listen well without arguing, or

---

11. R. C. Sproul, *The Intimate Marriage: A Practical Guide to Building a Great Marriage* (1975; Phillipsburg, NJ: P&R, 2003), 10.
12. Sproul explains that 1 Corinthians 7:1–5 expressly commands husbands and wives not practice abstinence from sex in marriage except for a brief season of prayer (*Intimate Marriage*, 120–23). He adds, "Thus we have in this text the clear teaching that sex is a fundamental obligation of marriage. That obligation must not be violated or abused if the marriage is to be healthy" (123). Sproul's use of *obligation* does not imply demand or coercion, rather the circle of healthy marriages leads to sexual intimacy; sexual intimacy feeds a healthy marriage.
13. Andreas Köstenberger and David Jones, *God, Marriage, and Family: Rebuilding the Biblical Foundation*, 2nd ed. (Wheaton, IL: Crossway, 2010), 80.

you'll likely shut off communication. Even when you disagree, do so as two committed to each other in love, standing upon the foundation of the gospel. Express forgiveness at an offense. Verbally reinforce your love and affection for each other.

Third, cherish your relationship. Value it as a gift from God. Treat it as a treasure to admire, enjoy, and delight in. The way you talk, look, touch, and show intimacy will communicate the way you treasure your marriage. By consistently cherishing your marriage, as the years roll on, the relationship grows stronger and more enjoyable.

Summary

Marriage shouldn't be complicated. Yet the sinful dispositions we bring into it multiply complications. That calls for building marriage upon the solid foundation of the gospel, honoring Christ by the way the husband and wife relate to each other. Husbands strengthen their marriages through intentionally nurturing their wives spiritually and emotionally by paying attention to them and living with them in an understanding way. People in strong marriages give attention to growing in communication: talking, listening, knowing, and growing in intimacy. The kind of marriage that reflects Christ and the church does not grow strong by passivity (Eph. 5:22–33). It calls for daily action.

REFLECTION QUESTIONS

1. What are the biggest hindrances faced by pastors and wives to a healthy, fulfilling marriage?

2. Why is the gospel foundational to marriage?

3. In what ways does the gospel inform and work out in the realities of marriage?

4. What is necessary for a husband to nurture his wife?

5. What's involved in marital communication?

How Can Pastors Shepherd Their Families?[1]

We're fortunate to have so many good books available on marriage and parenting.[2] Yet with all the good counsel, we must be careful not to latch onto a cookie-cutter approach to family life. Doing so forces unique personalities and God-designed lives into someone else's idea of what your home should look like. No doubt, we find plenty of good ideas, concepts, strategies, and illustrations to help us shape our homes. But those writers do not live with your wife or children. They do not know the unique way God designed your family to *image* his creativity and glory in the home. That's where Proverbs 24:3–4 offers guidance, as we consider the materials the Lord provides for us to strengthen and build our homes for his glory and our joy.

> By wisdom a house is built,
> And by understanding it is established;
> And by knowledge the rooms are filled
> With all precious and pleasant riches.

---

1. Some pastors do not have families, but their ministries regularly intersect and influence families. My hope in this chapter is that the principles considered will serve pastors as they serve their congregations.

2. See the previous question on books related to marriage. For parenting, consider Tedd Tripp, *Shepherding a Child's Heart*, rev. and updated (Wapwallopen, PA: Shepherd, 1995); Robbie Castleman, *Parenting in the Pew: Guiding Your Children into the Joy of Worship* (Downers Grove, IL: InterVarsity, 2013); Josh Mulvihill, *Preparing Your Children for Marriage: How to Teach God's Good Design for Marriage, Sex, Purity, and Dating* (Phillipsburg, NJ: P&R, 2017); Paul David Tripp, *Parenting: Fourteen Gospel Principles That Can Radically Change Your Family* (Wheaton, IL: Crossway, 2016); Julie Lowe, *Child Proof: Parenting by Faith, Not Formula* (Greensboro, NC: New Growth Press, 2018); Rachel Jankovic, *Loving the Little Years: Motherhood in the Trenches* (Moscow, ID: Canon, 2010).

If you're building a house, you must have the right kind of materials to get started. You wouldn't find a couple of pallets of modeling clay and boxes of building toys at the job site. It takes materials conducive to constructing a home for it to be built to live in.

In the same way, Solomon points to the materials God provides for building our homes. Wisdom, understanding, and knowledge, the wisdom writer states, are essential materials for building homes that taste and experience God's glory and joy. He does not use them as abstract concepts. Instead, the Lord utilized the same trio when he created the world: "The Lord by *wisdom* founded the earth, by *understanding* He established the heavens. By His *knowledge* the deeps were broken up and the skies drip with dew" (Prov. 3:19–20, emphasis added). The Creator created the creation with wisdom, understanding, and knowledge. That's how God built the universe. He modeled these materials for us as image-bearers in building our homes. With the unique challenges of shaping a family in the midst of pastoral ministry, using God-designed materials to build our homes gives encouragement even when the strain of ministry and family cause us to struggle.

Seek Wisdom

"By wisdom a house is built." Wisdom, in this use, has nothing to do with how smart one might be but points to how God reveals himself and his ways through the revelation of Holy Scripture. Wisdom looks to God's ways for the details of life. It sees truth for life, especially centered on God's revelation of himself in Christ as declared in the gospel. God reveals himself in his Word for believers to study, interpret, and apply (2 Tim. 2:15; 3:16–17). That's especially helpful for fathers seeking to strengthen their families. Rather than the frustration of trying to decide whose principles and ideas from the latest books will set his family on a good trajectory, he starts with God revealing himself in Christ as foundational.[3]

Paul saw wisdom with clarity. He spoke of the struggle he had on behalf of the believers in Colossae and Laodicea, "that their hearts may be encouraged, having been knit together in love, and attaining to all the wealth that comes from the full assurance of *understanding* [there's the application to all of life], resulting in [so he's showing continuation or progress] a true *knowledge* of God's mystery, that is, Christ Himself, *in whom are hidden all the treasures of wisdom and knowledge*" (Col. 2:1–3, emphasis added). He explains that the wisdom appropriate for every need, including the family, will be found in

---

3. I'm not suggesting tossing out books on the family! Plenty of good resources are available to aid our journey in strengthening families. Yet, as this passage shows, each family has its unique personalities and challenges and so must not simply follow a "canned" approach to family life. Learn from the ideas, concepts, illustrations, and recommendations offered, but sift them through the wisdom, understanding, and knowledge that God gives to build each home.

Jesus Christ. In that sense, the apostle teaches us that *wisdom is chiefly relational rather than informational.*

The entry into relationship with Christ, though, merely starts a life of discovering all the treasures of wisdom and knowledge hidden in him. Dick Lucas explains that trusting Christ as revealed in the gospel "is not the end but the beginning of life." We keep building upon the foundation of Christ as Lord and Life, and all the "growth and progress in the Christian life must be entirely consistent with its beginning."[4] *Wisdom, then, implies that God's revelation in the Word points supremely to Christ and the gospel as the foundation for everything needed to live faithfully before the Lord.*

While many things make a home, and many details we put into action we learn from various Scriptures, the revelation of God in Christ remains the most critical. If we do not start with the revelation of Christ as the foundation of all wisdom, then we randomly collect verses and principles that can be turned into a legalistic frame for family life. Relationship to Christ through the gospel must shape and hone character, conversation, attitudes, actions, love, service, forgiveness, and kindness as father and mother lead their children. As we apply the gospel to the whole of life, we model for our children the impact and power of the gospel for all of life. The gospel affects everything in our homes. That's why wisdom builds our homes. We're learning to build it on Christ and his gospel.

Exercise Understanding

"And by understanding it is established" (Prov. 24:3). *Understanding* has more to do with wisdom than simply an "ah-ha" moment. We can relegate understanding to just knowing some things in better fashion. But the idea expresses knowing something by applying it. When Solomon writes, "By understanding He [the Lord] established the heavens" (Prov. 3:19), he doesn't just mean he comprehended how to establish the heavens. Instead, he did it. Understanding, in this use, refers to action rather than simply a cognitive concept.

Here's where "understanding" becomes particularly helpful. "By understanding it [the home] is established." Wisdom involves revelation, grappling with truth in Christ until that truth becomes real to you. Understanding takes the truth and begins to work it out in the details of life. For instance, as we come to terms with the way Jesus came to serve (John 13), then that truth works out into the way we model service to our family. Therefore, as we set the example, we have a framework to teach service to our children, tailoring it to their particular circumstances. Wisdom reveals service; understanding applies it. In addition to the "service" of Christ, one might add the way that Jesus modeled forgiveness, care for others, value of relationships, generosity,

---

4. Dick Lucas, *The Message of Colossians and Philemon*, BST (Downers Grove, IL: IVP Academic, 2014), 87.

sacrifice, selflessness, humility, and so on. There are endless areas of wisdom in Christ that we can grapple with, practice, model, and train our children in.

The application of God's revelation in Scripture varies from one family to another. The revelation is the same. Truth doesn't vary. Truth is truth (2 Tim. 3:16). But how that truth gets applied in decisions, conversations, parenting, relationships, discipline, and a thousand other things will differ from family to family. Will there be some similarities? Certainly, but the important point to see is that a cookie-cutter approach to building a family ignores the healthy application of truth. A rigid list of do's and don'ts pasted together with random verses has the effect of taking *understanding* out of the picture. One need not use one's mind if a list of do's and don'ts controls the actions of the family. But one does need to think upon the revelation of God in the Word, and how that revelation works into the particular details of one's family.

1. Personalities

Each person in your home has a distinct personality. There may be similarities, but each differs from the other. Each personality processes conversations, body language, and correction in diverse ways. Each views responsibility with varying attitudes and work ethic. Each reacts to demands, stress, and challenges with a range of emotions, levels of angst, and action or inertia. Each has varying interests, goals, and levels of personal discipline. Maturity can't be squeezed into a one-size-fits-all approach to home life.

An amalgamation of varying personalities, interests, viewpoints, levels of maturity, grasps of Scripture, stages of spiritual development, and temperaments lives within the walls of your house. So, do you just pull a ten-step plan for the family out of someone's book and rigidly squeeze everyone in the family into that author's idea of what *your family* ought to look like? You can do that, but in the process you will miss out on securing your home with the kind of love, joy, and Christ-saturated attitudes that should befit homes led by Christians. You'll stifle some of the creativity and delights that grow when you take the time to thoughtfully apply the truth of Holy Scripture to each personality. Tailored application doesn't squash people but rather leads to freedom in Christ.

That's certainly what Paul had in mind when he wrote, "Fathers, do not provoke your children to anger" (Eph. 6:4). An approach to training children that ignores the personality of each child may do more damage than good. Instead of provoking to anger by ignoring a child's personality, hurts, or fears, or by failing to appropriately listen to better understand what causes a child to act the way he or she does, we're to "bring them up in the training and instruction of the Lord" (Eph. 6:4 NIV). To "bring up" is the same word translated as "nourishes" in Ephesians 5:29, a term of warmth that means "to feed," or with children, "to rear."[5] "Training" carries both the ideas of education and correc-

---

5. BDAG, ἐκτρέφω, 311.

tion. In a true sense, it expresses *discipling*. That's what happens through the application of wisdom to the particulars of a child: parents discipling their children. "Instruction" translates a word meaning "to put in mind."[6] So the parent pays attention to the individual receiving the "instruction," tailoring application to fit that one's understanding, situation, and need. Both must be done with an aim to cultivate the heart toward the Lord.[7]

2. Providences

Watching what happens in the details of God's unfolding providences in the families where I've pastored staggers my imagination. Each uniquely experiences a wide array of what God brings into their lives: odd circumstances, difficulties, challenges, hardships, joys, and opportunities. No home equates with the next. Here, the lively, ongoing grasp of God's revelation in Scripture specifically applied to the circumstances of our family members, with their varying personalities and life experiences, throws out the cookie-cutter approach to family life.[8] Instead, providence gives way to faces bent in prayer over the Word. It follows after faithfulness to Christ. In providence, we begin to see how the Lord has ordered life details, so we grow in grace, learn more God-dependence, develop in spiritual disciplines, and exercise the fruit of the Spirit in family relationships.[9]

3. Application

For instance, "understanding" or application of the Word may cause you to address or discipline one child differently than another. Application makes you sensitive to where each child stands with the Lord. One who's unbelieving you nurture toward seeing his or her sin and the beauty of Christ revealed in the gospel. One who's a believer you help nurture away from legalism into a walk in the Spirit.

With the use of "understanding," or application, in the home, we must regard the distinct personality, temperament, interests, life stage, sensitivities,

---

6. "Instruction," νουθεσία, comes from νοῦς (mind) and τίθημι (to place or to put) (*NIDNTTE*, 3:423). I prefer the idea of "to lay on the mind," as that's what we're doing as we instruct our children. We must keep in mind how each one learns and seek to lay on their minds the truths they need to live with a heart bent to the Lord.

7. John R. W. Stott, *The Message of Ephesians*, BST (Downers Grove, IL: InterVarsity, 1979), 249–50.

8. This might involve a child making a team or not making it; acceptance or nonacceptance into a club; a friend's father's sudden death; a friend in an accident leaving him or her paralyzed; misunderstandings with classmates; criticism or verbal attacks; struggles with a new teacher; the challenge of moving to a new city, etc. In each, how does God's Word speak to these providences? How do you teach, train, pray, and walk with your child through these providences? Here's where wisdom and understanding play out in family life.

9. As we train them by the wisdom in Christ, we also have the joy of showing our children just how practical theology is for all of life.

and challenges of each child. How do you apply the Word to each one? Will that take more effort than following a "packaged" approach to home life? Yes, it certainly will, but the effect will be much richer and fuller in the long run.

Live in Knowledge

"And by knowledge the rooms are filled with all precious and pleasant riches" (Prov. 24:4). Wisdom involves revelation from God's Word. Understanding implies the appropriate application of God's revelation. *Knowledge* means that you're continuing to grow in wisdom and understanding of the Lord and his ways. We might even call knowledge an *amplification* of truth for all of life. In one sense, it's an ongoing combination of wisdom and understanding. We see this in Solomon's statement about the Lord's creativity. "By His knowledge the deeps were broken up and the skies drip with dew" (Prov. 3:20). Here, Solomon doesn't use knowledge as a static grasp of information but as truth that continues to act to accomplish the purposes found in wisdom. In other words, he's emphasizing that by using *knowledge*, we're to actively apply the particular truth needed with the particular child and his or her particular needs. We're to think about the outcome of training, instruction, and discipline instead of just operating on autopilot as a parent.

The way Paul uses knowledge in his prayer for the Colossian Christians best instructs us: "For this reason also, since the day we heard of it, we have not ceased to pray for you and to ask *that you may be filled with the knowledge of His will in all spiritual wisdom and understanding*" (Col. 1:9, emphasis added). Paul relates knowledge to wisdom and understanding just as Solomon did. It's the growth in and grasp of the will of God found in wisdom (or revelation of God's Word) with a view toward applying it. "His will" points to knowing truth that God has revealed in the Word, instead of whether it's God's will to attend a particular school or to buy a new house or take a job offer. As we walk in "His will" revealed in Holy Scripture, we find other decisions falling into place. Walking with the Lord gives direction and clarity in how best to train and direct our children.

Paul explains, being filled with the *knowledge* of God's will in all spiritual *wisdom* and *understanding* affects (1) walking in a way that pleases the Lord, (2) bearing fruit in good works, (3) increasing in knowing God, (4) finding strength through God's power, (5) increasing in endurance and patience, and (6) living in joyous thanks to God (Col. 1:9–12). As we build our families with wisdom, understanding, and knowledge in the ways of God, changes occur in the way we think, act, talk, relate to others, view the world, and find joy.

Now, let's think about our homes. If our goal is to chisel out a certain type of family to rigidly follow another person's idea of the perfect home, then Proverbs 24:3–4 and the insights from Colossians has little to offer. But if our goal, *by the grace of God*, is to see the kind of fruit only God can produce, then we need to follow the pattern he has set forth. Does that mean if you have children, all will become Christians? We don't know. That's a sovereign work of God. But it does mean that by God's wisdom in the gospel, understanding in its outworking, and the amplification through knowledge of gospel truth, you've laid a solid foundation for their lives. You've anchored your life, home, and marriage in the revelation of God in Christ. And further, in the process, there will be surprising joys in seeing God at work through the application of his Word.

Summary

Parenting is no exact science. Instead, Christian parents learn to walk in wisdom, understanding, and knowledge as they teach, train, correct, and direct their children. This accounts for the personalities and emotional distinctions of each child rather than attempting to parent with a one-size-fits-all approach. Parents start with living in the wisdom found in Jesus Christ, exercising understanding in applying wisdom, and then amplifying wisdom and understanding by continuing in knowledge centered in Christ. This pattern lays a gospel foundation upon which to build our homes.

REFLECTION QUESTIONS

1. How does Solomon's use of wisdom, understanding, and knowledge in reference to the Lord God at creation instruct us in the application of this trio in the home (Prov. 3:19–20; 24:3–4)?

2. Ultimately, what is the wisdom upon which we build our homes?

3. What must be considered with each child in the application of wisdom?

4. How does Proverbs 24:3–4 navigate parents away from a one-size-fits-all approach to parenting?

5. How does knowledge relate to wisdom and understanding in the way it's applied in the home?

Do Pastors Need Pastoring?

The Pastoral Epistles model *pastoring* pastors. Paul pastored Timothy and Titus. He sent them to pastorally represent him with the church at Ephesus and churches on the island of Crete, respectively.[1] They faced the same kinds of issues confronting every pastor: personal struggles, opposition, distorted teaching, power groups, inconsistencies among members, inadequate leadership, questions about ministry, immaturity where there should be maturity, and temptation to withdraw or quit. In the midst of addressing the problems with the Ephesian and Cretan churches, Paul pastored Timothy and Titus to continue in faithful ministry. How did he do so?

In the Pastoral Epistles, he addressed particular issues faced while seeking to bring their congregations into more faithfulness as Christian churches. In 1 Timothy, the apostle has a "polemical edge" to address the heterodox teachers threatening the church's stability. In 2 Timothy, Paul's last letter, he urges Timothy to faithfulness in the face of opposition, relying on the promises inherent in the gospel. To Titus, Paul "calls for the nurturing of a clear sense of Christian identity and community" through the ethical transformation that marks true followers of Christ.[2] But woven throughout the letters, Paul reminds these men of essential, foundational issues in their Christian walks and public ministries.

---

1. John Stott suggests Timothy's role was "a kind of embryonic 'bishop'" (*The Message of 2 Timothy*, BST [Downers Grove, IL: InterVarsity, 1973], 19). But a better title is that of "apostolic delegate," since Paul knew nothing in the church of the sort of hierarchy conveyed by current usage of *bishop*. Derek Tidball uses the term "delegates" for Timothy and Titus (*Ministry by the Book: New Testament Patterns for Pastoral Leadership* [Downers Grove, IL: IVP Academic, 2008], 149–51); Andreas Köstenberger calls them "apostolic delegates who are temporarily assigned to their present location in order to deal with particular problems that have arisen in their respective churches and require special attention" (*Commentary on 1–2 Timothy and Titus*, BTCP [Nashville: Holman Reference, 2017], 9).

2. George M. Wieland, "The Function of Salvation in the Letters to Timothy and Titus," in *Entrusted with the Gospel: Paul's Theology in the Pastoral Epistles*, eds. Andreas Köstenberger and Terry Wilder (Nashville: B&H Academic, 2010), 171–72.

Pastoral Reminders

In reflecting on the Pastoral Epistles, at least five reminders stand out in the way Paul encouraged Timothy and Titus in their walks and ministries. These reminders serve as good content for how pastors can pastor their fellow elders. Paul puts into remembrance the things that matter most as we serve one another in pastoral ministry.

1. Remind One Another of the Gospel—Its Power, Effectiveness, and Promises

George Wieland points out that the Pastorals contain at least thirteen distinctly salvific passages.[3] Significantly, for our purposes, Paul weaves many of his exhortations to the young men with gospel roots. To encourage Timothy to steadfastness, Paul talks about the Lord's faithfulness toward him despite his former life as a persecutor of the church (1 Tim. 1:12–17). After discharging responsibilities for church leadership, he breaks out into a christological confession, reminding Timothy on the basis of Christ's faithful work how he ought to conduct himself in God's household (1 Tim. 3:14–16). To encourage Timothy to act in boldness, the apostle sets his counsel in the certainty of gospel assurance (2 Tim. 1:8–12). Before reminding Titus of his reason for leaving him in Crete, Paul reminds him of the hope of eternal life found in the gospel he proclaims (Titus 1:1–3). To help Titus speak to and correct the Cretan Christians with authority, the apostle grounds the exhortation in one of the most magnificent gospel declarations in all of Scripture (Titus 2:11–14). Pastors need gospel reminders as much as Timothy and Titus did. For only as we continue to believe and live in the gospel will we walk in faithfulness.

2. Remind One Another of Living Holy Lives and Regularly Fighting Sin

Paul presumed nothing with these two young men he had faithfully mentored.[4] Derek Tidball explains that even with the detailed instructions for their church responsibilities, "there seems an equal, if not greater concern about their characters and how they are to perform it. . . . He was concerned about their achieving the task, but was even more concerned about the kind of people they were."[5] Paul allowed no youthful excuses from Timothy, but insisted, "in speech, conduct, love, faith and purity, [to] show [himself] an example of those who believe" (1 Tim. 4:12). Timothy was to keep "faith and a good conscience" (1 Tim. 1:19), pay close attention to himself and his teaching, persevere in faithfulness to Christ (1 Tim. 4:16), not entangle

---

3. Wieland, "Function of Salvation," 155–62. The passages are as follows: 1 Tim. 1:1; 1:15–16; 2:1–7; 2:15; 4:10; 4:16; 2 Tim. 1:8–10; 2:8–10; 3:14–15; 4:16–18; Titus 1:1–14; 2:11–14; 3:4–7.
4. See Phil A. Newton, *The Mentoring Church: How Pastors and Congregations Cultivate Leaders* (Grand Rapids: Kregel Ministry, 2017), 53–57, 64–66.
5. Tidball, *Ministry by the Book*, 149.

himself in worldly affairs (2 Tim. 2:2), and "flee from youthful lusts and pursue righteousness, faith, love, and peace, with those who call on the Lord with a pure heart" (2 Tim. 2:22). Holding one another accountable as pastors/ elders to live holy lives sharpens our fight against sin.

3. Remind One Another of the Constant Need to Persevere in the Faith

While telling Timothy to flee the snares of temptation for riches, he exhorts, "Fight the good fight of faith; take hold of the eternal life to which you were called, and you made the good confession in the presence of many witnesses" (1 Tim. 6:11–12). Perseverance assures the genuineness of our faith in the Lord Jesus Christ. Assurance of salvation never breeds passivity but spurs the Christian—including pastors—to endure. John Stott explains that taking hold of eternal life meant that "although Timothy had already received eternal life, Paul urged him to seize it, grasp it, lay hold of it, make it completely his own, enjoy it and live it to the full."[6] Pastors must encourage each other toward perseverance in the faith, for in perseverance we experience more delight in what Christ has accomplished on our behalf in his death and resurrection.

4. Remind One Another to Be Men of the Word, Students of Holy Scripture

While one might think pastors need no reminder, if Paul had to remind Timothy to be diligent in improving his study and grasp of God's Word, then we need the same reminder: "Be diligent to present yourself approved to God as a workman who does not need to be ashamed, accurately handling the word of truth" (2 Tim. 2:15). Seminary president and former pastor Ligon Duncan comments, "Here we have an apostolic directive for a young minister to study with the equivalent exertion and effort of a tireless day-laborer. The true minister is a workman (Paul really likes this metaphor!). He works hard at his task. The true minister is to work hard at study so as to know and preach the truth rightly."[7] Regularly discussing truths we're learning from the study of God's Word spurs fellow pastors to dig deeper and study fervently.

5. Remind One Another to Stay Clear of Speculative, Specious Arguments That Profit Nothing

How easy it is for pastors to be trapped by worthless arguments made by (sometimes) well-meaning people. We must help guard one another from falling prey to wasting good pastoral time and effort on mere speculation. Paul reiterated this in several passages (1 Tim. 4:6–7; 6:20–21; 2 Tim. 2:14–19,

---

6. John Stott, *Guard the Truth: The Message of 1 Timothy and Titus* (Downers Grove, IL: InterVarsity, 1996), 157.
7. Ligon Duncan, "Keep Studying," in *Dear Timothy: Letters on Pastoral Ministry*, ed. Thomas Ascol (Cape Coral, FL: Founders, 2004), 197–98.

22–26; Titus 2:1–15; 3:9). Addressing error is one thing: we must do so (Titus 1:10–11). But the fruitless, speculative talk about peripheral issues in eschatology, spiritual gifts, numerology, and so on needs to be left alone.

Pastors Need Pastoring

Paul's reminders to Timothy and Titus help frame the sort of content that needs to be part of pastors pastoring fellow elders. The gospel, holy living, perseverance in the faith, studying Scripture, and avoiding speculative arguments compose a breadth of material for discussion and sharpening one another. While busily engaged in shepherding the flock entrusted to the elders' care, elders must keep an eye on one another.

Paul certainly had this in mind when he told the Ephesian elders, "Be on guard *for yourselves* and for all the flock" (Acts 20:28, emphasis added). "Yourselves" implies fellow elders. Watch out for your fellow elders just as you also watch out for the members of the flock. Or from a different angle, just as you would not think of failing to care for the body, even so don't think of failing to care for your fellow elders.

Yet we can easily presume upon one another. We have expectations with our fellow elders that we all have our acts together. Maybe sometimes we do. But what about the other times when we don't? If the shepherds of the flock don't care for one another, who will? Here are some suggestions to make pastoring pastors happen.

1. Pray Daily for One Another

Just as you pray daily for your own spiritual needs and those of your family, pray for your fellow elders. Those you regularly hold before the throne you hold closest to your heart. That act of daily prayer brings to mind the needs of your fellow elders. You're praying for what you've observed concerning them and what you've learned in conversations with them. You've been sharing life together, so most naturally, you share their needs with the Father.

Pay attention to your fellow elders. Communicate with them about their families, work, and shepherding in the body. Discern where the adversary assaults them. Observe their strengths and weaknesses. They serve arm in arm with you, so lift them before the Lord. Plead for their personal disciplines, marriages, children, and ministry.

2. Be Friends, Not Business Partners

We can fall into the trap of treating fellow elders or members of the church staff as though merely fellow board members. That's one reason I prefer not to use the term "elder board." We're not a board. We're a body who serves the congregation together in the name of Christ. Board members can be somewhat indifferent to each other as long as the board functions. They can discuss, deliberate, make decisions, and think their responsibilities are completed when gaveled adjourned. Yet isn't it hypocritical when we just go through the motions of acting as a board while failing to truly care for and serve each other? But as members of a body you learn to love each other, care for one another, weep and laugh together, know one another's struggles, carry one another's burdens.

As fellow elders, we've joyously shared in births of children and grand-children. We've wept over deaths of parents and siblings. We've labored in prayer over struggles with our children and grandchildren. We've walked through pains, emergencies, and celebrations. Friends care enough to know and serve one another.

3. Speak into One Another's Lives

When we're friends as fellow elders, rather than just board or staff members, we have the right to speak into one another's lives. Paul's encouragement in the body's growth, development, and doctrinal clarity necessitated speaking the truth in love (Eph. 4:14–16); elders were not excluded. His reminders to Timothy and Titus give plenty of content to think about as we speak into one another's lives. If elders don't speak the truth in love to one another, then they likely do little of it with the flock.

Yet to speak into another's life calls for a dual posture. The one speaking must approach his brother with humility, love, and willingness to listen and walk alongside the other. The one approached must share that same humility in listening, love in accepting correction, and willingness to submit to a brother's admonishing word. Both the one speaking and the one listening must readily maintain teachable hearts. Elders who think they never need correction and admonition should not be elders. Until we stand before Christ without spot or blemish, we need others to speak into our lives, especially those fellow elders who pray for us, love us, and hold us in their hearts.

4. Pay Attention to Pastoral Opportunities with Elders

One of our elders and his wife faced the intense grief of a son dying less than an hour after his birth. I will never forget the scene of my fellow elders and their wives gathered around the bedside weeping, praying, and loving on this brother and his wife. We must not presume we never need pastoral care.

Pastoral care can come in many ways. It can be during a family illness or death; the departure of a child heading to college or the military; the birth of a child or grandchild; adverse changes in life or job or family. Sometimes it's the sensitivity to raging spiritual conflicts that calls for fellow pastors to come alongside their brothers.

Don't presume another elder will serve the brother in his time of need. Take the opportunity to pastor your fellow pastors. The time will likely come when you will be on the receiving end of such ministry, so faithfully minister to your brothers in times of need. I'm writing this chapter during a time when I've been physically laid aside and isolated due to four months of chemotherapy treatment. The care from my fellow elders has lifted my spirits again and again.

5. Live Life Together in the Body

By living life together in the body, I'm thinking of the kind of things we do as members of the congregation, but in this case, even intensified with fellow pastors. We read books and talk about them. We share stories of how God has worked in some opportunity or need. We discuss sermons and Bible studies we're preparing to teach. We open up about our weaknesses. We talk about struggles with sin. We visit needy church members. We participate in mission trips. We work side by side in various church projects or workdays. We share table fellowship. We attend events together. We pray. We laugh. We do life together.

Yes, pastors need pastoring by their fellow elders. We can certainly develop formal structures for doing so (e.g., accountability times, Bible studies, peer reviews, etc.). But I'm advocating for something more holistic—life on life in the crucible of ministry. Know each other well. Pastorally serve each other faithfully.

Summary

Learning from Paul's exhortations to Timothy and Titus offers some tangible areas where pastors need to keep pastoring one another: gospel, holiness, perseverance, study, and focus. Practically, as we pray for one another, build friendships, speak into one another's lives, pay attention to pastoral opportunities, and live life together, we will both give and receive pastoral care to each other as fellow pastors.

REFLECTION QUESTIONS

1. What similar issues did Timothy and Titus face that you face as a pastor?

2. Why did Paul spend so much time reminding Timothy and Titus about the gospel?

3. What are the categories Paul had in mind as he sought to pastor Timothy and Titus?

4. Can you think of other categories that might be present in the Pastoral Epistles that would serve to help pastors to pastor one another?

5. What are the practical ways pastors might regularly serve and pastor their fellow elders?

How Can Pastors Deal with Discouragements in Pastoral Ministry?

As a college student, I served on staff with a pastor that seemed to be discouraged every Monday. He didn't see the response he had hoped for from his preaching; what he thought would be a great sermon fell flat; an older member complained about something in the service; a deacon spoke to him unkindly; the finances didn't meet budget. Consequently, his motivation starting the week sank. He complained, wallowed in misery, and seemed lethargic instead of actively pursuing the joy that would liberate him from discouragement.

Since that time, I've served for more than forty years as a pastor. I can testify that discouragements aim at pastoral targets on a regular basis. If the pastor has no shield to deflect them, he will succumb to the ingratitude, pride, complaining, and lethargy that discouragement often brings. Here's my observation: we best deal with discouragements by concentrating most on true joy.

What Credit Is a Miserable Pastor?

In one of his expositions on the Epistle to the Philippians, the twentieth-century London pastor Martyn Lloyd-Jones asked the question, "What credit to God is a miserable Christian?"[1] Or, borrowing from Lloyd-Jones, "What credit to God is a miserable pastor?" A little experience in pastoral ministry exposes levels of misery *and* joy. At times, pastors, representing through shepherding and proclamation the one whom to know is "fullness of joy," project the contrary (Ps. 16:11; John 15:11). Their struggles with a congregation may seep through sermons, hallway conversations, and pastoral visits. Their unsettled feelings over whether their ministries have achieved "success"

---

1. Martyn Lloyd-Jones, *The Life of Peace: An Exposition of Philippians*, 2 vols. (Grand Rapids: Baker, 1999), 14.

tend to keep them lurching in directions to find the elusive ministry "sweet spot." They may become calculated in their ministry pursuits in the attempt to find joy, yet rarely experience joy because they try to find it in the wrong places. Discouragement settles in.

Joy should be front and center in pastoral ministry. This doesn't mean challenging issues in ministry won't battle joy. Those battles happen in the normal practice of serving a congregation. Yet precisely at this point, pastors must learn where to find deep, satisfying, and contagious joy. If pastors do not walk in joy, then they will scarcely be able to point their flock to living in joy.

Jesus's Path to True Joy

It's helpful to track along Luke's Gospel to see how the intense life of following Jesus and dying to self doesn't contradict living in indescribable joy. Jesus told us if we wish to follow him, we must deny ourselves, take up our cross daily, and keep following him (Luke 9:23). In doing so, we're brought into levels of joy the world cannot comprehend.

As he spoke that decisive word on being a disciple, Jesus began his path to Jerusalem. He told the disciples of his impending suffering, death, and resurrection (Luke 9:22, 44). Knowing what lay ahead, Jesus set his face toward Jerusalem, a city that had killed prophets of old and rebelled against God under a thin veneer of faithful religious practice (Luke 9:51). Along the way, he countered soft professions partnered with caveats, excuses, and self-centered priorities with the terse statement, "No one, after putting his hand to the plow, is fit for the kingdom of God" (Luke 9:62). Jesus only wants disciples that go the way of the cross. And yet, it's the way of the cross that leads to true joy.

Amazingly, we get a hint of the spirit among his followers when Jesus sent out the Seventy (Luke 10:1–20). He sent them "as lambs in the midst of wolves," with no provisions and the certainty that some would listen to them and others, reject them (Luke 10:3–12). Did they return with dull, discouraging, and despondent spirits? Instead, "the seventy returned with joy" (Luke 10:17).

Luke stays on that theme of joy as he narrates the story of Jesus receiving the seventy disciples after their mission into the Galilean cities. In doing so, he helps us to *listen* to the tone of Jesus and his followers, discovering the immeasurable joy of belonging to him. *Jesus wants his followers to live in the joy of belonging.* That's particularly true of his undershepherds, whom he calls to lead his people into greater joys. But how do we live in that kind of joy?

Joy in Unusual Places

Six times in Luke 10:17–24, the scene describing the Seventy's return, Luke uses four different terms that express *joy, rejoicing,* or *happiness* (v. 17, *chara*; v. 20, *chairos*; v. 21, *agalliaō*; v. 23, *makarios*). Clearly, he presses that point in this context. Jesus set his face toward Jerusalem, the cross, resurrection, and ascension, and "for the joy set before Him, endured the cross" (Heb. 12:2). He called his followers to joy and exemplified it even with the days of his passion just ahead. But to Jesus, joy didn't equate to giddiness or absence of troubles, but rather the deep elation and exuberance that wells from our hearts when we know we belong to God through Christ. It is consciousness of relationship and hope for eternity. External circumstances cannot deter it or control it—not even disagreeable leadership or failed plans or cantankerous sheep. This joy, as Lloyd-Jones put it, "is the product, almost the by-product, of my concentration upon my relationship to God in Jesus Christ."[2] Jesus directs the disciples to this kind of joy when they return from their mission.

We need to get the picture. He told the Seventy as they headed out into ministry to expect "discouragements (10:2), dangers (10:3), and deficits (10:4)," as James Edwards notes (citing Luke). "The stage seems to have been set, in other words, for the poorly equipped and underprepared disciples to return limping in defeat."[3] It was the perfect formula for discouragement! But just the opposite happened. "The seventy returned with joy, saying, 'Lord, even the demons are subject to us in Your name'" (Luke 10:17). Here they knew the joy of success in their work. That's certainly commendable and normal. That's where we typically find our joy—accomplishments, abilities, successful tasks, and satisfactory experiences. Joy, the way the Seventy saw it, depends on what we do or experience. If we preach a great sermon or counsel a poor marriage back to harmony or lead a church to adopt elder plurality or welcome lots of new members, we feel joy. But herein lurks danger: that kind of joy is temporary and may unwittingly be dependent upon personal success. J. C. Ryle warns, "The time of success is a time of danger to the Christian's soul."[4] And why is that so? That type of joy might blind us to true, lasting, richer, fuller joy in Christ.

Jesus responded to the Seventy's elation with a gentle redirection: "But He said to them, 'I was watching Satan fall from heaven like lightning'" (Luke 10:18). That could have been a prophetic word anticipating the cross,[5] Jesus acknowledging the original fall of Satan,[6] or Jesus seeing the impact of the nearness of the kingdom of God in the overthrow of Satan applied in that mission.[7] Maybe there's a combination of all three, although I tend to think the theme of the coming near of the kingdom of God, as expressed in Luke 10:9 and 11, is the point. The disciples were seeing evidences of the

---

2. Lloyd-Jones, *Life of Peace*, 15.
3. James Edwards, *The Gospel according to Luke*, PNTC (Grand Rapids: Eerdmans, 2015), 311.
4. J. C. Ryle, *Expository Thoughts on the Gospels*, 4 vols. (Grand Rapids: Baker, 2007), 2:359.
5. David Gooding, *According to Luke: The Third Gospel's Ordered Historical Narrative* (Belfast: Myrtlefield House, 2013), 207.
6. Ryle, *Expository Thoughts*, 362.
7. Philip G. Ryken, *Luke*, REC, 2 vols. (Phillipsburg, NJ: P&R, 2009), 1:525.

inbreaking of God's kingdom! Edwards is right: "Whenever the kingdom of God is truly proclaimed, the work of God is accomplished in ways that even its proclaimers are often unaware of."[8] More happened than these disciples anticipated.

But thoughts of personal success must be quickly corrected. Jesus does just that since true joy doesn't hinge on things we accomplish: "Behold, I have given you authority to tread on serpents and scorpions, and over all the power of the enemy, and nothing will injure you" (Luke 10:19). In other words, Jesus reminded them that they did not *succeed in casting out demons by their own authority*. That authority over evil came through Christ. Satan and his minions cannot ultimately conquer Christ's followers. Romans 8:31–39 is true![9]

Joy through Settled Assurance

So true joy is not found in success itself but *only when achievement turns us to glory in the Lord*. Rightly understood, any success should be attributed to the grace of God shown to us for that particular act. In this way, we turn our achievement back to the Lord with thanks and glorying in him. Otherwise we enter the danger zone of pride. It lurks to destroy us, especially in pastoral ministry! "Pride goes before destruction, and a haughty spirit before stumbling" (Prov. 16:18). As Thomas Watson warns, "Pride is apt to breed in our holy things as the worm breeds in sweetest fruit."[10] We don't find true joy in the pathway of pride. It's only found in the humble road of cross bearing and seeing our joy in belonging to Jesus.

"Nevertheless," Jesus stops the train of thought and elation in the Seventy's apparently successful ministry. Jesus calls us to live in far richer joy: "Nevertheless do not rejoice in this, that the spirits are subject to you, but rejoice that your names are recorded in heaven" (Luke 10:20). *Here is true joy, taking greatest pleasure in what God has done for eternity through Christ on our behalf.* The ancient world used "recorded" for inscribing someone's name on an official register or citizenship roll.[11] The divine passive verb indicates God as the one who has recorded our names in heaven. What he records cannot be removed (as the perfect passive expresses). So, the call to "rejoice," as Moisés Silva notes, is in finding "joy in God's electing love."[12]

A shift must take place in our ministry thinking. Here's where we need to find our chief joy. We discover God's electing love that chose us before

---

8. Edwards, *Luke*, 312.
9. Edwards, *Luke*, 313.
10. Thomas Watson, *The Godly Man's Picture* (1666; Edinburgh: Banner of Truth Trust, 1997), 79.
11. *NIDNTTE*, ἐγγράφω, 1:593–94.
12. *NIDNTTE*, 4:647.

the foundation of the world (Eph. 1:3–6), called us through the gospel of Christ by the Holy Spirit (Eph. 1:7–14), regenerated us and gave grace to repent and believe the good news of Christ (Eph. 2:1–10), sealed us with the Spirit until he brings us into his presence (Eph. 1:13–14), adopted us into his family forever (Gal. 4:1–7), and gives us an eternal hope in Christ—these are quite enough to produce joy every day (Eph. 1:18–23). The weight of assurance that fills us with joy is, then, not on our success with the church's leadership or perceived level of ministry effectiveness or how much approval we receive from our congregation. Instead, it rests on the faithfulness of the God that chose us, pursued us, and loved us enough to send his Son to the cross on our behalf. Jesus told his disciples, "What you did on your mission was wonderful, but that's not where you're to find your joy. It's found in what God has done by calling you his own and se-curing you forever." That's where pastors must find true joy that conquers discouragement.

Summary

So how do we deal with discouragement in pastoral ministry? Here are seven actions to regularly take to counter discouragement by pursuing the joy of settled assurance.

1. Contemplate the faithfulness of Jesus Christ in his death and resurrection.

2. Think on God's faithfulness to his promises to save all that repent and believe the gospel.

3. Intentionally repent of self-trust, reliance on our deeds, or any pos-turing to think that our successes increase our standing with God.

4. Ponder and give thanks that Jesus has indeed paid our sin debt and reconciled us to God through his death and resurrection.

5. Focus on the greatness of God's electing love, Christ's atoning death and triumphant resurrection, and the Holy Spirit's regenerating and experiential witness of the work of God in us.

6. Find our joy in Jesus—belonging to him, being united to his family, and being secure in his faithful love. He is sufficient in all the Father gave him to do to redeem a people. We can rest in him.

7. Focus on the truth that in the end, the Lord rewards persevering faith rather than great performance (2 Tim. 4:6–8).

REFLECTION QUESTIONS

1. What discouragement points do you face in pastoral ministry?

2. Why is a pastor's joy so critical to the rest of the congregation?

3. How does Luke's Gospel lead the reader to the pathway of true joy?

4. Where did Jesus redirect the Seventy's joy?

5. What are some regular actions to take to pursue true joy in the face of discouragements?

How Do Pastors Endure in Their Ministries?

During a daylong pastors' conference, I joined two other pastors in a panel discussion on endurance in pastoral ministry. We averaged twenty-eight years in the same church. Since that may seem daunting to a young pastor, the moderator asked if we originally planned to stay so long in our ministries.

His question sent me drifting back over three decades to the start of my present pastorate. I don't remember consciously thinking at that stage, "I'm planting my life in Memphis." Many in my generation tended to go light on ecclesiology, and so thought of climbing the ministerial ladder instead of staying with one congregation. Discussions of moving on to bigger and better things frequently marked pastoral gatherings. Staying in one place, planting your life, enduring the many changes accompanying any congregation, just didn't seem to be the focus.

However, after years of involvement in pastoral ministry, I think *staying long should be the rule rather than the exception.*[1] Certainly, one might posit Paul's missionary church planting ministry, staying a few months to a maximum of three years, as one possible pastoral template. Yet Paul's calling "to preach the gospel, not where Christ was already named," differs from the pastor's call to "shepherd the flock of God among you" (Rom. 15:20; 1 Peter 5:2). As his normal practice, Paul turned the shepherding role over to local church elders/pastors (Acts 14:23) while he pressed on to new regions with

---

1. My thesis is not intended to bind anyone's conscience, nor does it fail to take into consideration that the first or second church a man pastors may not be a place where he can spend his life. I pastored three churches in a span of almost ten years before planting South Woods Baptist Church in Memphis where I've continued in pastoral ministry since 1987. Looking back, I cannot see planting my life in the other places where I served. But I am grateful for the experiences in those churches that helped to prepare me for planting my life and ministry in one place. A *good* short pastorate should prepare for a long pastorate.

the gospel. Meanwhile, pastors stayed long to teach, train, shepherd, correct, admonish, counsel, and encourage the local congregations.

Why Stay Long?

Admittedly, some churches make staying long difficult due to lack of support, power groups, poor financial compensation, neglect in caring for pastors, and ongoing dissatisfaction with pastors (yes, I've been there). Yet, out of the Lord's kindness, many congregations provide a good foundation for long tenures. Hunger for Christ, desire to reach the community and beyond with the gospel, appreciation for faithful pastoral care, and respect for the pastoral office tend toward encouraging longer pastorates. These kinds of churches just need faithful pastors to stay and endure the difficulties until they can work toward strong health for the congregation.

Yet sometimes pastors move too quickly to enjoy what the Lord has rooted in these churches. A few problems arise, and the pastors update their résumés. These pastors fail to realize they will likely face the same kind of issues in the next pastorate. By my observation, few men inherit healthy churches. Healthy churches do not mean problem-free churches. Congregations must be shepherded toward good health over a long stretch, requiring endurance from the pastoral team that desires to see Christ formed in the church (Gal. 4:19).

Granted, a lot needs to happen for a church to develop into a healthy fellowship of believers. The rough edges of doctrinal clarity need to be smoothed (1 Tim. 4:16). The practice of biblical exposition must be cultivated (1 Cor. 2:1–5; 2 Tim. 4:1–5). Biblical church polity must be established (1 Tim. 3:1–13; Titus 1:5–9). Relationships must be strengthened in gospel application (Eph. 4:4–6:9). Confessional bonds will need to be taught (1 Tim. 3:14–16). A mission trajectory needs to be set in place (Matt. 28:18–20; 2 Cor. 5:16–21). But how will these kinds of healthy church practices happen if pastors keep moving on?[2] It likely will not take place without pastoral stability.[3]

Some churches that could have a strong community impact as they grow in health and Christlikeness instead just "do church" with little biblical aim. They're satisfied with *business as usual*, having little to do with biblical Christianity. They pass for a Christian church because of regular services and programs identified as *Christian*. Pastoral hopping saps their life. Until a pastor commits to stay through the difficult days to lead them toward health—and these days come with any pastorate—those churches will likely flounder.

---

2. A good place to start when thinking about the areas a church needs to move toward biblical health is Mark Dever, *Nine Marks of a Healthy Church*, exp. ed. (Wheaton, IL: Crossway, 2004). For a companion volume that helps to flesh out *how* to move in a healthy direction, see Mark Dever and Paul Alexander, *The Deliberate Church: Building Your Ministry on the Gospel* (Wheaton, IL: Crossway, 2005).

3. For a perspective on longevity, see Question 40.

Pastoral longevity tests and shapes the character and gifts of the pastor. It challenges him to work through more of God's Word with the congregation instead of repeating the same one hundred sermons he has stuffed into file folders to cart from one church to the next. It gives the congregation a more balanced diet of Scripture, as the pastor works through book after book—Old Testament and New Testament—to expound the riches of the Word. Longevity stretches him to grow in his hermeneutical and homiletical abilities. It stretches his devotional life, as he must go deep in seeking the Lord if he would go long in serving his church. Pastoral longevity gives time to develop solid disciples who know the Word, understand how to interpret Scripture, and apply it to the whole of life. It offers a chance to build a congregation that's passionate about gospel work locally and among the unreached people of the world.

Staying long means the pastor's prayer life will change—both privately and in pastoral prayers during worship services. He will spend more time knowing the flock he shepherds, which will bring more and more needs into his praying. The longer he stays, the more he realizes it's not his power or ability that brings change to the church—it's the power of God (Acts 6:2, 4). As he prays publicly, he also finds his desires building to see the body develop in private and corporate prayer for one another. His burden for his people he has loved and served for years through trials, heartaches, joys, and challenges will be evident in the way his prayer life changes and affects the congregation around him.[4]

As he endures in his pastoral charge, the pastor will discover more and more of what it means to live in the grace of God, to "venture all on God," as John Bunyan expressed it.[5] He will inevitably face battles. Power groups that have held the church in bondage, if they would be dissolved, must be met head-on with a faithful man of God standing upon the Word, protecting the body from spiritual rogues, and boldly proclaiming the truth, not leaving his post for an easier situation. Over time, his boldness and humility, his power and grace exposes false teaching and faulty ecclesiology, while correcting sloppy living and anemic congregational relationships. He leads them out of human-centered worship toward a robust, joyous, and gospel-centered worship of the living God. He sets the example in witness and mission, changing the culture of the church toward the unbelieving world.

None of this happens in a short pastorate. A pastor may attempt to do some good things for a church, but unless he endures, little lasting change will

---

4. One need only look at Paul's prayers for the churches to be moved by his pastoral passion for those congregations (e.g., Eph. 1:15–23; Phil. 1:9–11; Col. 1:9–14). Note how pastoral praying deepens over time.
5. For an encouraging look at Bunyan's endurance, see Roger Duke and Phil A. Newton, *Venture All for God: The Piety of John Bunyan* (Grand Rapids: Reformation Heritage Books, 2015).

happen. I agree with Mark Dever: "Staying with a congregation through thick and thin helps the church to see that you're not with them because it's easy, or because everything goes your way. You're with them because you love them, and you rely on God. You endure for his sake, for the love he has given you for his people."[6] Staying long and staying faithful for the long run, by the grace of God, can bring about healthy changes in the church.

What's Needed for Staying Long?

While any pastor that has stayed long might come up with additional necessities, the following five top my list.

1. Patience

That's a word that may get under your skin; it does mine. We want what we want *now*! Just as you can't bring your own body into good health with rash, impatient practices, you can't lead the church to health without patience. It takes patience to cultivate listening ears, to make significant polity changes, to instill a mission heart, to see transformation in relationships, and to find renewal in corporate worship. That's why Paul partnered "great patience" with preaching God's Word to the flock (2 Tim. 4:2). John Stott wisely writes, "However solemn our commission and urgent our message, there can be no possible justification for a brusque or impatient manner."[7] Short pastorates attempt to squeeze quick results instead of patiently—through faithful instruction in God's Word and dependence upon the Holy Spirit—trusting God's promises to transform the congregation. Often, those changes take many years, followed by patiently continuing to hone each facet of a healthy church life.

2. Contentment

Congregations can be tough on pastors. They may complain, fail to show appropriate gratitude, ignore pastoral pleas, reject biblical instruction, refuse loving leadership, and so on. Our pastoral expectations run high. We want quick responses so that we can move on to the next big plan on our agenda.

But staying long calls for contentment with the little incremental changes: the one person that seems to "get it" when you've taught; the surprising volunteer for a mission team; the testimony of a student that has led a friend to Christ; the unexpected tears in the middle of worship; the kindly act toward an easily passed over attender; the selfless service shown toward a needy member. When these little things start to emerge from the congregation after

---

6. Mark Dever, "Staying for the Glory of God: Sibbes, Simeon and Stott Model," *9Marks*, December 20, 2010, https://www.9marks.org/article/staying-glory-god-sibbes-simeon-and-stott-model.
7. John R. W. Stott, *The Message of 2 Timothy: Guard the Gospel*, BST (Downers Grove, IL: InterVarsity, 1973), 108. Stott writes, "We must never resort to the use of human pressure techniques, or attempt to contrive a 'decision'" (108).

years of faithful ministry, the contented pastor finds the satisfaction to keep enduring in service with the flock. Just like Jesus, who would not crush the bruised reed or put out the smoldering wick "until He leads justice to victory" (Matt. 12:20), so pastors must show contentment in the little things *until* gospel transformation takes place in their congregations.

When Paul wrote the Philippian church about contentment, he addressed the subject in the context of his life *and* ministry. They had supplied some of his needs while in prison in Rome, but he let them know that, while grateful, his sufficiency lay elsewhere. He could do all things through Christ who strengthened him (Phil. 4:10–14). Contentment, then, is not so much about how many things a pastor sees happening that would gratify his ministry longings, but rather about how sufficient Jesus Christ is for him in the daily demands of life and ministry, whether he fares well or with little.

3. Vulnerability

Healthy, long-term relationships require a measure of vulnerability. Others will see us for what we are. They will know our strengths, certainly, but they'll see our weaknesses because we're living life among them. As I'm getting closer to others through an enduring ministry, they will see that I don't always have my act together, that I sometimes need a good kick to start moving, that I occasionally face despondency, that I wrestle like they do with finding my joy in Jesus each day. They will know I'm not Mr. Super Christian but a fellow struggler learning to deny myself, take up my cross daily, and follow Jesus (Luke 9:23).

Vulnerability means willingness to risk failure for the sake of faithfulness. Pride gets smashed, a certain projected image gets shattered, and in the process, we stay long enough for a congregation to know that we're truly disciples (*mathētēs*), *learners of Jesus Christ*. As Paul admitted to the Philippians, he had not arrived, but he was still seeking, he says, to "lay hold of that for which also I was laid hold of by Christ Jesus" (Phil. 3:12–16). Vulnerability makes us personally uncomfortable but makes us *real* with our people.

4. Courage

Just check the examples of courage in the book of Acts and beyond. Philip's church planting in Samaria and up the coast to Caesarea during a time of persecution took courage (Acts 8:4–40). Paul, Barnabas, Silas, and Timothy established new churches in Asia Minor, and then all the way to Europe. That took courage (Acts 13–16). The pastors in Lystra, Iconium, and Derbe, where Paul had been stoned, faced the daunting task of continuing pastoral work where opposition existed—that took courage (Acts 14:23). Pastors in Ephesus, Galatia, Corinth, Rome, Philippi, and Colossae lived in places unwelcoming to the gospel with notable opposition. They had to be courageous to continue to faithfully serve their congregations.

The church grew by courageous pastors enduring suffering in order to establish the gospel firmly in their congregations. The rest of church history agrees. Athanasius faced exile for his stand on the deity of Christ. A converted Patrick returned as a gospel missionary to the land of his captors. John Wycliffe preached, translated, wrote, and counseled while serving the English people amid regular threat and opposition. Luther spent years pastoring in Wittenberg under threat of death. Calvin got run out of Geneva only to return and spend the rest of his life serving the St. Pierre Church that impacted Europe with the gospel. Charles Simeon endured incredible opposition and hardship at Holy Trinity Church, Cambridge, continuing with a ministry that lasted fifty-four years. Martyn Lloyd-Jones endured the World War II years in London and opposition from those resistant to his doctrinal expositions, staying for nearly thirty years. Courage stays because much fruit can only be seen over time.

5. Trust

More than anything, neglecting to cultivate trust in the Lord speeds pastoral departures. That doesn't mean every short pastorate exposes unbelief. But sometimes it does. Learning to trust the Lord, especially when adversity dogs the pastor's steps, is the only way to stay long.

Trust in Christ grows when we live in the gospel, continue steadily in our devotional life, increase in praying instead of worrying, delight in the Lord instead of perceived success, and rely upon the promises of God to his people. Like barbells to the weightlifter, the difficulties we face in pastoral ministry serve to build our trust in the Lord as we endure instead of giving up for an easier path.

Summary

Maybe you've run into a wall in your pastoral work. Instead of updating your résumé, consider what might happen *if* through patience, contentment, vulnerability, courage, and trust in the Lord you manage to stay longer? Twenty-five years from now a healthy church and a maturing pastor might bear testimony to God's grace in endurance. The trying years that brought pain and heartache will give way to the joy of seeing a congregation grow more into the image of Christ. Short pastorates won't allow you to learn much about yourself and where you need honing, nor will you learn much about the flock and where they need tending. But endurance brings the pastor and the church into a deepening relationship with one another and the Lord. That's worth the price it takes to endure.

REFLECTION QUESTIONS

1. Do you agree with this chapter's thesis that "staying long should be the rule rather than the exception"? Why or why not?

2. What circumstances make a long ministry difficult?

3. Why do we find ourselves impatient in our pastoral ministries?

4. What stands in the way of pastors being content in their pastorates?

5. How can a pastor cultivate and strengthen his trust in God?

How Do Intra-Pastoral Connections Strengthen Patient Endurance?

The pastor checks his calendar and wonders how he can finish his "to-do" list for the day. He knows what he misses today will face him tomorrow. But some things can't wait. Feeling the pressure of preparation for Sunday's sermons, making another call, checking on the latest church visitor, driving to the hospital to visit a member having surgery, and rushing back in time to do the pre-marriage counseling arranged two months earlier when his calendar looked blank will leave him little time to complete today's tasks. He repeats the hurry-up schedule tomorrow, the next day, and the next. By Friday, when the sermons appear ragged, the meeting for Sunday afternoon is still unplanned, and the need arises to return to the hospital to see another ailing member, he leans back in his chair and wonders how long he can continue this pace. He loves his flock and loves what he does. But he doesn't love the frantic feeling that hits him every Friday afternoon. Can he endure long enough to develop a team that will stand with him to serve the body? Can he persevere until his discipline and experience allow him to cut through a lot of the encumbrances to his week?

This pastor needs a pastoral network, a fellowship of fellow shepherds, a fraternal brotherhood in the trenches that will help him navigate through the pace of ministry. But he feels so busy that he fears giving time to such a gathering. Yet that kind of intra-pastoral connection may be just what he needs to patiently endure in pastoral ministry.

Pastors should not function solo in pastoral labors. Aside from the fellowship that's nurtured in a healthy elder plurality, making connections with other pastors—locally and beyond—that share similar doctrine, passion for pastoral work, and desire to see the gospel proclaimed will help to spur pastors on in their work. To demonstrate this thesis, we'll look at intra-pastoral connections biblically, historically, and contemporarily.

Biblical Intra-Pastoral Connections

By *intra-pastoral connections*, we're considering how pastors holding similar convictions in theology, ecclesiology, and pastoral ministry affiliate together in what might be called a network, group, fellowship, or association for the purpose of mutual encouragement, fellowship in the gospel, counsel for ministry, and learning from one another. How these gatherings look may vary from one group to another, but they will share similar traits of building relationships centered in gospel ministry for the purpose of faithful endurance. The relationships bond over time through meeting together and/or contacting one another through various means between gatherings. *Pastoral friendships* might be the best way to put it, but these are friends that help each other continue pressing on in faithfulness in the ministries entrusted to each one.

When it comes to biblical precedent for intra-pastoral connections, we don't find commands or instructions detailing what to do, other than those related to relationships between believers (e.g., Rom. 12:9–13; Eph. 4:1–6; Phil. 2:1–4; Col. 4:7–17). Yet we do see patterns suggesting that some of the relationships between pastors/elders with those outside their local gathering may have strengthened fellowship and deepened bonds of ministry.

One must certainly consider Paul and Barnabas with others from Antioch[1] traveling to Jerusalem to meet with the apostles and elders in order to settle the confusion stirred by Judaizers, as one such intra-pastoral connection (Acts 15). While the theological agenda had to be addressed, we must not think it to be sterile, stilted theological disputations. Here were pastors, missionaries, elders, apostles, and leaders of various churches gathered around the gospel. That's central to intra-pastoral connections. Fellowship takes place. The unity wrought through the work of Christ manifests itself. The challenge to expand gospel work spreads through the conversations. Encouragement to persevere in ministry happens. Admittedly, calling this an "official" intra-pastoral connection might stretch the term. Yet what happened among them describes what takes place in some pastoral networks, with theology discussed, issues ironed out, doctrinal statements made, and continuation in ministry encouraged.

Paul had a network of relationships with people who regularly crossed paths or traveled with the apostle in his missionary labors.[2] One such "network" took shape after leaving Ephesus and traveling through Greece. Luke identifies Paul's company as "Sopater of Berea . . . Aristarchus and Secundus of the Thessalonians, and Gaius of Derbe, and Timothy, and Tychicus and Trophimus of Asia" (Acts 20:4). This eclectic group of companions knew each other through Paul. He brought them together for more than company on a

---

1. Could it have been Titus and Luke traveling with them, since they likely were part of this church?
2. Robert J. Banks, *Paul's Idea of Community: The Early House Churches in Their Cultural Setting*, rev. ed. (Grand Rapids: Baker, 1994), 149–51.

long journey. He taught, trained, and shaped them for ministry.[3] Throughout, these men bonded in gospel relationships, mutually fellowshipping, sharpening, and discussing the things they were learning from Paul. They formed an intra-pastoral connection to spur one another on in faithfulness to Christ and ministry. Whether they all met again as a group, we're not told. But the time together surely affected their endurance in the years ahead.[4]

Historical Intra-Pastoral Connections

In the second century, Ignatius of Antioch sent epistles to the Ephesians, Magnesians, Tralians, Romans, Philadelphians, Smyrneans, and to Polycarp, Smyrna's bishop. In each, he demonstrated concern for other congregations' spiritual health, polity, unity, and maturity, as well as, emphasis on the churches following their pastoral leaders.[5] His letter to Polycarp exudes tenderness and love for a fellow worker in the gospel, offering encouragement, exhortation, and counsel, all with local church consciousness.[6] Centuries later, we can learn from the warmth of intra-pastoral connection recorded in these ancient letters.

In sixteenth century Geneva, John Calvin engaged in intra-pastoral connections in his ministry. The *Vénérable Compagnie* or Company of Pastors, organized by Calvin, met on Friday mornings to talk theology, ecclesiology, membership issues, and to engage ministry candidates. The company comprised eight to ten from churches in the city, with another ten or eleven from small parish churches around Geneva. As an added benefit, Calvin allowed ministry trainees to be part of this gathering in order to learn from seasoned pastors.[7]

The seventeenth-century Particular Baptists of England made "interchurch communion" part of their practice, best demonstrated in the formation of *associations*. Even during times of persecution under Charles II and James II, they still attempted to meet with their association when possible. They did not consider the gatherings to hold formal authority over any of the churches. But they did see themselves as a body useful to give advice and to maintain "peace,

---

3. See Phil A. Newton, *The Mentoring Church: How Pastors and Congregations Cultivate Leaders* (Grand Rapids: Kregel Ministry, 2017), 63–82.
4. The long list of greetings in Paul's epistles indicates that likely some elders/pastors/missionaries living and/or serving throughout the Roman Empire were part of Paul's ministry network. They had fellowshipped around the gospel at some point and probably offered mutual encouragement in doing pastoral and missionary work with each other (Rom. 16:1–14; 1 Cor. 1:15; Eph. 6:21; Phil. 4:18; Col. 4:10, 12, 17; 2 Tim. 4:10, 12; Titus 3:13). While the greetings do not make them "pastoral networks," they indicate affection, unity, and gospel kinship in sending greetings. That's the fruit of intra-pastoral connections.
5. *ANF* 1:45–104.
6. *ANF* 1:93–96.
7. Scott Manetsch, *Calvin's Company of Pastors: Pastoral Care and the Emerging Reformed Church, 1536–1609*, Oxford Studies in Historical Theology, ed. David Steinmetz (New York: Oxford University Press, 2013), 2. See also Newton, *Mentoring Church*, 90–91.

union, and edification" among the churches. Their pastoral fraternal included persecuted and imprisoned pastors that endured suffering in long ministries. They gained strength in the bonds of fellowship formed in their associations.[8]

The eighteenth-century New Brunswick Presbytery formed by the Philadelphia Synod (Presbyterian) brought together like-minded pastors with similar training, passion for spiritual awakening, and diligence for seeing genuine conversions. They included Gilbert Tennent, William Tennent Jr., John Cross, Samuel Blair, and Eleazar Wales, names associated with the First Great Awakening. They shared efforts to train and set apart gospel ministers to be sent out. This intra-pastoral connection saw much gospel fruit in long ministries.[9]

One of the most significant pastoral fellowships began in 1792 with the formation of the Particular Baptist Society for the Propagation of the Gospel amongst the Heathen, or the Baptist Missionary Society. Eleven pastors, a deacon, and a ministry student gathered in a small living room around a commitment for the work of global missions. S. Pearce Carey, great grandson of William Carey, one of the members, noted that they were "pastors of obscure little village causes . . . of no fame and of scantiest salary."[10] Yet the names of Carey, Andrew Fuller, John Sutcliff, John Ryland Jr., and Samuel Pearce still echo in discussions of local church involvement in global missions. Their gospel-centered focus, theological discussions, mission strategy, deep friendship, mutual encouragement, and ecclesiological precision helped sustain them in ministry while supporting Carey in India. Michael Haykin comments that the pastors were "faithful to their calling and laboured for God's approval, not that of men." Only one among them failed to keep the faith and maintain the close friendship, fellowship, and missionary support to their dying day.[11]

Under London pastor Martyn Lloyd-Jones's leadership, the Westminster Fellowship, or "Fraternal," began meeting quarterly in 1941. They focused on "experimental and practical issues" through a theological address, discussion, and models of how to apply basic biblical theology to the range of issues facing the church. Their number included Alan Stibbes, Philip Edgcumbe Hughes, Earnest F. Kevin, J. I. Packer, Iain Murray, Geoffrey Thomas, and others. Without question, their faithful endurance in gospel ministry continues to

---

8. James M. Renihan, *Edification and Beauty: The Practical Ecclesiology of the English Particular Baptists, 1675–1705*, Studies in Baptist History and Thought 17 (Eugene, OR: Wipf & Stock, 2009), 154–66. Their number included early Baptist leaders Nehemiah Coxe, Benjamin Keach, Hanserd Knollys, William Kiffin, Hercules Collins, and John Spilsbury.

9. Thomas S. Kidd, *The Great Awakening: The Roots of Evangelical Christianity in Colonial America* (New Haven, CT: Yale University Press, 2007), 36–37.

10. Michael A. G. Haykin, *One Heart and One Soul: John Sutcliff of Olney, His Friends and His Times* (Durham, UK: Evangelical Press, 1994), 220. Pearce Carey used the word "causes" to refer to the small churches.

11. Haykin, *One Heart*, 219–223. See also Timothy George, *Faithful Witness: The Life and Mission of William Carey* (Birmingham: New Hope, 1991), 67–69. These biographies, along with others about these men, reveal the fruitfulness found in intra-pastoral connections.

affect the evangelical world, with much of their insights for the church forged through the Westminster Fellowship.[12]

Contemporary Intra-Pastoral Connections

Over the years, I've always had connections with other pastors. Sometimes friends from college or seminary days constituted that number. They proved to lift my spirits during the frequent challenges of early ministry. Yet these connections did not go deep theologically or ecclesiologically. During a particularly difficult time when I faced the genuine possibility of being dismissed from my church due to renewed theological clarity, the Lord brought a fellowship of pastors into my life that loved to talk theology, church, missions, and gospel work. Although we only saw each other a couple of times a year, those days of fellowship sustained me through some of the darkest seasons of ministry. I endured, in part, due to their encouragement, insight in Scripture, shared experiences, intense prayer, and regular contact with one another.

In the last number of years, a local fellowship of like-minded pastors has brought great encouragement and opportunity to deepen bonds of fellowship. We help each other during times of difficulty. As one of the senior members, my role has shifted a bit in spending more time offering counsel to the many younger pastors to endure in ministry. Along with the local fellowship, I'm involved with a broader network of pastors scattered in many places. Much of our contact happens through email, texts, or calls, although we try to get together intentionally to deepen fellowship, discuss theology, sharpen ecclesiology, spur gospel proclamation, and strengthen expository preaching. We find that tossing out a quandary one pastor faces gives opportunity to speak into his life and offer counsel for action. We share burdens, pray for one another, and urge each other to continue on with endurance in pastoral work.

Suggestions for Intra-Pastoral Connections

If you see the need for the kind of pastoral fellowship or fraternal this question addresses, then consider what might be available in your area. Do existing pastoral networks with like-minded pastors function in your community but you've not attempted to get involved? Or do you need to consider starting a pastoral fellowship in your community? It need not be large. Our local pastoral network ranges from ten to twenty in gatherings, but I know of some with much smaller fellowships that serve pastors well. Here are a few ideas to think about.

(1) *Keep it simple.* Think about what pastors in your area need to keep persevering in pastoral work. The most beneficial things you do will not cost financially. Be practical rather than theoretical. Be local-church centered.

---

12. Iain H. Murray, *The Life of Martyn Lloyd-Jones 1899–1981* (Edinburgh: Banner of Truth Trust, 2013), 240–41, 375.

(2) *Keep it focused.* Develop an agenda for the gathering. If you decide you will meet for one morning a month (that's our local fellowship's plan, except summers), then divide the time to introductions to one another, opportunity to pray for one another, listening to an exposition or a theological topic, discussing the address, offering counsel to any brother in need, and then meeting for an inexpensive lunch at a local restaurant.

(3) *Keep it relational.* Pastors need good relationships with other pastors. Make sure your agenda doesn't lose sight of that. Invite local pastors to be part of the fellowship who you think will contribute to other pastors or might be walking through struggles and need other pastors' input.

(4) *Keep it useful.* Talk about real ministry issues, recommend good books, identify helpful commentaries for expositional preaching, listen to and offer counsel for pastors facing crises, build lasting friendships, and even give away a few books now and then.

Summary

From Paul's traveling companions to Lloyd-Jones's Westminster Fellowship to my local pastoral fellowship, intra-pastoral connections continue to strengthen pastors to remain steady in ministry. While the size, shape, formality, regularity, and agenda differ from one pastoral network to another, the main point is that pastors need these connections to sharpen thinking, offer support, spur holiness, and provide good ministry models. If a pastor cannot locate a suitable network, he should consider starting one for his community.

REFLECTION QUESTIONS

1. What kind of discussions, do you suppose, would have taken place with Paul and the small group that traveled with him, as recorded in Acts 20:4?

2. How did John Calvin utilize his intra-pastoral connections?

3. How did the Baptist Missionary Society founded in 1792 shape the pastors who were part of it, and ultimately, the evangelical world?

4. What might a pastoral fellowship/network/fraternal look like?

5. What should an interested pastor maintain as priorities in starting a pastoral fellowship?

PART 3

Pastoral Practices

What Is the Biblical Aim of Pastoral Ministry?

Where does a pastor begin when he first arrives to serve a congregation? For that matter, what if he's been there for a while? He may see so many needs before him: division, confusion, bloated membership rolls, lifeless worship, neglected discipleship, apathetic leaders, unqualified teachers, pointless activities, and so on. He cannot simply decree these things away. Nor can he change the list of weak points overnight.

The pastor need not scavenge to find a new list of programs to install or activities to present to the church. Those things might get a few more people involved in doing "stuff," but they cannot improve the church's health. Instead of rolling out new ideas that will not transform lives, the pastor must lead his congregation toward the biblical aim that remains the same for every church. Paul made the aim totally clear in the only passage where the title "pastor" (shepherd, *poimēn*) is used in the New Testament (Eph. 4:11).[1] We will consider the aim for pastoral ministry by investigating its means and aim detailed in Ephesians 4:11–16.[2]

The Means of Pastoral Ministry

By *means*, we refer to what the Lord of the church has entrusted to pastors in order to faithfully accomplish pastoral ministry. Jesus gave "some as

---

1. Some translations use "shepherds" rather than "pastors" (e.g., ESV). As we've noted in several of the questions, the terms pastor, elder, and overseer are used synonymously throughout the NT. Yet only in Ephesians 4:11 do we find the nominal use of *pastor* as descriptive of an office serving the local church. Note the verbal use in Acts 20:28 and 1 Peter 5:2 in connection with the *work* of elders/overseers.
2. Question 2 asks, "What Is Meant by Pastoral Ministry?" It looks at a definition of the *nature* of pastoral ministry. While some overlap will occur in the present question, the goal is to think more narrowly on the *how* and *why* of pastoral ministry.

pastors and teachers" to serve the local church toward a particular purpose.[3] This means that teaching-pastors[4] need not resort to novelty when it comes to *what* their role is to the church. Jesus Christ has made that perfectly clear. They must seek to fulfill that role by the power of the Spirit in dependence upon the Lord of the church (1 Cor. 2:4–5). Equipping the saints to build up the body of Christ takes place through the means common to pastors—for instance, preaching, teaching, prayer, counsel, exhortation, and setting an example for the church in living as disciples.

1. Proclaim God's Word

Paul explains the means of ministry in the churches when he declares, "We proclaim Him, admonishing every man and teaching every man with all wisdom" (Col. 1:28). "Him" stands in the emphatic position in the Greek, emphasizing that the focus of proclaiming God's Word centers on Jesus Christ and the gospel. "This Christ, whose life flows in all his people," writes F. F. Bruce, "is the one whom the apostle and his associates proclaim. He is the sum and substance of their message. . . . He is indeed the embodiment of divine wisdom, but the exploration of the wisdom that resides in him is the task of a lifetime."[5] Since "the equipping of the saints" seeks to bring the church into "the unity of the faith, and of the knowledge of the Son of God," it cannot be done other than through the proclamation of God's Word (Eph. 4:12–13). That's why Paul emphatically told Timothy, "Preach the word!" (2 Tim. 4:2)

When Mark Dever interviewed for the senior pastor position at Capitol Hill Baptist Church in Washington, DC, he explained his focus would be on preaching, praying, discipling, and patiently waiting on God to work instead of adding new programs to the church. He wrote, "What I wanted to get across was that there's only one thing that's biblically necessary for building the church, and that's the preached Word of God."[6] The work of equipping to build the church doesn't rely on clever techniques or expensive programs. It

---

3. For discussion on whether apostles, prophets, and evangelists in Ephesians 4:11 remain as current offices for the church, see Benjamin L. Merkle, *Forty Questions About Elders and Deacons* (Grand Rapids: Kregel Academic, 2008), 46–53.

4. The Greek, τοὺς δὲ ποιμένας καὶ διδασκάλους utilizes one article (τούς) with the two plural nouns (ποιμένας καὶ διδασκάλους), which indicates Paul does not identify two different roles but rather describes how this one role/office functions with the church. These are pastors that teach or teachers that shepherd. The use of καί may be explicatory rather than conjoining two separate nouns, so "pastors *that are* teachers." F. F. Bruce notes, "Teaching is an essential part of the pastoral ministry; it is appropriate, therefore, that the two terms, 'pastors and teachers,' should be joined together to denote one order of ministry" (*The Epistles to the Colossians and Philemon and to the Ephesians*, NICNT [Grand Rapids: Eerdmans, 1984], 348).

5. Bruce, *Epistles*, 86.

6. Mark Dever and Paul Alexander, *The Deliberate Church: Building Your Ministry on the Gospel* (Wheaton, IL: Crossway, 2005), 33.

depends on the faithful proclamation of the Word (see 1 Tim. 4:11; 2 Tim. 2:15; Titus 2:1, 15, reminding us that faithful proclamation includes diligent study and doctrinal clarity).

Dever explains why that always remains true: "God's Word is His supernatural power for accomplishing His supernatural work. That's why our eloquence, innovations, and programs are so much less important than we think; that's why we as pastors must give ourselves to preaching, not programs; and that's why we need to be teaching our congregations to value God's Word over programs." He continues on the primacy of teaching our people the gospel: "Preaching the content and intent of God's Word is what unleashes the power of God on the people of God, because God's power for building His people is in His Word, particularly as we find it in the Gospel (Rom. 1:16). God's Word builds His church."[7]

2. Shepherd God's People

As pastors shepherd the flock, they get involved with the congregation to cultivate in them faithful understanding and application of God's Word. Paul and Peter exhort elders "to shepherd the church of God which He purchased with His own blood" (Acts 20:28; 1 Peter 5:2). This lovely metaphor reminds pastors of their personal engagement with the body of Christ to admonish, explain, instruct, exhort, and patiently lead the church in following after Christ. Much shepherding work takes place through proclamation, but not all of it. Personal labors in knowing the flock, praying for them, helping to apply the gospel in their lives, and encouraging their obedience to Christ in all things takes place in conversations, notes, counsel, group gatherings, and personal visits.[8] Just as a good shepherd knows his sheep (John 10:11–15), those shepherding local churches need to know the spiritual condition of the members of their flock so they might shepherd them toward the kind of corporate maturity described in Ephesians 4:13.

3. Model Spiritual Maturity

Peter called for pastors to "be examples to the flock" (1 Peter 5:3). Similarly, Paul told Timothy, "Show yourself an example of those who believe" (1 Tim. 4:12). The pastoral writer of Hebrews explained that those who had spoken the Word of God to them—presumably pastors/elders—were to be imitated in the way they practiced the Christian faith (Heb. 13:7). Paul had no hesitation to encourage the young churches to imitate him and the others that led them in the faith (1 Cor. 4:16; Phil. 3:17; 1 Thess. 1:6; note the use of "us" refers to Paul, Silas, and Timothy). Modeling what we preach offers

---

7. Dever and Alexander, *Deliberate Church*, 35.
8. See Charles Bridges, *The Christian Ministry: With an Inquiry into the Causes of Its Inefficiency* (1830; Edinburgh: Banner of Truth Trust, 1967).

visual illustrations of how to apply God's Word to daily life. Obedience, love, holiness, and service must mark pastors as they model the gospel for their congregations, equipping them for service.

Jesus Christ has given pastors the means toward his aim for pastoral ministry: proclamation, shepherding, and modeling spiritual maturity.

The Object of Pastoral Ministry

While pastoral work always seeks to make new disciples (Matt. 28:18–20; 2 Tim. 4:5), it primarily focuses on the body of Christ. "For the equipping of the saints for the work of service" gives laser approach to pastoral preaching and shepherding work.[9] Pastors are to *equip* the church so that the corporate body engages in ministry to one another[10] and gospel work in the community. Paul knew nothing of church ministry belonging only to the pastors. He understood the congregation laboring together in the work of ministry—learning how to serve one another in the body (1 Cor. 12:7–26; Gal. 6:1–2; Eph. 4:15–16; 5:19–21; Phil. 2:1–4; Col. 3:12–17) and those outside the faith as ambassadors for Christ (Matt. 28:18–20; Rom. 12:14–21; 2 Cor. 5:16–20; Col. 1:27–28).

For the church to do ministry, it must be equipped. *Equip* expresses, "to put in order, restore, prepare."[11] Originally, it meant setting a broken bone to restore to use, mending broken nets for usefulness, and supplying the right equipment for an expedition. It conveys the idea of training, correcting deficiencies, making the right provisions (the Word), and disciplining for effective service.[12] Pastors will stay busy equipping! It means giving ourselves tirelessly to make sure the body is taught the Word, trained as followers of Christ, and is provided good examples and applications. It involves modeling personal discipline and modeling how Christ shapes our lives to serve one another with humility and love demonstrated by Christ for his church (John 13).

As the well-equipped church engages in the work of service, it results in "the building up of the body of Christ" (Eph. 4:12). It's no longer a few believers that happen to get together occasionally for spiritual endeavors but a Christ-mirroring edifice under construction to display the glory of God. The construction terminology pictures the church as a house or a temple (1 Cor. 3:9; Eph. 2:19–22; Heb. 3:5–6; 1 Peter 2:4–5) that is built on a good foundation as a strong structure that can withstand the elements, that serves a grand purpose, and that aesthetically catches the attention of those outside (Matt. 5:14–16; 7:24–25; 1 Cor. 3:10–17; 1 Peter 2:12; 3:15–16). Jesus designs and

---

9. Note that *saints* is Paul's common term for the church (see Rom. 1:7; 1 Cor. 1:2; Eph. 1:1; Phil. 1:1; Col. 1:2).
10. More than forty times in the NT we find "one another" passages, sometimes called "reciprocal living" passages, instructing the church in how they're to live in relationship to one another.
11. *NIDNTTE*, καταρτισμός, 1:408.
12. BDAG, καταρτίζω, καταρτισμός, 326.

builds the church so that it lives, breathes, and acts together to display the glory of God.[13]

Through proclamation, shepherding, and modeling gospel faithfulness, pastors equip the church to regularly and naturally engage in the work of service (ministry) that results in building up the church. In other words, as pastors teach and train, and as the church responds by exercising love and care for one another and doing gospel work in the community (and beyond), the church naturally grows *inwardly* to mature the body and *outwardly* to make disciples of the nations. Instead of pastors/elders attempting to do all the work of ministry, they're equipping the body to serve one another and witness to the world. Jesus never intended his body to be spectators when it comes to ministry, but as the "Head" engages in ministry, the body follows (Eph. 4:15–16).

The Aim of Pastoral Ministry

In the following verse, "until" provides an explanatory rationale, or *aim*, for why pastors equip the saints to do the work of ministry that builds up the body: "until we all attain to the unity of the faith, and of the knowledge of the Son of God, to a mature man, to the measure of the stature which belongs to the fullness of Christ" (Eph. 4:13). If we read this passage as though written only to individuals, then we miss the meaning. Paul wrote to the church. *The aim for the body is nothing short of corporate unity, experiential knowledge of Christ, and full maturity.* Here, pastors must fix the aim of their pastoral labors. Other things must not sidetrack them. Even noble endeavors that fall short of local congregations displaying the fullness of Christ among them through unity, experience of Christ, and maturity must be laid aside.

1. Unity of the Faith and of the Knowledge of the Son of God

Since the apostle already stated unity as a gift from the Holy Spirit (Eph. 4:3), and "one faith" constitutes part of the narrow confessional statement (Eph. 4:4–6), Paul's intentional prepositional phrase explains the kind of unity he has in mind as he refers to unity *in the body of faith*—the truths of Holy Scripture. In light of the rampant doctrinal deviations that plagued the young churches (Eph. 4:14), unity of the Spirit coalesces around doctrinal truth, not a warm feeling.[14]

The church finds unity in the objective "faith" that we know as the body of truth called the gospel *and* in the *experiential* knowledge[15] of the Son of God. Paul locates the church's corporate unity in *relationship* to Christ

---

13. See Mark E. Dever, *A Display of God's Glory: Basics of Church Structure—Deacons, Elders, Congregationalism, and Membership* (Washington, DC: 9Marks, 2001).

14. That's all the more reason to major on expositional preaching through God's Word as the means to train our congregations in "the whole purpose of God" (Acts 20:27).

15. "Knowledge" (ἐπίγνωσις) means "knowledge directed toward a particular object," so experiential knowledge focused upon Christ the Lord (*LEKGNT*, 441).

himself revealed and declared in the gospel. As pastors equip the saints, they continually bring the church into the depths and heights of the gospel so that they're corporately nurtured in their mutual relationships with Christ as Lord. This brings the experience of unity into every facet of relationship and church life. In the ongoing experience (knowledge) of the gospel (faith), the church grows into maturity.

2. To a Spiritually Mature Body

"To a mature man" envisions the many in the local church as *one* together in maturity in Christ. Paul leaves no room for inactive church members or peripheral members or nonparticipatory members. That's why pastoral ministry engages in continually discipling every member of the body. Paul calls for every person that belongs to a local congregation to be under the equipping work of pastors to build up the church toward the aim of unity in the faith and the knowledge of Jesus Christ. As that happens, the church corporately grows to spiritual maturity. Ultimately, maturity finds itself in "the measure of the stature which belongs to the fullness of Christ," which John Stott explains as "the fullness which Christ himself possesses and bestows."[16] In this phrase, the apostle bridges the *now* and the *not yet*, as he looks to the maturity of the church. *Now*, the church presses on into more and more likeness to Christ in every aspect of character and life.[17] *One day*, we will see him as he is in all his fullness (1 John 3:1–2). That's why Paul kept praying to that end for the churches, since the ultimate goal for the body, corporately, is to reflect the Lord Jesus in his fullness in every way (Eph. 1:16–19; Phil. 1:9–11; Col. 1:9–12).

The aim of pastoral ministry, then, encompasses this massive goal of "the unity of the faith and of the knowledge of the Son of God, to a mature man, to the measure of the stature which belongs to the fullness of Christ." No wonder the apostle uses terms expressing the most arduous, labor-intensive effort to describe pastoral ministry (Col. 1:29). With the labor, he also declares the necessity of dependence upon the active, energetic power of Christ working through pastors, in order to "present every man complete in Christ" (Col. 1:28–29).

Summary

So much emphasis in church life today falls upon the individual pastor, but not so in the NT. There the emphasis constantly focuses on the corporate body maturing, growing, serving, and witnessing together. A return to the NT aim for pastoral ministry—laboring *until* attaining the unity of the faith and

---

16. John R. W. Stott, *The Message of Ephesians*, BST (Downers Grove, IL: InterVarsity, 1979), 170.
17. Colossians 3:12–17 offers a good picture of what this kind of maturity looks like in the church.

of the knowledge of the Son of God—will build healthy, maturing churches that endure through every struggle. But to do so, pastors must lay aside the proclivity toward adding new programs instead of relying upon the power of God's Word proclaimed, shepherded, and modeled for the body of Christ.

REFLECTION QUESTIONS

1. What three elements are identified as "the means of pastoral ministry"?

2. Evaluate how much *proclamation* is valued in your pastoral ministry. How might this improve?

3. How does equipping for ministry lead to the building up of the body of Christ?

4. What is the *aim* of pastoral ministry according to Paul in Ephesians 4:13?

5. What should corporate maturity look like with a local church?

What Should the First Year of Pastoring Look Like?

Throughout the year, young men (and sometimes older men) anxiously wait for their first pastoral charge. They work through various networks to get their names before churches for consideration as pastoral candidates. Inquiries come, questionnaires get completed, and sermon videos get sent along with other material. After a flurry of activity follows the sound of silence. Pastoral searches seem notoriously slow to update the process or to let a candidate know his status. But finally, a church invites the candidate to visit, meet with leaders, and preach before the church.

The waiting continues for the church's vote. Finally, with the vote completed, the call comes. The process of accepting the church's call begins with discussing compensation, working out details for moving, wondering about whether the "no" votes implied stubborn opposition, fretting over what to preach, mulling over the first leadership meeting, feeling concern over whether the compensation will be adequate, and being anxious over sending the kids to a new school. The new pastor and his family pack up their belongings and move to a new community where they do not have close friends or know if they will truly be accepted. The first year of pastoring begins.

I remember my first pastorate, too. I began serving a small church in rural southwest Mississippi during my last year of seminary. On graduation day, a couple of the members helped load our furniture and kitchen wares onto a cattle trailer and moved us into the church pastorium (a house provided by the church for the pastor). I didn't know what I was getting into or what I needed to do while embarking on my first year as a pastor.

Every pastor must experience the first year of pastoring in order to start laying groundwork for a lifetime of ministry. No two pastorates are the same. Yet we can learn from others that have walked that road before us. So, what should a new pastor focus on during that year?

Learn to Expect the Unexpected

A young pastor wrote me about his first year of ministry. I grinned widely as I read about the "firsts" he was experiencing and thought of my own first year. In a typical church, the first year includes experiences of the first baptism, first Lord's Supper, first wedding, first funeral, first deacons' meeting, first business meeting, and first conflict. Nothing in seminary can quite get the young pastor completely ready for that series of "firsts." Here were a few of my unexpected "firsts":

- An absentee pulpit search committee that communicated nothing of the church's expectations

- A five-dollar-a-week raise when moved from part-time to full-time

- Bivocational ministry meant finding another job—and not knowing ahead of time how hard it would be in a depressed community that was not the least impressed with my bachelor and master of divinity degrees

- Celebrating the one-hundredth birthday of a member who had not attended the church for decades and whom I had never met, and then doing her funeral a few weeks later

- Living in a church-owned house that no one took the time to look after to make sure it remained livable

- The loneliness faced in a small church and rural community where three or four families composed the congregation, and who, without realizing it, excluded us from their lives

- The challenge of attempting to prepare two sermons for Sunday and a midweek Bible study while working bivocationally

I could add more, but you get the point. Nothing you read and no one you talk with can fully prepare you for the unexpected things that will happen in the first year of pastoring (or latter years, for that matter). So, expect the unexpected—not in an anxious way but by cultivating a healthy devotional life that keeps you steadfastly trusting in the Lord. Realize every event that unfolds comes by God's wise, providential governing over your life, so you can trust him for wisdom, strength, power, honing, disciplining, and preparing you to serve him with greater faithfulness (Ps. 139; 2 Cor. 12:1–10; Rom. 8:26–39; Heb. 12:1–17; 1 Peter 1:3–16). Strengthen yourself for the unexpected by making use of good resources, helpful blogs and podcasts, and refreshing conferences.[1]

Be Diligent to Remain Teachable

One serious malady that often afflicts those freshly minted with a Bible college or seminary degree is *I-know-it-all-now-itis*. They may hold a degree, having taken a range of ministry-related subjects in preparation for pastoral work. That's a good thing to have, and it does lay groundwork for readiness. But a seminary or Bible college degree only gets a pastor started. It exposes him to a lot of good things and rich truths, but it will take years to solidify, hone, and in some cases prune what he's learned to become useful in pastoral work.

Meanwhile, it's okay that new pastors have yet to master ministry. The early years of pastoral work become part of the wonderful process through which the Lord teaches and trains a man so that he can faithfully serve the body of Christ for decades to come. So what should he do?

(1) *Read voraciously.* Continue to stay fresh with biblical languages and theological, exegetical, and homiletical books. Read good sermons to help to expand your creativity and jumpstart stagnant days. Read good devotional material to stimulate prayer, meditation, praise, and worship. Read the Puritans who understood Scripture, application, and dependence upon the Lord like no other generation of ministers. Read good biographies and church history. At points along my pastoral journey, good biographies rescued me from despair, big mistakes, and cynicism.

(2) *Develop friendships with older, experienced pastors instead of only inexperienced peers.* In my first pastorate I had two pastor friends around my age with whom to share burdens and pray together. But I needed an older pastor that could give me guidance. Thankfully, in my second pastorate, an older minister took me under his wing to help me. I'm forever grateful for his encouragement, counsel, and help as I sought to navigate pastoral ministry. Seek help without apology. Most pastors who've been at it for a while will gladly assist a younger brother in ministry. All of us need it!

(3) *Listen to your wife.* She may not hold a seminary degree, but she likely has a better eye on details than you do. Don't push her ideas and corrections

---

1. See the selected bibliography for useful pastoral ministry resources. Additionally, Brian Croft has a series of books that he has authored, coauthored, or sponsored within his Practical Shepherding series (Zondervan), as well as the blog, podcast, and workshops available at http://practicalshepherding.com. 9Marks Ministries has books, podcasts, articles, conferences, and workshops that can be sourced at https://www.9marks.org. The Gospel Coalition has books, podcasts, articles, and conferences geared to help pastors that may be sourced at https://www.thegospelcoalition.org.

aside. She is the Lord's chosen instrument to help you see things more clearly. Plus, she knows you, your weaknesses, and your struggles. She's out to help you, so listen to her.

(4) *Listen to your congregation.* They were part of the church long before you arrived. Take the time to just listen rather than always instructing them. Two older men served as deacons in my first pastorate. They were quiet gentlemen with little education but a lot of wisdom. I profited from their insights as I sought to get my feet on the ground in serving this congregation.

Labor to Establish Priorities

You may have just finished seminary or Bible college, or just quit a profession to start up pastoral work. Go ahead and admit to yourself that you do not have everything well ordered in your life. Then begin to work on establishing healthy priorities that will carry you through life.

(1) *Major on developing a strong devotional and prayer life.* Nurture your walk with Christ. Let nothing substitute a joyous, vibrant relationship to Christ. Get into a regular pattern of devotional time that will feed your soul.[2]

(2) *Develop your ability to expound and pastorally apply God's Word.* Biblical exposition, if handled properly, will open the text and let the text speak to the needs of the congregation with sensitive, pointed application. Never stop growing in this area. Always be a student of the Word. Always look for ways to apply Scripture to your congregation. That's a major part of shepherding the flock.[3]

(3) *Be attentive to your marriage and family life. Attentive* means that you lay aside the unending demands of ministry to focus on your wife—serving her, loving her, and enjoying her. Your children need that kind of attentiveness too. Don't overschedule yourself in ministry so that your family only gets the crumbs of your time and energy. A congregation will allow you to fill every moment serving them. You must set the agenda to make sure your family gets some of the very best of your time and focused attention (Eph. 5:22–6:4).[4]

(4) *Gather around you a few men in whom you can pour your life in a disciple-making relationship.* Read and study the Word together. Pray together. Hold one another accountable. Serve Christ together. Do gospel work together (2 Tim. 2:1–2).

---

2. See Questions 6 and 7.
3. Questions 21–25 will amplify a number of aspects toward preaching well.
4. See Questions 8 and 9.

(5) *Patiently listen, shepherd, and serve the body entrusted to you, while being slow to make significant changes.* Some pastors rush in as the "professionals" ready to make massive changes in a church. They generally have short pastorates. Take the time to know your flock. Learn to genuinely love them. Don't try to make major changes in the first year, maybe not even the second or third. Focus on incremental changes in important areas essential to the church's health. Lay biblical, theological groundwork for changes so they come more naturally as the body learns the Word and applies it (Acts 20:28).

Concentrate on a Few Things

Ministry will be filled with highs and lows, ups and downs. That's normal. So just when you think a particular low or downtime spells the end of your pastoral tenure, realize it's part of the cycle of serving a congregation through the rugged issues of life. Persevere through the difficulty. We live in a fallen world. Your ascendency to the pulpit hasn't changed that reality. So, concentrate on a few things:

(1) *Be faithful as a Christian, husband, father, friend, student of Scripture, and pastor.*

(2) *Preach well.* A lot of things can be excused, but never sloppy, atheological, poorly exegeted, unorganized, sentimental, applicationless preaching (2 Tim. 4:1–5). Don't let leisure, lack of discipline, social media, or stubbornness get in the way of good preaching.

(3) *Shepherd faithfully.* You've been entrusted as an undershepherd by the Good Shepherd to care for one of his little flocks. One day he will ask for an accounting of how you cared for, loved, served, and pastored his people (Heb. 13:17). Be ready to give an account of faithfulness.

(4) *Set an example as a believer.* Concentrate on living a joyfully holy life (1 Tim. 4:12).

(5) *Let Scripture drive you and your ministry.* Don't waste time focusing on the latest fads on social media. Put into practice dependency upon the sufficiency of God's Word.

(6) *Find the greatest joy.* As Jesus told the Seventy, joy is found not in what you might accomplish in pastoral work, how great you imagine your preaching to be, how many have been added to the church's membership, or in the esteem of others toward you, but in that your name is written in heaven (Luke 10:20).

Summary

Enjoy the process of pastoral work. Not every day will be rosy or bleak. Unexpected demands and challenges will keep you dependent on Christ. Learn that the Lord faithfully abides with you as you, in weakness and sometimes fear, shepherd the flock of God. Work hard at remaining teachable—a stubborn, know-it-all pastor creates misery for everyone around him. You can't do everything you will want to do, so concentrate on what matters most. Make sure your priorities for walking with Christ, family relationships, preaching, shepherding, and discipling keep you focused so that when the unexpected happens, you remain steady and faithful in all things.

REFLECTION QUESTIONS

1. If you're in your first couple of years of pastoral ministry, what "firsts" are you walking through?

2. What will help the pastor be prepared and remain faithful when the unexpected happens?

3. What part does remaining teachable have in ministry?

4. What are your priorities in life and ministry?

5. If you cannot do everything that you would like to do in life and ministry—and no one can—then what areas need your concentration?

How Should the Practice of Not "Crushing a Bruised Reed" Shape Ministry?

Jesus's approach to ministry showed his deep consciousness of the people he served. With the broken, suffering, rejected, impoverished, and weak that often followed him, Jesus showed extraordinary gentleness (Matt. 11:25–30; Luke 13:10–17; 18:35–43; 19:1–10). With the Pharisees, however, he did not hesitate to call attention to hypocrisy or to declare a series of woes (Luke 11:37–52). As Puritan pastor Richard Sibbes put it, "The wounds of secure sinners will not be healed with sweet words."[1]

In the midst of pastoral ministry, both secure sinners and broken, wounded sinners need a pastoral word. But the same tone and approach to both will not meet them at the point of need. Jesus set the example throughout his ministry. Matthew calls particular attention to the way Jesus dealt with "a bruised reed" and "a smoldering wick," using metaphors in Isaiah's first Servant prophecy to describe the poor, outcast, and needy whom the Messiah served with gentleness (Matt. 12:15–21; Isa. 42:1–4).[2] His model of compassion establishes the approach for effective pastoral ministry with those who feel the weight of their sin and weakness.

1. Richard Sibbes, *The Bruised Reed*, Puritan Paperbacks (1630; Edinburgh: Banner of Truth Trust, 1998), 24.
2. Isaiah 42:1–4 is the first of four Servant prophecies referring to Jesus the Messiah fulfilling Israel's failure as Yahweh's servant: 49:1–12; 50:4–9; 52:13–53:12. See Craig Blomberg, "Matthew," in *Commentary on the New Testament Use of the Old Testament*, eds. G. K. Beale and D. A. Carson (Grand Rapids: Baker, 2007), 42; and D. A. Carson, ed., *NIV Biblical Theology Study Bible* (Grand Rapids: Zondervan, 2018), 1238.

The Example of Compassion

Matthew 12 records stories of the Pharisees' failure to show compassion for the needy, while they criticized Jesus for doing so. First, the disciples, hungry on the Sabbath, gathered handfuls of grain to eat as they passed through a field. Rather than concern for the men's hunger, the Pharisees could only think of their rigid approach to Sabbath-keeping. Jesus rebuked them, "But if you had known what this means, 'I desire compassion, and not sacrifice,' you would not have condemned the innocent" (Matt. 12:1–7; Jesus cites Hos. 6:6).[3]

Second, on the same day in the synagogue, Jesus healed a man with a withered hand. The Pharisees questioned the lawfulness of healing on the Sabbath. Jesus questions which of them would leave one of their sheep in a pit on the Sabbath. Then he quickly adds, "How much more valuable then is a man than a sheep! So then it is lawful to do good on the Sabbath" (Matt. 12:9–14). This left the Pharisees scheming to destroy him.[4]

Knowing the Pharisees' plot, Jesus withdrew from the scene but not without followers: "Many followed Him, and He healed them all" (Matt. 12:15). Matthew explains, Jesus's approach with the infirmed, poor, and needy fulfilled Isaiah's prophecy about Yahweh's Servant (Isa. 42:1–4; Matt. 12:17–21). The Servant chosen and beloved by Yahweh would by the Spirit proclaim justice to the nations, yet would not do so with fanfare. With gentleness and compassion he would serve the downtrodden, needy, broken, and weak "until He leads justice to victory," not allowing evil to triumph. "And in His name the Gentiles [nations] will hope" (Matt. 12:20–21). Leon Morris comments, "With his broad vision the prophet sees them all [the nations] as coming within the scope of God's compassionate love and of the servant's saving activity."[5] In the midst of Messiah's work, we find the model of compassion and gentleness with battered reeds and smoking flax as metaphors for the overlooked and needy. Both reeds and flax/wicks were fragile and in abundance, so they were usually replaced instead of salvaged for continued use.[6] Jesus never saw the weak and helpless as *replaceable* or *expendable*. Unlike the Pharisees who lost sight of people in their rigid application of the law, with compassion and gentleness Jesus served needy people.

The Bruised Reeds

In his classic work *The Bruised Reed*, Richard Sibbes offers pastoral wisdom for how to serve the needy and broken, following the merciful pattern

---

3. See Blomberg, "Matthew," 40–42, for Jesus's use of Hosea 6:6.
4. Another story shows them blaspheming Jesus when he healed a demonized man (Matt. 12:22–32).
5. Leon Morris, *The Gospel according to Matthew* (Grand Rapids: Eerdmans, 1992), 311–12.
6. Morris, *Gospel according to Matthew*, 311–12.

of Jesus. He describes *bruised reeds* in eight ways so we might recognize those among us suffering under the weight of sin, guilt, and trials—and like Jesus Christ, serve them with compassion and gentleness.

(1) Bruised reeds have been brought low especially by seeing their sin and feeling its crushing power, guilt, and judgment. They may have experienced "crosses" as well, that is, particular acts of God's providence that discipline or bring the person low.

(2) Bruised reeds see the evil of sin—so they think biblically about sin even though they may lack understanding of God's remedy for sin in Christ. In light of sin's evil, they also recognize God's favor as the greatest good known to man.

(3) Bruised reeds long for mercy by reason of the personal awareness of sin and the weakness sin creates.

(4) Bruised reeds feel deeply their unworthiness of any kindness from the Lord.

(5) Bruised reeds have sympathy for others living under difficult providences or conviction of sin. Instead of criticizing or condemning, they *feel* with them.

(6) Bruised reeds consider the happiest people in the world those who walk in the comforts of the Holy Spirit. They long for this happiness, but it seems far away.

(7) Bruised reeds tremble at God's Word while honoring those proclaiming the Word. They respect pastors seeking to speak the Word into their lives.

(8) Bruised reeds have no interest in formality or show. They are "taken up with the inward exercises of a broken heart" and "careful to use all sanctified means to convey comfort."[7]

Bruised reeds may be unbelievers struggling to believe the gospel. Or they may be Christians that have fallen under the weight of sin or "crosses," and so wrestle with believing the power of the gospel to lift them to joy and happiness in Christ.

Unlike the Pharisaic spirit that values formality, the letter of the law, tradition, and the supposedly spiritual elite, those characterized as bruised reeds recognize their weaknesses, unworthiness before God, brokenness over sin,

---

7. Sibbes, *Bruised Reed*, 10–11.

and wounds over bitter providences. They long for God's mercy but struggle to believe the Lord God will meet them in their brokenness. They need to see that bruising levels "all proud, high thoughts, and that we may understand ourselves to be what indeed we are by nature," helpless sinners in need of a merciful Savior.[8] And in so doing, humbled before the Lord, bruised reeds meet the compassion and gentleness of Christ through his servants ministering the Word of God.

The Practice of Compassion

Pastors can get frustrated with weak, needy people that fail to respond quickly to their exhortations or counsel. "Why can't they just do what I've told them to do?" a pastor might ask, feeling imposition upon his time by someone who seems overburdened by sin or some difficulty. Instead of following instructions laid out, they continue to struggle and groan under a weight the gospel could lift. Without realizing it, pastors may slip into Pharisaic mode, placing higher expectations upon a person than he or she can meet. Sibbes seeks to help pastors move away from any Pharisaic attitude in serving broken and needy people in order to follow the compassionate practice of Jesus Christ with the needy. What do we see in Jesus that models pastoral ministry to *bruised reeds*? We'll let Sibbes help us.

1. Mercy

Cloistered by ministerial practicality, pastors can drift into smugness toward those appearing to offer little contribution to the body because of their weakness. Yet they need mercy, not smugness. Sibbes writes, "That spirit of mercy in Christ should move his servants to be content to abase themselves for the good of the meanest" [i.e., those of little importance].[9] A humble spirit extends mercy toward those considered "the meanest." Yet too often, we can look down on the lowly. Sibbes counsels, "Misery should be a lodestone [magnet] of mercy, not a footstool for pride to trample on."[10] How do we deal mercifully toward others? Sibbes quips, "In the censures of the church, it is more suitable to the spirit of Christ to incline to the milder part, and not to kill a fly on the forehead with a mallet, nor shut men out of heaven for a trifle."[11] Extending mercy better suits the spirit of Christ than a heavy hand that tends to crush the broken.

2. Humility

Jesus told the broken and needy, "Come to Me, all who are weary and heavy-laden, and I will give you rest. Take My yoke upon you and learn from Me, *for*

---

8. Sibbes, *Bruised Reed*, 4.
9. Sibbes, *Bruised Reed*, 27.
10. Sibbes, *Bruised Reed*, 31.
11. Sibbes, *Bruised Reed*, 30.

I am gentle and humble in heart, and you will find rest for your souls" (Matt. 11:28–29, emphasis added).[12] The humble King of glory welcomed "weary and heavy-laden" people to himself so he might bear them up in his strength. This kind of humility crushes the natural disposition of pride and superiority that can affect pastors accustomed to attention and commendations. "The best of men," counsels Sibbes, "are severe to themselves, tender over others."[13] Instead of superiority that disdains those not progressing as they wish, pastors should follow the practice of Martin Bucer: "After long experience he resolved to refuse none in whom he saw *aliquid Christi*, something of Christ. The best Christians in this state of imperfection," Sibbes notes, "are like gold that is a little too light, which needs some grains of allowance to make it pass."[14] Only humble hearts will show that kind of tenderness toward the weak.

3. Gentleness

Gruff, bombastic, and heavy-handed preachers thundering away at straw men garner applause at conferences. Yet Jesus modeled the opposite. Sibbes explains, "That great physician, as he had a quick eye and a healing tongue, so he had a gentle hand and a tender heart."[15] The "woes" reserved for the hypocritical religious leaders gave way to the gentle heart of Jesus with the broken and weary. "Some think it strength of grace to endure nothing in the weaker," writes Sibbes, "whereas the strongest are readiest to bear with the infirmities of the weak."[16] We're to be like Jesus in gentleness with the weak. "He is a meek king; he will admit mourners into his presence, a king of poor and afflicted persons" is our model.[17] With gentleness, we're to bear the infirmities of the weak (Rom. 15:1), just as Jesus did with Thomas's doubts (John 20:27), Peter's denials (Luke 22:61), and the poor man's unbelief (Mark 9:24).[18]

4. Grace

Grace experienced should motivate us to show grace to others, even when we see little grace in them. Sibbes points out, "We must remember that grace sometimes is so little as to be indiscernible to us."[19] Some we think not Christian may be weak believers that need our gentleness urging them to rely on Christ and the gospel. We must patiently take them back to gospel truths they should know by now. We must show grace to them in the way we speak and act. Others

---

12. See Dane Ortlund, *Gentle and Lowly: The Heart of Christ for Sinners and Sufferers* (Wheaton, IL: Crossway, 2020).
13. Sibbes, *Bruised Reed*, 23.
14. Sibbes, *Bruised Reed*, 33.
15. Sibbes, *Bruised Reed*, 34.
16. Sibbes, *Bruised Reed*, 33.
17. Sibbes, *Bruised Reed*, 8.
18. Sibbes, *Bruised Reed*, 20–21.
19. Sibbes, *Bruised Reed*, 37.

we may think to judge instead of serve because their spiritual lives seem weak when we expect them to be strong. Yet, writes Sibbes, "a spark of fire is fire, as well as the whole element. Therefore we must look to grace in the spark as well as in the flame."[20] Consequently, we must guard against falling into a pattern of law in the way we shepherd them instead of shepherding in grace. "Moses, without any mercy, breaks all bruised reeds, and quenches all smoking flax," notes Sibbes concerning the distinction between the law and the covenant of grace. "Christ comes with blessing, even upon those whom Moses had cursed, and with healing balm for those wounds which Moses had made."[21] So, too, do we who've received the grace of God shepherd bruised reeds in the rich, full grace of Christ.

Jesus demonstrated mercy, humility, gentleness, and grace over and over to the bruised reeds and smoking flax that he encountered. That's the model of compassion for pastors to embrace in their shepherding work.

Summary

Studying the pastoral example of Jesus Christ helps strip from pastors the tendency to function with impatience, harshness, judgmentalism, and censoriousness. Throughout his ministry, Jesus came face to face with bruised reeds who carried heavy burdens. Pastors face twenty-first-century versions of bruised reeds, with the weakness, guilt, fear, and weightiness shared in the first century. As Jesus modeled, pastors must learn to deal with bruised reeds in mercy, humility, gentleness, and grace. This kind of compassion honors Christ and lovingly shapes pastoral ministry.

REFLECTION QUESTIONS

1. What's the context for the Matthew 12 use of the Isaiah 42:1–4 prophecy?

2. How would you pastorally describe the metaphors of *bruised reeds* and *smoking flax*?

3. Who comes to mind when you think about *bruised reeds* and *smoking flax* in your pastoral context?

4. What are the characteristics of the practice of compassion evidenced by Jesus toward the needy and broken?

5. Which of the four practices of compassion considered in this chapter seems most difficult for you at this point, and why?

---

20. Sibbes, *Bruised Reed*, 36.
21. Sibbes, *Bruised Reed*, 36–37.

What Are Some Dangers to Avoid in Pastoral Ministry?

The dangers of pastoral ministry can be a loaded topic that might expand to book length. But since some of the other questions consider many of the dangers, I simply want to call attention to a few very present ones and offer observations that might help a fellow pastor steer clear of them.

After more than four decades in ministry, I've witnessed fellow pastors falling prey to various dangers that cost them their ministries and, sometimes, their families. The good intentions with which we begin pastoral work cannot be done on autopilot. The adversary shows no mercy to us in areas of weakness or neglect, but rather exploits them to destroy us, and the churches we serve (1 Peter 5:8). We're engaged in spiritual conflict day in and day out, so we must learn to "be strong in the Lord and the strength of His might," putting on "the full armor of God, so that [we] will be able to stand firm against the schemes of the devil" (Eph. 6:10–11).[1]

Recognizing dangers and hazards in our paths provides one of the best ways to engage in spiritual battle. While every Christian faces spiritual dangers, pastors seem to have a few unique to our work. We'll look at them under personal and ministry headings.

Personal

The personal dangers can bleed over into ministry and vice versa. But for the sake of getting our heads around them, we'll consider the following as personal dangers.

---

1. See D. Martyn Lloyd-Jones, *The Christian Warfare: An Exposition of Ephesians 6:10–13* (Grand Rapids: Baker, 1998); and D. Martyn Lloyd-Jones, *The Christian Soldier: An Exposition of Ephesians 6:10–20* (Grand Rapids: Baker, 1998).

1. Carelessness in Personal Holiness

Since the Lord is holy, Peter writes, "be holy yourselves also in all your behavior" (1 Peter 1:15–16). He adds, "Beloved, I urge you as aliens and strangers to abstain from fleshly lusts which wage war against the soul. Keep your behavior excellent among the Gentiles, so that in the thing in which they slander you as evildoers, they may because of your good deeds, as they observe them, glorify God in the day of visitation" (1 Peter 2:11–12). Holiness follows union with Jesus Christ (Rom. 6:5–7). Yet that's no call for passivity but rather an urgent reason for actively fighting to not let sin reign in us (Rom. 6:12–14).[2] Robert Murray M'Cheyne said, "The greatest need of my people is my personal holiness."[3] And if only for your people, it's your greatest need in your personal life.[4]

2. Letting Offenses Fester

Pastoral ministry provides a laboratory of opportunities for offense. So does a sinner living in a home with other sinners. Remaining bitter, seething over something spoken, nursing a cross look, or fuming over a neglected act sours the heart against others. We must "put away" bitterness, wrath, anger, clamor, slander, and malice, responding as forgiven people with kind, tenderhearted acts of forgiveness (Eph. 4:31–32). Don't call it a bad mood, call it by its real name: *sin that needs repentance*. Go to Christ daily, throughout the day, to keep the heart free of bitterness (1 John 1:7–9). Forgive others as those forgiven by God.

3. Putting Off Development in Personal Discipline

We're to discipline ourselves for the purpose of godliness (1 Tim. 4:7). A life of discipline means we've given attention to ordering our lives before God so that he has preeminence in all things (Col. 1:18). Neglecting discipline becomes self-defeating (Prov. 15:32). Discipline involves developing good habits to cultivate the spiritual life, exercising restraint on desires, making good use of time, focusing on priorities, and enduring through difficult days (Prov. 12:1; 13:18). It doesn't happen overnight. But it won't happen without attention to the details needed for a healthy walk and faithful ministry.

4. Neglecting Physical Health

Malachi rebuked the priests that offered sickly and deformed sacrifices on the altar (Mal. 1:6–14). If we're to be "living sacrifices" (Rom. 12:1), then

---

2. See the warning against unholy "shepherds," Israel's spiritual leaders, in Ezekiel 34:1–10.
3. Quoted in Olford, S. F., & Olford, D. L. *Anointed Expository Preaching* (Nashville: Broadman & Holman Publishers, 1998), 221).
4. See John Owen, *Overcoming Sin and Temptation*, eds. Kelly Kapic and Justin Taylor (Wheaton, IL: Crossway, 2006); J. C. Ryle, *Holiness: Its Nature, Hindrances, Difficulties, and Roots*, abridged (Chicago: Moody, 2010); J. I. Packer, *Rediscover Holiness: Know the Fullness of Life with God* (Grand Rapids: Baker, 2009).

it stands to reason that while the physical life never takes priority over the spiritual (1 Tim. 4:7–8), it's also not to be taken for granted. God has gifted us with our bodies, so we must care for them by staying in shape, eating well, exercising, and getting sufficient sleep. Otherwise we shortchange families, congregations, and ourselves when we're not in the kind of physical health needed for maintaining a robust schedule.[5] Schedule an annual physical. Discuss with your physician the kind of exercise appropriate for your age, physical condition, and health. Then do it. Work on eating and sleeping habits that will enable you to maximize each day for the glory of God. Be willing to get help for any of the areas necessary for staying in good health.

5. Taking Marriage for Granted

Be intentional with your marriage. An automobile in neutral will do okay going downhill, but that won't last long. Just letting your marriage coast along, taking what comes, equates to leaving it in neutral. Look for ways to daily serve your wife. It may be helping with things around the home or helping with the children or volunteering to shop for groceries. Be creative. Your wife will love seeing you seek out ways to intentionally serve her. She will feel loved by your selfless service.

6. Neglecting Time with Your Children

Paul's simple exhortation "Fathers, do not exasperate your children, so that they will not lose heart" demands we evaluate the way we relate to our children (Col. 3:21). Sometimes our absence, while doing good things, speaks volumes to them about our concern for their struggles and challenges. Take time to be involved in their interests (sports, music, outdoor activities). Help with their schoolwork. Allow them room to speak, even complain, with an attentive ear and without a harsh reaction. Exercise self-control when correcting and disciplining. Apologize when you've failed them in any way. In short, be Christians in all things with your children.[6]

7. Neglecting to Take Time Off

When the Twelve returned from their first solo ministry, Jesus listened to their reports and then "withdrew" so that they might rest (Luke 9:10).[7] Call it withdrawing or a day off. Jesus knew they could not maintain a torrid pace without taking a break to relax. Neither can pastors. Pastors must prioritize a day off from ministry labors. I've taken Mondays off for the past thirty years

---

5. A disability or chronic illness will make this difficult, but even with it, pastors should do all they can to maintain the best health possible.

6. Paul David Tripp, *Parenting: Fourteen Gospel Principles That Can Radically Change Your Family* (Wheaton, IL: Crossway, 2016).

7. "Withdraw," ὑποχωρέω, used with the preposition ἐν gives the sense "retire to a place and spend some time there" (BDAG, 1043).

and have found that to refresh me with new vigor for the week. The congregation respects that time, so I'm rarely called upon to do ministry on Mondays (although I'm willing to do so when needed). Schedule vacations *in advance*, and as you do, *make sure* the pulpit and other responsibilities are covered in-house or with a guest. See it as a stewardship on your part to take time off.

8. Spending Too Much Time on Social Media

It's amazing how much time can be frittered away in a day! Checking all the social media accounts several times each day, adding new posts, and interacting with friends about what someone else posted can suddenly cost an hour or two or four in a day that should be devoted to better things. Limit your social media. Discipline yourself to find a non-working time when you will check them out (keep in mind they can be destructive to family life, too). Stay away from sites that engage in needless arguments (2 Tim. 2:14–19). Guard against lingering where enticements toward sinful thoughts or acts would tempt you (1 Tim. 6:3–16). Use accountability partners to ensure you exercise good restraints on media use.[8]

Ministry

To say that ministry contains minefields does not exaggerate the dangers each pastor faces. That can be said of other occupations, for sure, yet ministry has unique challenges we need to understand and take action to address.

1. Lacking Accountability

Pastors are not excluded from being tempted to sin, making poor choices, becoming complacent, developing a poor attitude, or going rogue. God designed plurality for pastoral (elder) work as built-in accountability.[9] If your church doesn't have elder plurality, then initiate bringing a couple of godly men into your life as accountability partners until elder plurality might be established. Be open enough to share life together, discuss struggles, pray for one another, and demand holy living from each other. Pastors living solo set themselves on a dangerous trajectory.

2. Thinking That You Are Irreplaceable

Or to expand this danger: *attempting to do the church's ministry alone.* Sometimes it's a control issue, other times it's a pride or arrogance issue, and still other times it's a fear issue that keeps us thinking we must do all ministry alone—the visits, teaching, meetings, administration, and so on. "No one else can do it as well!" "No one else will do it the way I want it done!" In doing so,

---

8. See Tony Reinke, *Twelve Ways Your Phone Is Changing You* (Wheaton, IL: Crossway, 2017).
9. See Phil A. Newton and Matt Schmucker, *Elders in the Life of the Church: Rediscovering the Biblical Model for Church Leadership* (Grand Rapids: Kregel Ministry, 2014).

we develop the mentality that we're irreplaceable. Before long, we put more confidence in our abilities and insights than depending upon the Lord. Yet since the church belongs to Jesus and he promised to build it (Matt. 16:18), we can be assured that Jesus can replace us. He does not need us. He has been pleased to entrust the flock to us for a time, but it's his flock and we're his undershepherds to serve at his pleasure. Pastors must guard against the pride that makes them feel irreplaceable. Otherwise, a pastor will wear himself out trying to keep up that faulty image.

3. Getting into Compromising Relationships or Situations

Proverbs warns against the adulteress or enticing woman, and the pit-falls of being in places or situations that make us more vulnerable to sexual temptation (Prov. 5–7). Those aren't wasted warnings. Counseling a woman with a closed door or with no one else in the office compromises the pastor. Visiting women in their home alone compromises the pastor. Daring to surf the Internet to pursue lusts compromises the pastor. Establish policies for counseling or visiting that prevents compromise. Utilize filters and account-ability to keep from *accidentally* getting onto porn websites. When we stand before the Lord to give an account for how we discharged our responsibilities as his undershepherds, let there be no instances where we've compromised moral purity and played loosely with the holy work he has given us.[10]

4. Failing to Utilize the Body's Gifted People

The Lord has sovereignly worked in the church to gift its members for ministry (Rom. 12:3–8; 1 Cor. 12:1–31; Eph. 4:11–16; 1 Peter 4:9–10). The pastor's responsibility, instead of doing all the ministry, is to equip and release the church's members to get involved in the work. We suffer under the weight of an unbiblical spectator type of church life. Pastors groan at how much they have to do when part of the problem rests squarely on their failure to get the body involved. This means intentionally *training up spiritual leaders* that can serve the congregation faithfully.[11] It means watching for giftedness in the members and putting them to work. Never hesitate to personally ask people to get involved in ministry. Don't rely upon pulpit or email announcements, but personally recruit members for service.

5. Chasing After Every Negative Comment

The public nature of pastoral work means we're open to criticism, as well as ample misunderstandings. With that territory comes negative comments,

---

10. See Brian Croft, *Help! He's Struggling with Pornography* (Wapwollepen, PA: Shepherd, 2014).
11. See Phil A. Newton, *The Mentoring Church: How Pastors and Congregations Cultivate Leaders* (Grand Rapids: Kregel Ministry, 2017).

complaints, and barbs. At times, when they rise to the occasion of causing division in the church, the elders need to address them. Most of the time, however, those comments serve as choice instruments to humble us to depend upon the Lord and cast our fretfulness upon him (1 Peter 5:6–7). Some people tend to be negative, so negative comments may not mean anything ill; it's just a personality trait. Consider the source of the comment in such case, and don't take it too seriously. If there's a kernel of truth to the complaint, learn from it; perhaps even thank the complainer for the insight.

6. Forgetting to Regularly Express Gratitude to Those Serving with You

Gratitude should characterize every Christian (Eph. 5:20). Pastors should model it for the congregation. Notice how others serve, the effort they put into their labors, the sweet attitude they bring to the work, the cooperative spirit with fellow workers, the sacrificial mind in serving, and so on—and express gratitude. It does not take a lot of effort to be gracious in offering thanks to others. It just takes noticing them as fellow servants of Christ. A card, note, text, email, or call might lift a brother or sister to a new level of service because the pastor notices and expresses thanks.

7. Failing to Exercise Wise Caution and Godly Courage

By *wise caution*, one follows carefully the teaching of Scripture, with attentiveness to the working of the Holy Spirit when making a decision, not giving way to a timid spirit. While ready to move forward with an exciting decision in one church that I served, I sensed a check in my spirit on the day the decision was to be made. I had no hesitation before, so it puzzled me. This led to spending the day seeking the Lord in Word and prayer. Late in the afternoon, when I read Proverbs 17:4, peace broke into my heart that had been absent the entire day. I was able to be decisive without fearfulness, knowing the Lord had given me wise caution on moving ahead.

Yet we can allow a natural tendency to shrink from conflict or hard decisions to excuse constant caution. The church will not make good progress with a pastor that is always *too cautious* to make decisions that might "rock the boat." In such case, we need to exercise *godly courage* (e.g., Josh. 1:6–7; 2 Tim. 1:7). Courage doesn't mean brashness or a natural insensitivity to others or running over people to do what we want. Instead, godly courage "speaks God's truth into a world and a culture that is going to be offended by it," writes John MacArthur. "But you do it because you've been called to do it and you know it honors the Lord."[12] When it's our pride at stake, it's not courageous to act. It's time for restraint. Godly courage takes action when God will get all the glory.

---

12. John MacArthur, "Why Churches Languish Under Cowardly Pastors," Crossway, May 17, 2019, www.crossway.com.

8. Falling into Unhealthy Patterns of Sermon Preparation

Here are a few unhealthy patterns of sermon preparation: (1) waiting until Saturday to start preparing for Sunday; (2) trying to come up with applications without first grounding them in sound interpretation; (3) attempting to be clever in preaching instead of focusing on faithfulness to the biblical text; (4) borrowing ideas and lengthy quotes from others without giving appropriate credit; (5) cutting and pasting other pastors' sermons without taking the time to thoughtfully develop a homiletical structure; (6) failing to pray and meditate on the text; (7) making assumptions about a text without the diligent effort to properly understand it; and (8) failing to humbly depend on the Holy Spirit in preparation. When the pastor recognizes he's fallen into some unhealthy preparation patterns, then he needs to take immediate action to remedy how he prepares. He's preaching God's Word to God's people, so that calls for his best efforts each week.

Summary

The common adversary of all believers carefully aims his fiery darts at pastors, knowing that when they succumb to temptation or indiscipline or complacency or bitterness, the entire congregation will be impacted. Recognizing personal and ministry dangers allows the pastor the keenness in prayer, application of the Word, and accountability to avoid falling into traps laid by the adversary. The eternal importance of the pastor's work urges him to faithfulness in all things.

REFLECTION QUESTIONS

1. In what ways are pastors' dangers unique from the average church member?

2. What warnings in areas of the personal life seem most pertinent in your life?

3. Which personal danger do you observe most pastors struggling to address?

4. How has God provided accountability for pastors?

5. Why is neglect in expressing gratitude to coworkers a danger to avoid?

How Should Pastors Handle Opposition?

Pastors need not think it strange when facing opposition. It goes with the territory of pastoral ministry. One need only read the Pauline and Johannine epistles to realize opposition seemed to weave its way into most every church in the first century (e.g., 1 Cor. 1:10–17; 2 Cor. 10–13; Gal. 1:6–2:14; Phil. 3:17–19; 2 John 7–11; 3 John 9–10). The same continues in our day. Some may see disagreements, differing opinions, or different ways of handling issues as *opposition*. However, some disagreements can be healthy when they lead us to irenically search the Scriptures together for answers. Opposition, on the other hand, rises to a level that threatens the church's stability.

Early in my second pastorate, a disgruntled community member sent letters making harsh accusations to three ladies in our congregation. With the letters unknown to me, it happened that the following Sunday my sermon picked up some themes in the letters—albeit with a completely different aim than the letter writer (that's called God's providence!). I addressed them with biblical application. After the morning worship, one of the recipients began to grumble to others that I was the perpetrator, even though nothing I said that morning gave credence to the content of the unflattering letters.

In my present pastorate, I spoke one Sunday evening from 2 Timothy 4:1–5 on why I preach expositionally. One of the leading Sunday school teachers defiantly walked out in the middle of the sermon, making visible his opposition to exposition.

When working through establishing plural elder leadership in our congregational polity, one man abruptly quit attending while murmuring to others on the way out. After talking with him, he admitted he didn't care that it was biblical to have elder plurality, but it wasn't Baptist, so he rejected it.

That's just a few of the times I've felt the strong weight of opposition. Even people I had spent lots of time serving during sickness and loss felt no loyalty when it came to opposing me. The question I faced, as with every pastor, was how to deal with the opposition and continue in faithful pastoral ministry. We'll think about this with six considerations.

Pray Often

Opposition may be spiritual warfare. Attacks may come in different shapes, forms, and with an array of people and circumstances. When it involves the church's health, its leadership, the congregation's unity, the church's corporate witness, and faithfulness to the lordship of Christ, *it is* a spiritual issue. This requires spiritual leadership to face it whether confronting or laboring in prayer to see matters changed. Paul's exhortation in Ephesians 6:10–20 appropriately calls for pastors and congregations to "be strong in the Lord and the strength of His might" and be clothed in the armor of God (vv. 10–11).[1] John Stott explained this as "the proper combination of divine enabling and human co-operation."[2] Paul calls for exercising it with "all prayer and petition," praying "at all times in the Spirit" (v. 18). "It [prayer] is to pervade all our spiritual warfare," wrote Stott. He continues, "Equipping ourselves with God's armour is not a mechanical operation; it is itself an expression of our dependence on God, in other words of prayer."[3]

Prayer for wisdom, discernment, power, humility, clarity, and grace should accompany any thought of confronting opposition. It may be that in prayer the pastor realizes the matter does not warrant confrontation, so he leaves it in the hands of the Lord. At other times, when the gospel is at stake, he knows he must confront those in opposition, so he bathes his steps and words in prayer, knowing if the Lord does not act on his behalf, his efforts will be in vain.

Walk in Humility

The call to humility mirrors what we find in the Lord Jesus Christ (Matt. 11:29). He knew when to confront and when to remain silent. He kept the larger purpose of his mission and kingdom at the forefront of every confrontation without using it for selfish motives.

Humility must not be confused with mousiness. Rather, humility means the pastor recognizes the truth about himself and God and doesn't confuse them. He realizes he does not have the power to change the heart in opposition, but God does. He knows that despite his persuasiveness, someone else can persuade otherwise. So, he approaches addressing opposition with the

---

1. See Martyn Lloyd-Jones, *The Christian Soldier: An Exposition of Ephesians 6:10–20* (Edinburgh: Banner of Truth Trust, 1977); and William Gurnall, *The Christian in Complete Armour*, 3 vols. (17th c.; Edinburgh: Banner of Truth Trust, 1990).
2. John R. W. Stott, *The Message of Ephesians*, BST (Downers Grove, IL: InterVarsity, 1979), 266.
3. Stott, *Ephesians*, 283.

deep consciousness that he must simply be a vessel that the Lord might use, not the hero of sorting out a church conflict. He consciously gives glory to God for any change, repentance, and correction.

Keep Your Heart Warm

By that, I mean keep your relationship to the Lord warm and renewed. Few things can be worse than an angry, bitter pastor attempting to deal with opposition from a church member. This kind of impoverished spiritual walk leaves fractures in its wake, with some that may never heal. Before confronting opposition, a pastor needs to know he's dealt with his sinful attitudes and bitter spirits (Eph. 4:29–5:2). He must know he's living in forgiveness toward those that created the opposition or else he will defend himself and his rights without thought of the glory and honor of God and the gospel. He must know he's walking carefully in the will of the Lord and the fullness of the Holy Spirit (Eph. 5:15–21). Check your heart and your walk before taking one step toward dealing with opposition. It may be that the biggest problem is not in someone else but in the pastor that has allowed bitterness to fester. The unity of the church and testimony of the gospel is at stake in such times.

It seems important in these occasions for pastors to hide God's Word in their hearts. Passages dealing with humility (1 Peter 5:6–7), gentleness (2 Tim. 2:25), wisdom (James 1:5–6), and speech (Prov. 15:1) would be good to commit to memory and rehearse throughout the time of preparing for and confronting opposition.

Discern If It Is Best to Let It Go or to Confront

If someone makes a stinging or untrue remark—and it will happen time and again—the pastor will need to decide if it's an instrument serving to humble him to trust the Lord more, something unfair but not worth taking a chance on ruining relationships, or a matter that affects the church's unity and gospel message. Often, experience testifies, the little nipping at the heels or nicks on the shins, so to speak, just do not merit the time it takes to unravel who said what and why it was said. Unless it affects the church's unity, gospel testimony, corporate worship, polity issues regarding membership and leadership, or mission, then it may not rise to the need for confrontation.

But if the matter or nature of opposition rises to the point of needing confronting, then the pastor should never do so alone. He should have at least one more elder (preferably a non-staff elder) join him in the confrontation. These men should pray through and discuss how they will handle the situation, with each holding the other accountable for humility, gentleness, and love accompanying their conversation and demeanor.

It may be—and I personally think this happens often—the matter of opposition is simply a misunderstanding. In such case, approaching it with gentleness and grace may diffuse any tension and anger. Or it may be that in the conversation the pastor realizes personal blame in something said or done or neglected. In such cases, he needs to receive correction with humility and ask for forgiveness. If the other person(s) involved has started rumors or spoken without merit, then the pastor and elder should point out the issue, get clarification, and then explain through Scripture why it must be stopped, and hopefully, apologies are made commensurate with the offense. If the matter rises to the level of church discipline due to false doctrine or disrupting the unity of the church, then anyone involved should be approached in the spirit of Matthew 18:15–17, recognizing the seriousness of the matters at hand. Here, the pastor and his fellow elder will need to stand firmly upon truth, keeping aware of any threat to the church's testimony or unity.

Keep Preaching God's Word

Only in extreme circumstances should a pastor change his expositional series to publicly address the opposition. He must guard the pulpit from being a "bully pulpit." He never wants to be accused of misusing the pastoral office to attack someone else or someone's position in order to make himself appear justified in the face of opposition. I've found it remarkable how often the normal planned series of expositions through a book of the Bible timely addresses an issue that has arisen. Publicizing the preaching schedule ahead of time eliminates accusations of shifting sermons to attack someone else. God's sovereign hand at work in the church must not be forgotten!

More importantly, the regular ministry of the Word must remain the priority for the pastor. He must guard against the tendency of being sidetracked by opposition so that he loses sight of the first concern of feeding the flock the Word of God—that's one of the adversary's strategies. He must also know the Holy Spirit works through the preaching of the Word to accomplish far more than he will ever know. So be faithful in preaching God's Word.

Leave the Matter in God's Hands

When the pastor has prayed, approached the situation with humility, prepared his heart before God, and discerned the best way to act or to remain silent, he must entrust the opposition and its dangling effects to the hands of God. The Lord who created the heavens and the earth has ample power to work in the situation that has caused so much angst. Sometimes matters of opposition seem to never end. Other times, the Lord acts to bring them to a grinding halt in ways the pastor realizes were far beyond his own ability to change. But other matters must be considered regarding opposition and God's ultimate hand at work.

The Lord may be pruning the pastor and/or the church. The time of opposition takes the pastor deeper into dealing with his sin and walking with the Lord. It takes the church into more intense repentance, prayer, and obedience.

The Lord may be teaching the pastor to rely on him. So often, in my own ministry, that's been the case. I've learned more lessons of God's faithfulness when facing opposition than when all seemed to be going well.

The Lord may be exposing error and ungodliness in the church. In such cases, that may mean confrontation or even church discipline. Or it may be a call to deep repentance for the congregation. At other times it means the Lord may do the painful work of purging the church to purify it.

The Lord may be setting the stage for future changes in the church that will expand its gospel testimony and ministry. We walked through a three-year period of opposition, with rumblings under the surface that could not be pinpointed to address. It proved to be one of the most painful times in ministry, especially since much of it centered on the gospel. Yet God used that time to humble, purify, and change us. Our church is not the same church—and thank God for that, as it has given rise to new levels of gospel testimony and ministry locally and globally.

Summary

Pastors and churches may expect occasional disagreements, misunderstandings, and personal conflicts as normal aspects of learning to live together as followers of Christ. Opposition that undermines gospel unity arises from time to time as spiritual conflict. As spiritual, it mustn't be dealt with apart from consciously depending upon the Lord's power and provision for his people. Prayer, humility, and devotedness to Christ must precede any thought of confronting opposition. Discerning God's desire in whether or not to confront will only be known through the Word and prayer. Confrontations, when necessary, must be done with gentleness, humility, and love with an aim toward restoration and unity. Ultimately, pastors must learn to trust the Lord with opposition, as well as learn the lessons he would teach his undershepherds and congregations.

REFLECTION QUESTIONS

1. Why is spiritual warfare a critical aspect of handling opposition?

2. How does humility become a necessary trait when facing opposition?

3. When should opposition be confronted and when should it be left alone?

4. How should the pastor use the pulpit in times of opposition?

5. What might the Lord be teaching the pastor and congregation through opposition?

How Does the Pastor Lead an Elders' Meeting?

I led the first elders' meeting that I attended.[1] That's probably not the best way to get started. But when our congregation voted to establish elder plurality leadership as our governing structure, very few churches in my denomination had elders. All of the churches I knew about in my area had a range of pastor/deacon, single pastor, or committee-led churches. I had no model on which to base my actions that afternoon.

That was more than twenty-five years ago. I can't remember all we did in that first meeting, but I do remember through the years elders' meetings developing into times of rich fellowship and prayer, spiritual sensitivity, burden for needy members, laughter and tears, affirmation and wise counsel.

How a pastor leads an elders' meeting may vary. Yet it seems we will have similar templates for considerations during our meetings even though we move the pieces around or approach them with differing emphases. We will utilize a few questions to help us think through how the pastor might lead an elders' meeting.

Why Are You Gathered?

We need to start at the beginning. Elders focus on four areas: doctrine, discipline/member care, direction, and modeling the Christian life. The latter remains a tangential part of the meeting without being part of the agenda. Attitudes, discussion, decisions, and changes will reflect how well elders

---

1. The lead pastor is not the only possible leader of elders' meetings. Potentially, any man among them could be a possible leader on a rotating basis. Some lead pastors prefer not to lead the elders' meeting but defer to a man chosen among them. Unless a church's polity insists otherwise, it's likely the lead pastor will at some point lead elders' meetings. Without doubt, even when he quietly sits in a meeting, his leadership will be felt and needed among the elders. I've written the chapter with this in view.

model the Christian life within their council and with the congregation. Items on the agenda should fit under the other three categories—doctrine, discipline/member care, and direction/leadership. If an item proposed for discussion does not fit under these categories—that is, within the elders' reason for calling and service—then the pastor can remove it from the agenda and delegate that item to the appropriate person, group, team, or committee.

What Are the Hinge Points for Elders and Their Meetings?

The nature of an elders' meeting is determined long before the meeting itself begins, that is, in the careful process of a congregation choosing qualified men as elders. Paul helps us to understand that not everyone fits well into the culture of equality, confidentiality, and humility necessary for all elders' meetings: "An overseer, then, must be above reproach . . . temperate, prudent, respectable, hospitable, able to teach, not . . . pugnacious, but gentle, peaceable, free from the love of money" (1 Tim. 3:2–3). Likewise, to Titus, he writes, "For the overseer must be above reproach as God's steward, not self-willed, not quick-tempered . . . not pugnacious, not fond of sordid gain, . . . loving what is good, sensible, just, devout, self-controlled, holding fast the faithful word which is in accordance with the teaching, so that he will be able both to exhort in sound doctrine and to refute those who contradict" (Titus 1:7–9).

Without retracing every detail, one notes that the character of the elder must hold priority over his abilities, gifts, and prominence in the church. He cannot be a loose cannon or else he will sink the entire body of elders with his temper, tongue, and unbridled actions. He can't be a bully but must be characterized by gentleness and peace. He needs to exercise good sense and sound thinking. He can't be controlled by the idea of personal gain. He must be preeminently a man of the Word who knows how to apply and follow the teaching of Holy Scripture for the areas that elders consider.

These character traits must never be left at the door when a *meeting* begins. They must permeate the atmosphere of the gathering. Prepare early for healthy elders' meetings by selecting and affirming men with the kind of character that Paul sets forth as essential for overseers. If an elder has a weak moment and lapses in one of these areas, then the remainder of the council has the responsibility to correct and admonish him.

How Do You Model Elder Leadership While Leading the Meeting?

The lead pastor has the most public exposure and pulpit time and could come across to the rest of the elders as being the *most* important among the elders. But he's not. He's equal to the others, although first among them in terms of responsibilities and accountability before the congregation.[2] He

---

2. See Benjamin L. Merkle, *Forty Questions About Elders and Deacons* (Grand Rapids: Kregel Academic, 2008), 174–75.

cannot and need not change the latter, but he can work consciously to build equality among the elders. One way that he expresses equality with the balance of the elders will be the way he handles leading the meetings.

The pastor's *commitment* to the elders as fellow-pastors of the flock will be evident in the way he enjoys spending time with them, daily intercedes for them, and affirms their gifts and service in the body. Just to be with his fellow elders counts as a privilege and gift from the Lord. His commitment to them communicates that attitude. He *knows* the other elders' families well, calling upon the Lord to work mightily among the elders' wives and children.

The pastor's *humility* in the way he handles attention from the congregation, including compliments and complaints, serves to put the other men at ease as equal participants in the meeting. "Genuine humility is something of a built-in shock absorber—it diffuses both the potential offensiveness of some positive ideas, and the potential defensiveness that some criticisms might otherwise engender."[3] His *exercise of biblical authority* by the way he handles the Scripture and directs discussion in the clear teaching of God's Word builds an atmosphere where the elders delight in following sound doctrine. His ability to *listen well*, being slow to speak and avoiding dominating the meeting, communicates to the others that their views hold as much importance as his own thoughts. His *patience* when facing disagreements, met with grace and a warm spirit, will go far in helping the council to find a solution to any impasse. The way he *values* others' input and decisions, particularly when he might have wanted to go in a different direction, builds respect and unity among the elders. His openness to *correction* and godly criticism as a means of grace to sharpen him spiritually and in his pastoral responsibilities will open the other elders to receive the same kind of warm criticism to best serve the body of Christ. His *humor* and ability to laugh at himself as they gather will build camaraderie.[4]

What Preparation Goes into the Elders' Meetings?

Elders' meetings start far earlier than the gathering time. A week, two weeks, and even a month out may be needed to help to prepare for the discussion and actions to be taken. Part of the challenge with non-staff elders will be holding enough information prior to an elders' meeting to participate in discussion and move toward a decision. It's easy to presume these men—wise and thoughtful as they are—will catch up during the meeting with what the staff elders have discussed at length. But such presumption

---

3. Mark Dever and Paul Alexander, *Deliberate Church: Building Your Ministry on the Gospel* (Wheaton, IL: Crossway, 2005), 191.
4. Dever and Alexander note that humility, biblical warrant, patience, willingness to yield, giving and receiving godly encouragement and criticism, and humor are good qualities for the lead pastor to model. Some of their ideas have shaped my comments (*Deliberate Church*, 191–92).

will likely stifle discussion and potentially breed resentment. So, the staff elders must be diligent and thoughtful to prepare enough material or have enough discussions with non-staff elders to help them have ready minds for the discussion. This might happen through a series of emails or letters or hand-delivered packets containing up-to-date information on members, budget issues, mission requests, ministry recommendations, and doctrinal controversy.[5]

During one period, our elders had to deal with a member's doctrinal aberration. Several of us had discussions with him. Three or four of us engaged in lengthy email dialogues in an attempt to show his exegetical and theological error. We passed the notes along to each other and disclosed the conversations in emails for the other elders to prepare to discuss the situation. Apart from that kind of communication, some of the elders would have been hamstrung in the tedious dialogue that ensued in our meeting.

Most of the out-of-meeting discussions will not have that gravity, but they're important to allow each elder to feel a part of the discussion. A side benefit of this kind of communication will be strengthening the relationships and bonds among the elders. When equality and plurality get demonstrated at a ground level, like pre-meeting communication, it reinforces the way elders will serve with each other when gathered.

We've chosen to divide various ministry responsibilities among a team of elders (e.g., worship, missions, Sunday school, etc.), allowing teams to meet prior to the regular monthly elders' meeting to discuss details. By the time we meet, they have generally ironed out most details and provide readily accessible information for discussion and decision making. In leading the meetings, I will call attention to particular matters that arise and delegate them to the elder teams. They will have a deadline to report back to the larger body of elders after their research.

Often, I assign a specific agenda item to an elder to lead in the meeting. I do this for two reasons: first, he probably knows more about the subject than I do, so he can speak to it with greater clarity; second, this allows equality to be expressed even as the meeting agenda unfolds.

What Does an Elders' Meeting Look Like?

Preparation for the meeting culminates in an *agenda* that sets the pace for the meeting. While I will give an example of an agenda below, first it's important to think about some of the broader categories that will likely be part of most, although not every, meeting.

(1) *Devotion, Scripture reading, and prayer.* Elders' meetings are spiritual meetings. They will tend to drift into corporate business meetings unless

---

5. Dever and Alexander, *Deliberate Church*, 179–80.

anchored in the Word of God and prayer (Acts 6:4). The approach may vary from one meeting to the next. Sometimes we have a devotion, other times we read a lengthy portion of Scripture to aid our hearts toward prayer. The pastor may assign this responsibility to one of the elders to begin the tone of the meeting in God's Word.

If you ask our elders about the most important part of our meetings, hands down everyone will answer our times of prayer. We bare our hearts before the Lord for the congregation, for members in spiritual need, for physical needs in the body, for our walks with Christ, for our wives and children, for unbelieving relatives and friends, for people visiting our congregation and considering membership, for global missions, for our local mission and ministry work, for our worship gatherings. Discussion is good; prayer is best.

(2) *Membership issues and needs.* Each elder has responsibility for a "shepherding group" that represents all our members and regular attenders. We seek to do pastoral care through the shepherding group. In this way each of us has more up-to-date information on particular members under our direct care. While we all serve the broader church family, the shepherding groups give us better management of our pastoral care. We'll often make assignments during this period for further contact, an exhortation, a movement toward the process of church discipline, a pastoral visit, a discussion about calling or ministry, an invitation to participate in a mission project, and so on. During this time, we keep abreast of infirmed members and how we might care for them.

(3) *Minutes and/or unfinished agenda items from the last meeting.* We need to backtrack to make sure we've covered the bases from the previous meeting, particularly any assignments made. Inevitably, we'll have unfinished items.

(4) *Ministry and mission in the church.* This broad category discusses everything from mission trips, adopting an unreached people group, local work at a needy school, refugee work, Sunday school and Bible study classes, midweek study time, future preaching planning, and more.

(5) *Administration.* Details related to the building, for which the deacons might ask for our input, needs we recognize in our organizational structure, finances, schedules, personnel changes, and so on fall under this category. While our deacons handle most of the physical needs around the facility, sometimes they need direction from the elders in order to do their work.

(6) *Theological discussion and/or training.* During periods of selecting new elders, we engage in theological training with the candidates. On other

occasions, we read through a book together with discussion or hammer out a theological issue we think needs greater clarity in the body.

These six categories cover the reason that we gather for meetings. They are based on the elders' biblical focus in doctrine, discipline/member care, and direction/leadership. Here's a typical agenda to consider.

- Scripture and prayer
- Review contacts with members, identifying needs and further contacts
- Study and present research on current doctrinal issue
- Discuss a potential church discipline case
- Work on ministry team selections
- Discuss new teachers for upcoming Bible classes
- Plan next year's Sunday school and Wednesday night studies
- Discuss requests for mission support
- Discuss a new local ministry opportunity
- Review pastoral internships
- Discuss summer evangelistic outreach[6]

Summary

While elders' meetings represent a fraction of the time elders engage in ministry to the body, it happens to be the time that the pastor sets the trajectory for the elders' ministry. Care must be given to ensure that faithful, humble men serve as elders. The pastor models for the elders the kind of humility, prayerfulness, listening ear, cooperative spirit, warmth, and patience needed in all. Categories noted for consideration in meetings may not all be utilized but should be considered for every meeting. Communicating appropriate information prior to each meeting will help toward good discussion and wise decisions. An agenda provides a roadmap to keep the meeting on target. Certainly, the Holy Spirit might disrupt the agenda for grander purposes, but apart from his leadership, following an agenda will allow the elders to accomplish more than thought possible at the start.

REFLECTION QUESTIONS

1. Why do elders gather for meetings instead of just shepherding?

---

6. Adapted from Phil A. Newton and Matt Schmucker, *Elders in the Life of the Church: Rediscovering the Biblical Model for Church Leadership*, 9Marks (Grand Rapids: Kregel Ministry, 2014), 209.

2. What are the hinge points necessary for elders to gather in unity and good purpose?

3. What qualities does the pastor need to exhibit to model elder leadership?

4. What does preparation for elders' meetings look like?

5. What broad categories may be part of any elders' meetings?

How Can Pastors Mentor Future Pastors and Leaders?

Pastoral ministry follows the example of Jesus, Peter, and Paul when it trains future pastors and church leaders. Jesus trained the Twelve and the Seventy, who in turn continued the ministry of Jesus while training others (Luke 9–10). Peter took along some brothers from Joppa to help with ministry to Cornelius (Acts 10:23). That Cornelius and others had been baptized indicates they had received training and been set apart to leadership in the Joppa church (Acts 10:48). Paul regularly took along those he trained to do gospel ministry where he had planted churches (e.g., Acts 16:1–3; 17:4; 20:4–5; Gal. 2:1). Faithful pastoral ministry follows the same pattern (2 Tim. 2:2).

Granted, the idea of training others for gospel work seems daunting. One might think that work belongs to theological institutions rather than the local church. But seminaries and Bible colleges, while helpful in multiple ways, never replace local churches to hone and shape the spiritual and ministerial fabric of future pastors, missionaries, and Christian leaders. A preaching class might critique a sermon, a hermeneutics class might correct an interpretation, and a Greek class might sharpen the understanding of the use of verbs in a text. All these things are necessary and helpful for future ministers (and with capable pastors doing the mentoring, these things may be done in the local church, too). Yet for someone preaching a sermon in a congregation where one is a member, regularly living life in the body, any critique goes beyond homiletic structure. The pastor walks alongside the trainee observing his walk with Christ, evaluating study of the biblical text, discerning pastoral application in the sermon, and noting passion in proclamation. He's been living life with the trainee as part of the body, so he has an advantage over a professor who might see the student only a few days a week.

Instead of seeing mentoring as requiring a complicated program, see it as the natural outworking of pastoral relationships with those God may be raising up to be elders, pastors, missionaries, and leaders. How can pastors faithfully mentor others for ministry?

The Context of Community

Mentoring takes place in close association or "consociation," as Günter Krallmann helpfully expresses. He notes that Jesus saw "consociation with him as the most fertile soil for his disciples' growth relative to character, understanding and skill. Hence he made the experience of his with-ness the pivot of their training."[1] The idea of "with-ness" must be central to what we're doing in mentoring. By the uniqueness of pastoral relationships, the trainee begins to live in the atmosphere of ministry as he relates to his pastoral mentor.

Michael Crow concurs, adding that the limitation of *content*-driven training, such as is found in seminary classrooms, lectures, or conferences, calls for *mentoring*-driven training that adds the personal dimension to shape the trainees. He rightly urges for building training curriculum around the mentoring relationships just as Jesus did:[2] "Jesus mentored in ways tailored to each individual."[3] The local church provides the most consistent atmosphere for the one-on-one approach of mentoring. Like Jesus with the Twelve and the Seventy, it includes *mentoring in the context of community*. This position does not disparage intense academic training but rather puts it into perspective by insisting on the local church's ability to shape ministers for the practical demands of ministry.[4] Seminaries and Bible colleges supplement *in partnership* with the local church, where the church may lack the capacity to offer a thorough theological education. Ideally, training for future pastors and missionaries should include an intensive theological education, as well as intensive local church pastoral mentoring.

In my pastoral context, we've mentored some men prior to their theological training. With others, we've come alongside during seminary to keep their local-church edge sharpened, to develop their ministry gifts, and to help them grapple with the complex issues arising in pastoral ministry. With still others, we've mentored them upon completing their seminary work. This kind of mentoring keeps them from simply looking at ministry training as an academic exercise. It's more. It's spiritual development that doesn't neglect

---

1. Günter Krallmann, *Mentoring for Mission: A Handbook on Leadership Principles Exemplified by Jesus Christ* (Waynesboro, GA: Gabriel, 2002), 53.
2. D. Michael Crow, "Multiplying Jesus Mentors: Designing a Reproducible Mentoring System—A Case Study," *Missiology: An International Review* 36, no. 1 (January 2008): 93.
3. Crow, "Multiplying," 92.
4. As an example, see Warren Bird, "Churches Taking Back the Task of Theological Education," *Leadership Network*, March 13, 2012, http://leadnet.org/wp-content/uploads/2014/02/2012-06-12_Churches_Taking_Back.pdf, who discusses Sojourn Church's (Louisville, KY) church-based theological education in partnership with the Southern Baptist Theological Seminary.

the academic training. It helps trainees to understand that a seminary degree doesn't necessarily qualify one to shepherd a congregation.

How does this spiritual development work out? Through contact with Jesus, E. F. Harrison explains, the Twelve "almost unconsciously absorbed from him. They must have learned something about the art of meeting people and handling situations as they witnessed their Master threading his way through life with its maze of difficult circumstances occasioned by the public character of his work."[5] Although inadequate on our part, the best way to maintain a strategy with future gospel workers (pastors, church planters and revitalizers, and missionaries) similar to what Jesus modeled is for faithful pastors to bring them into a mentoring relationship in a local church context. As with Jesus's mentoring, it costs time and personal involvement. It demands working through the sometimes messy nature of relationships, but it yields much fruit in future years. Those mentored *absorb* from their mentors the relational skills, application of doctrine, and insights in handling difficulties by the "with-ness" in the mentoring relationship. Five replicable aspects of the impact of mentoring are observed from Jesus and his disciples.

Following Jesus's Model

First, Jesus provided an example for mentors to follow. By contrast, Jewish rabbis expected their disciples to attend to them. Jesus not only declared himself to be among them as one that served (Luke 22:26–27) but he also did it in practice.[6] The disciples watched Jesus care for the poor, show compassion to the downtrodden, demonstrate tenderness toward little children, confront the arrogance of religious hypocrisy, and suffer on behalf of others. His example never left the disciples' minds as they took on the responsibility for gospel work after the resurrection (e.g., 1 Peter 2:21–25; 1 John 1:1–3). Contemporary mentors must never minimize the power of example in shaping their trainees.

Second, Jesus demonstrated the priority of relationships with his trainees. His discipleship framework revealed this priority, as the intimacy of living in relationship to both Jesus and the small community of followers shaped life-long friendships.[7] Krallmann poignantly clarifies: "Yet Jesus did not go about establishing an academy, he went about establishing a fellowship; he first majored on making friends and only later on sending out apostles (cf. Mark 3:14)."[8] Contemporary mentors will make friendship the first order of attachment to

---

5. E. F. Harrison, *A Short Life of Christ* (Grand Rapids: Zondervan, 1968), 143.

6. Martin Hengel, *The Charismatic Leader and His Followers* (Eugene, OR: Wipf & Stock, 1968), 51–52.

7. Michael J. Wilkins, "Disciple, Discipleship," in *Evangelical Dictionary of World Missions*, eds. A. Scott Moreau, Harold Netland, and Charles Van Engen (Grand Rapids: Baker, 2000), 279.

8. Krallmann, *Mentoring for Mission*, 55. He further writes, "A mentoree is not a project but a person. Mentoring implies more than a lecturer-student connection, *it is friendship*" (emphasis added).

trainees. Rather than seeing mentoring as a project with a long list of goals and objectives, think of it as friendship that goes deep and lasts a lifetime.

As I pray each week for those we've trained and sent out to serve in various places around the globe, I feel the depth of friendship more than I do a trainer/trainee relationship. We continue to interact, laugh together, encourage one another, talk about ministry and family, counsel one another, and maintain the relationships that began in mentoring. I love to visit with them, when possible, and see how their walks with Christ, family lives, and ministries continue in the grace of God. Relationship trumps a programmatic approach to training.

Third, Jesus modeled love and service in leadership. As Jesus taught on true greatness when correcting the sons of Zebedee jockeying for lordly positions in the future kingdom, he explained greatness is to be found in service, "just as the Son of Man did not come to be served, but to serve, and to give His life a ransom for many" (Matt. 20:28). Jesus's life and teaching modeled generosity, forgiveness, service, and humility (Luke 16:1–31; 17:1–10; 18:9–30).[9] Mentors must consciously model service and love with their trainees, for this shapes the trainees to do the same.[10] "Ivory tower" mentors may feed information to trainees, but they do little to help them become true leaders. Of course, this means a mentoring pastor must be one who gladly loves and serves his congregation.

Fourth, Jesus mentored with the cross in view. Jesus journeyed toward destiny with the cross where he secured redemption for his people. He regularly pointed toward that destiny as he trained his disciples (Luke 9:22, 43–45; 18:31–34). Likewise, he demonstrated that the terms of following him require a cross (Luke 9:23). Mentors do well to keep their trainees focused on the sufficiency of Christ in his death and resurrection, while also modeling the necessity of dying to selfish desires and embracing adversities, trials, and hardships as the means of throttling the natural tendency toward vanity.[11]

Fifth, Jesus's mentoring included correction. When John sought to hinder those attempting to cast out demons in Jesus's name, Jesus corrected him (Luke 9:49–50). When James and John wanted to call fire down from heaven because of perceived insult from some Samaritans, Jesus told them, "You do not know what kind of spirit you are of" (Luke 9:51–56). He "exposed and rebuked and corrected" the sins and infirmities of the disciples.[12]

---

9. Darrell Bock, *Luke 1:1–9:50*, BECNT (Grand Rapids: Baker, 1994), 24.
10. Derek Tidball explains that Paul viewed service as "the constant subtext of his understanding of Christian leadership" (*Ministry by the Book: New Testament Patterns for Pastoral Leadership* [Downers Grove, IL: IVP Academic, 2008], 121). In Paul's theology, the gospel requires service.
11. J. Schneider identifies six possible interpretations of taking up one's cross, but concludes that it is "a vivid metaphor for self-denial" (σταυρός, *TDNT*, 7:578–79).
12. Harrison, *Short Life of Christ*, 144–45.

Mentors must seek to correct sinful tendencies in their trainees in order to uproot attitudes and rash behavior that would hinder their spiritual walks, family lives, and ministries, thereby distracting from the gospel (Gal. 6:1–5). Only by first focusing on relationship-building can this kind of correction naturally take place.

Summary

In the intimacy of one-on-one and small group mentoring, local church mentors are well positioned to impact their trainees.[13] Their example in relationships, love, service, and dying to self gives future gospel workers a better picture of how to live faithfully as servants of Christ. Effective mentors give priority to relationships with their trainees rather than depending upon a finely polished program. The relationships shape future pastors, missionaries, and leaders into more effective pastoral workers.

REFLECTION QUESTIONS

1. What are some examples from Jesus, Peter, and Paul of training future leaders?

2. How do seminaries and local churches partner in training for ministry?

3. Why is *community* a critical component of pastoral mentoring?

4. Why does *friendship* play a large part in pastoral mentoring?

5. Identify the five areas Jesus modeled in training for ministry.

---

13. For a more detailed look at mentoring in the local church, see Phil A. Newton, *Mentoring in the Local Church: How Pastors and Churches Cultivate Leaders* (Grand Rapids: Kregel, 2017).

PART 4

Pastoral Preaching

What Distinguishes Pastoral Preaching from Simply Preaching?

Five young pastors, serving their churches from three to five years, recently told me of the challenges they faced in early pastoral work. Some served older congregations stuck in a 1950s time warp. Another congregation balked at even the hint of change. Still others showed animosity to the exposition of Scripture. These young pastors have experienced the brunt of gossip, nasty business meetings, movements to remove them, and the loss of members. They've also witnessed people coming to Christ, believers growing in gospel application, new levels of sacrificial service and giving, revitalized practices in membership, and renewed worship of the living God. In such a short time, they've discovered that pastoral work requires more than simply preaching each Sunday, even while, by their own testimony, preaching remains at the center of their work. They stay in the trenches, facing obstacles along the way, confident in the gospel's power at work in their congregations. They did not accept their pastorates merely as preaching posts. They labor to preach Christ and shepherd the flock until Christ is formed in the congregation (Gal. 4:19).

Not all preachers grasp what these young men have. Some men, even good men, seem to be enamored with preaching. That's understandable, given the uniqueness of preaching. Yet preaching is such a high, holy calling and weighty responsibility that one must never enter into it without counting the cost. At just this point lies a critical issue among those desiring to preach the gospel. Does a man just want a place to preach or does he long to preach to a people whom he will shepherd as Christ's followers?

Pastoral Preaching

A preacher can study a biblical text, do superb exegesis, and develop a true-to-the-text homiletical exposition, yet still not preach pastorally. Pastoral preaching does involve study, exegesis of the text, and wrestling with theme and structure, but it takes another step. As Tony Sargent explained when discussing the preaching of Martyn Lloyd-Jones, "He is not commenting on a text [as though giving a running commentary on a passage], he is expounding Scripture with a view to the needs of his pastoral charge"[1] This last phrase, "with a view to the needs of his pastoral charge," distinguishes pastoral preaching from simply preaching a good textual sermon.

John Calvin describes pastoral preaching as the primary way God has been pleased to grow and develop his church: "We see how God, who could in a moment perfect his own, nevertheless desires them to grow up into manhood solely under the education of the church. We see the way set for it: preaching of the heavenly doctrine has been enjoined upon the pastors."[2] Sitting under the regular teaching of faithful pastors, congregations learn to listen and apply the exposition of God's Word toward growth and maturity. Calvin notes that through pastoral preaching, "God appears in our midst, and, as Author of this order [i.e., of pastoral exposition], would have men recognize him as present in his institution."[3] The congregation, recognizing this God-appointed means for the church's growth and maturity, submits "with a gentle and teachable spirit [so that] they may allow themselves to be governed by teachers appointed to this function."[4] Faithful, consistent, pastoral preaching to a congregation who loves and welcomes God's Word into their lives leads to a healthy, vibrant, and Christ honoring church.

In a day when social media gives access to more sermons, teaching, and lectures than anyone could listen to in a hundred lifetimes, God has still appointed pastoral preaching *in the local church* as the means for the body's growth, maturity, and unity. Ephesians 4:7–16 explains the ascension gifts of Jesus to the church, and among them the gifts of pastors and teachers. "And He gave some as . . . pastors and teachers," or "shepherd teachers." One article controls both nouns in the Greek, suggesting "one office with a dual function"[5] or a single office of "teaching shepherds."[6] And for what reason were these gifts given to the church? "For the equipping of the saints for the work of service, to the building up of the body of Christ; until we all attain to the unity of the faith, and of the knowledge of the Son of God, to a mature man, to the measure of the stature which belongs to the fullness of Christ" (Eph. 4:12–13). When the church functions under faithful pastoral teaching, it gets anchored in sound doctrine, discerns doctrinal error, grows in Christ,

---

1. Tony Sargent, *The Sacred Anointing: The Preaching of Dr. Martyn Lloyd-Jones* (Wheaton, IL: Crossway, 1994), 85.

2. *Calvin*, 4.1.5.

3. *Calvin*, 4.1.5.

4. *Calvin*, 4.1.5.

5. Curtis Vaughan, *Ephesians*, Founders Study Guide Commentary (Cape Coral, FL: Founders, 2002), 94.

6. Markus Barth, *Ephesians*, 2 vols. (Garden City, NY: Doubleday, 1974), 2.438–39.

finds its unique area of ministry and service to and with one another in the body, and continues to grow in love (Eph. 4:14–16).

After considering these Ephesians 4 truths, Calvin notes, "Paul shows by these words that this human ministry which God uses to govern the church [referring to pastoral ministry] is the chief sinew by which believers are held together in one body. He then also shows that the church can be kept intact only if it be upheld by the safeguards in which it pleased the Lord to place its salvation." He adds, God manifests his power through this appointed pastoral office: "This is the manner of fulfillment: through the ministers to whom he has entrusted this office and has conferred the grace to carry it out, he dispenses and distributes his gifts to the church; and he shows himself as though present by manifesting the power of his Spirit in this his institution [of pastoral preaching], that it be not vain or idle."[7]

Why is pastoral preaching so critical? Pastors maintain sensitivity to the needs of the congregation as they open God's Word in the corporate gathering. Sargent amplifies, "The prime responsibility of the preacher is to determine what the Holy Spirit wants to say to his congregation from that passage [that he's studying]."[8] With the aim of equipping and building up the body, the pastor studies his text and then expounds it with a passion for his congregation, knowing it desperately needs God's Word to grow and mature in love and holiness.

Preach the Word!

Consider Paul's instruction to Timothy in 2 Timothy 4:1–5 as defining the scope of pastoral preaching. With good reason, this text likely finds its way into more ordination services than others. But here are the questions that confront us. Was Paul charging Timothy with preaching generically or preaching to a particular people? And so, do we approach this passage as a general instruction on preaching, or does it have striking emphasis on preaching to a given people as a shepherd?

After highlighting the solemnity of the responsibility of preaching, Paul charges, "Preach the word" (2 Tim. 4:2). Certainly, that must be our rallying cry with any sermon in any setting. Timothy knew, as John Stott notes, that *the word* "is the body of doctrine which he has heard from Paul and which Paul has now committed to him to pass on to others."[9] William Mounce states quite simply, it "is the gospel."[10] So the content in pastoral preaching is clear: the Word of God or, more pointedly, the gospel of our Lord Jesus Christ as the focus of the whole

---

7. *Calvin*, 4.3.2.
8. Sargent, *Sacred Anointing*, 85.
9. John R. W. Stott, *The Message of 2 Timothy: Guard the Gospel*, BST (Downers Grove, IL: InterVarsity, 1973), 106.
10. William D. Mounce, *Pastoral Epistles*, WBC 46 (Nashville: Nelson, 2000), 573.

of Scripture.[11] To *preach* the word implies preachers "have no liberty to invent our message, but only to communicate 'the word' which God has spoken and has now committed to the church as a sacred trust."[12] The call to faithfulness in opening and expounding what God has spoken cannot be clearer!

Yet the balance of what Paul intended appears to tip the scale toward pastoral preaching. "Be ready in season and out of season," meaning any time, any occasion. "Reprove, rebuke, exhort, with great patience and instruction" (2 Tim. 4:2). *Who* is being reproved, rebuked, and exhorted? Does that describe a one-time preaching engagement? Perhaps, but without knowing the people to whom he preaches, how will he appropriately reprove, rebuke, and exhort with effectiveness in a solitary sermon to a congregation? Paul's descriptive terms for preaching application lend themselves best in consecutive expositions with a given congregation.

Why the need for "great patience and instruction" (2 Tim. 4:2)? A continual expositional ministry to a particular people requires the preacher to show humility and patience in bringing them along in understanding and applying God's Word. That's one of the great challenges in pastoral preaching: it's slow, humble, patient, careful labor with one congregation week by week, year by year, until Christ is formed in them. The preacher's love and service will be tested as he shepherds the church through the Word. "Instruction," or doctrinal teaching, demands the regular ministry of layering one biblical doctrine upon another. The implication is, it seems, that while we accept "preach the word" as a rallying cry for all preaching, the particular details that follow best fit the ongoing expository ministry of a pastor faithfully serving a congregation.

Paul continues by warning of a time ahead "when *they* will not endure sound doctrine" (2 Tim. 4:3; emphasis added). Does he speak generically of all people, or did he have in mind the people of Ephesus where Timothy served? The latter best fits the context.[13] So Paul exhorts Timothy, who by this time may have lived with a knot in his stomach over the problems existing in the church (2 Tim. 1:6–7), "Fulfill your ministry" (2 Tim. 4:5). Don't cut it short. Don't give up. Don't compromise what has been entrusted to you. Don't just preach, but "fulfill your ministry."

H. B. Charles Jr. discussed two well-known pastors who had influenced him; one, in particular, modeled pastoral preaching. The first preached hermeneutically sound, doctrinally clear sermons. One could listen to the sermon a hundred years from now and still get the same truths out of it as the day it was delivered. But if someone listened to the other, while still theologically sound

---

11. See Edmund Clowney, *Preaching Christ in All of Scripture* (Wheaton, IL: Crossway, 2003), 11–44.

12. Stott, *2 Timothy*, 106.

13. Andreas J. Köstenberger, *Commentary on 1–2 Timothy and Titus*, BTCP (Nashville: Holman Reference, 2017), 273.

in every way as the first preacher, there would be portions of the sermon that the hundred-year-later listener might not understand. Why the difference? The latter preached pastorally to his congregation, applying the Word of God in ways specific to his hearers so that only investigation would yield all the specifics of his sermon. Charles points out that true pastoral preaching has the congregation in view with the sermon, expounding the biblical text and applying it with rigorous specificity to a particular people.[14]

I discussed this subject with one of our pastoral interns who had preached at a church giving consideration to him as a pastoral candidate. I counseled, "You have to discern whether you are looking for a place to preach or whether you are committed to shepherding that congregation." There is a difference. In the former, one might polish his sermons, add oratorical flash, and expect compliments that he has preached a solid sermon. In the latter, he feels the weight of the congregation's needs as he approaches the pulpit with the Word of God. He's conscious that from his trembling lips come life for the man he's counseled over and over for habitual sin; hope for the lady recently diagnosed with terminal cancer; a vision of the sufficiency of the gospel for the one struggling to put one foot in front of the other; and clarity in the call to serve Christ internationally in the Spirit's power for the couple burdened for unreached people groups. This kind of preaching takes place when a pastor lives with, prays for, loves, invests in, and faithfully shepherds his flock in all the ups and downs of pastoral ministry. Is it just a preaching point? No, but rather a people entrusted to him by the Lord of the church to pastorally preach week after week after week, even when things get difficult, even when those very people rise up in rebellion, and even when the preacher is no longer popular—that's the call to pastoral preaching. And so he preaches until Christ is formed in that congregation.

Summary

We may characterize pastoral preaching in the following five ways:

1. Pastoral preaching feels the weight of the biblical text and the weight of shepherding the congregation in holy tension.

2. Pastoral preaching lives with the burden of shepherding the flock of God until Christ is formed in them (1 Peter 5:2; Acts 20:28; Gal. 4:19).

---

14. H. B. Charles, "Ten Preachers Who Have Influenced My Preaching," *The On Preaching Podcast*, March 1, 2019, episode #065, https://www.hbcharlesjr.com/2019/03/01/065-10-preachers-who-have-influenced-my-preaching.

3. Pastoral preaching thinks and prays for the body and visualizes specific needs of individual members that can be met through the Word, even while working through the text to preach.

4. Pastoral preaching develops homiletical structures that clearly reflect the text, but it aims for the people for whom the pastor has been praying, teaching, counseling, and loving throughout the week.

5. Pastoral preaching expounds the Word with eyes on the flock, emphasizing, pressing, and directing to them words of comfort, exhortation, admonition, and consolation.

So, preach the Word whenever the opportunity arises. Take advantage of filling a pulpit. But don't accept a church's call as pastor to simply have a place to preach. This Christ-accountable labor belongs to the man committed to shepherding Christ's flock.

REFLECTION QUESTIONS

1. How is pastoral preaching distinguished from *simply* preaching?

2. What was John Calvin's point about pastoral preaching?

3. In what specific ways does the pastor/teacher gift aid the body of Christ, according to Ephesians 4:9–16?

4. What is the content of "the word" in Paul's exhortation "Preach the word"?

5. How does Paul's exhortation to Timothy in 2 Timothy 4:1–5 point specifically to pastoral preaching?

What Should Pastors Teach Their Congregations?

I've been a Southern Baptist all my life, but I've never heard these things. Why didn't they teach this to me?"[1]

The question struck a nerve. I had just finished an hour-long discussion with several people, including the lady asking the question. We talked about basic teaching concerning the Old and New Testaments. Our talk focused on what Jesus declared to the pious elite who hid behind their religious facade, "You search the Scriptures because you think that in them you have eternal life; it is these that testify about Me" (John 5:39). Jesus also set the example for what he meant when he met the two disciples on the road to Emmaus after his resurrection: "Beginning with Moses and with all the prophets, He explained to them the things concerning Himself in all the Scriptures" (Luke 24:27). All Scripture *ultimately points* to Jesus Christ, God's work of redemption through him, how he has accomplished the work necessary to bring sinners into his family, and how everything culminates in the revelation of his glory.

Yet the perplexed lady had never heard this basic biblical teaching. So how would this affect the way she reads the Bible? What kind of applications would she make from scattered texts pulled together with no christological continuity in her mind? Would she grasp the relationship between the testaments? Would she understand the first gospel statement in Genesis 3:15, and the way God's redemptive message continued through Malachi? How would she handle the seminal promise to Abraham in Genesis 12:3? Would she grasp what redemption, atonement, propitiation, and reconciliation mean through the way both testaments develop these doctrines?

---

1. The Southern Baptist Convention happens to be my denomination, but the same could be said for other denominations.

If our members have little exposure to "the whole counsel of God," they will be ill prepared for everything in life and death (Acts 20:27). Our responsibility is to make sure we "preach the word" in such a comprehensive way that they think and live biblically. To help us to do so, we have the disciplines of biblical and systematic theology to accompany our preparation and preaching.

Make Good Use of Biblical Theology

A pastor must teach his congregation how to interpret Scripture in light of its salvation-historical fulfillment in Christ. When the Jews accused Jesus of breaking the Sabbath because he healed a lame man, he began to explain the relationship between the Father and the Son. He showed that the one honoring the Father will honor the Son (John 5:19–23). He then explained that the witness of John the Baptist (John 5:31–34), Jesus's attesting miracles (John 5:36), the Father (John 5:37–38), and the Scriptures (John 5:39–40) testified in concert to the authenticity of Jesus as the Messiah. In his argument, he said of the Scriptures, "You search the Scriptures because you think in them you have eternal life; it is these that testify about Me" (John 5:39). The "Scriptures" of which he spoke refers to the whole Old Testament revelation. Jesus declared that the Old Testament Scriptures centered on him. If the interpreter properly interprets and understands the Old Testament, then he or she must see their place in the biblical narrative centered on Jesus and the gospel, especially the way the NT writers quote and imply OT texts.[2]

After the resurrection, Jesus appeared to two disciples walking on the road to Emmaus who did not recognize him. They were despondent over the death of Jesus, whom they hoped would "redeem Israel" but who died at the hands of the chief priest and rulers (Luke 24:21). They expressed skepticism about the resurrection reports from a few who witnessed the empty tomb. Then Jesus upbraided them for the way they had failed to properly interpret Scripture. He went straight to good hermeneutics that lead to sound, robust biblical theology: "O foolish men and slow of heart to believe in all that the prophets have spoken!" (Luke 24:25). They had read the prophets but were slow in believing their intended message, believing instead the popular interpretations of the day. "Was it not necessary for the Christ to suffer these things and to enter into His glory?" (Luke 24:26). In other words, Jesus called attention to the way they had read Scripture without rightly interpreting it from a christological hermeneutic.[3] Luke tells us what happened next: "Then beginning with Moses and with all the prophets, He explained to them the things

---

2. The most useful tool to help with the way the NT writers utilized the OT is G. K. Beale and D. A. Carson, eds., *Commentary on the New Testament Use of the Old Testament* (Grand Rapids: Baker Academic, 2007).

3. Dennis E. Johnson, *Walking with Jesus through His Word: Discovering Christ in All the Scriptures* (Phillipsburg, NJ: P&R, 2015), 11.

concerning Himself in all the Scriptures" (Luke 24:27). Just as Jesus had told his religious opponents, he told his disciples: the Scriptures are about him. So, if we would interpret them properly, we must see each passage in light of the revelation of Jesus Christ. Biblical theology helps us in this aim.

Later, when gathered with the disciples, he gave them marching orders to be his witnesses (Luke 24:48) but only after he corrected their hermeneutics and centered their biblical theology grid on himself and the gospel. As Jesus declared, the way we interpret and apply the Scriptures affects everything in life and ministry.

> Now He said to them, "These are My words which I spoke to you while I was still with you, that all things which are written about Me in the Law of Moses and the Prophets and the Psalms must be fulfilled." Then He opened their minds to understand the Scriptures, and He said to them, "Thus it is written, that the Christ would suffer and rise again from the dead the third day, and that repentance for forgiveness of sins would be proclaimed in His name to all the nations, beginning from Jerusalem." (Luke 24:44–47)

Paul preaching "the whole counsel of God" dovetails with what Jesus did with the disciples on the Emmaus road and those gathered in the closed room. A right interpretation of Scripture inevitably points to Jesus Christ directly or indirectly, as preparatory for his coming, as an explanation or illustration or symbol or parallel statement explaining his redemptive work, or as a picture of the culmination of the redemptive work of Jesus. That's why Dennis Johnson rightly asserts, "Jesus is the central figure in the outworking of God's plan for human and global and cosmic history, the divine agenda that unifies everything in the Bible, from Genesis to Revelation."[4] Therefore, if we would teach our congregations the Bible, we must focus on the whole Bible's revelation of Jesus Christ (Eph. 1:3–12; 3:8–12).

Biblical exposition, then, must be done from a biblical-theological aim. The expositor does his exegetical work looking grammatically, historically, and contextually into his passage, while he simultaneously examines "the individual parts to see how they fit into the big picture" of the biblical narrative, all of which points to Christ.[5] Michael Lawrence offers this helpful explanation about why biblical theology must guide our interpretations and applications from the text we consider: "Biblical theology is about reading the Bible, not as if it's sixty-six separate books, but a single book with a single plot—God's

---

4. Johnson, *Walking with Jesus*, 3.
5. Graeme Goldsworthy, *Gospel-Centered Hermeneutics: Foundations and Principles of Evangelical Biblical Interpretation* (Downers Grove, IL: IVP Academic, 2006), 68.

glory displayed through Jesus Christ."[6] So the pastor seeks to understand the doctrines in the text before him by how they are worked out in the biblical narrative and how they find their shape in the revelation of Jesus Christ. He interprets them in this light rather than simply as an individual text isolated from the biblical narrative and story line. In doing so, as he preaches, he's displaying the unity and fullness of Scripture in its focus of summing up all things in the revelation of Jesus Christ (Eph. 1:9–11).

As the pastor works through the language, background, history, and context of his passage, he's alert to the biblical theological implications from the text. He's considering how his passage fits into the book's immediate theological context and then, more broadly, to the grand narrative of Scripture focused on the revelation of Jesus Christ. Lawrence explains, "Biblical theology is therefore about discovering the unity of the Bible in the midst of its diversity. It's about understanding what we might call the Bible's metanarrative."[7] The pastor cannot be satisfied until he sees the text's place in this biblical metanarrative. Then he's ready to preach *Christ* to his congregation from the Sunday's text. If he neglects to preach Christ, he fails at what must be taught to his congregation.

Some have tried to squeeze square pegs into round holes when it comes to an attempt to preach from a Christ-centered theology. Not every text offers implicit teaching on Christ.[8] Here the expositor must see what place the text has in the storyline of Scripture, culminating in the revelation of Jesus Christ.[9]

Preaching through a book of the Bible, whether OT or NT, if done properly, can never take place in isolation from the rest of Scripture. Each biblical book has been informed by and/or connected with other portions of Scripture. Faithful exposition does biblical theology as the sermon unfolds. Preaching/teaching consecutively through a book also teaches Christ-centered hermeneutics, so those listening learn through the process how to properly interpret God's Word. Expositions should model how to study, interpret, and think theologically about God's Word.

When we preach theological expositions, we're giving our congregation "the whole counsel of God." They don't need moral lessons or therapeutic

---

6. Michael Lawrence, *Biblical Theology in the Life of the Church: A Guide for Ministry*, 9Marks (Wheaton, IL: Crossway, 2010), 15.

7. Lawrence, *Biblical Theology*, 15.

8. See Edmund Clowney, *The Unfolding Mystery: Discovering Christ in the Old Testament*, 2nd ed. (Phillipsburg, NJ: P&R, 2013); Sidney Greidanus, *Preaching Christ from the Old Testament: A Contemporary Hermeneutical Method* (Grand Rapids: Eerdmans, 1999); Sidney Greidanus, *Preaching Christ from Genesis: Foundations for Expository Sermons* (Grand Rapids: Eerdmans, 2007); Goldsworthy, *Gospel-Centered Hermeneutics* (2006); Johnson, *Walking with Jesus* (2015).

9. My expositions through Genesis and Esther may offer some examples of how to preach Christ in all of Scripture. For Genesis, see http://www.southwoodsbc.org/posts/biblebook/genesis; for Esther, see http://www.southwoodsbc.org/posts/biblebook/esther.

pep talks. They need Jesus Christ in all of Scripture. As our people begin to see Christ in all of Scripture, it changes the way they apply the Word to daily life. Their applications begin to be clearly gospel-centered, so that they root their sanctification in what Christ has done for them instead of what they can do for him.

Make Good Use of Systematic Theology

A pastor must teach his congregation how to interpret Scripture logically in light of other passages. The fruit of biblical theology during sermon preparation leads to the practical categories and applications of systematic theology.[10] While biblical theology shows a doctrine's development in Scripture, systematic theology summarizes "in an orderly and comprehensive manner what the whole Bible has to say about" this topic.[11] It shows the doctrine's "practical value for living the Christian life," since "nowhere in Scripture do we find doctrine studied for its own sake or in isolation from life."[12]

Paul told the Ephesian elders during his last visit with them, "For I did not shrink from declaring to you the whole purpose of God" (Acts 20:27).[13] The phrase "whole purpose" is translated "whole will" (NIV) and "whole counsel" (ESV), and expresses "the divine will" the Lord God purposely determined.[14] David Peterson explains, "the purpose of God" used "in parallel with 'the kingdom' (v. 25) suggests that it refers more precisely to the whole plan of God for humanity and the created order revealed in the Scriptures and fulfilled in Jesus Christ (Cf. Luke 24:24–27, 44–49)."[15] Here the apostle offers a glance at the content of his teaching with the Ephesians and, we can suppose, with other churches he planted. He did not avoid the difficult doctrines or the full-orbed look at the Law, Prophets, and Writings with their fulfillment centered in Jesus Christ and his redemptive work.[16]

---

10. See, e.g., Wayne Grudem, *Systematic Theology: An Introduction to Biblical Doctrine* (Grand Rapids: Zondervan, 1994); John M. Frame, *Systematic Theology: An Introduction to Christian Belief* (Phillipsburg, NJ: P&R, 2013); Robert Letham, *Systematic Theology* (Wheaton, IL: Crossway, 2019); Robert L. Reymond, *A New Systematic Theology of the Christian Faith*, 2nd ed., rev. (Nashville: Thomas Nelson, 2010); W. G. T. Shedd, *Dogmatic Theology*, ed. Alan Gomes, 3rd ed. (Phillipsburg, NJ: P&R, 2003).
11. Lawrence, *Biblical Theology*, 89.
12. Grudem, *Systematic Theology*, 23.
13. "Shrink" (ὑποστέλλω) expresses avoiding a matter due to fear (BDAG, 1041).
14. BDAG, βουλή, 182. In two other uses of the word in Acts (2:23; 4:28), βουλή is modified by ὁρίζω "to make a determination about an entity, determine, appoint, fix, set" and προορίζω "decide upon beforehand, predetermine," respectively (BDAG, 723, 873). The other use in Acts 13:36 expresses God's purposes worked out in respect to David with their ultimate fulfillment in Jesus Christ's resurrection.
15. David G. Peterson, *The Acts of the Apostles*, PNTC (Grand Rapids: Eerdmans, 2009), 567.
16. See Johnson, *Walking with Jesus*, 11–13, on these threefold genres of the OT.

But was Paul an aberration in the early church? Peterson explains Paul simply followed the same pattern Jesus established with all of his disciples: "Such an understanding of the term ['the whole counsel of God'] is consistent with the scriptural framework and foundation of Paul's gospel presentation in Acts 13:16–41, which parallels the outlines of Peter's preaching in many respects (Acts 2:15–39; 3:13–26)."[17] In other words, Paul did not establish a lonely seminary in Ephesus where he could deal with the heady matters of doctrine. He did this kind of systematic theological teaching *regularly* with his churches, and even in his evangelistic work (Acts 17:22–31).

What does that teaching include? Peterson notes, "The breadth and depth of Paul's teaching about *the whole will of God* can be discerned from an examination of his letter to the Romans, which he had just written and sent ahead of him at this time."[18] So, for example, if we glance at Romans, what theological categories would we find to help us consider essential matters to teach our congregations?

- The gospel's connection to OT prophetic teaching in Trinitarian efficiency (Rom. 1:1–17)
- The reality of human depravity that leaves all under condemnation (Rom. 1:18–3:20)
- The righteousness of God applied by faith rather than through law-works (Rom. 1:17; 3:24–32)
- The doctrines of justification, redemption, and propitiation (Rom. 3:24–26)
- The distinction between law and gospel (Rom. 3:22–31)
- The OT view of justification shown parallel to the NT teaching (Rom. 4:1–25)
- The effects of justification in union with Christ (Rom. 5:1–21)
- Sanctification and the mortification of sin (Rom. 6:1–23)
- Union with Christ in spiritual conflict (Rom. 7:1–25)
- God's works of providence, foreknowledge, predestination, calling, justification, and glorification (Rom. 8:1–39)
- God's sovereignty in salvation (Rom. 9–11)
- The details of sanctification worked out in obedient faith in the believer (Rom. 12–15)[19]

That systematic summary offers distinct points for evaluating the content of our teaching. Here's the closest we come to Paul's *systematic theology*. This

---

17. Peterson, *Acts*, 567–68.
18. Peterson, *Acts*, 568 (emphasis original).
19. No doubt, this list only selected *some* of Paul's doctrinal instruction to the Romans. For a more thorough look, consider commentaries by Leon Morris, Thomas R. Schreiner, John Murray, John Stott, and others.

discipline synthesizes the Bible's teaching on a doctrine so that by utilizing systematic theologies, pastors may effectively explain and apply the doctrine in preaching. While biblical theology traces a doctrine in its biblical-historical development, arriving at a proper interpretation in light of its place in the redemptive story, systematic theology puts together the whole picture and gives the pastor clarity in applying the doctrine to his congregation.[20] Seeing the broad-to-narrow categories in systematic theology gives direction to the pastor for ensuring well-rounded teaching of Scripture in his church.[21]

In addition to making good use of systematic theologies, pastors may find it useful to consider how confessions of faith offer a compendium of what we *must* teach over a period of years with our churches. A church's doctrinal standards should be covered by theological expositions in the normal schedule of preaching, as a means of teaching "the whole counsel of God."

Apply Biblical and Systematic Theology

A pastor must teach his congregation how to apply Scripture to life's realities in light of interpretations rooted in biblical and systematic theology. Several years ago, it hit me that a major part of my pastoral role is to help people face trials, adversity, and death. Rarely do we have warning that these ever-present realities of living in a fallen world are about to meet our people with shocking force. But if they are rooted in faithful interpretation and application worked out in biblical and systematic theology, then when we come to the moments of bringing comfort and encouragement, we're not scrambling to make up for lost years. We have readied them for most everything providence lays at their feet.

Over a two- or three-year period, we walked through great trials with three of our families, each of whom lost a child. We wept with them as we sought to encourage them through the weightiness of a child's death. Yet as we journeyed, each made some comment to the effect that the Lord had been preparing them through his grace to bear up under their loss. Scripture they had stored up came to the forefront of their need. Rich theological discussions and applications made years earlier prepared them for the present difficulties.

What are you teaching your congregation? Let it never be said of us, "They didn't teach me these things." Instead, proclaim Jesus Christ, admonish and teach every person under your charge with all wisdom, in order that you

---

20. Lawrence, *Biblical Theology*, 89–92.
21. A pastor will find books on *historical theology* useful, as well, in seeing how various doctrines have been worked out historically, especially in light of the many theological controversies throughout Christian history. See Gregg Allison, *Historical Theology: An Introduction to Christian Doctrine* (Grand Rapids: Zondervan, 2011); Alister E. McGrath, *Historical Theology: An Introduction to the History of Christian Thought*, 2nd ed. (West Sussex, UK: Wiley-Blackwell, 2013); Geoffrey W. Bromiley, *Historical Theology: An Introduction* (Grand Rapids: Eerdmans, 1978).

might present him and her complete in Christ. Labor to do so in Christ's power that works mightily within you (Col. 1:28–29).

Summary

Pastors face the responsibility of teaching the whole counsel of God to their congregations. Such a challenge requires them to faithfully exegete each week's texts while seeing their connection to the metanarrative of Scripture. Sound exegesis and biblical theology lay the foundation for theological exposition. The discipline of systematic theology provides a practical summary of the doctrines unpacked through exegesis and biblical theological interpretation. As pastors preach through books of the Bible, they will encounter the multiplied doctrines in Scripture, allowing them to journey through the ongoing practice of teaching the whole counsel of God. Apart from this practice, a congregation will lack the biblical foundation and knowledge to handle life's realities. Paul's letter to the Romans, systematic theologies, and faithful doctrinal statements offer pastors a good framework for teaching the whole counsel of God.

REFLECTION QUESTIONS

1. How does Jesus's view of Scripture affect the way pastors approach the content of their preaching?

2. How would you relate systematic theology to Paul's teaching on "the whole counsel of God"?

3. How did the juncture of Jesus's post-resurrection instructions on biblical interpretation and theology impact his commission to the disciples as witnesses to his death and resurrection?

4. How does biblical theology inform our understanding of what to teach our congregations?

5. What part do biblical and systematic theologies have in our regular sermon preparation?

How Does a Pastor Prepare a Pastoral Exposition?

With all of the tasks facing pastors, they can count on one constant: preparing to preach on Sunday. Pastors need to regularly read and study works on hermeneutics/exegesis, sermon preparation, and the act of preaching as they face the challenge of weekly exposition of God's Word to their congregations.[1] Developing as faithful expositors in the midst of busy pastoral ministry presents no small challenge. Pastors must not fear the shifts and changes taking place as they grow in ability to expound the Word to their people. Just as "there is an artistic element in a sermon"[2] that takes shape over time with sweat and labor,[3] so too the artistry of the preacher takes shape over years of faithfully laboring to expound God's Word book by book. How he preaches at the start of his pastoral work will be honed in advancing years by the power of the Word, the work of the Spirit, the nurturing of his faith in Christ, the providence of God, his growing love for his flock, and the prayers and responsiveness of his congregation. He must see pastoral preaching as

---

1. E.g., Sidney Greidanus, *The Modern Preacher and the Ancient Text: Interpreting and Preaching Biblical Literature* (Grand Rapids: Eerdmans, 1988); Tremper Longman III, *Reading the Bible with Heart and Mind* (Colorado Springs: NavPress, 1997); Andreas Köstenberger and Richard Patterson, *For the Love of God's Word: An Introduction to Biblical Interpretation* (Grand Rapids: Kregel Academic, 2015); Edmund Clowney, *Preaching Christ in All of Scripture* (Wheaton, IL: Crossway, 2003); Dennis E. Johnson, *Him We Proclaim: Preaching Christ from All the Scripture* (Phillipsburg, NJ: P&R, 2007); John Piper, *The Supremacy of God in Preaching* (Grand Rapids: Baker, 1990); J. W. Alexander, *Thoughts on Preaching* (1864; Edinburgh: Banner of Truth Trust, 1988); John Stott, *Between Two Worlds: The Art of Preaching in the Twentieth Century* (Grand Rapids: Eerdmans, 1982); D. Martyn Lloyd-Jones, *Preaching and Preachers*, 40th anniv. ed. (Grand Rapids: Zondervan, 2011).
2. Lloyd-Jones, *Preaching*, 89.
3. Lloyd-Jones, *Preaching*, 90.

an ongoing development of his gifts and abilities in weekly preparation and exposition of the Word as a faithful shepherd of Christ's church (Acts 20:28).

My venture in discussing sermon preparation does not attempt to replace lengthier treatments of this holy work. But as a *learner* that has preached thousands of sermons (many fit for the shredder), I simply want to walk you through my approach from text to pulpit. While I have adjusted, refined, re-worked, and retooled my process over the years, I still follow a general pattern of expository sermon preparation taught by a seminary professor and then reinforced through books, seminars, discussions, and lectures from noted ex-positors. So, I'm not claiming originality to my method. Rather, I'm *talking aloud* about what has worked well for me over the past forty years in sermon preparation, while keeping in mind John Stott's wise word, "There is no one way to prepare sermons. Every preacher has to work out his own method, which suits his temperament and situation."[4]

Get the Text into Your Heart

After deciding on an appropriate book to preach through for your con-gregation's spiritual welfare, it's time to get the Sunday text into your heart.[5] This comes by reading, meditating, and memorizing at least portions of it. While a lengthy narrative text may be difficult to fully memorize in the short span of a week, get as much of it into your heart and mind as possible.[6] Some of the best sermon work happens away from the study as you mentally work through the text, considering its areas of emphasis, the beauty of the language, the historical and theological context and implications, its noticeable themes, and its structure. While most of that work happens in the study, I've found that pondering the text while driving, walking, or even lying in bed gives light to the sermon.

Do Translation Work

Even with excellent translations, doing the work yourself of getting into the original language of the text, seeing the nuances in the grammar, under-standing how the same biblical writer uses in other places words and phrases in your text, and savoring the beauty of the language written to the original audience opens the biblical text in a fresh way. I've actually found that the slow work of translation aids in memorizing the text. I type out my transla-tion double- or triple-spaced, making parenthetical explanatory notes from

---

4. Stott, *Between Two Worlds*, 213.

5. Knowing his gifts, schedule, temperament, and family life, the pastor needs to experiment until finding the appropriate weekly rhythm from start to final manuscript.

6. Andrew M. Davis, *An Approach to Extended Memorization of Scripture* (Greenville, SC: Ambassador International, 2004).

the translation aids in the body,[7] and then use the one to three pages (generally) to jot notes on each verse to build my understanding of the text (hermeneutics) with an aim toward structuring it for preaching (homiletics). By the time I'm finished, I generally write all over the page/pages of the translation with different colors of ink, experimenting with themes at the top and structural divisions in the margin. Most of the explanations, applications, quotes, and illustrations that will be part of the sermon manuscript will be jotted on my translation pages.

Understand the Text

My first goal is to understand what the text meant when originally written. "In order to arrive at this you will have to learn how to ask questions of your text," Martyn Lloyd-Jones reminds us.[8] The faithful preacher, David Helm insists, "gives the biblical context (rather than his own context) control over the meaning of the text."[9] Until understanding the Holy Spirit's intention through the human author, I do not move on to the sermon (2 Peter 1:20–21). Otherwise, I will impose a meaning upon the text instead of expounding its meaning. The goal in exposition is always to be a "mouthpiece" for the text.[10] However long it takes to grapple with the text's meaning until its light breaks forth in the heart, stay at it! I agree with Leander Keck: "Preaching is truly biblical when (a) the Bible governs the content of the sermon and when (b) the function of the sermon is analogous to that of the text."[11] The hard work of digging into words and phrases, grappling with the historical background, seeing the OT in the NT and the NT fulfilling the OT, thinking from a biblical theology angle, wrestling with the text's place in the larger canon, and seeing the text's intended meaning must continue until I know what the text means. Long before preparing to feed the flock on Sunday, I'm feeding my own soul on the richness of God's Word as I study and prepare.

After translating and meditating on the text, jotting ideas along the way toward its meaning and exposition, I will read through a number of commentaries and expositions. I do this for at least four reasons: (1) I want to check and refine my interpretation in light of other pastors, theologians, and scholars that have labored in my text; (2) I want to reinforce my sermon with appropriate material or quotes suitable to explain or illustrate the text; (3) I

---

7. E.g., BDAG, *TDNT*, *NIDNTTE*, and *LEKGNT* for Greek; *NIDOTTE*, *TWOT*, and BDB for Hebrew.
8. Lloyd-Jones, *Preaching*, 214. See pp. 214–15 for suggestions of questions. He calls this learning to talk to your text: "They talk to you, and you must talk to them. Put questions to them" (215).
9. David Helm, *Expositional Preaching: How We Speak God's Word Today*, 9Marks Building Healthy Churches Series (Wheaton, IL: Crossway, 2014), 40.
10. J. I. Packer, *God Has Spoken* (Grand Rapids: Baker, 1979), 28.
11. Leander Keck, *The Bible in the Pulpit: The Renewal of Biblical Preaching* (Nashville: Abingdon, 1978), 106, quoted in Greidanus, *Modern Preacher*, 10.

want to stretch my thinking with good scholarship; and (4) I want to expose my congregation to faithful interpreters, theologians, and preachers.[12]

Identify the Theme

As I work through the text's meaning, I look for the thread that runs through it, holding together its words, phrases, sentences, and theology to give them a unified meaning. That's the text's theme, "dominant thought,"[13] essence, or "the central truth."[14] Write it out in a complete sentence—as briefly, concisely, and poignantly as possible. I labor over this sentence, trying to use as much active (nonpassive) language as possible. I want the sentence to jump out when spoken because, in a sense, it's stating the whole sermon in one sentence.[15] It may be an indicative or imperative, while conveying the present implication of the sermon.[16] I always place this thesis statement in my sermon introduction, adding verbal emphasis when stating it, so that the congregation knows precisely what I'm preaching. Charles Simeon explained that this "categorical proposition" is "*the great secret* of all composition for the pulpit."[17] He further described it as a way to "screw the word into the minds of your hearers," so that "when it has turned a few times, scarcely any power can pull it out."[18]

Develop the Structure

The structure of the sermon *must* be anchored in the text as expressed by the sermonic theme. By structure, I'm referring to the form or divisions or skeleton upon which you build the sermon. Chiefly, we do this via some type

---

12. To identify good commentaries, consult Tremper Longman III, *Old Testament Commentary Survey*, 4th ed. (Grand Rapids: Baker, 2007); D. A. Carson, *New Testament Commentary Survey*, 6th ed. (Grand Rapids: Baker, 2007). For expositions on each book of the Bible, see https://www.monergism.com/scripture.
13. Stott, *Between Two Worlds*, 224–25.
14. Alec Motyer, *Preaching? Simple Teaching on Simply Preaching* (Ross-shire, Scotland: Christian Focus, 2013), 33–35.
15. Some recommend stating in one sentence the theme of the text and a second sentence identifying the theme of the sermon. I opt for one theme since my sermon should clearly mirror the meaning of the text.
16. The theme is not a historical reflection (there may be exceptions to this on occasion) but a statement of divine action that has bearing on the past, present, and given the context, future. As an example, my theme from 1 Corinthians 2:1–5, "Faithful gospel ministry centered in Christ crucified runs counter to everything that boasts in human wisdom, ability, and achievement," captures the historical context but also moves to the point of the sermon and its present application.
17. Charles Simeon, *Horae Homileticae* (11 vols.), XXI, n.p. (emphasis orig.), quoted by Stott, *Between Two Worlds*, 226.
18. Charles Simeon, in the *Christian Observer* (Dec. 1821), in Hugh Evan Hopkins, *Charles Simeon of Cambridge* (London: Hodder & Stoughton, 1977), 59, quoted by Stott, *Between Two Worlds*, 226.

of outline. Lloyd-Jones helpfully writes, "Never force a division," so don't try to create an outline that fails to be well represented by your text as stated in your theme. He adds, "The headings [of the outline] should be natural and appear to be inevitable"[19]—so nothing contrived by cleverness. By "natural," use language that communicates and fits the rest of the sermon. Avoid awkward phrases, obtuse words, archaic expressions, colloquialisms, and overly lengthy sentences. Be crisp and clear with the use of vivid, active words.

In a recent sermon on Luke 15:11–24, on the prodigal son, my exposition focused on the central idea that the parable teaches us about the gracious father more than about the two sons. Yet to get to the focal point, I had to unpack the way back to the father (this sermon only looked at the first part of the parable). My theme, "The Father shows extravagant joy in celebrating repentant sinners," had two headings aimed toward a climatic conclusion. In order to show the Father's joy, I expounded the prodigal's prodigality and ultimate repentance that brought him into the father's joyous celebration. The outline unfolded as follows:

I. The Bent of the Heart Away from God
    1. By a self-focused and self-centered heart attitude
    2. By intentional distancing from spiritual influences
    3. By careless indulgence in sin
    4. By blindness to sin's consequences

II. The Way of Repentance toward God
    1. As a change of mind
    2. As a new attitude or new way of thinking
    3. As a decisive turn away from one life to another
    4. As a clear ownership and admission of sin
    5. As recognition of the need for mercy
    6. As humble trust in God's mercy and grace

The conclusion focused on how the father responded with mercy, grace, reconciliation, and celebration—the very same way the heavenly Father does with us, which was the point Jesus made in the three facets of the one parable (lost sheep, lost coin, lost sons). The outline followed the story Jesus told about the wayward son who finally came to his senses, humbly returning to the father. The context shaped my theme (Luke 15:1–2). In it, Jesus told the parable to explain to the Pharisees and scribes that their view of God failed to understand his gracious way with sinners. Instead of casting aside the tainted, nonreligious tax collectors and general sinners, the Lord pursues them until he brings them into his joyous celebration that one who was "dead has come

---

19. Lloyd-Jones, *Preaching*, 220.

to life again" and one who was "lost . . . has been found" (Luke 15:24). What the Pharisees and scribes thought worthy of their grumbling, Jesus declared to be the way of God with sinners.

Theologically, the parable teaches about total depravity, God's mercy and grace, repentance and faith, the failure of works righteousness (with the older brother), and God's nature as loving, merciful, gracious, forgiving, generous, and joyous. Yet the overarching theme, while helping us grapple with soteriological concepts, brings us to understand the nature of God with sinners through the father's celebration.

Compose the Manuscript

The exposition will likely contain an introduction, the body of the sermon, and a conclusion. We're accustomed to this form when writing an essay. But a sermon rises above an essay in that it's not simply a well-researched idea. It's a mouthpiece for a particular text from God's Word. Given the genre of the text, the three-phase structure may vary. For instance, a narrative sermon should reflect *story*, so a typical introduction and conclusion found in a more didactic passage may be wrapped into the narrative style of preaching. Most expositions should make application throughout the sermon. But a narrative sermon may backload the application as a conclusion.

The *introduction*, as Stott maintains, (1) "arouses interest, stimulates curiosity, and whets the appetite for more," and (2) "genuinely 'introduces' the theme by leading the hearers to it."[20] Many recommend writing the introduction after finishing the body of the sermon. I take the approach that the introduction, with its aim to introduce the theme, should help to shape the flow of the sermon. With that in mind, I almost always write my introduction first after establishing a clearly worked out homiletical structure. The introduction sets the stage for the sermon. It gives a rationale for why the congregation should listen to the sermon. It raises questions critical for the hearers answered by the expounded text.

Introductions may vary in approach. Often, I like the first line in the introduction to be as pithy and arresting as possible. Let me offer a few examples. "The unexpected happens" (Ps. 42–43, "Hope in God"). "A distant God is not much of a concern or threat" (Ps. 139, "God Is There"). "Details matter" (Luke 1:57–80, "His Name Is John"). "Jesus saves those we may think unsavable" (Luke 8:26–39, "He Does Great Things"). Or, if not pithy, I tell a story that the hearers can relate to that lays groundwork for declaring the sermon's theme. Or, when helpful, I use a quote from a sermon or an article or current event or historical figure that will grab the listener's attention. If the introduction does not hold the congregation's interest, then the sermon probably will not either.

---

20. Stott, *Between Two Worlds*, 244.

Normally, I state the exposition's theme toward the end of the introduction, followed by a question or two that will challenge the mind to engage in the work of thinking about the text. Pastoral expositions should always cause the congregation to think on the text: what does it mean, why was it written, how does it lay claim on my life, why does it matter, how must I respond, and so on.

The *body of the sermon* follows the logical progress of the outline that has been worked out during preparation. It should reflect the expositor's grasp of the text's meaning, its historical and theological context, its place in biblical theology, its systematic theological implications, and its application. But it should not read like a commentary or a lecture. It should be, as Lloyd-Jones so ably stated, "Logic on fire! Eloquent reason! . . . It is theology on fire."[21] The way each one approaches this task of composing the body of the sermon varies from one preacher to another. But getting it on paper (whether longhand or printed) allows us the chance to pore over it with an eye to scrutinize every word and detail. It gives us a chance to test the sermon's theology and application arising from the biblical text. It provides time to not only clean up poor wording, grammatical irregularities, and verbosity, but also to purge from it those tendencies of the flesh to draw attention to self in a public setting.

The *conclusion* should be just that: conclude the sermon; don't re-preach it. The conclusion should go "beyond recapitulation to personal application,"[22] reiterating previous applications made during the sermon and/or bringing the major application to the fore as the sermon closes. It may end with a sobering awareness pressed by the text or, such as is the case with the previously mentioned Luke 15 sermon, with a joyous anticipation of heaven erupting with celebration at a sinner repenting. Let your conclusion spur thought and action on the part of the congregation.

Summary

Finishing the sermon manuscript means the pastor understands the text's historical context and theological implications. He's identified the theme and the supporting structure reflecting the theme. His introduction, sermon body, and conclusion explain and apply the text. But the preparation is not over. The goal should never be to read the manuscript to the congregation. Preach the text, not the manuscript. By that, I mean, so live in the text that it becomes part of your thinking and living. The manuscript serves as a tool to guide you along the way, but it mustn't keep you from feeling the weight, joy, seriousness, delight, power, and authority of the biblical text. While the sermon manuscript remains important, the text must be all-important. Plead for the Holy Spirit to work through your weakness

---

21. Lloyd-Jones, *Preaching*, 110.
22. Stott, *Between Two Worlds*, 246.

to speak with authority and power. Pray that the Word will impact the congregation's thinking and action.

Prayerfully work through your sermon manuscript enough times that you can preach it effectively with good eye contact throughout. Every pastor will need to find a rhythm that will help him to preach without overreliance on his manuscript. If that's three, four, or ten times, go over the manuscript, thinking and praying about those who will listen on Sunday and feeling the burden of serving as a "mouthpiece" for the text.

REFLECTION QUESTIONS

1. What are the initial recommendations in this chapter on getting into the biblical text?

2. What must be understood about the text before developing the sermon?

3. Why is the sermon theme of critical importance?

4. What recommendations on developing structure or form for the sermon proved useful to you?

5. What part does the introduction play in the sermon?

Why Should Pastors Preach through Books of the Bible?

Expressing his conviction of the pastor as shepherd of God's flock, John Stott observes, "For the chief responsibility of the pastor who 'tends' his sheep is to 'feed' them."[1] He explains feeding as a metaphor "for teaching the Church. So, the pastor is essentially the teacher."[2] If Stott is right, and I certainly think he is, then the pastor will need to decide what to feed his congregation. Similar to a home setting, all meals are not equal. Some have good nutritional value aiding cell development and growth, while others—that is, junk food—simply fill an empty spot. Pastors feeding their flocks must never fall prey to filling an empty spot. They're to feed the flock of God with his Word (Ps. 19:7–14) so that the flock grows "up in all aspects unto Him who is the head, even Christ" (Eph. 4:15).

But how do we supply this food for the flock? A fellow pastor and I discussed his conversation with a group of pastors on what they were preaching in their churches. While most seemed to agree biblical exposition must have priority in the church, few thought it wise to preach consecutively through books of the Bible—particularly with series extending beyond twelve weeks. The nineteenth-century Presbyterian pastor and professor J. W. Alexander disagreed. He wrote, "The expository method of preaching is the most obvious and natural way of conveying to the hearers the import of the sacred volume."[3] By *expository*, he focused directly upon addressing the congregation consecutively through one book of the Bible, dealing with its entirety,

---

1. John R. W. Stott, *Between Two Worlds: The Art of Preaching in the Twentieth Century* (Grand Rapids: Eerdmans, 1982), 118.
2. Stott, *Between Two Worlds*, 118.
3. J. W. Alexander, *Thoughts on Preaching* (1864; Edinburgh: Banner of Truth Trust, 1988), 229.

considering its context and theology, and allowing the week's chosen text to serve as the entire focus of the sermon. Each week's text connects with what came before and what will follow. Welsh pastor Martyn Lloyd-Jones, who followed this plan in his London pastorate, shows how the book's context affects each consecutive exposition. He writes, "In [an expositional] sermon the theme or doctrine is something that arises out of the text and its context, it is something which is illustrated by that text and context."[4] Alexander points out that the two greatest preachers in the Greek and Latin churches, Chrysostom and Augustine, followed this expositional pattern. So, too, did the sixteenth-century reformers Luther and Calvin, and seventeenth-century Nonconformists. He adds that "exposition in regular course was considered a necessary part of ministerial labour" for the Nonconformists.[5]

One may understand the challenge of preaching longer series through books of the Bible. But the value of training a congregation in regularly expounding the Scriptures far outweighs concern for series' lengths. Alexander told of Scottish peasants surpassing more sophisticated congregations in their grasp and application of God's Word due to consistently following "in their little Bibles" the pastor's weekly exposition through books of the Bible. He mused, "There is something beautiful in the very idea of training up a whole congregation in the regular study of the holy Scriptures."[6]

My own experience has proven this over and over. The forty-four sermons I preached through Ephesians in 1990–91 literally transformed my life, theology, and congregation. Eight or ten sermons would not have sufficed to uproot faulty theology and set us on a right course. The fifty-two sermons in Hebrews in 2000–01 sharpened our understanding of the gospel and its application to the whole of life. The forty-two sermons through Revelation in 2006–7 led us to depths of worship and understanding of Christ's redeeming purposes for the church we had yet to fathom. It seems we must decide our aim: to merely expose a congregation to a book or to thoroughly expound it, so they grasp its import, doctrines, and applications.

Why preach consecutively through books of the Bible? Here are seven important reasons.

1. Pastors have the responsibility to preach the whole range of biblical revelation.

Paul told the Ephesian elders, "For I did not shrink from declaring to you the whole purpose of God" (Acts 20:27). He could not simply address his favorite issues, but rather he intentionally sought to comprehensively proclaim

---

4. D. Martyn Lloyd-Jones, *Preaching and Preachers*, 40th anniv. ed. (Grand Rapids: Zondervan, 2011), 82.
5. Alexander, *Thoughts on Preaching*, 231–33.
6. Alexander, *Thoughts on Preaching*, 236–37.

God's will for sinners and the redeemed. Standing before the Lord to give an account likely motivated Paul's thoroughness. "Consequently, he cannot be held responsible if any of them might perish."[7] Australian pastors Phillip Jensen and Paul Grimmond explain that genuine expository preaching not only respects the whole Bible as God's Word, but "it means planning to preach the whole of the Bible rather than just the parts that we find enjoyable or comfortable."[8] Picking easier texts or "hobby horses" might simplify the pastor's preaching task but will simultaneously starve the congregation, ensuring spiritual anemia.

"The whole purpose of God" refers "to the whole plan of God for humanity and the created order revealed in the Scriptures and fulfilled in Jesus Christ."[9] Alexander reminds pastors that "insulated texts at random" will neglect "many important doctrines or duties." How do we remedy this negligence? "But the regular exposition of a few entire books, well selected, would go far to supply every defect of this nature."[10] Simply doing topical doctrinal preaching on difficult doctrines will not suffice. As Alexander explained, only when the pastor sets forth those doctrines "in their scriptural connection" by exposition through books do the doctrines get clearer, and the congregation better grasps the whole counsel of God.[11]

2. Preaching consecutively through a book allows the pastor and congregation the opportunity to better absorb the purpose of God and the text's impact upon the original audience.

Not long ago, I completed preaching fifty sermons through Genesis. What amazed me as I studied and preached was how the biblical narrative presented several points of crescendo that we would have missed had I only preached a few selected texts. For instance, Abraham offering Isaac at God's command is certainly one of the most magnificent Old Testament scenes that gave assurance to God's purpose for his people, while also pointing to Christ as our substitute. But if we simply preach Genesis 22 without having walked the long journey from Genesis 12, where God called Abraham out of paganism and then faithfully preserved him through many ups and downs as he waited for the unfolding of God's promise of a son, then we miss something of the pathos intended for the original audience. Can you imagine the first audience of Genesis listening to the buildup of the story—hearing the promises of God that depended upon the solitary heir of the patriarch—gasping

---

7. John Stott, *The Spirit, the Church, and the World: The Message of Acts* (Downers Grove, IL: InterVarsity, 1990), 326.

8. Phillip Jensen and Paul Grimmond, *The Archer and the Arrow: Preaching the Very Words of God* (Kingsford, Australia: Matthias Media, 2010), 40.

9. David G. Peterson, *The Acts of the Apostles*, PNTC (Grand Rapids: Eerdmans, 2009), 567.

10. Alexander, *Thoughts on Preaching*, 240–41.

11. Alexander, *Thoughts on Preaching*, 240.

at the seemingly out-of-the-blue command from God to sacrifice his "only son"? The knife rose above the very one holding the key to everything God had promised in the previous ten chapters. Then God provided a substitute—and in so doing preserved the line of Abraham that eventually came to grand fruition in the blessing of the nations through the person of Jesus Christ. The emphasis on *substitute* takes on more intense meaning with this background. Yes, we can just preach Genesis 22, and it will be powerful, but I suggest it loses something of its effect when we skip over living together each week in the previous ten chapters.

3. Preaching consecutively through books of the Bible gives the pastor and congregation a better understanding of a book—and if properly expounded, a fuller grasp of biblical theology.

I can preach Ephesians 2:8–10, exhorting my hearers to depend upon the grace of God in Christ alone. But if I've taken my congregation to the theological mountain top in chapter 1, descended to the darkest depths of human sinfulness in the opening of chapter 2, and then listened to Paul's declaration of grace, "But God," in Ephesians 2:4, then I find Ephesians 2:8–10 generates greater power to my hearers. The theological context gives weight to the passage expounded. As Lloyd-Jones insists, "preaching must always be theological," which presents a challenge when preaching isolated texts.[12] Short series that skip over the broader doctrinal context may shorten preaching and make things more palatable to biblically illiterate congregations, but it also weakens the doctrinal impact that would build up and mature the church. Have no fear that doctrinal exposition may come across as dry. Tim Keller writes, "The point of preaching is not just to expound doctrine, but to make the doctrine real to the heart and therefore permanently life-changing."[13] Theology rightly understood brings heart change.

4. Preaching consecutively through books of the Bible challenges the pastor's study, discipline, hermeneutics, homiletical strengths, pastoral insight, and prayer life.

Expository preaching is hard work. "The observation is very common," remarked Alexander, "that expository preaching is exceedingly difficult."[14] A pastor will need to "love his work" and "be possessed of enthusiasm which shall never suffer him to forget the impending task."[15] He must diligently work through the text to understand its meaning in its original context (2 Tim. 2:15). He translates, meditates, compares translations, treads into the contextual

---

12. Lloyd-Jones, *Preaching*, 76.
13. Timothy Keller, "A 'Tract for the Times,'" in Lloyd-Jones, *Preaching*, 94.
14. Alexander, *Thoughts on Preaching*, 242.
15. Alexander, *Thoughts on Preaching*, 235.

meaning of particular words and phrases, thinks about theological implications of a preposition, reads comments from others, weighs positions, and wrestles with the right interpretation before he gets anywhere close to composing a sermon. Taking into account his diligent study, he now struggles to discern the text's theme as the focal point of his exposition. He studies to see how the various strands of the sermon emerge from the theme in the text. He considers how the broader context affects interpretation and application, and refers back to the larger context without cutting and pasting from a previous sermon. Concurrently, he prays for his flock, seeking to know how to apply the meaning of the passage to their pressing needs. He feels the weight of text and congregation pressing him toward Sunday's exposition. The clock ticks, other duties call, but he must remain steady to open God's Word to those for whom he will give an account (Heb. 13:17). He's also learning to trust in the grace of God and the Holy Spirit's power in preparation and preaching. The time in the study deeply impacts the expositor before it ever does the congregation.

> ### 5. Preaching consecutively through books of the Bible focuses the pastor on the biblical story line, lest he skip those uncomfortable texts he otherwise would never preach.

Tim Keller explains, "The key to preaching the gospel every time is to preach Christ every time, and the key to that is to find how your particular text fits into the full canonical context and participates as a chapter in the great narrative of the Bible, which is how God saves us and renews the world through the salvation by free grace in his Son, Jesus Christ."[16] In my Genesis expositions, I wrestled through Noah's drunkenness, Lot's incestuous acts, and Judah's adultery with his daughter-in-law. I would not voluntarily pick those texts for topical expositions! But they are part of the storyline of Scripture that help us understand the fallen condition, the promise of the Messiah King, and the necessity of God's grace to redeem sinners. Those texts helped my congregation grasp the message of Genesis, hammering home that the living God preserves his people despite their messy lives. It also demonstrated, through Judah's lineage, the true humanity of our Lord Jesus so that he might become the perfect Redeemer (Heb. 7:14; 2:14–18).

> ### 6. Preaching consecutively through books of the Bible gives congregations a chance to meditate more deeply upon a particular book, mining its riches, soaking up its doctrines, and making pointed applications to daily life.

For instance, if you work through a book, you regularly consider the book's context until it begins to stick into the congregation's mind (not to

---

16. Timothy Keller, *Preaching: Communicating Faith in an Age of Skepticism* (New York: Viking, 2015), 70.

mention your own mind). The logic of a particular text fits into the grand logic of the larger context you've woven into the exposition, and that into the framework of Holy Scripture. Over a period of years, through steady expository preaching, the congregation begins to think biblically. As they read and think upon passages in that book or others in their personal devotion and study, the contextual understanding informs their interpretation, as does their ability to recognize the doctrines found in the text. Such reading of the Word results in more faithful application to daily life. Alexander observes, "The mental habits of any Christian community are mainly derived from the preaching which they hear."[17] Regular exposition teaches sound hermeneutics to the church as they listen with open Bibles. Their meditation upon the text, consequently, will be done contextually, by which richer understanding of doctrine and application will be developed. One can microwave a beef roast and serve it to guests (short series through books), but the slow roasting in the oven (full book exposition) will soak up the flavors, tenderize the meat, and make for a more satisfying meal. Regular biblical exposition, book by book, provides local congregations a privileged feast to participate in.

Consistent exposition through books combats biblical illiteracy in the pew. Rather than being fearful to preach longer expositions due to a congregation's poor grasp of Scripture, just the opposite should be true. As my pastor friend Chris Spano put it, "It should be obvious that the best way to combat biblical illiteracy is not to teach people less of the Bible, but far more of the Bible."[18] So, start with smaller books and/or series (Philippians, 1 Thessalonians, Malachi, etc.) but then move toward more substantial messages whether from a small or large book of the Bible. Instead of ten sermons in Philippians, preach twenty. Instead of staying in books under five chapters, you move on to preach through a gospel or Romans or Hebrews or an Old Testament narrative. Your congregation will profit from faithful, patient exposition.

7. Preaching consecutively through books of the Bible, once the congregation is trained to listen, will prove far more interesting than the method of skipping through the Bible or preaching topical series.

No doubt, many people can't wait to hear what their pastor will say— or do—from the pulpit on any given Sunday. But that's not common with churches where consecutive exposition will be heard week by week. Instead, the congregation comes because they can't wait to hear what God's Word declares. The pastor realizes he's just "a mouthpiece for his text."[19] Rather than pulpit antics to keep people returning, faithful expositors depend upon the sufficiency of Holy Scripture to do its work as the Holy Spirit moves among

---

17. Alexander, *Thoughts on Preaching*, 240.
18. Personal correspondence, March 22, 2019.
19. J. I. Packer, *God Has Spoken* (Grand Rapids: Baker, 1979), 28.

them. Such "pure teachings of the Spirit, accompanied with suitable explanation, necessarily occupies the mind of the preacher" as he expounds through books of the Bible week by week.[20]

Summary

Am I suggesting we all preach thirteen years through Romans, as did Martyn Lloyd-Jones (without finishing it)? Or preach forty-plus years through Job, as did the Puritan Joseph Caryl? Or even preach 180 sermons through Genesis as James Montgomery Boice? Not at all! Rather, let's think of a measured way to work adequately through a book of the Bible, giving us time as preachers to absorb it, and giving our congregations a chance to grapple with its message.[21]

The pastor must decide what he can handle and what the congregation can absorb—this will vary from one congregation to another and one pastor to another. Admittedly, many congregations are not ready to spend a year or two in Genesis or Romans or John. The pastor may not be quite ready either. That takes training for pastors and congregations, starting with smaller books and working toward longer ones, while teaching the congregation how to read, listen, meditate, and interpret the Word. But in the end, as pastor and congregation grow together in expounding and hearing God's Word, a depth and satisfaction with the sufficiency of Holy Scripture will certainly take place. I cannot imagine any pastor preaching through books of the Bible and then looking back and saying, "I wish that I had not spent so much time preaching through books of the Bible to the people for whom I will give an account to God."

REFLECTION QUESTIONS

1. How did you react to the J. W. Alexander quotation, "There is something beautiful in the very idea of training up a whole congregation in the regular study of holy Scriptures"? Do you agree?

2. What does preaching "the whole purpose of God," in Paul's comment to the Ephesian elders, imply for contemporary preaching?

---

20. Alexander, *Thoughts on Preaching*, 236.
21. As a suggestion, I've found it useful to check websites of expositors to see how they have broken down various books into preaching segments. One may also find help in Kent Hughes's Preach the Word series (Crossway), as well as the Reformed Expository Commentary series (P&R).

3. How does consecutive preaching through books of the Bible affect a congregation's grasp of biblical theology?

4. What will be necessary for a pastor to keep pace with preaching through books of the Bible year after year?

5. J. I. Packer states that the pastor is "a mouthpiece for the text." How does that statement reflect the way you're currently preaching God's Word to your congregation?

How Should a Pastor Decide Which Book to Preach to His Congregation?

Dining in a school cafeteria for twelve years accustomed me to eating repetitive meals. With sparse variety, the same food cooked in large batches did little for my taste buds and probably less for my dietary needs. I wished for something different that went beyond meat, beans, and potatoes, but the staff focused on convenience rather than on a wide culinary range.

Similarly, pastors can grow complacent in what they serve from the pulpit, focusing on convenience in preparation rather than a wholesome diet for the congregation. With busy administrative, pastoral, and counseling demands, pulpit fare can stay locked on a few themes or limited biblical genres, instead of on "the whole counsel of God" (Acts 20:27 ESV).

Preaching the whole of Scripture challenges pastors and congregations in preparation and listening. Yet, since the *entire* Bible is God's infallible Word, by which he intends his people to be trained and equipped, giving consideration to the range of Scripture must take center stage in the church's preaching and teaching ministry (2 Tim. 3:16–17). Training a congregation to attentively listen to God's Word may require some time, discussion, and exposure to various biblical genres. Doing so proves necessary to the health and vitality of the local church.

How should a pastor, then, decide which books of the Bible to preach to his congregation? We'll embark upon this question by giving consideration to some critical evaluations that will inform the decision, both in the initial planning for early in the pastor's ministry, and for long-term planning of pastoral preaching.

Critical Evaluations

Pastors must not presume upon their congregations or themselves when planning their preaching. At least four areas need to be considered to lay groundwork for planning which books to preach.

1. Be Committed to Biblical Exposition in Your Weekly Pulpit Ministry

Commitment to ongoing exposition lashes the pastor to the Bible as the basis for his preaching. Letting a congregation know from the start that he intends weekly exposition through books of the Bible will hold him accountable against the temptation to take an easier route. As he works through the Bible book by book, he builds interest with the congregation that discovers the richness of God's Word applying to the whole of life. As the congregation develops faithful listening skills, it grows in hunger for the whole counsel of God.[1] When the congregation grows in listening and applying God's Word, the pastor feels an increased demand for diligent preparation to expound the Word. Pastor and congregation grow together under this commitment to weekly biblical exposition.

2. Evaluate the Doctrinal Understanding of Your Congregation

Sometimes, well-meaning pastors begin their ministry at a new church by plunging immediately into a lengthy treatment of a doctrinally heavy book like Ephesians or Romans. He needs to preach these books, but maybe not at the start of his ministry. He must first discern how well the congregation knows the gospel. Can they clearly explain the gospel? Do they understand who Jesus is, why he came in the incarnation, what he accomplished through his death and resurrection, and what he has promised to those who believe?

Beyond the basics of the gospel, what do they know about essential Christian doctrine? Can they discuss God's purpose in the creation, humanity's fall into sin, Jesus's redemptive work, and God's reconciliation of everything in Christ? Do they understand the meaning of predestination, justification, redemption, adoption, sanctification, and glorification? Do they grasp the person and work of the Holy Spirit? What do they understand about the nature and mission of the church?

One series through a book will not change their grasp of these truths, but it can advance their understanding in the right direction. Foremost on the preaching agenda should be discerning what books might help (a) move the church toward maturity in gospel understanding and application, and thereby (b) develop greater unity as the body of Christ.

3. Evaluate Where You Need to Be Theologically Challenged, Refined, and Strengthened to Preach to Your People

H. B. Charles exhorts, "Stretch yourself. Pick texts that will force you to work and think and grow."[2] Pastors should always be pushing themselves to

---

1. Ken Ramey, *Expository Listening: A Handbook for Hearing and Doing God's Word* (Woodlands, TX: Kress Biblical Resources, 2010). In the foreword, Lance Quinn writes, "Actively listening to the preaching of God's Word requires mental alertness, focused attention, and a spiritually receptive heart" (xi).
2. H. B. Charles, *On Preaching: Personal and Pastoral Insights for the Preparation and Practice of Preaching* (Chicago: Moody, 2014), 56.

grow exegetically and theologically. They may find it helpful to stretch to preach through one book that would prepare them to preach through a more challenging book. For instance, preaching through Zechariah stretched me, but it prepared me to step up to the bigger challenge of preaching through Revelation. Preaching through several shorter Pauline Epistles laid groundwork for preaching through Romans. I initially preached through Ephesians in the early '90s because I needed to work through its many doctrinal emphases. It proved to strengthen me and to challenge many in our congregation. Keep in mind, if you personally grow in doctrine and practice as you prepare to preach, so will your congregation. As you stretch yourself personally, you will help the body to do the same.

4. Evaluate How Well Your Congregation Listens to Expositions

If you're new to a church or new at biblical exposition, begin weekly preaching with shorter series of expositions. With this approach, you teach your congregation what is involved in expository preaching while building their biblical understanding and contextual application. Pay attention to their attentiveness, questions after the sermon or during the week, reactions to doctrinal explanations, and evidence of growth in the faith. If their progress appears slow, continue with shorter expositional series in order to give them time to learn to better listen. Where congregations have had little exposure to faithful exposition, the challenge will be greater. But a pastor's diligence, gentleness, and patience in preaching through books week by week help the body grow in their habits of listening.

Sometimes it proves helpful to provide outlines of the sermon for taking notes or just following the reasoning through the text. I provide copies of my sermon manuscript prior to the service as a listening aid and for further study during the week. Occasionally do a brief testimony or interview with someone in the church that seems to have come alive in listening to the Word. When going through more difficult or challenging books, I have sometimes taken a Sunday evening or midweek service to answer questions and expand explanation. Approach these as teaching opportunities rather than a time of pulpit defense. Initial planning of preaching series will aim to teach the body to listen faithfully.

Initial Planning

When following a pastor that has steadily expounded God's Word book by book for many years, a new pastor will likely have much freedom to start his ministry with longer expositional series. He still needs to discern where the church stands in spiritual health and doctrinal understanding. That will likely dictate where he starts his longer expositional series. But where consecutive exposition has not been the practice, starting slowly to acclimate the congregation to the meaty diet of doctrinal exposition may take one to two years. The pastor needs to think about what the church needs to move them forward in doctrine, spiritual health, and breadth of biblical knowledge. He will be wise to work through various biblical genres in order to demonstrate the christological focus of all of Scripture.[3] Ultimately, the pastor's faithfulness in preaching the biblical text, whatever book he chooses, will be used by God to impact the church.

To help with some ideas toward developing shorter series throughout the Bible, I'll offer an overall title for each series and suggested textual units for exposition. The pastor may choose to rework these series and textual units as fits his pastoral context. The sermon series represent five biblical genres and alternate between New and Old Testaments. The Old Testament textual units need to be preached christologically.

(a) Titus (7 sermons)—*Be Gospel-Centered People*: Titus 1:1–4; 1:5–9; 1:10–16; 2:1–10; 2:11–15; 3:1–7; 3:8–15

(b) Ruth (4 sermons)—*The Kinsman-Redeemer*: Ruth 1; 2; 3; 4

(c) Jude (5 sermons)—*Contending for the Faith*: Jude 1–2; 3–4; 5–16; 17–23; 24–25

(d) Haggai (2 sermons)—*A Call to Perseverance*: Haggai 1; 2

(e) 2 Timothy (10 sermons)—*The Christian's Endurance*: 2 Timothy 1:1–7; 1:8–18; 2:1–7; 2:8–13; 2:14–19; 2:20–26; 3:1–9; 3:10–17; 4:1–8; 4:9–22

(f) Malachi (6 sermons)—*A Call to Faithfulness*: Malachi 1:1–4; 1:6–2:9; 2:10–16; 2:17–3:7; 3:8–15; 3:16–4:6

(g) Philippians (12–13 sermons)—*United in Joy*: Philippians 1:1–11; 1:12–26; 1:27–30; 2:1–11 (or 2:1–4 and 2:5–11); 2:12–18; 2:19–30; 3:1–7; 3:8–11; 3:12–16; 3:17–4:1; 4:2–9; 4:10–23

(h) Judges (10 sermons)—*Mercy and Deliverance*: Judges 1–3; 4–5; 6; 7–8; 9–10; 11–12; 13–14; 15–16; 17–18; 19–21

(i) Mark (16 sermons with key texts from each chapter rather than verse by verse and with recommended titles)—*The Kingdom Has*

---

3. See Edmund P. Clowney, *Preaching Christ from All of Scripture* (Wheaton, IL: Crossway, 2003); and Dennis E. Johnson, *Him We Proclaim: Preaching Christ from All the Scriptures* (Phillipsburg, NJ: P&R, 2007).

Come: Mark 1:1–15 (The Way into the Kingdom); 2:13–28 (The Kingdom Clarified); 3:13–35 (The Kingdom Distinguished); 4:1–34 (The Kingdom Explained); 4:35–5:43 (The Kingdom in Power); 6:1–6 (The Kingdom Rejected); 7:1–23 (The Kingdom Heart); 8:27–38 (The Kingdom's King); 9:30–40 (The Narrow Way of the Kingdom); 10:13–31 (The Single-Mindedness of the Kingdom); 11:1–10 (The Humble King of the Kingdom); 12:28–37 (Not Far from the Kingdom); 13:1–37 (The Kingdom That Lasts); 14:12–26 (The Kingdom Meal); 15:1–47 (The Kingdom's King at the Cross); 16:1–8 (The Kingdom's King Triumphs)

(j) Psalms (15 sermons)—*The Ascension Psalms: Trusting along the Journey*: Psalms 120–134

Long-Term Planning

Planning the textual units for weekly exposition needs to be done at least three months out (six to nine months is better). The pastor also needs an idea of where he will head when he completes his current series. He must have in mind the spiritual development of his congregation as he plans instead of just preaching what interests him. Here, the input of his fellow elders will help him to see the breadth of the church's needs as he plans his next preaching series. Although daunting to me, I remember, with the counsel of my fellow elders, deciding to preach through Genesis. I hesitated due to its length, some of the difficult texts, and the lengthy narratives. It proved to be foundational for our congregation and an enormous joy for me.

Plan your preaching to help the church to understand the gospel, mature in the faith, grow in its mission, cultivate service toward one another, and experience deeper worship. This means when you see an area that needs honing or teaching or training or correction, aim for a book that will help toward that end. Here are a few ideas in various areas of the congregation's needs.

(a) *Intensifying worship*: Job, selected Psalms, Isaiah 40–66, Lamentations, Ezekiel, the Gospels, Romans, Ephesians, Hebrews, Revelation

(b) *Spiritual maturity*: Genesis, Deuteronomy, Joshua, 1–2 Samuel, Job, selected Psalms, Isaiah, Jeremiah, Daniel, the Gospels, Acts, Romans, 1–2 Corinthians, Galatians, Ephesians, Philippians, Colossians, Hebrews, 1–2 Peter, 1 John

(c) *Cultivating service and relationships*: Ruth, 1–2 Samuel, Nehemiah, selected Proverbs, Micah, the Gospels, Acts, Romans, Ephesians, Philippians, 1 Timothy, Philemon, James, 1 Peter, 2–3 John

(d) *Developing in missions*: Jonah, the Gospels, Acts, Romans, Ephesians, Philippians, 1 Peter, 3 John, Revelation

(e) *Holiness and sanctification*: The Pentateuch, Joshua, Judges, 1–2 Kings, 1–2 Chronicles, selected Psalms and Proverbs, Hosea, Joel, Amos, Micah, Haggai, Malachi, the Gospels, Romans, 1 Corinthians, Galatians, 1 Thessalonians, Hebrews, James, 1–2 Peter, 1 John

(f) *Building deeper doctrinal roots*: Genesis, Leviticus, selected Psalms, Isaiah, Jeremiah, Ezekiel, Daniel, Micah, Haggai, Zechariah, Malachi, the Gospels, Romans, Galatians, Ephesians, Colossians, Hebrews, 1 Peter, 1 John, Jude, Revelation

(g) *Enduring suffering*: Ruth, 1–2 Samuel, Job, selected Psalms, selected Proverbs, Ecclesiastes, Lamentations, Daniel, Habakkuk, the Gospels, Acts, Romans, 2 Corinthians, Ephesians, 2 Timothy, Hebrews, James, 1–2 Peter, Revelation

(h) *Establishing healthy ecclesiology*: Matthew, John, Acts, Romans, 1–2 Corinthians, Ephesians, Philippians, Colossians, 1 Thessalonians, 1–2 Timothy, Titus, Hebrews, 1 Peter, Jude, Revelation

(i) *God's sovereignty and providence*: Genesis, Exodus, Numbers, Joshua, Judges, 1–2 Samuel; 1–2 Kings, 1–2 Chronicles, Ezra, Nehemiah, Esther, Job, Psalms, the Major Prophets, the Minor Prophets, the Gospels, Acts, Romans, Ephesians, Hebrews, 1–2 Peter, Revelation

(j) *Perseverance and building endurance*: Genesis, Exodus, Joshua, 1–2 Samuel, 1–2 Kings, 1–2 Chronicles, Ezra, Nehemiah, Esther, Job, selected Psalms, selected Proverbs, Daniel, Habakkuk, the Gospels, Acts, Romans, Ephesians, Philippians, 2 Thessalonians, Hebrews, James, 1–2 Peter, 1 John, Jude, Revelation

(k) *Gospel proclamation*: the entire Bible, especially the Gospels, Acts, Romans, Ephesians, Colossians, Hebrews, 1 Peter

(l) *The nature and attributes of God*: The Pentateuch, Esther, Job, Psalms, Proverbs, the Major Prophets, the Minor Prophets, the Gospels, Acts, Romans, the Prison Epistles, Hebrews, Revelation

No doubt, other pastors will add books to the various categories I've proposed. But the point of the categories and recommended books demonstrates that every biblical genre has something to offer the church on any given Sunday's gathering. Working through the Scripture book by book and genre by genre exposes the congregation to the wealth found in God's Word, transforms their Bible reading, and enables them to see the applicability of all of Scripture to the whole of life.

I've found that generally alternating longer book series with shorter book series allows a little time to catch my breath in preaching and the congregation's, in listening. Occasionally in a longer series, I might interrupt it for a short excursus on a related theme. For instance, when preaching Matthew 16 on the first mention of the church, I took five additional weeks to expound other ecclesiological texts.

Most importantly, pray for God's direction in which book to preach at a given timeframe. The needs may be many, so don't fret over whether you've selected *just* the right book since so many, as illustrated above, can fit the need. Your faithfulness to the biblical text will bear fruit. As the Lord gives discernment on the state of the church and its pressing needs, evaluate potential books for consideration. Read through them. Which book do you sense a burden to dig into and expound? With dependence upon the help and power of the Holy Spirit, begin the process of understanding that book, laying out the textual units for preaching, and then expounding it weekly to the congregation.

Summary

Deciding which book to preach at a given time will always be a spiritual and practical process. The pastor's walk with Christ, growing devotional life, and time in prayer will prepare him to be sensitive to the Lord directing him in his preaching plans. Practically, reading through the Scripture yearly to grow familiar with each book, discussing preaching plans with fellow elders, and engaging with other pastors on their preaching will give insights on where to head next in preaching. Starting with shorter series allows a congregation time to learn to listen well. Longer series may occasionally have brief interruptions to explore similar themes in another genre. Working through the broad range of God's Word will strengthen the spiritual health and faithful application of the Word with the congregation.

REFLECTION QUESTIONS

1. What particular truths do you look for when evaluating a church's doctrinal understanding?

2. Why should a pastor stretch himself in preaching through unfamiliar books of the Bible?

3. What should a pastor look for, to discern how well his congregation is listening to the preaching of the Word?

4. What kind of shorter expositional series are recommended for a pastor newly beginning his pastoral ministry?

5. Why is a mixture of biblical genres important for a long-term preaching plan?

How Should a Pastor Lead the Congregation in Worship?

Early in the Reformation, Emperor Charles V enacted "equal laws" for Protestants and Catholics regarding religious practice. Knowing they differed, the emperor sought to quell some of the conflict by treating them with deference. But the Roman pontiff objected, strongly expressing the emperor "put heretics on a footing with Catholics." To clarify *why* the Reformation arose and *what* differences existed among them, John Calvin wrote a small treatise to the emperor, *The Necessity of Reforming the Church*. Theodore Beza, Calvin's successor in Geneva, commented on this work, "I know not if any writing on the subject, more nervous [bold] or solid, has been published in our age."[1]

Calvin boiled the Reformation down to two issues in the church. First, "a knowledge . . . of the mode in which God is duly worshipped." While we generally think of justification by faith as the *first* matter in the Reformation, here Calvin chose to identify worship as primary. Second, "of the source from which salvation is to be obtained." He explained when the mode of worshiping God and the source of salvation get laid aside, "our profession is empty and vain."[2] He further added, "All our controversies concerning doctrine relate either to the legitimate worship of God, or to the ground of salvation."[3] Jonathan Gibson and Mark Earngey note, "For the Reformers, the Reformation was not simply about recovering true doctrine; it was ultimately about recovering pure worship. . . . The recovery of the gospel in the Reformation was ultimately a worship war—a war against the idols, a war for the pure worship of God."[4]

---

1. John Calvin, *The Necessity of Reforming the Church*, trans. Henry Beveridge (Dallas: Protestant Heritage Press, 1995), 5, following the publisher's introduction citing Beza.
2. Calvin, *Necessity of Reforming*, 15.
3. Calvin, *Necessity of Reforming*, 41.
4. Jonathan Gibson and Mark Earngey, eds., *Reformation Worship: Liturgies from the Past for the Present* (Greensboro, NC: New Growth Press, 2018), 49.

Since pure worship and a right understanding of the gospel go together, the pastor must not fail at giving leadership to the former while speaking to the latter. Sound theology fuels healthy, joyous doxology. As pastors preach and lead their congregations to be a people of *the Book*, they must never see this as merely increasing biblical knowledge. Their aim must be worship "that consciously shows how magnificent God is."[5] In considering pastoral leadership in worship, we will look at the rationale for the pastor leading corporate worship, the Word of God regulating worship, and the shaping of a worship service.

The Pastor(s) Should Lead Corporate Worship

With the stress on individualism still flourishing since the Enlightenment, building healthy congregational life demands returning to the biblical emphasis on the corporate body (Acts 2:42–47; 4:23–35; Eph. 2:11–5:21). Worship remains at the center of corporate life just as it did with ancient Israel.[6] Writing about congregational worship, nineteenth-century Scottish theologian James Bannerman explained God's corporate blessing rising above the individual blessing: "The outward provision which Christ has made for social Christianity, as embodied and realized in the communion of the Church, is richer in grace and more abundant in blessing by far than the provision made for individual Christianity, as embodied and realized in separate believers."[7]

And who leads these corporate gatherings of the church? The pastors whom God appointed for equipping, training, instructing, and shepherding God's flock lead the corporate gatherings, particularly when the body meets for worship (Acts 20:28; Eph. 4:11–12, 16; 1 Tim. 3:2; 4:11–16; Titus 1:9; 1 Peter 5:1–4). In the corporate gatherings, pastors find some of their most effective times of instruction, shepherding, and modeling of the Christian life. Teaching doctrine through faithful exposition magnifies the character, attributes, works, and ways of God, leading to worship.

Consideration and meditation on God's Word leads to worship (Ps. 19; 104:31–35). As the pastor lives in the text he expounds, he may naturally

---

5. John Piper, *Expository Exultation: Christian Preaching as Worship* (Wheaton, IL: Crossway, 2018), 28. Calvin's definition of worship expands Piper's short explanation of worship: "Its chief foundation is to acknowledge him to be, as he is, the only source of all virtue, justice, holiness, wisdom, truth, power, goodness, mercy, life, and salvation; in accordance with this, to ascribe and render to him the glory of all that is good, to seek all things in him alone, and in every want have recourse to him alone" (Calvin, *Reforming the Church*, 16). So, in Piper's words, worship "consciously shows how magnificent God is."

6. See J. Ligon Duncan III, "Does God Care How We Worship?," in *Give Praise to God: A Vision for Reforming Worship—Celebrating the Legacy of James Montgomery Boice*, eds. Philip G. Ryken, Derek W. H. Thomas, and J. Ligon Duncan III (Phillipsburg, NJ: P&R, 2003), 17–50.

7. James Bannerman, *The Church of Christ: A Treatise on the Nature, Powers, Ordinances, Discipline, and Government of the Christian Church* (1869; Edinburgh: Banner of Truth Trust, 2015), 347.

be caught up in a spirit of worship as he preaches. He ponders the magnificence of God revealed in the Word. He exults in the person and work of Jesus Christ. He glories in the sovereign work of the Holy Spirit. As he worships by proclaiming God's Word, he leads his people to worship. There's no demarcation between supposed "worship time" and "preaching time." Biblical preaching is an act of worship. Piper concurs: "Since Paul tells us to preach the Scripture, therefore, *the nature and aim of Scripture dictate the nature and aim of preaching*. Both Scripture and preaching aim at worship and are worshipful."[8]

Therefore, the pastor must not be hands-off when it comes to other portions of the worship service. He is a derelict shepherd if he allows hymns, music, and elements of worship lacking doctrinal clarity as part of the service. Mark Dever and Paul Alexander comment, "Part of pastoral leadership [in light of Eph. 5:19], then, is to facilitate this kind of edifying worship. . . . It does mean . . . you as the pastor must be theologically discerning in what you encourage and lead your congregation to sing."[9]

Consequently, pastors may be the ones selecting the congregational music. At minimum, they must work in concert with those leading the worship service to insure the doctrine taught through music or other worship components maintains biblical clarity.

The Word of God Must Regulate Worship

Jesus gave no room for creative meddling with worship when he spoke to the Samaritan woman: "God is spirit, and those who worship Him must worship in spirit and truth" (John 4:24).[10] *If worship aims to glory in God,* then worship planning must not veer into the tendencies of the flesh to make worship about us. Calvin warns, "For men pay no regard to what God has commanded, or to what he approves, in order that they may serve him in a becoming manner but assume to themselves a license of devising modes of worship, and afterwards obtruding them upon him as a substitute for obedience."[11]

---

8. Piper, *Expository Exultation*, 77 (emphasis added). Piper argues that Scripture's "ultimate goal for the reader and the preacher is that God's infinite worth and beauty would be exalted in the everlasting, white-hot worship of the blood-bought bride of Christ from every people, language, tribe, and nation" (77).

9. Mark Dever and Paul Alexander, *The Deliberate Church: Building Your Ministry on the Gospel* (Wheaton, IL: Crossway, 2005), 84.

10. D. A. Carson states, "There are not two separable characteristics of the worship that must be offered: it must be 'in spirit and truth' [one preposition governing both], i.e., essentially God-centered, made possible by the gift of the Holy Spirit, and in personal knowledge of and conformity to God's Word-made-flesh, the one who is God's 'truth,' the faithful exposition and fulfilment . . . of God and his saving purposes" (D. A. Carson, *The Gospel according to John*, PNTC [Grand Rapids: Eerdmans, 1991], 225).

11. Calvin, *Reforming the Church*, 23.

Scripture clearly teaches the specifics for how God must be worshiped as well as how he must *not* be worshiped.[12] He accepted Abel's worship but not Cain's (Gen. 4:3–5). Countering prevailing approaches to worship, Yahweh narrowed how he must be thought of (truth) and the manner in which he must be worshiped (spirit) in the first two commandments (Exod. 20:1–6). The Lord wholly rejected attempts to imaginative worship when Aaron and Israel made the golden calf (Exod. 32–34). He immediately judged Nadab and Abihu when they put their spin on worship (Lev. 10). The prophets reproved Israel for worship displeasing to God, culminating in the postexilic prophet Malachi declaring, "Oh that there were one among you who would shut the gates, that you might not uselessly kindle fire on My altar" (Mal. 1:10). Calvin notes, "For, next to idolatry, there is nothing for which they [the prophets] rebuke the people more sharply than for falsely imagining that the worship of God consisted in external show."[13]

Jesus corrected the worship of the Pharisees and scribes, calling their worship "vain" (Matt. 15:1–9). He reiterated how God may be worshiped in his encounter with the Samaritan woman (John 4). Here he taught, as Ligon Duncan explains, a *"redemptive historical shift regarding the place of worship. . . . That worship is response to revelation and thus must be according to revelation. . . . [and that] Jesus reemphasizes the importance of worship in the new-covenant era."*[14] Paul corrected the faulty worship influenced by the Colossian heresy (Col. 2:16–19), as well as specified parameters for gathered worship in Corinth (1 Cor. 14).

Duncan summarizes, "God's word itself must supply the principles and patterns and content of Christian worship. True Christian worship is by the book. . . . The Bible alone ultimately directs the form and content of Christian worship."[15] Since the Reformation, this view has been called the *Regulative Principle* of worship, meaning Scripture alone establishes who God is, how he is to be worshiped, and what does and does not constitute worship. Some practice the *Normative Principle* of worship, accepting legitimacy of any form or type of worship as long as Scripture does not expressly forbid it. Yet, Bannerman warns, this theology of worship thinks "it were competent or right for men to worship God at a venture, and by such means as, appointed by them in their ignorance." But if we follow the sufficiency of Scripture, that "cannot be known to be acceptable to Him."[16]

The pastor must lead his congregation in understanding the nature of God, his works and ways, and how he has prescribed worship for his people.

---

12. The next two paragraphs follow Duncan, "Does God Care How We Worship?," 28–50.
13. Calvin, *Reforming the Church*, 46–47.
14. Duncan, "Does God Care How We Worship?," 42–44 (emphasis original).
15. Duncan, "Does God Care How We Worship?," 20.
16. Bannerman, *Church of Christ*, 397–98.

With the prominence of human-centered worship services, one must not assume a congregation has a clear theology of worship. The pastor's high view of God and reverence in worship, including theologically strong congregational singing, biblically saturated pastoral prayers, attention to the public reading of Scripture (1 Tim. 4:13), and doctrinally faithful exposition, will build a healthy theology of worship for his church. Moving away from faddish elements that exalt people may take the pastor time, but with prayer, wisdom, and diligence, he can shape congregational worship according to Scripture.

Shaping a Service of Worship

Biblical worship must aim toward "the glorification and enjoyment of God."[17] But we tend to miss worship's focus. James Montgomery Boice pointed out "pervasive triviality," human-centered self-absorption, and being "oblivious to God" as characteristics affecting modern worship services. To remedy this deficiency, he called for a return to "service elements that have always been associated with God's worship": praying (1 Tim. 2:1–4), reading God's Word (1 Tim. 4:13), expositing Scripture (1 Tim. 4:13; 2 Tim. 4:1–4), confessing sin (Prov. 28:13; 1 John 1:9), and singing hymns (Eph. 5:18–21; Col. 3:16).[18] To these we would add the ordinances and giving (1 Cor. 11:17–34; 16:1–2). Planning the worship service, then, considers the elements God's Word identifies in contributing to God-glorifying worship.

How, when, and what manner the pastor includes these elements of worship into the Sunday gathering may vary. That's where the use of creativity and cultural affinities work into the planning.

1. The Reading of Scripture

Oddly, many liberal Protestant and Catholic services feature more public reading of God's Word than churches professing to believe in the inerrancy and sufficiency of Scripture. God's Word must be prominent in our worship gatherings. We utilize a *scriptural call to worship* to start our service. Later we do a *scriptural responsive reading* so that the body engages in reading the Word, followed later by the *reading of the text to be expounded* by the pastor. We want our worship to be scripturally saturated. Typically, Reformation worship "services included various readings from the Old and New Testaments, the Gospels, and the Psalms."[19]

---

17. Duncan, "Does God Care How We Worship?" 25.
18. James Montgomery Boice, *Whatever Happened to the Gospel of Grace? Rediscovering the Doctrines That Shook the World* (Wheaton, IL: Crossway, 2001), 176–80.
19. Gibson and Earngey, "Worshiping in the Tradition," *Reformation Worship*, 55.

2. Prayers

Prayers—plural—should be interwoven in the worship service. Not just perfunctory prayers simply because we're a Christian gathering, but serious prayers of confession, thanksgiving, intercession, and petition. We follow our scriptural call to worship with a *corporate prayer of confession*. We print these prayers in our Sunday worship bulletin for further use during the week by our members. The *pastoral prayer* should include praise and thanksgiving for God's mercies. As so evident in the Psalms and the prophetic books, the pastoral prayer will often include lament.[20] This prayer needs to be shaped by meditation upon God's Word. It should include prayers of intercession for needs of members and others in the community, the broader Christian church, unreached people groups, gospel outreach in the community and beyond, leaders in church and government, international missions, including missionaries and pastors sent out by the congregation. We identify one or two unengaged, unreached people groups in our Sunday worship bulletin for our congregation to pray for even as the pastor does in the pastoral prayer. Part of shepherding the flock is petitioning needs of members that can be publicly mentioned in the pastoral prayer. The pastor or others may *pray for God's blessing on the ministry of the Word, for the contributions,* and *for dedication of members sent out for service.* At the conclusion of the service, a *benediction* or *blessing* may be offered that either directly comes from Scripture or summarizes the biblical content of the exposition (e.g., Num. 6:23–26; Rom. 15:13; 1 Cor. 13:14; Gal. 6:18; Eph. 3:20–21).

3. Congregational Singing of Psalms, Hymns, and Spiritual Songs

A church learns and reinforces much of its theology through its music. It serves as a means of praise, thanksgiving, and positive *creedal* confession of what we believe concerning God, the Trinity, salvation, eternity, and the church. Bannerman called praise "the natural and necessary utterance towards God of the gratitude or adoration of a creature for blessings enjoyed, or because of Divine glory exhibited and seen."[21] Duncan correctly states, "What we mean by 'sing the Bible' is that our singing ought to be biblical, shot through with the language, categories, and theology of the Bible. It ought to reflect the themes and proportion of the Bible, as well as its substance and weightiness."[22] It should include a variety of older and newer hymnody that exposes the congregation to the way many generations confess the Christian faith in a sound, memorable, theological fashion.

---

20. Mark Vroegrop has served the church with this penetrating work on lament's place in Christian worship (*Dark Clouds, Deep Mercy: Discovering the Grace of Lament* [Wheaton, IL: Crossway, 2019]).
21. Bannerman, *Church of Christ*, 345.
22. Duncan, "Foundations for Biblically Directed Worship," 67.

4. Biblical Exposition

Preaching should serve to not only instruct and exhort, but also demonstrate a biblical framework and means to worship. As the pastor *exposits* the biblical text, he brings the congregation's attention to truths about the Lord God and his ways that give vent to praise, thanksgiving, confession, reverence, awe, and rejoicing. Piper calls this "expository exultation." He explains, "Preaching shows God's supreme worth by making the meaning of Scripture known and by simultaneously treasuring and expressing the glories of God revealed in that biblical meaning."[23]

5. The Ordinances of Baptism and the Lord's Supper

While baptism may be an occasional celebration in the church, as it acknowledges a new believer, it should be viewed as an act of worship in gratitude to Jesus Christ for his saving work. It's how the church confirms and identifies with a new brother or sister in Christ—and that calls for praise to the Lord.

Paul told the church, "For as often as you eat this bread and drink the cup, you proclaim the Lord's death until He comes" (1 Cor. 11:26). The Lord's Supper may be observed "as often" as the church chooses. Many churches observe the Supper weekly, others monthly, and still others quarterly. We've opted for a monthly celebration of the Lord's Table, giving attention to its covenant significance for the body. We read a portion of our church covenant, welcome new members to sign the covenant, and initiate formal discipline on those occasions.

6. Giving

Churches have various positions on how to approach members giving to support its local ministry and mission work. Paul indicated this as a significant part of the obedience and involvement of the church in broader gospel work (1 Cor. 16:1–4; 2 Cor. 8–9). Since believers give in gratitude to the Lord, it's part of our worship service (we do it as the conclusion of the service followed by the benediction).

7. Doctrinal Confessions

There's strong evidence doctrinal confessions were part of the liturgy of local churches in the first century (e.g., Phil. 2:5–11; 1 Tim. 3:16; note especially Paul's reference to the latter as "by common confession"). Confessing our faith together may be done through a biblical text (e.g., Eph. 1:3–14; Col. 1:15–20; Rev. 1:4–8) or through the confessions recognized by the church through the centuries as faithful representations of biblical teaching (e.g., Apostle's Creed, Nicene Creed, Athanasian Creed). These confessions declare what the church believes and affirms together.

---

23. Piper, *Expository Exultation*, 51.

Summary

Worship planning should focus on *worship*, never pounding members into a particular form or liturgy, as though Scripture necessitates only one form.[24] The various *elements* of worship are found throughout the Bible, not usually in one passage. Gibson and Earngey note, "Despite the inevitable diversity, the Magisterial Reformers—following Martin Luther's lead—strenuously aimed for unity in the gospel, but liberty and charity in church liturgy. The great Reformers Thomas Cranmer and John Calvin both understood the contextual nature of liturgical diversity in reforming the Church, and wisely encouraged liberty and charity where necessary."[25]

While "worship wars" may emerge in churches, it often happens for the wrong reasons—musical preference or style—rather than clearly theological ones. Pastors must *lead* in this regard, teaching what it means for the gathered church to worship. It may be a slow process to see significant changes occur, but in doing so, the life of the congregation changes from shallowness to a spiritual depth that can only come by the body of Christ encountering the Lord God.

Here is one example of an order of worship:

> Scriptural Call to Worship
> Corporate Confession of Sin
> Choral Call to Worship
> Congregational Hymn
> Doctrinal Confession
> Pastoral Prayer
> Scriptural Responsive Reading
> Congregational Hymn
> Choral Message in Music
> Sermon
> Concluding Prayer of Blessing
> Congregational Hymn
> Worship through Offerings
> Benediction

---

24. Gibson finds a liturgical pattern of call to worship, response, and fellowship meal in biblical narratives that may be fleshed out in various ways (Gibson and Earngey, *Reformation Worship*, 2–22). He elaborates on a fuller liturgy in Revelation (18).
25. Gibson and Earngey, *Reformation Worship*, 45.

REFLECTION QUESTIONS

1. Why did John Calvin position the church's worship as a primary focus in the Reformation?

2. Why should pastors lead the congregation in worship?

3. What is the Regulative Principle of worship?

4. Why is practicing the Regulative Principle critical to a church's worship?

5. Can you identify the biblically expressed elements of worship?

How Should a Pastor Conduct Funerals?

Funerals may be the most difficult and yet most rewarding opportunities for pastoral ministry. The difficulty comes as we deal with depths of grief, questions of why, consciousness of loss, and suddenness of death. But in the midst of grief and loss, we have the privilege of ministering the good news of Jesus Christ to grieving family and friends. We have the only message that can give comfort to those working through the anguish of a loved one's or friend's death (2 Cor. 1:3–7; 1 Thess. 4:13–18). In his wisdom, God has placed you in the lives of the grieving so that you might shepherd them in the gospel of Christ.

How shall we shepherd family and friends through the time of loss culminating in a funeral? We'll think on this question under the categories of responsibilities and practices in pastoral care.[1]

Responsibilities for Pastoral Care

Whether the deceased is a faithful church member, a relative of a member, a known unbeliever, or someone unknown to you, the pastor has the responsibility to shepherd families and friends when faced with death. The funeral director and his or her associates will handle details related to the funeral and burial, but the pastor will be the one to come alongside the grieving with comfort and hope in the Scriptures. Six areas of responsibility need to be considered.

1. Offer Guidance and Care[2]

The pastor need not be an expert on handling funerals to provide the kind of care needed by a grieving family. His presence, more than anything else,

---

1. Brian Croft and I wrote *Conduct Gospel-Centered Funerals: Applying the Gospel at the Unique Challenges of Death* (Grand Rapids: Zondervan, 2014). I will follow portions of it in responding to the question on conducting funerals. However, space will not allow the examples of funeral sermons, eulogies, orders of service, and music that we suggest for funerals.
2. This section follows the outline in Croft and Newton, *Funerals*, 18–23.

offering prayers and appropriate Scripture along with occasional comments, will be most welcomed during these times. He, in a sense, will be guiding families in grieving, as he grieves along with them in their loss. He shows through confidence in Christ and the gospel that his grief aims to find comfort in Christ. He realizes that the immediacy of the death, visitation, and funeral only lays groundwork for serving the grieving family in the weeks and months ahead. Consider the period when the family first learns of a loved one's death as the start of giving care, not the end.

2. Offer Comfort through God's Word and Pastoral Presence

When one of our older members faced the death of a loved one, I came alongside her and read the Word, offering just a few simple comments. Years later, she recalled to me the passage I read and the comments I made during that time. I could remember no details, but she did. Taking the time to select passages that might breathe peace and comfort for those grieving will bear fruit in years ahead. As the shepherd of those going through loss, consider their walks with Christ, experiences in life (maybe they've faced much loss), and what they face in the days ahead. As much as possible, choose biblical texts that fit their present need. I was with a family that had just lost a fairly young family member in an unexpected death. Their world had caved in. So I read Psalm 46, a passage appropriate to the collapse of everything around, but one that sets our minds on the Lord's immutability and presence. It served them at that crisis moment.

3. Represent Christ, the Church, and the Gospel

While we can never replace the Christ who loves us and gave himself for us (Eph. 5:2), we're his servants (1 Cor. 3:9). We're bringing Christ to the grieving through Word and prayer. We're meeting them with the consciousness of *Christ with us* to serve them. Alongside comes the church, which we represent as its shepherd, ready to love and care for the grieving. We're to be alert to ways the larger body might serve the family in their time of need, perhaps offering assurance to the family of ways the church will be helping them—and reporting back to the church for organized action (e.g., meals, visits, childcare, cleaning their home, etc.). We want the family to know that our only comfort and hope is in the gospel of the crucified and resurrected Lord Jesus Christ. Our prayers, Bible reading, and comments need to display the gospel of Christ.

4. Declare the Sufficiency of the Gospel

Whether in visits with the family or at the funeral service, we want to declare the sufficiency of the *good news*. A family at loss may not feel this sufficiency at the moment, even though theologically they know better. So our communication of the gospel will be essential. By this, I do not mean that we look at the funeral and surrounding events as solely an evangelistic outreach. I've been around this approach a few times and it unfortunately comes across as trite and offensive, as though the minister plays on the emotions of the grieving in order to get an evangelistic decision. Far be it from us to neglect the gospel at such times! The gospel is our comfort and peace. The gospel gives direction when life throws obstacles in the way. The gospel sets hopes and affections on the eternal rather than the temporal. In that kind of gospel-sufficient reality, we may have wonderful opportunities to talk to family and friends about the gospel of Christ—opportunities that will need to be followed up on beyond the funeral.

What if the deceased gave no evidence of having believed the gospel of Christ? Then continue to focus on the gospel with application to the family and friends. Our responsibility at the funeral is not to make an eternal judgment on the deceased. We're not preaching them into heaven or hell. Ours is to hold forth Christ who conquered sin and death, having triumphed over it in his death and resurrection (1 Cor. 15:1–28; Col. 2:13–15). We're to help them see Jesus Christ as sufficient in their loss and for their future.

5. Build Deeper Relationships

There's something unexplainable about the bond that often takes place when a pastor comes alongside a family soon after a death and continues to minister to them throughout their grief. They've shared life and sorrow together at the most vulnerable time. They've listened to each other, wept together, shared stories, and heard the Word of God comfort them in need. They've listened to the pastoral prayers that have held the grieving family before the throne of grace. Relationships forged during such times provide many opportunities to later shepherd those family members in the truths of the Word. For instance, maybe you want to address an area in a family member's sanctification. The deepening relationship through loss provides an increased level of trust *later on* when continuing to shepherd in areas of Christian growth and maturity. In God's providence, the difficulty of a funeral provides a larger platform to serve the family in the name of Christ.

6. Be Ready to Serve and Counsel in the Long Term

Your responsibilities at the funeral may only be the start of a chance to serve the grieving family in extensive ways in the months ahead. Grief only begins at the death and subsequent funeral. Although burial provides one level of closure, it doesn't end the grief a family may feel for years to come. Pastoral visits, phone calls, emails, texts, and notes in the days ahead will be useful in serving them. Build on what you've been teaching them in the exposition of Scripture, helping them to make application of the gospel to their loss. You can do that personally and through notes.

Practices at the Funeral Service

The following will offer some guidance around the logistical issues of funerals and the service itself.

1. Connect with the Funeral Director for Service Details

As a professional, the funeral director knows everything he or she will need to do for the service and burial except one thing: how you will lead the service. The director should lead everything else, but the service, as a time of worship, will need your decisive leadership. Plan to give the director an outline of how you will conduct the service, for example, opening Scripture reading, prayer, hymn, eulogy, hymn, message, closing prayer. The director will know that when you close in prayer, he or she will take over once again.

2. Give Permission for Attendees to Grieve

Grieving is part of humanity. God gave us the capacity to grieve when facing loss. There's nothing unspiritual about it unless our grief exceeds the boundaries of those who live in the hope of Christ (1 Thess. 4:13). Even Jesus wept at Lazarus's graveside (John 11:35). Sometimes it serves the family to help them understand grief as a gift from the Lord to vent the emotions they feel from the loss.[3] But use this as a time to help them turn their grief to the hope that is in Christ, so that while sorrowing, they know the future remains far brighter than they can imagine.

3. Focus on Hope in Christ through the Gospel

The gospel is full of hope (Titus 2:11–14). "Christ in you" is "the hope of glory" (Col. 1:27). Even our God is called "the God of hope" who fills us with joy and peace in believing the gospel of Christ, "so that you will abound in hope by the power of the Holy Spirit" (Rom. 15:13). Hope sets our thoughts beyond this world to one that never ends, with no more death or sorrow or pain (Rev. 21:1–4). Hope provides the confident expectation that what Jesus secured for us in his death and resurrection will be consummated one day at his return (1 Cor. 15:1–58). Gospel preaching at a funeral helps the believer to feel the tug of "the hope of His calling," "the riches of the glory of His inheritance in the saints," and "the surpassing greatness of His power toward us who believe" (Eph. 1:18–19). This kind of hope-filled gospel needs to be the mainstay of our funeral services. It should be evident in the Scripture reading, singing, praying, and preaching.

---

3. James W. Bruce III, *From Grief to Glory: A Book of Comfort for Grieving Parents* (Edinburgh: Banner of Truth Trust, 2008). Discussing lament might also prove to be useful during this time. See Mark Vroegop, *Dark Clouds—Deep Mercy: Discovering the Grace of Lament* (Wheaton, IL: Crossway, 2019), for a helpful discussion on lament. For a perspective on death that will help with pastoral care, see also Matthew McCullough, *Remember Death: The Surprising Path to Living Hope* (Wheaton, IL: Crossway, 2018).

4. Instruct in the Gospel and Its Multiple Applications

Teach the gospel at funerals.[4] Don't just use the word *gospel*, but explain the gospel of Jesus Christ, the Son of God Incarnate, who lived a sinless life, died a substitutionary death, bore the wrath and judgment of God, crushed the power of sin and death at the cross, rose from the dead as the conqueror of sin and death, ascended to reign as Lord, and will one day return in glory. If I'm preaching from Psalm 23, I'm going to explain how Jesus shepherds us through the valley of the shadow of death by means of explaining the gospel. If I'm preaching John 14 about the dwelling places Jesus has prepared for his followers, I'm going to explain what he did to make that preparation as explained in the gospel. If I'm preaching 1 Thessalonians 4 about the return of Christ and the resurrection of the dead, I'm going to explain what precedes his return and why it matters by discussing the gospel. Out of this kind of gospel explanation, I can make applications—for example, Jesus has conquered death, our believing loved one will be bodily raised from the dead, the sting of death does not last forever, and the hope secured by Christ will comfort the grieving. As you set forth the gospel, you're pointing family and friends to the only hope for sinners; you're explaining *how* the gospel becomes personal through repentance and faith in Christ; you're assuring those who believe of the gospel's power to overcome their grief and loss.

5. Show Honor and Respect to the Deceased

I think it's appropriate, especially if doing a brief eulogy, to speak about the deceased. I do not think the funeral service should be all about the deceased. The funeral is about Christ, the gospel, and the hope that belongs to those believing. But we do want to give honor where honor is due by making appropriate remarks.[5] Having listened to family and friends during the visitation and other times, the pastor will likely have a few comments, an anecdote, or a testimony to share about the deceased. If fitting for the person and time, even a humorous anecdote may suit the occasion, although the pastor doesn't want anything to draw undue attention away from the gospel.

---

4. I suggest funeral messages be no longer than twenty minutes. Many attendees have left work or other responsibilities to attend. Family members are generally tired from the days preceding the funeral, so their attention span may be limited. I try to expound a text for fifteen to twenty minutes, which allows enough time to press home the gospel of Christ. The entire service should normally last no more than forty-five to sixty minutes, giving opportunity for singing, praying, Scripture reading, eulogy, and message. There are exceptions but they should be rare.

5. See Brian Croft's helpful remarks on eulogy in *Conduct Gospel-Centered Funerals*, 44–48, 107–17.

6. Keep on Shepherding

The pastor shepherds during the funeral as he points to the sufficiency of Christ. But he follows afterward by continuing to shepherd the grieving family by helping them to live in the hope that belongs to us through the gospel of Christ. A phone call or card or visit in days subsequent to the funeral will go a long way in helping the family to work through painful loss. The pastor's and other members' conscientiousness may help the family become a comfort to others walking through loss.

Summary

Funerals and the time of grief surrounding them provide the pastor with many opportunities to shepherd members of his congregation, as well as to extend the reach of the church to friends and extended family. The time invested in serving families in need will be a balm to them and an encouragement to the community that looks on and sees the care shown by pastor and congregation. The time of serving the family needs to center on the sufficiency of Christ in the gospel to comfort and heal the brokenhearted. Shepherding families through the immediate days of loss and subsequent months will provide families much needed comfort as they work through grief.

REFLECTION QUESTIONS

1. What are the challenges that most concern you with conducting funerals?

2. What seems most important from a grieving family's standpoint regarding the pastor's care during their loss?

3. What should be kept in mind when selecting Scripture passages to read with the family prior to and during the funeral service?

4. How should the message of hope in the gospel permeate the pastor's care during the funeral?

5. How might the pastor continue to shepherd the family that has walked through loss?

How Should a Pastor Conduct Marriage Ceremonies?

When I was a twenty-two-year-old newlywed, having been set apart as a gospel minister in my denomination, a college friend asked me to conduct his wedding. To say that I sweated through it would be understating my nervousness. But everything came together. We worshiped the Lord while witnessing my friends united in marriage. Utilizing a traditional marriage ceremony, we walked through the wedding without a hitch.

Since that time, I've seen several changes in wedding ceremonies. One or two couples wrote their own vows. Others added symbolic elements to the ceremony. Some desired music that appeared out of place. A few requested marriage homilies that clearly proclaimed the gospel to their guests. The general framework remained the same, but each wedding had its own uniqueness that made it special to the bridal couple.

What does a pastor need to keep in mind when approached to conduct a wedding? We will investigate this question by looking at general considerations, wedding policies, thoughts on premarriage counseling, and the elements of a wedding ceremony.

General Considerations

Civil authorities did not initiate marriage—God did. Before any other human institution, the Lord God formed the woman from Adam's rib "and brought her to the man" (Gen. 2:22). This act of God shows the primacy of marriage in human society. It fulfilled what he saw as "not good" in the creation. After naming the animals, no creature corresponded to Adam (Gen. 2:20). Man needed one like him—another human—but *unlike* him, one that would complement and complete him, one that would fulfill and delight him. The first poetry in Scripture arose out of Adam's exclamatory reaction when he first saw his wife.

This at last is bone of my bones,
> and flesh of my flesh;
she shall be called Woman,
> because she was taken out of Man. (Gen. 2:23 ESV)

Ray Ortlund captures this poetic moment.

> The man is not threatened by the woman's obvious equality with him. That heartwarming reality is the very thing that pleases him. With relief ("at last"), he greets her as his unique counterpart within the whole of creation. He intuitively identifies with her. His heart is drawn toward her. He prizes her. He rejoices over her. He praises God for her. And in thanking God for her, he perceives her as intimate with himself. . . .
>
> With his last act as duly authorized namer in the garden, the man identifies himself and the woman as of one kind, yet distinct from each other. The ultimate human relationship is presented to us as a complementarity of differences, not a duplication of sameness.[1]

With that beautiful picture of the first marriage as the foundation, a pastor faces the challenge of incorporating the wonder, beauty, joy, and God-ordained purpose in marriage as he meets with a couple and becomes part of their wedding planning. He must keep in mind the divine plan for marriage as he counsels and prepares to serve in joining a man and woman in marriage. The couple enters into the marriage covenant that calls for the permanence, sacredness, intimacy, mutuality, and exclusiveness of marriage.[2] To add accountability as the couple begins the journey of marriage, the public ceremony confirms the marriage covenant.[3]

Yet, a pastor begins the *marriage conversation* with the couple without knowing their understanding of what they're entering into. Do they know Jesus Christ as Lord and Savior? Are they growing in the grace and knowledge of Christ? Are they faithful members of a local church? Do they seek to guard their lives from the world? Do they see marriage as a picture of Christ and the church? Are they committed to following biblical teaching on marriage

---

1. Ray Ortlund, *Marriage and the Mystery of the Gospel*, SSBT, eds. Dane C. Ortlund and Miles Van Pelt (Wheaton, IL: Crossway, 2016), 27.
2. Andreas Köstenberger and David W. Jones, *God, Marriage, and Family: Rebuilding the Biblical Foundation*, 2nd ed. (Wheaton, IL: Crossway, 2010), 77–78.
3. Köstenberger and Jones define the covenantal model of marriage, in contrast to sacramental and contractual models, "as a *sacred bond between a man and a woman instituted by and publicly entered into before God (whether or not this is acknowledged by the married couple), normally consummated by sexual intercourse*" (*God, Marriage*, 73, emphasis original).

and family? Do they understand marriage as an inviolable covenant? These kinds of questions need to be part of the initial conversation *before the pastor agrees* to conduct the wedding. Paul warns of being "bound together with unbelievers" (2 Cor. 6:14). So the pastor needs to determine before the initial meeting whether he will only conduct the wedding of two believers. What if neither bride nor groom follows Christ? Then he needs to decide whether his conscience will allow him to officiate their wedding.[4]

Wedding Policies

Each church needs officially documented wedding policies. "Officially documented" means these policies will be adopted through the church's governing body and will identify specific use of the church facility and parameters for its pastors in conducting weddings. In that respect, the pastor follows the dictates of the church's governing body. That protects him and the church when difficult decisions must be made that affect a couple's wedding plans regarding the church and its pastors.

The wedding policies need to address the church's position on marriage (e.g., a covenant between one man and one woman before God committed to faithfulness to the marriage vows, as a picture of Christ and the church; Eph. 5:22–33), and the desire to glorify God in the rehearsal, ceremony, and reception. Unless a couple agrees to the wedding policies, the pastor and church may decline participation and facility use.

Policy should determine the rights and procedures for members and nonmembers on the use of the church facilities, as well as the pastor's (and/or church staff) involvement. Identifying parameters for scheduling weddings held at the church facility will protect the church's preparation for the Lord's Day services. The church's requirement of premarriage counseling by one of its pastors, even if the church's pastors do not conduct the ceremony, helps to guard the church's biblical position on marriage.[5] Details on the nature of

---

4. Second Corinthians 6:14–18 makes clear that believers and unbelievers should not be united in marriage. This passage presents a big challenge for the pastor to maintain the biblical teaching when unbelieving children of church members request a church wedding. But the question of whether to conduct a ceremony of two unbelievers is not addressed, and should be a matter of personal conviction on the part of the pastor. Obviously, he will wonder why they would want him to officiate their wedding since he will approach it from a decisively Christian perspective.

5. The church should not agree to members' or nonmembers' use of the facilities until the initial premarriage counseling. This session may uncover a reason why proceeding would be unwise. Stating in the wedding policy that agreement for using the church facilities or the pastor's participation will be evaluated and decided upon by the church's elders happens after the initial premarriage counseling session. For this reason, it would be wise to require notification of interest in use of the church facility or pastor officiating at least three to six months prior to the proposed wedding.

the marriage ceremony, the type of music permitted,[6] use of decorations, use of the church's musical instruments and sound system, and participation of photographer and videographer should be spelled out so that the church and pastors do not find themselves in compromising or awkward positions. Any fees for members' and nonmembers' use of the facility will need to be stated. There should also be a statement specifying the wedding party to be responsible for any damages to the church property, as well as costs, if in addition to facility usage, for custodial services. The signed and dated wedding policy should be filed in the church office with a copy given to the bridal couple.

Premarriage Counseling

Nothing will be more important to the wedding than the time the couple spends in premarital counseling with one of the church's pastors. Not only will this allow time for the pastor to know the couple better so that he might shape his remarks to fit their unique relationship, but primarily it gives opportunity to discuss what it looks like to have a marriage reflecting the beauty of Christ and the church (Eph. 5:22–33). Each couple brings the positives and negatives of their background, personalities, proclivities, and understanding of marital roles into the marriage. So, the pastor should assume nothing, even if the couple has grown up under his pastoral leadership.[7]

What is the pastor trying to accomplish in the premarriage counseling? He cannot teach them everything they need to know about marriage in a few sessions. They will learn much in the years ahead by the give-and-take relational work that furthers sanctification through marriage. I consider ten categories for discussion, recommending resources with some of them, and extending some sessions when it seems more pertinent for the couple.

1. Christian testimony
2. The couple's involvement in the local church
3. The interweaving of personalities and gender distinctions
4. The meaning and purpose of marriage
5. Developing personally and together in spiritual maturity
6. Learning to communicate
7. Money and work
8. Children

---

6. We require the musical selections to be approved by our worship pastor. While each selection may not be Christian music, depending on the church's position, it should be tasteful and appropriate.
7. I utilize a questionnaire that helps to consider the couple's backgrounds, personalities and temperaments, the shape of their relationship, their Christian faith, and plans for finances, children, and views on fidelity in marriage. This shapes the discussion in premarriage counseling. It might also reveal reasons for postponing the wedding or requiring additional counseling or the pastor not agreeing to conduct the wedding ceremony.

9. In-laws
10. Marital intimacy

Depending on areas needing additional attention, I will recommend or give them a book to read, discuss together, and report back to me with some of what they learned.[8] I usually have in mind how many premarriage counseling sessions that I plan to do—two or three. But as I get into the sessions, I may find the need to extend the sessions to address areas with more depth. Approach premarriage counseling with some goals, but realize the couple may have needs that stretch your counseling template. You may also find it useful to bring in another elder or pastor to assist with certain areas you think they can speak on with more clarity.

I have, from time to time, set up follow-up sessions with couples *after* their marriage. Recognizing that only the experience of life together will bring some things to the surface that I think may be latent, I will ask them to meet me for *tweaking* their new marriage.

Generally, at the start of the premarriage counseling I will ask about proposed details for the wedding: time, place, coordinator's name, music, plans for the marriage license, ceremony details, size of the wedding party, and any unusual circumstances I should be made aware of.[9] I make copious notes I can review closer to the rehearsal and ceremony.[10]

---

8. Here are a few possibilities: R. C. Sproul, *The Intimate Marriage: A Practical Guide to Building a Great Marriage* (Phillipsburg, NJ: P&R, 2003); Raymond C. Ortlund Jr., *Marriage and the Mystery of the Gospel* (Wheaton, IL: Crossway, 2016); Paul David Tripp, *What Did You Expect? Redeeming the Realities of Marriage* (Wheaton, IL: Crossway, 2010); Timothy and Kathy Keller, *The Meaning of Marriage: Facing the Complexities of Commitment with the Wisdom of God* (New York: Dutton, 2011); Dave Harvey, *When Sinners Say, "I Do": Discovering the Power of the Gospel for Marriage* (Wapwallopen, PA: Shepherd, 2007); Bryan Chapell, *Each for the Other: Marriage as It's Meant to Be* (Grand Rapids: Baker, 2006); Larry Burkett, *Complete Financial Guide for Young Couples* (Nashville: David C. Cook, 2002); Daniel Akin, *God on Sex: The Creator's Ideas about Love, Intimacy, and Marriage* (Nashville: B&H, 2003); Clifford and Joyce Penner, *The Gift of Sex: A Guide to Sexual Fulfillment* (Nashville: Thomas Nelson, 2003); Gary Thomas, *Sacred Marriage: What If God Designed Marriage to Make Us Holy More Than to Make Us Happy?* (Grand Rapids: Zondervan, 2000).

9. The latter could include details on family dynamics, divorced parents uncomfortable being with each other, someone other than the bride's father giving her away, estranged family members, a Christian couple desiring that the gospel be proclaimed in the ceremony, etc.

10. Some pastors have stand-ins for the rehearsals (e.g., an assistant). While that's understandable in a large congregation with weddings almost every weekend, it seems preferable to be part of the rehearsal in order to make sure that the coordinator and pastor are in sync, as well as to utilize the time for shepherding the couple and the wedding party.

Elements of the Wedding Ceremony

Practices for traditional wedding ceremonies may vary from one denomination to another.[11] Basically, they contain similar elements that may be observed in various orders in different traditions.

1. *The announcement of marriage.* "Dearly beloved, we are gathered in the sight of God, and the presence of these witnesses, to join together this man and this woman in holy matrimony. . . ." The pastor may choose to read Genesis 2:18–25; Psalm 127:1–2; Ephesians 5:22–33; Colossians 3:12–19; Hebrews 13:4; 1 Peter 3:1–7; or John 2:1–11 as part of his announcement and brief explanation of marriage.
2. *The charge to the marital couple.* "I require and charge you both, as you stand in the presence of God, before whom the secrets of all hearts are disclosed, that having duly considered the holy covenant you are about to make, you do now declare before this company your pledge of faith, each to the other."
3. *The marriage homily.* The pastor will offer a biblical foundation for marriage. Here he has opportunity to proclaim the gospel through the picture of marriage in Ephesians 5, offering portions of the bridal couple's testimonies, Jesus's performing his first miracle at the wedding in Cana of Galilee that attested to his redemptive work (John 2), God's intention in the first marriage to prefigure the marriage of Christ to his bride (Gen. 2; Rev. 19, 21–22), or other appropriate passages. As a homily, he needs to keep it brief and to the point. Five to seven minutes is appropriate.
4. *The intention for marriage.* "Will you have this woman [man] to be your wedded wife [husband] to live together in the holy estate of matrimony?"
5. *The giving away of the bride.* "Who gives this woman to be married to this man?" The father (generally) responds, "Her mother and I." When someone other than the father gives the bride away, the response may be "I do."
6. *The marital vows.* "I . . . take you . . . to be my wedded wife [husband]; and I do promise and covenant before God and these witnesses to be your loving and faithful husband [wife], from this day forward, for better, for worse, for richer, for poorer, in sickness and in health, to love and to cherish, till death do us part, according to God's holy ordinance; and thereto I pledge you my faith."

---

11. In this outline, I've borrowed portions of the traditional marriage ceremony from the United Methodist Church, United Presbyterian Church, and Anglo-Genevan Psalter marriage liturgies.

7. *Prayer of consecration.* "Father, we commend this man and woman in the inviolable bonds of marriage, that you might set them apart to serve you by displaying the beauty of Christ and the church in their relationship. . . ."
8. *The exchanging of rings and the ring vows.* "In token and pledge of our constant faith and abiding love, with this ring I thee wed, in the name of the Father, and of the Son, and of the Holy Spirit. Amen."
9. *Pronouncement as husband and wife.* "I pronounce you husband and wife. The Father of all mercies, who by his grace called you to this holy state of marriage, bind you together in true love and faithfulness, and grant you his blessing. Amen."
10. *The husband and wife kiss.*
11. *Prayer and blessing, followed by presentation and recessional.*

With this general framework, the pastor may work with the bridal couple to add or remove elements that will best serve them. As long as he maintains reverence, a biblical view of marriage, the centrality of the gospel to all of life, the mutual responsibilities in marriage, and marriage as a covenant, then changing language, removing some of the traditional phrases, adding appropriate music, and supplying other variations are certainly permissible.[12]

As a final legal act, the pastor needs to sign, date, and mail the marriage license back to the appropriate government agency handling marriage licenses in his state. I make it a practice to have a stamp with me and drop off the completed license at a local post office after the ceremony.[13]

Summary

Preparation remains key to a worshipful marriage ceremony. The church and pastor prepare for a wedding by a well-thought out marriage policy approved by the church's governing body. Thoughtful premarriage counseling prepares the couple for marriage. The pastor prepares by asking questions, taking notes, and understanding his role in discussion with the marital couple. The bridal party and guests prepare to worship and rejoice by a reverent, biblically thoughtful ceremony that sees the gospel as foundational to life and marriage.

---

12. We do not grant requests for communion since it is a church ordinance practiced corporately by the body. I've witnessed parents giving testimonies or expressing blessings for their children during the ceremony. The pastor needs to assess requests for additional elements to the ceremony by whatever maintains the dignity and honor that should be present. Musical contributions often accompany various portions of the ceremony. Here, the pastor needs to give freedom unless he deems it obtrusive and out of place. Discussing these matters early in the premarriage sessions will keep surprises from arising the night of the rehearsal.
13. This practice began when I discovered three days after a ceremony that the license was still in my coat pocket. I did make the delivery within the allowable timeframe!

REFLECTION QUESTIONS

1. How does Genesis 2:17–25 establish a foundation for marriage?

2. What areas should a church's wedding policies address?

3. What should a pastor discuss in premarriage counseling?

4. How does the pastor keep the gospel central to the marriage ceremony?

5. What are the traditional elements to a marriage ceremony?

The Church and Pastoral Ministry

What Is the Church?

W*hat is a church?* We might presume to already know the answer when reading a book on pastoral ministry. Yet how we view the church will shape and hone understanding and practice of pastoral ministry. Without clarity on the church, we fail to have clarity on pastoral ministry.

- If a pastor views the church as merely *a religious organization*, he will treat pastoral ministry as just a job with benefits and a salary.

- If a pastor sees the church as a *cultural phenomenon*, he will treat pastoral ministry as a cultural experiment whose most significant feature will be how the church influences its surroundings. Pastoral ministry, then, centers on shaping the community without reference to making and shepherding disciples.[1]

- If a pastor holds the church as his *personal kingdom*, he will treat pastoral ministry selfishly, focusing on what furthers his career, aims, goals, and image.

- If a pastor considers the church as *a denominational entity*, he will treat pastoral ministry as a means to promote the denomination's programs and objectives and further his chances to better his position.

But if the church is what Jesus describes in Matthew 16:13–20 and 18:15–20, its *raison d'être* differs profoundly from previous misconceptions. Consider the content of how Jesus describes the church in these verses:

---

1. That's not to say that a healthy church does not affect the community. It does, yet that is not primary for the church.

- The church is built upon a clear doctrinal confession of Jesus Christ as God's Son, promised Messiah, and King of an eternal kingdom.

- The church *belongs* to Jesus; he promises to build it, taking on its welfare, existence, and future.

- The church cannot be overpowered by death, which no other institution can claim.

- The church is anchored by apostolic authority and gospel proclamation (after the ascension).

- The church is corporately, not individualistically, focused.

- The church lives with concern for character, faithfulness, obedience, and holiness among its members.

- The church maintains mutual care for one another, especially in how the members reflect obedience to Christ's commands.

- The church exercises authority over those it admits and dismisses.

- The gathered church is assured of Christ's presence as it exercises its disciplinary prerogatives.

And that's just in two passages! What of the other 106 references to the church in the New Testament, not to mention the nearly one hundred metaphors used to describe it?[2] So grand is God's purpose and design for the church that he sent his Son to die for it, secure it, and welcome its members as his people (John 17:6–26; Acts 20:28; 1 Peter 2:9–10). To think on the church, we will consider some definitions, defining marks, and distinguishing metaphors for the church.

---

2. The NT uses ἐκκλησία 114 times, with 109 referring to the church. Out of the 109, at least 96 refer to local assemblies of believers while the others, primarily in Ephesians, point to the universal church. The word typically means "an assembly," which highlights the *local* understanding of the church gathered to worship, pray, fellowship, receive the Word, observe the ordinances (sacraments), serve, and minister. See Mark Dever, "The Church," in *A Theology for the Church*, ed. Daniel L. Akin (Nashville: B&H Academic, 2007), 770–73, and John S. Hammett, *Biblical Foundations for Baptist Churches: A Contemporary Ecclesiology*, 2nd ed. (Grand Rapids: Eerdmans, 2019), 29–34. For metaphors on the church, see Paul S. Minear, *Images of the Church in the New Testament* (Philadelphia: Westminster, 1975).

Definitions of the Church

When asked the meaning of the church, Martin Luther responded, "Why, a seven-year-old child knows what the church is, namely, holy believers and sheep who hear the voice of their Shepherd."[3] He emphasizes a regenerate, holy people with faith in Christ constituting the church. In his *Institutes*, John Calvin states, "The church includes not only the saints presently living on earth, but all the elect from the beginning of the world." He then looks at the present church as those "spread over the earth who profess to worship one God and Christ."[4] Calvin identifies the church as both eternal and actively present.

Nineteenth-century Baptist theologian J. L. Dagg explained, "A Christian Church is an assembly of believers in Christ, organized into a body, according to the Holy Scriptures, for the worship and service of God."[5] Dagg presses the local assembly idea inherent in the term *ekklesia*, with its formation by Scripture for worship and service. The late nineteenth-century church leader Charles Octavius Boothe explained the church's identity as twofold. It includes "the whole family of the redeemed of all ages" and "a body of believers, united together in one place according to the teachings of the New Testament."[6] Boothe mirrors Calvin's assessment of the church, while emphasizing its local gathering.

Theologian Gregg Allison states, "The church is the people of God who have been saved through repentance and faith in Jesus Christ and have been incorporated into his body through baptism with the Holy Spirit."[7] Similarly, but with emphasis on the church's togetherness and service in the world, Mark Dever notes, "The church is the body of people called by God's grace through faith in Christ to glorify him together by serving him in this world."[8] Wayne Grudem puts it simply: "The church is the community of all true believers for all time."[9]

I would define the church like this. The church is God's people redeemed by Jesus Christ and baptized into his body by the Holy Spirit to glorify God through Christ-centered worship, service, and witness. This definition, and the others, tells us about the people called the church. But what marks individual congregations?

3. Timothy George, *Theology of the Reformers*, rev. ed. (Nashville: B&H Academic, 2013), 88.

4. *Calvin*, 4.1.7.

5. J. L. Dagg, *Manual of Church Order* (1858; Harrisonburg, VA: Gano Books, 1990), 74.

6. Charles Octavius Boothe, *Plain Theology for Plain People* (1890; Bellingham, WA: Lexham, 2017), 113–14.

7. Gregg R. Allison, *Sojourners and Strangers: The Doctrine of the Church*, Foundations of Evangelical Theology, ed. John Feinberg (Wheaton, IL: Crossway, 2012), 29.

8. Dever, "Church," 768.

9. Wayne Grudem, *Systematic Theology: An Introduction to Biblical Doctrine* (Grand Rapids: Zondervan, 1994), 853.

Defining Marks of the Church

The earliest nonbiblical, comprehensive marks of the church came in the A.D. 325 Nicene Creed, known as the *notae ecclesiae*: one, holy, catholic (universal), and apostolic church. *One* refers to the church's unity in the oneness of God, countering the claim of Arianism that denied Christ's deity. *Holy* reacted to the third-century Novations and fourth-century Donatists by asserting the church's holiness in its head, Jesus Christ. Ultimately, as the Reformers noted, it points to the church's holy status from justification onward. *Catholic* or *universal* indicates a shared faith and mission in a definitive orthodoxy among all people groups. *Apostolic* refers to the church's doctrine governed by the revelation of Holy Scripture of which the apostles were foundational (Eph. 2:20; 2 Peter 1:16–21). In other words, to be apostolic means that we hold to the same teaching proclaimed by the apostles revealed in Scripture.[10]

The Reformers did some of their finest work on identifying what constitutes a true church. Calvin, while wanting to show grace and gentleness toward struggling churches, saw the marks of the church in minimalistic fashion. He writes, "Wherever we see the Word of God purely preached and heard, and the sacraments administered according to Christ's institution, there, it is not to be doubted, a church of God exists."[11] The gospel proclaimed and the sacraments observed *marked* true churches even when these churches struggled in other areas. Later, Calvin explained that Satan attacks these two marks more than anything, for he knows destroying them will remove the church's distinction as a true congregation of God. He explained that simply wearing the name *church* did not make it one. Rather, "Every congregation that claims the name 'church' must be tested by this standard as by a touchstone. If in Word and sacraments it has the order approved by the Lord, it will not deceive. . . . But again, if, devoid of Word and sacraments, it advertises the name of church, we must just as scrupulously beware such deceits, as we must avoid rashness and pride on the other side."[12]

Martin Bucer, Calvin's mentor in Strasbourg, agreed with these two marks but added, "There cannot be a Church without *ein Bann* (excommunication)."[13] As Paul Avis explains concerning Bucer, "The quality of Christian discipleship becomes a mark of the Church. Love and discipline must be added to word

---

10. This section closely follows Hammett, *Biblical Foundations*, 57–69 and Dever, "Church," 775–78. While space does not allow for delving into the various interpretations of the *notae*, the Reformers corrected some post-Nicene interpretations, including reacting against Augustine's "mixed body" explanation of the church to reinforce its holiness by the status wrought in justification. Some viewed apostolicity as apostolic succession, an idea not found in Scripture and soundly countered by the Reformers.
11. *Calvin*, 4.1.9.
12. *Calvin*, 4.1.11.
13. Paul D. L. Avis, *The Church in the Theology of the Reformers* (Eugene, OR: Wipf & Stock, 2002), 45.

and sacrament to form the true church."[14] Bucer found the heart of what's involved in a church exercising its responsibility to discipline (formative and corrective) by adding "the possession of suitable ministers" as another mark of the church. He believed preaching the gospel and administering the sacraments required suitable ministers who would also be engaged in shepherding the church in "righteousness and holiness of life."[15]

English Puritans William Perkins and Thomas Cartwright came close to agreeing with Bucer but differed by explaining discipline as necessary for the church's well-being (*bene esse*) but not its being or existence (*esse*).[16] John Knox, the hearty Scottish reformer, agreed with Bucer that church discipline rightly administered should be added to the two primary marks.[17]

John Hammett's summary of the Reformers' views on the marks of the church clarifies, "If it [the church] loses the gospel message, a group of people is no longer a true church."[18] That should be uppermost in identifying a true church and evaluating pastoral preaching.

Mark Dever takes an expanded look at the marks of the church. While agreeing with these two essential marks, Dever also identifies nine marks "that set off healthy churches from true but more sickly ones."[19] While the Reformers sought to recognize *any* true church by the mark of gospel proclamation, however weak and sickly, Dever seeks to identify nine marks that, when practiced, tend toward improving and strengthening the church's health. He does not hold that churches neglecting these nine marks are not true churches—as long as the gospel is faithfully proclaimed and the ordinances observed—but rather, when neglected, they will not be *healthy* churches.[20] He identifies them as follows: expositional preaching, biblical theology, the gospel, a biblical understanding of conversion, a biblical understanding of evangelism, a biblical understanding of church membership, biblical church discipline, a concern for discipleship and growth, and biblical church leadership. His work continues to help pastors build on gospel proclamation while improving church health and, consequently, its witness in the world.

---

14. Avis, *Church in the Theology of the Reformers*, 48.
15. Avis, *Church in the Theology of the Reformers*, 48–49. While he added "the possession of suitable ministers" as more of an explanatory mark, Bucer is still known for agreeing with Calvin but adding church discipline as essential to identify a true church. Apart from discipline exercised, the church fails to be the body of Christ "gathered by the Spirit of Christ" (49).
16. Avis, *Church in the Theology of the Reformers*, 46.
17. Avis, *Church in the Theology of the Reformers*, 50–51.
18. Hammett, *Biblical Foundations*, 70.
19. Mark E. Dever, *Nine Marks of a Healthy Church*, expanded ed. (Wheaton, IL: Crossway, 2004), 24.
20. Dever, "Church," 778–91.

Distinguishing Metaphors for the Church

Grudem points out that the multiplied use of NT metaphors explaining the church means we need to guard against focusing "exclusively on any one."[21] With so many varying metaphors—ninety-six according to Paul Minear—pastoral preaching should broaden a congregation's understanding and joy in thinking of the church that Jesus redeemed and secured.[22] It should also help pastors focus their ministries in shepherding the church. Here we will look at four metaphors used for the church.[23]

1. The People of God

Both testaments use the phrase "My own possession" or "My people" to refer to God's people he has elected and redeemed for himself (Exod. 19:5–6; Hos. 1:10; 2:23; Titus 2:14; 1 Peter 2:9–10).[24] The language does not mean two *different* people but one people of God who became his possession by the redemptive work of Jesus Christ (Titus 2:14). Peter explicitly refers to descriptive phrases for Israel *now* applied to the church: "a chosen race, a royal priesthood, a holy nation, a people for God's own possession" (1 Peter 2:9). Paul ties this together with his explanation about God's elect people from out of Israel—correcting Gentile pride (Rom. 11:1–2)—united as one with his elect from the Gentiles (Rom. 15:7–12). The apostle did not hesitate making application to the Corinthian church as God's people, citing Leviticus 26:12 and Jeremiah 32:38, thus referring to his people in both testaments as one people (2 Cor. 6:16).[25]

As the people of God, the church has its identity in God's gracious act of redeeming a particular people from all of those in the world to be his own possession (Titus 2:14). Belonging to the Lord, then, affects the way the church lives out the gospel in contrast to the rest of the community. It assures the church of God's care, while also urging perseverance as his people. Pastors

---

21. Grudem, *Systematic Theology*, 859.
22. While some of Minear's choices in *Images of the Church* may be disagreeable to other interpreters, most give visuals for the church to better understand who they are in God's sight and mission.
23. Other metaphors to consider: bond-servants, bride of Christ, fellow citizens, flock of God, general assembly, God's building, Israel of God, new creation. Also, consider the use of terms such as saints, brethren, friends, chosen of God, and disciples of the Lord used synonymously with the church, expressing some distinguishing truths about the body of Christ.
24. Hammett explains the continuity between OT and NT people of God while holding to discontinuity due to the indwelling Spirit making "the church the new creation of God" (*Baptist Foundations*, 39–42).
25. Paul also draws the conclusion in this passage that God dwelling among his people in the tabernacle (temple) now makes reference to the church as that temple (see also Eph. 2:21–22).

must think of how their sermons, personal example, and leadership offer the reassurance and distinction as God's people.

2. The Body of Christ

Body of Christ language looks at the *nature* of those in relationship to Christ and the *function* as those united in Christ.[26] They differ in emphasis and approach but relate to each other. As to the *nature* of the body, Paul calls the church "His body" in which God reconciles Jews and Gentiles into "one body" through the death of Christ (Eph. 1:23; 2:16). Jesus is "the head of the church, He Himself being the Savior of the body" (Eph. 5:23). So closely does the body relate to Christ that Paul compares the husband and wife relationship to it as the one flesh union mirrors "the church" as "members of His body" (Eph. 5:28–29). Jesus is "head of the body, the church" (Col. 1:18, 23).

Consequently, by *function*, the church must see each member as sovereignly placed for the good of the entire body (1 Cor. 12:18). This calls for members to exercise their spiritual gifts for the good of others (Rom. 12:4–8; 1 Cor. 12:7–11), while also holding each member in love and regard (1 Cor. 12:14–27).

Pastors, then, will learn to prioritize building healthy relationships in the body. Unity must be nurtured by the way members treat one another and how they serve each other through their gifts and ministries. Equipping the church for ministry will build up the body of Christ into a healthy church (Eph. 4:12–16; Col. 2:19).

3. The Household of God

The general term *household of God* encompasses a number of phrases that express either directly or metaphorically the idea that the church is the family of God. The writer of Hebrews calls the church "His house" (Heb. 3:4–6). Most of the terms express a *family* concept: "children of God" (John 1:12; Rom. 8:16; 9:8; 1 John 3:1–2); "children" (Heb. 2:13–14); "sons of God" (Rom. 8:14; 9:23–26); "sons" (2 Cor. 6:18); "heirs of God" (Rom. 8:17; Gal. 4:7; Eph. 1:18); "beloved of God" (Rom. 1:7; Col 3:12). While the writers infer nothing biological, the family ideas offer some of the richest assurances of relationship to God that can be understood in normal family constructs.

The family language urges pastors to help the congregation to understand the church as family.[27] That changes the dynamics of relationships from people meeting weekly to brothers and sisters learning to live life and serve

---

26. Grudem notes, "We should not confuse these two metaphors in 1 Corinthians 12 and Ephesians 4, but keep them distinct" (*Systematic Theology*, 858–59), i.e., the former uses *body* in a functional way, as with the use of spiritual gifts; the latter considers the organic nature of the church.

27. For a superb treatment of this subject, see Joseph Hellerman, *When the Church Was a Family: Recapturing Jesus' Vision for Authentic Christian Community* (Nashville: B&H Books, 2009).

Christ together. This calls for counseling and exhorting when family relationships fray. It demands teaching on the selfless love and the practice of forgiveness to characterize the church (Eph. 4:29–5:2).

4. The Temple of God

Since the temple held vital significance in the OT economy as the place
where God dwelled among his people (Exod. 40:34–35; 2 Chron. 5:14–6:2),[28]
the temple motif fittingly expresses the Holy Spirit dwelling in the church
(Eph. 2:21–22).[29] Just as the indwelling Holy Spirit characterizes true believers
(Rom. 8:9–11), so, too, his indwelling characterizes a true church corporately
(2 Cor. 6:16). Peter's description of "a spiritual house for a holy priesthood to
offer up spiritual sacrifices acceptable to God through Jesus Christ" alludes to
a *new* temple—the church—with Jesus Christ as the "precious cornerstone"
upon which the whole church exists (Ps. 118:22–24; Isa. 28:16; 1 Peter 2:4–
8). The temple language leaves the church with a deeper consciousness of its
priestly role before God—not to offer animal sacrifices, for that is fulfilled
in Christ (Heb. 10:1–18), but to praise him and to proclaim his gospel (Heb.
13:15; 1 Peter 2:9; Rev. 1:6; 5:10).

The church as the temple of the Lord helps the pastor understand the
significance of every worship gathering. The Lord has come near his people
who gather to offer sacrifices of praise and to proclaim his excellence, as well
as to do the priestly work of intercession for one another. The pastor, therefore, labors to make sure no member of the church sees himself or herself as
a spectator, but rather that they all see themselves as priests serving in the
temple of the Lord.

Summary

Seeing the church as the people of God redeemed by Christ and indwelled
by the Holy Spirit changes the dynamics of every gathering. Rather than
having a complacent attitude toward the church, the faithful pastor needs to
feel the wonder that the Lord has been pleased to let him serve his Spirit-
indwelt people. Not every church that advertises the name, as Calvin noted,
is a true church. Rather, genuine churches must be marked by regular gospel
proclamation and proper administration of the ordinances. God's estimation
of the church redeemed by Christ looms so large that no one term can adequately explain it. It takes metaphors and images to help us grasp the wonder
of God's family—the church.

---

28. See Ezekiel 37:24–28 for how this works out through Jesus as the Davidic heir.
29. The root stem -τηριον in κατοικητήριον, translated as "dwelling," indicates a "place
    where something happens" (BDAG, 534–35). This indicates that the Spirit's dwelling in the
    church is never passive.

REFLECTION QUESTIONS

1. After reading through the various definitions of the church, how would you define it?

2. Why is any brief definition of the church inadequate?

3. What are the *notae ecclesia* and their significance?

4. What two marks of the church must be present for a church to be a true church?

5. What metaphor for the church did you find most helpful in understanding better how to do pastoral ministry?

What Kind of Authority Does Scripture Give to Pastors of Local Churches?

Authority carries broad meaning, evoking various responses and reactions. For those living under a dictatorship, authority expresses absolute life and death power over a people's daily existence. Quite differently, for those electing governing officials every two to six years, authority has limits controlled by a constitution and elections. We may complain about elected officials misusing authority, but those kinds of complaints don't take place in a dictatorship. Dictators misuse authority on a totally different scale.

Abuse of authority gets enough attention to spur complaints about all authority. Yet that fails to consider that every aspect of corporate life—public and private—must have some measure of authority to continue to exist. Levels of authority remain necessary for peace, productivity, discipline, and order in society. Company management exercises authority to maintain the company's goals and employees' productivity. School administrators hold authority over students and staff in order to maintain a safe learning environment. Even a pickup basketball game at a local gymnasium must have someone in charge—hence exercising authority—to keep the teams rotating and fair.

Not surprisingly, a church needs a level of authority to maintain membership, stay focused on its mission, manage its ministries and activities, and ensure its ongoing spiritual maturity and unity. But how does that authority work out in church life? How do those appointed as pastors and elders exercise authority? We will investigate this subject by looking at textual implications for pastoral authority, the meaning of delegated authority, and the use of authority.

Textual Implications of Pastoral/Elder Authority

Where do we find biblical warrant for pastoral authority? An Israelite king and local church pastor have little in common except faithfulness to God in the sphere of their calling. Even the authority Jesus gave the Twelve and the Seventy does not constitute the basis for understanding the breadth and limits of pastoral authority (Luke 9:1–11; 10:1–20). Jesus built his church on the apostles and prophets exercising authority he had given them to speak the foundational truths of the Christian faith (Matt. 16:17–19; 1 Cor. 3:5–11; Eph. 2:19–22; 3:1–13). We learn from them about trusting Christ in our mission, but we guard against claiming authority uniquely given to them for a time. Benjamin Merkle rightly points out, "The New Testament does not explicitly spell out how much authority the elders [pastors] of a local church should have."[1] That leaves us to consider the extent of and limits on pastoral authority implied by a few biblical texts.

1. Have Charge Over, Manage, Rule (1 Thess. 5:12–13; 1 Tim. 3:4–5; 5:17)

Paul writes in his letter to the Thessalonians, "But we request of you, brethren, that you appreciate those who diligently labor among you, *and have charge over you in the Lord [prohistēmi]* and give you instruction, and that you esteem them very highly in love because of their work" (1 Thess. 5:12–13). The NIV translates the key phrase as "who care for you in the Lord." The title of *elder, overseer,* or *pastor* is not used in this earliest Pauline epistle,[2] as the titles for church leaders had yet to be worked out.[3] Years later, in 1 Timothy 3:4–5, Paul compares an elder managing (*prohistēmi*) his household with taking care of (*epimeleomai*)[4] God's household. Just as a father manages his household by leading and showing care to his family, elders/pastors will do the same with God's household. Given the broad range of *prohistēmi* in the Greek language, Paul uses the terms as synonyms to emphasize that pastoral leadership and management focus on taking care of those under their charge.

In 1 Thessalonians 5:12, Paul identifies the pastors as those diligently *laboring* among them, *exercising leadership* over them, and *instructing* them. The word *prohistēmi*, translated as "have charge over," conveys the idea "to place or put or stand before,"[5] indicating a level of authority for a particular purpose in a group's existence. While metaphorically implying leadership, it certainly indicates one standing before the church to instruct them in God's Word. Much of the care shown by pastors will take place by exercising the

---

1. Benjamin L. Merkle, "The Biblical Role of Elders," in *Baptist Foundations: Church Government for an Anti-Institutional Age*, eds. Mark Dever and Jonathan Leeman (Nashville: B&H Academic, 2015), 276. See also Benjamin L. Merkle, *40 Questions About Elders and Deacons* (Grand Rapids: Kregel Academic, 2008), 95–100.
2. Charles A. Wannamaker, *Commentary on 1 and 2 Thessalonians*, NIGTC (Grand Rapids: Eerdmans, 1990), 38.
3. Luke identifies "elders" in Acts 11:30 and 14:23, but that would have been written after Paul's first imprisonment, at least ten or eleven years after the apostle penned 1 Thessalonians in Corinth.
4. Jesus used the same term to describe the Samaritan's care for the wounded man, Luke 10:34–35; ἐπιμελέομαι (BDAG, 375).
5. The prefix πρό, meaning "before," joins the verb ἵστημι, "to place, put, stand."

authority of proclaiming God's Word. This authority does not inherently reside in the pastor but in the Word of God he proclaims. J. L. Dagg makes clear, "The only rule which they [pastors] have a right to apply is that of God's Word; and the only obedience which they have a right to exact is voluntary."[6]

The NIV's translation "care for" also expresses the shape of this authority by serving a congregation in a shepherding role. Silva writes, "But 'to stand before' can also imply protection and aid, so the vb. [verb] takes on such meanings as 'to help, support, guard, care for.'"[7] Without contradiction in meanings, with the ancient Greek usage in military and political realms for someone heading or leading or directing others, Silva concludes on 1 Thessalonians 5:12, "The apostle clearly is making ref. [reference] to a group exercising leadership in the church."[8]

The same prominent idea appears in Paul's use of *prohistēmi* in 1 Timothy 5:17: "The elders who *rule* well are to be considered worthy of double honor, especially those who work hard at preaching and teaching."[9] Some elders ruled more effectively than others, particularly through their ministry of preaching and teaching. The authority indicated by "rule" did not mean dictatorial powers over the congregation. Instead, as John Hammett explains, "The way leaders exercise their authority in the New Testament is never dictatorial but with a humble spirit, open to the input of others and seeking to 'lead the church into spiritually minded consensus.'"[10] *Prohistēmi* expresses authority exercised for the care, protection, and nurturing of the church.

2. Lead, Leading (Heb. 13:7, 17, 24)

New Testament writers frequently use *hēgeomai* with two distinct meanings. First, the term can express "to regard," "to consider," and "to count,"[11] indicating *a way of thinking*. Second, reinforcing that context determines the meaning of words; the word can identify someone "leading" or "governing," indicating *authority*. In Matthew 2:6, both plural and singular use of *hēgeomai* identifies "*leaders* of Judah" and "a *Ruler* who will shepherd [*poimēn*, pastor] My people Israel." When Jesus settled a dispute with the disciples on who should be regarded the greatest among them, he declared, "The greatest

---

6. J. L. Dagg, *Manual of Church Order* (1858; Harrisonburg, VA: Gano Books, 1990), 264.

7. *NIDNTTE*, προΐστημι, 4:140.

8. *NIDNTTE*, προΐστημι, 4:140–41. By "group" he refers to plural leadership.

9. The NIV, as a dynamic rather than literal translation, expresses the meaning by translating it, "The elders who direct the affairs of the church well are worthy of double honor." The softening of "rule" by "direct the affairs" does not change the meaning in the least.

10. D. A. Carson, "Church, Authority in the," in *EDT*, 72; quoted in John S. Hammett, *Biblical Foundations for Baptist Churches: A Contemporary Ecclesiology*, 2nd ed. (Grand Rapids: Kregel Academic, 2019), 193–94.

11. Acts 26:2; 2 Cor. 9:5; Phil. 2:3, 6, 25; 3:7, 8; 1 Thess. 3:15; 1 Tim. 6:1; Heb. 10:29; 11:11, 26; James 1:2; 2 Peter 1:13; 2:13; 3:9, 15.

among you must become like the youngest, and the *leader* like the servant" (Luke 22:26). The combination of leader with servant maintains the same emphasis found with *prohistēmi*—a leader attentive in caring for others.[12]

With pastoral implication, the writer of Hebrews uses the term, translated as *led* and *leaders*, three times (Heb. 13:7, 17, 24). Borrowing from the civil and military world, the word means "to be in a supervisory capacity; lead, guide."[13] The writer repeats the same verb structure, roughly translated as "those who are themselves continuing to lead."[14] Each identifies a *plurality* of spiritual leaders working among them. What did this work involve? They engaged in leadership, taught God's Word, provided an example of faithfulness to Christ, and watched over the congregation's spiritual life (Heb. 13:7, 17). For their charge before God, they would give an account to "the great Shepherd of the sheep" (Heb. 13:17, 20). In responding to their leadership, the congregation was to remember the leaders with regard to their teaching, imitate their example of faith, obey and submit to their soul care, and do all without complaint or rebellion (Heb. 13:7, 17).

The call to "obey" (*peithō*) and "submit" (*hupeikō*) to these spiritual leaders has to do with the realm of spiritual care and watchfulness, not control or dominance over the flock.[15] Dagg notes, "So the spiritual rulers under Christ have no coercive power over the persons or property of those under their authority."[16] Their authority exists through proclaiming God's Word as they shepherd God's people, validating the authority through exemplary character and conduct while serving to care for the spiritual health of the church.

3. Elder, Overseer, and Pastor (Titus 1:5–9; 1 Tim. 3:1–7; Eph. 4:11)

The titles *elder*, *overseer*, and *pastor* identify the same local church office while emphasizing particular aspects of their role and authority in the church.[17] An elder (*presbuteros*) in ancient Jewish life had authority over a family or clan. He represented them in the larger gatherings of the tribe. The wisdom that came

---

12. *Hēgeomai* (ἡγέομαι) is translated as "*governor* over Egypt" in Acts 7:10 and "*chief* speaker" in Acts 14:12. Judas and Silas were called "*leading* men among the brethren" (Acts 15:22).
13. BDAG, ἡγέομαι, 434.
14. Present middle participle, third person plural: the middle voice stresses the subject's action. So, he emphasizes the act of continuing to lead the flock.
15. Merkle points out, "The normal word for 'obey' or 'to subject oneself' is *hupotassō*, which is a stronger word. Although the verb *peithō* demands obedience, it is 'the obedience that is won through persuasive conversation.' The second command, 'submit' (*hupeikō*), is found only here in the New Testament and means 'to submit to one's authority'" ("Biblical Role of Elders," 276). He cites William L. Lane, *Hebrews 9–13*, WBC 47B (Dallas: Word, 1991), 554.
16. Dagg, *Manual*, 264.
17. For consideration of elder and overseer as one office, see Benjamin L. Merkle, *The Elder and Overseer: One Office in the Early Church*, SBL 57, ed. Hemchand Gossai (New York: Peter Lang, 2003). He explains that the term "elder" describes the character of the office and "overseer" the function, 156.

with age and experience gave him respect with those he led. The emphasis on leadership, respect, maturity, and wisdom carry over into the NT church usage of the term, noted especially by the character qualities necessary for the office, along with teaching gifts (1 Tim. 3:1–7; Titus 1:5–9). Character and wisdom rather than age seems most prominent in the NT usage.[18]

Overseers (*episkopos*) arose from Greek life, with the concept of their duties built on a word meaning "one who watches." The term developed to identify those watching over or giving leadership to civil, military, and religious groups.[19] The NT writers (Luke, Paul, and Peter) swap use of the terms *overseer* and *elder* to indicate they refer to the same church office (Acts 20:17–31; Luke also uses the verbal form of *pastor* in 20:28; cf. Titus 1:5–9; 1 Peter 5:1–4—with Peter using verbal forms of *overseer* and *pastor*). Jesus is called the "Overseer of your souls" (1 Peter 2:25), indicating watchfulness in the office.[20]

Pastor (*poimēn*), the most familiar term for the office of leadership in the local church, can be found nominally (Eph. 4:11) and verbally (Acts 20:28; 1 Peter 5:2) as reference to the NT office. Elsewhere, the NT translates the term as "shepherd," indicating that just as the Lord as our Shepherd watches over us spiritually, those whom he appoints to this office do the same on his behalf (John 10). The pastor feeds, nurtures, and protects the flock.[21]

Each term—*elder, overseer,* and *pastor*—carries the idea of authority in that leading, watching over, nurturing, and protecting the church can only take place when the congregation recognizes pastoral authority established by the Lord of the church.

The three groups of terms convey a level of pastoral authority focused on the ministry of the Word and spiritual care for the church. Claim to more extensive authority cannot be validated by Scripture, and so must not be practiced in the church.

Delegated Authority

Peter reminds his fellow elders that they ultimately serve "the Chief Shepherd" in their pastoral office, not themselves (1 Peter 5:1–4). Paul told the Ephesian elders to carry out their pastoral duties with consciousness that the church did not belong to them but to Christ, who purchased the church with his own blood (Acts 20:28). Even the obedience and submission owed to these spiritual leaders comes with the understanding they will give an account for the way they've shepherded and cared for God's flock (Heb. 13:17). These inherent *limits to pastoral authority* should humble those serving in the

---

18. See *NIDNTTE*, πρεσβύτερος, 4:127–35; Phil A. Newton and Matt Schmucker, *Elders in the Life of the Church: Rediscovering the Biblical Model for Church Leadership* (Grand Rapids: Kregel Ministry, 2014), 46–47.
19. *NIDNTTE*, ἐπίσκοπος, 2:248–52.
20. Newton and Schmucker, *Elders*, 48.
21. Newton and Schmucker, *Elders*, 49.

office while building confidence in the church to regard their authority. "They derive their authority from the Word of God," Merkle notes, "and when they stray from that Word, they abandon their God-given authority."[22] As servant leaders, they exercise duties with a view to reporting to the Chief Shepherd. Jesus has therefore given them authority *under his watchful accountability* to shepherd his people. The Word of God, then, limits the church's obedience and submission to their pastors/elders. Pastors have no room under the guise of pastoral authority to manipulate, coerce, or use guilt tactics to get the church to act or follow them. That's not authority; it's abuse. "All coercion is inconsistent with the nature of the authority intrusted . . . to them," as Dagg explains.[23] Ultimately, the church obeys Christ, not mere men.[24]

But churches must recognize this God-given office to care for their souls. While waiting for the Shepherd's appearance (Titus 2:13–14; 1 Peter 5:4), his undershepherds give attention to training, equipping, teaching, guarding, and caring for the flock. Despising them in their ministry of the Word equates to despising the Good Shepherd who appointed them to serve the church until he returns.[25] Rather than fearing pastoral authority, the church must rejoice in it as a gift from God.

Use of Authority

A few guidelines on the use of pastoral authority may help pastors toward wise use of authority while alleviating the congregation's fear of authority.

1. Authority under the Congregation's Authority

Pastors/elders must not view themselves as holding ultimate authority in the church. Even their appointment to office comes via the church's recommendation and approval (Acts 14:23).[26] If they prove derelict in office, the congregation can remove them. Paul reminds congregations not to accept unwarranted accusations against elders, while also warning elders that "continue in sin" of potential public discipline before the ultimate human authority—the church (1 Tim. 5:19–20; Matt. 18:15–20).

2. Authority Exercised in Preaching and Teaching

The foremost passages indicating pastoral authority *also* stress that it happens primarily through the ministry of the Word (1 Thess. 5:12–13; 1 Tim. 5:17; Heb. 13:7). Merkle writes, "The authority that elders possess is not so

---

22. Merkle, *40 Questions About Elders and Deacons*, 97.
23. Dagg, *Manual*, 264.
24. Martin Bucer, *Concerning the True Care of Souls*, trans. Peter Beale (1538; Edinburgh: Banner of Truth Trust, 2009), 209.
25. Bucer, *True Care of Souls*, 202.
26. Simon Kistemaker writes, "The term *to appoint* actually means to approve by a show of hands in a congregational meeting" (*Acts*, NTC [Grand Rapids: Baker, 1990], 525,).

much derived from their office but from the duties they perform"[27] (e.g., preaching, teaching, and shepherding).

3. Authority Demonstrated in Spiritual Leadership

Those called to watch over, care for, exhort, reprove, correct, and give direction to the flock do so as spiritual leaders (Heb. 13:7, 17). The Lord of the church entrusts the care of his people to those appointed as elders/pastors of the church. That kind of authority comes from Christ in the limited realm of spiritual leadership, never life control.

4. Authority Shown in Humble Service

Just as Jesus came to humbly serve among his disciples and the masses, pastors must follow this same example (Matt. 20:28; Luke 22:26; John 13; Phil. 2:5–8). Pastoral authority finds acceptance through its humble service.

5. Authority Humbly Accepted, Not Demanded

Pastors have no reason to *demand* that a church submits to them. If they fall into this pattern, then humble service is nowhere to be found. In the role of shepherding the flock willingly and eagerly, "proving to be examples to the flock," pastors (gradually) receive authority from the people they serve (1 Peter 5:2–3).

6. Authority Focused on the Church's Health, Maturity, and Mission

Pastoral authority is no cul-de-sac; it must be channeled. It focuses on leading the church toward healthy maturity as a people engaged in service to one another and gospel mission to the world (Matt. 20:19–20; Eph. 4:11–16).

7. Authority Always Operating in Plurality

Pride and deceitfulness of heart can lead a pastor to misuse authority. But, when serving in a plurality of pastors/elders, as evident in NT practice, the potential misuse of authority gets crushed by the accountability of brothers, united and humbly serving Christ's flock (Acts 14:23; Titus 1:5).[28]

8. Authority Anticipates the Day of Accounting

Authority delegated, not inherently derived, means the one that did the delegating will call for an accounting. Jesus Christ delegates pastoral authority, and also holds pastors accountable for how they use their authority in serving the flock (Heb. 13:17; 1 Peter 5:4).

---

27. Merkle, "Biblical Role of Elders," 279.
28. Newton and Schmucker, *Elders*, 50–54.

Summary

With *authority* as a touchy word in our culture, pastors must approach its use with humility and servant-heartedness as those faithfully preaching and teaching God's Word. Recognizing the church as the ultimate authority humanly speaking,[29] pastors preach, lead, and care for the church with authority entrusted by the Lord. Passages regarding the church's spiritual leaders affirm the limits and extent of authority that comes with the pastoral office. Authority must always be measured by the consciousness of giving an account to the Lord for its use.

REFLECTION QUESTIONS

1. What is implied by the phrase in 1 Thessalonians 5:12, "have charge over you in the Lord"?

2. What pastoral practices accompany those leading the church (Heb. 13:7, 17)?

3. In what ways do the titles *elder*, *overseer*, and *pastor* convey authority?

4. Why is pastoral/elder plurality critical to good use of authority?

5. What role does the church have in response to pastoral authority?

---

29. Hammett, *Biblical Foundations*, 157.

How Is Good Pastoral Ministry Tied Directly to Healthy Ecclesiology?

Every church has an ecclesiology. That is, every church holds particular views and understandings of the church that work out in the congregation's practice. The source of these ideas might arise from the Bible, tradition, cultural concepts, government, leadership groups, or authoritarian rulers (religious or political).

Every church has an ecclesiology, but not every church holds or practices healthy ecclesiology. To practice *healthy* ecclesiology, the adjective must be qualified. Healthy ecclesiology cannot be measured by a full calendar of church activities or success in attracting large numbers or burgeoning financial resources. A church may possess all these things and not even be a true church. A true church must preach the gospel and rightly observe the church's ordinances.[1] Yet even those churches may not be healthy.

A healthy church evidences the qualities and practices we see in the faithful NT churches. Now, as then, despite persecution, struggles, errant members, doctrinal questions, and missteps with relationships, because these churches understand who they are as the body of Christ and the people of God, they can work through the problems toward good health. Each church has pastors and elders helping lead in the path of healthy ecclesiological life through preaching God's Word, shepherding the flock, and modeling the Christian life. Good pastoral ministry leads to healthy ecclesiology. We will

---

1. For a brief historical sketch of the marks identifying a true church from a false one, even if the true churches fail to be healthy, see Mark Dever, *Nine Marks of a Healthy Church*, expanded ed. (Wheaton, IL: Crossway, 2004), 21–33. While acknowledging more marks, he identifies nine marks of a church "that set off healthy churches from true but more sickly ones" (24). For an extended treatment of the Reformers' view of ecclesiology, see Paul D. L. Avis, *The Church in the Theology of the Reformers* (Eugene, OR: Wipf & Stock, 2002).

examine this proposition by considering the nature of healthy ecclesiology and the intersection of pastoral ministry and healthy ecclesiology.

The Nature of Healthy Ecclesiology

The fourth-century Nicene Creed used four adjectives to describe the nature of the church: one, holy, catholic, and apostolic.[2] No doubt, through the centuries various traditions have qualified the implications in the four *notae ecclesiae*, especially evident in the way the Protestant Reformation took issue with traditional Roman Catholic views on the church.[3] More recently, Mark Dever points out that since the late 1980s, various writers identify at least forty "prescriptions . . . for the problems of the local church" and offer their slant on a healthy church.[4] Some have biblical moorings; others do not.

What did Jesus have in mind when he called the body of redeemed people that he would build "the church"? The term *church* (*ekklēsia*) came out of the secular world, meaning "assembly." We find it used for a mob gathered in confusion (Acts 19:32) and citizens gathering to conduct legal issues (Acts 19:39). "Assembly," as Hammett notes, must be considered in some of the NT usage of the word as expressing "the gathered body" (Acts 14:23; 15:3–4, 22). The NT writers also borrowed from the Hebrew word *qāhāl*, "those who have heard the call and are following it," as they used *ekklēsia*, with each context weighting the emphasis. This background fits well with the etymology of *ekklēsia* (the prefix *ek*, "out," and root word, *klētos*, "call"), "the called out ones."[5]

To understand the nature of a healthy church, NT descriptions of "the called out ones" or the "assembly" of the saints will help pastors keep biblical characteristics of healthy ecclesiology in view while shepherding their churches to health. What does a healthy New Testament church look like?

- A self-disciplining community (Matt. 16:18–19; 18:15–20; 1 Cor. 5:1–13; Gal. 6:1)

- A Spirit-empowered and witnessing community (Acts 1:8; 4:23–31; Eph. 6:18–20)

---

2. John S. Hammett, *Biblical Foundations for Baptist Churches: A Contemporary Ecclesiology*, 2nd ed. (Grand Rapids: Kregel Academic, 2019), 57–69. See also "Defining Marks of the Church" in Question 29, "What Is the Church?"

3. For a Reformer's clarification on the nature and practice of the church, see John Calvin, *The Necessity of Reforming the Church* (Dallas: Protestant Heritage, 1995).

4. Dever actually calls these forty "a small sampling from recent authors" (*Nine Marks*, 249).

5. Hammett, *Biblical Foundations*, 29–30, citing L. Coenen, "Church," in *New International Dictionary of New Testament Theology*, ed. Colin Brown (Grand Rapids: Zondervan, 1975), 1:292–96.

- A Spirit-filled community (Acts 2:1–4; Eph. 5:15–21)[6]

- A worshiping, fellowshipping, praying, and selfless community (Acts 2:41–47; 4:32–35; 1 Tim. 2:1–8; 1 Peter 2:4–10)

- A sending community (Acts 13:1–3; 15:36–41; 20:4; Phil. 2:25–30; 3 John 5–8)

- A theological community (Acts 15:6–35; Eph. 2:19–20; 1 Tim. 3:14–16; 2 John 4, 9–11; 3 John 3; Jude 3)

- A hospitable community (Acts 28:14; Rom. 12:13; Titus 3:13–14; Philem. 22; 3 John 5–8)

- A serving community (Mark 10:41–45; John 13:12–17; Acts 4:32–35; 6:1–6; Rom. 12:10–13)

- A holy community (Rom. 1:7; 1 Cor. 1:2; Eph. 1:1; Phil. 1:1; Col. 1:2; 1 Peter 2:4–5, 9–10; 3 John 11)

- A Spirit-gifted community (Rom. 12:3–8; 1 Cor. 1:7; 12:7)

- A familial community (Rom. 12:10; 16:1–16; 1 Cor. 16:20; Gal. 4:5; 6:10; Philem. 7)[7]

- A generous community (Acts 2:44–45; 4:32–37; 1 Cor. 16:1–2; 2 Cor. 8–9; Phil. 1:5; 4:15–18; Heb. 13:16)

- A burden-bearing community (Gal. 6:2–5)

- A Holy Spirit–indwelled community (1 Cor. 3:16–17; Eph. 2:21–22)

- A unity-, maturity-, and love-pursuing community (Eph. 4:13–16)

- A kind, tender-hearted, and forgiving community (Rom. 15:7; Eph. 4:31–32; Phil. 4:2–3)

---

6. Derek Tidball, *Ministry by the Book: New Testament Patterns for Pastoral Leadership* (Downers Grove, IL: IVP Academic, 2008), 87–88.
7. For a detailed look at the church as family, see Joseph H. Hellerman, *When the Church Was a Family: Recapturing Jesus' Vision for Authentic Christian Community* (Nashville: B&H Academic, 2009). Note also, as with biological brothers and sisters, those in the Christian family must work at getting along and loving one another (e.g., 1 Cor. 1:10–13; 3:1–9).

- A sin-fighting community (Rom. 6:12–19; Eph. 4:17–5:14; 6:10–20; 1 Peter 5:6–9)

- A faithfully shepherded community (Acts 14:23; 1 Tim. 3:1–13; Titus 1:5–9; Heb. 13:7, 17, 24; 1 Peter 5:1–4)

- A joyful community (John 15:11; 17:13; Phil. 4:4)

- A hope-filled community (Titus 2:11–14; 1 Peter 1:3–5)

- A loving community (John 13:34–35; 1 John 2:10; 3:16; 4:7–12; 2 John 5–6)

No doubt, we can add to this list. But we don't want to simply think of the church as a group checking off performance boxes. Rather, think of the church as a body alive in Christ, united to one another in the redemptive work of Jesus and the indwelling Holy Spirit, whom Christ brought into relationship to learn to live life together as a display of his glory.[8] A healthy church reflects the effects of the gospel at work in their midst. As the new creation in Christ (2 Cor. 5:17), a healthy corporate body finds their attitudes, conversations, time management, discipline, relationships, and actions affected by what Christ has accomplished in them. Paul uses *plural* pronouns when he writes of the church laying aside the corrupt and deceitful "old self," being renewed in the spirit of the mind, and putting "on the new self, which in the likeness of God has been created in righteousness and holiness of the truth" (Eph. 4:22–24). That's corporate life in union with Christ found in faithful, healthy local churches.

The *radical individualism* in Western churches fights against healthy church life and practice. That seems apparent as church members regularly leave congregations when facing strained relationships or difficult people or a careless snub or simple misunderstanding, instead of embracing the sanctifying process of learning to live together in love, forgiveness, and service to one another. Good pastoral ministry shepherds the church to see the fault lines in attempting to live the Christian life without reference to the Christian community.[9] The testimony of the gospel in our neighborhoods and cities will be most noticed when the congregation lives as a community loving and serving one another. A healthy congregation takes seriously the forty-five "one another" exhortations given to the church in the New Testament.[10] When the

---

8. Mark E. Dever, *A Display of God's Glory: Basics of Church Structure* (Washington, DC: 9Marks, 2001).
9. Hellerman, *Church Was a Family*, 2–4.
10. John 13:34–35; 15:5, 12, 17; Rom. 12:10; 13:8; 14:13, 19; 15:5, 7, 14; 16:16; 1 Cor. 12:25; 16:20; Gal. 5:13, 26; Eph. 4:2, 25, 32; 5:19, 21; Phil. 2:3; Col. 3:9, 13; 1 Thess. 3:12; 4:9; 5:11;

church *moves* and *grows* in that direction, it is a healthy church. Although there may be setbacks and bumps along the way, the faithful movement in the effects of the gospel working out in relationships in the church makes for healthy ecclesiology in understanding and practice.

The Intersection of Pastoral Ministry and Healthy Ecclesiology

What part does the pastor have in shepherding his congregation toward healthy ecclesiology?

1. Be Servant Leaders Training Disciples

Christ gave pastoral ministry as the means to lead a church toward health, which spills over into affecting interpersonal relationships, home life, service, and mission. Pastors focus on discipling, which Derek Tidball describes (quoting R. T. France) as "'essentially a matter of relationship with Jesus' and through him with the trinitarian God."[11] These disciples (*mathetēs*), or learners, continue to grow under faithful biblical teaching, accountability, godly example, and occasional correction. As Tidball examines Matthew's view on disciple-making, he stresses "that this learning took place within a community and not the individual learning experience that has characterized so much of Western education. . . . Matthew's portrait of the church is one where brothers and sisters work and learn together." In this setting, pastors do not assume a hierarchical position but rather, through servant leadership (Matt. 23:8–12), teach and model the Christian life in community.[12]

2. Go Deep in Relationships

A pastor cannot lead the church to health by lecturing on the Christian life while standing aloof from relationships in the body. He must be involved with the body, building relationships, working through the messy issues of life with one another. Hellerman rightly explains, "One who has no true brothers in the congregation will be unable authentically and credibly to challenge others to live together as surrogate siblings."[13] Planting his life in the church, going deep in relationships, staying when difficulties arise, forgiving and loving abrasive members, and living out the truths he teaches *leads* the church toward health. He's not behind pushing but in front leading, modeling the powerful effects of the gospel in the healthy way he lives in community.

Heb. 3:13; 10:24, 25; James 5:9, 16; 1 Peter 1:22; 4:8, 9, 10; 5:5, 14; 1 John 1:7; 3:11, 23; 4:11; 2 John 15.

11. Tidball, *Ministry by the Book*, 22, quoting R. T. France, *Matthew, Evangelist and Teacher* (Exeter: Paternoster, 1989), 262.

12. Tidball, *Ministry by the Book*, 22–23.

13. Hellerman, *Church Was a Family*, 181.

3. Focus on the "Means of Grace"

Pastors should focus on the means of grace, that is, on what Christ has given his people to learn, grow, and mature in the faith: the Bible, proclamation of the Word (primary), corporate worship, prayer, the ordinances, fellowship, and Christian service. Each has its part to strengthen the community in its growth in grace. Pastors must refrain from using practices not clearly identified in God's Word. They must focus their energies on the things that will develop their congregation's spiritual health. While they may be tempted to *think* that other means will improve the congregation's health, they *know* God uses the means of grace to mature the church. So he keeps his focus on preaching and teaching God's Word, leading in Christ-centered worship, faithfully observing the ordinances (especially the Lord's Supper as the ongoing means of encouraging the church), and leading the body to pray, fellowship, and serve.

A few years ago, I worshiped with an underground congregation in a large Asian city. Attendees made their way to apartments turned into gathering places, under the watchful eye of government security cameras. They had the *means of grace* and nothing else for their growth and maturity. Although I couldn't understand their language, I felt their hearts—and mine—united in worshiping the crucified and risen Christ. I sensed gratitude and joy because of the forgiveness of sins. I watched them serving brothers and sisters confined to wheelchairs. Their hospitality humbled me. They talked, laughed, and encouraged one another, knowing that when they exited, the cameras would mark them as belonging to that gathering. But the government didn't really need the cameras. It only needed to see the joy and spiritual health robustly evident through the church to know that these members belonged to Jesus and to one another.

Summary

Every church has an ecclesiology, but only by seeking to live out the ecclesiological practices called for in the NT will churches be healthy. Faithful pastors hold a key role in leading a congregation toward healthy ecclesiology. They do so by not just teaching good ecclesiology but by modeling the kind of relationships we're called to as Christians living in community. The radical individualism in the West often challenges the pastoral aim to lead the church to good health. That's where the pastor's role takes on the responsibility of servant leadership, going deep in relationships, and focusing on the means of grace.

REFLECTION QUESTIONS

1. What is meant by "healthy ecclesiology"?

2. How does the Greek term *ekklēsia*, "church," help us to understand healthy ecclesiology?

3. Name five aspects of healthy ecclesiology identified in this chapter.

4. What part do pastors hold in leading congregations toward good health?

5. Why should the pastor focus on "the means of grace" in leading the church to health, instead of more pragmatic practices?

How Long Should a Pastor Wait to Make Changes in the Church's Ministry?

Upon his father's sudden death, H. B. Charles Jr. had the unusual challenge of following his father's forty-year tenure as senior pastor. Unprepared for a succession after a long ministry, the church leaders updated the church constitution in an effort to curb pastoral authority. Once Charles accepted the church's call a year-and-a-half later, he said "a tug-of-war for power" erupted. The church debated whether the pastor, deacons, or trustees held the authority for direction and leadership. Charles decided to go to God's Word to find the answers for who leads the church. He saw very clearly that "elders and deacons are the only biblical offices of church leadership. Elders serve by leading. Deacons lead by serving." But seeing that in Scripture and translating it into reality in his congregation were two different things, particularly in his denomination, which was not typically given to elder leadership.[1]

Realizing he needed godly counsel, Charles did the right thing. He sought out an older, faithful pastor for advice on how to proceed with the biblical pattern for church leadership. The sage pastor affirmed his biblical findings and explained how his church practiced the very same polity. Thrilled, Charles was ready to immediately return and start the process of changing the church's longstanding polity. But the pastor advised against any sudden changes. Counseling from 2 Timothy 4:2, he told him, preach the Word but do so "with great patience and careful instruction" (NIV). Charles called that "a knock-out punch." He realized that, while faithfully preaching and teaching

---

1. H. B. Charles Jr., *On Pastoring: A Short Guide to Living, Leading, and Ministering as a Pastor* (Chicago: Moody, 2016), 87–88.

God's Word, he must do so with "complete patience"—"patience with difficult people, not just difficult circumstances."[2]

Healthy and faithful pastoral work rides on the heels of patience and teaching. But the desire to see changes happen quickly often gets in the path of the biblical way to lead a church. Pastors think of their denominational standing, personal goals, vision for the church, and even, perhaps, where they would like to go in their next pastorate. So early in their pastorates, they move to make things happen fast. Disaster typically awaits, as personalities get tangled, power groups feel threatened, and untaught congregants remain confused as the pastor scrambles to make things happen. Even though the changes might eventually be good for the church, the church remains unhealthy and caustic, and may eliminate the problem by firing the pastor.

A little prudence will help the pastor in the early years to make sane, timely decisions in creating change in the church's polity, structures, ministry, and practices. That never means disagreements will flee, but they will be fewer than with impatient pastoral leadership. To tackle this question, we'll consider how *when* to make changes is a subjective issue by looking at criteria for evaluating the church. Then we'll examine a pattern for creating healthy change.

A Subjective Issue

While it may be true that no one can tell exactly when to make significant changes in your church, pastoral experience counsels a slower, more deliberate approach. Personally, I've seen my impatience in making changes too quickly backfire and create issues that otherwise I may not have faced. So, I write this chapter with an ache for moving too quickly and a smile at the amazing way pastoral patience brings about change in the church. A pastor will have to make changes if he is to lead the church toward health, but what should he consider in doing so?

1. Consider the Church's History of Change and Conflict

Take the time to investigate the church's historical documents, church minutes, and old church newsletters. Have candid conversations with older members and present leaders. Work to get a bead on how the church has handled change and conflict through the years. That should alert you to some patterns to avoid, power groups to consider, and situations to bathe in prayer and the ministry of the Word.

In one pastorate, I moved quickly to make changes in the worship service and in the church's evangelistic ministry. Both needed new life. But in doing so I had not taken the time to realize the church was in the middle of a huge rift, one that exposed forty years of fighting, splits, bickering, pastoral firings,

---

2. Charles, *On Pastoring*, 88–89.

and chaos. Had I spent a bit more time knowing my circumstances, I would have navigated with more wisdom.

2. Consider the Pastoral Tenure of Former Pastors

If the church is accustomed to short pastorates, expect them to buck at the suggestion of any change. It's partly justified, for without pastoral longevity, they've not learned to trust the love and judgment of their pastors. Or maybe a pastor had a long tenure but without much biblical ministry. That shouts for the new pastor to patiently teach God's Word before making changes.

3. Consider the Health of the Church

Where is the church in its understanding and articulation of the gospel of Jesus Christ? When John Calvin wrote that "the pure ministry of the Word and pure mode of celebrating the sacraments" suffice to show a true church exists, he followed with an important principle to consider: "We must not reject it [the church] so long as it retains them [Word and sacraments], *even if it otherwise swarms with many faults*."[3] Does the church proclaim the gospel with faithfulness, even if with weakness? Does the church understand the ordinances (sacraments) as *gospel ordinances*?[4] A pastor may find himself serving a church that has abandoned the gospel, and thus needs to lay a fresh gospel foundation for the people to hear and believe.

A church with concern for the gospel should also demonstrate it in their priorities, service, mission work, and ministry to one another. If that is not happening, then realize making change in polity and ministry is a moot point. Labor to teach them the gospel.

4. Consider Your Commitment to a Long Pastoral Tenure

Granted, some congregations may not be where a man will plant his life. In such cases, the pastor should not be making significant changes in the church. He takes a chance on disrupting the congregation for his successor. Preach and teach God's Word, and leave changes to someone who will commit to longevity. But if a pastor desires to stay long, then he must consider his willingness to bear up in the difficulty and pain that often accompanies significant change.

---

3. *Calvin*, 4.1.11 (emphasis added).
4. John S. Hammett notes regarding the ordinances that "(1) they must have been directly instituted by Christ, and (2) they must be directly related to the gospel" (*Biblical Foundations for Baptist Churches: A Contemporary Ecclesiology*, 2nd ed. [Grand Rapids: Kregel Academic, 2019], 297).

5. Consider What Kind of Leadership Support Stands with You

After a few months in a church, a pastor should have an idea of those who appear inclined to follow his leadership. This assumption, of course, must not be taken as absolute. Some only feign support. But those who love the Word, pastoral ministry, the congregation, seeing Christ manifested in the body, and humbly serving should be counted on to stand with the pastor when making changes. Even with this support, the pastor still needs to maintain a patient stance toward change. He may need to restrain those standing with him from moving too quickly before a good biblical foundation has been laid in the church's teaching ministry.

6. Consider What Major Changes Were Made before You Arrived as Pastor

Maybe no changes took place. Then the pastor will know he's blazing new territory with change, so he must wield his leadership mantle patiently and wisely. Or maybe some big changes happened that disrupted the fellowship. Then slow down. Wait for a good opportunity to lead toward more solid footing.

7. Consider What Changes the Pastor and Pastoral Search Committee Discussed before the Call to Ministry Took Place

I received a call from a new pastor asking me to speak to his church about changing polity to a plural elder leadership structure. I balked, fearing my teaching would result in his dismissal. But he assured me that the pastoral search committee presented the idea to him of changing the church's leadership polity to plural elder leadership. After a horrific experience with an immoral pastoral dictator, they realized God's Word spoke clearly on how to address their need, so they asked this new pastor to lead the charge. He did, quite patiently and deliberately, with much success.

After thinking through the subjective issues any church will face, the pastor will need to face reality. Changes may happen quicker than he thought due to the health of the church, its history, and its leadership. Changes may proceed at a slower pace than he anticipated due to past conflicts, short pastoral tenures, and lack of support. In making such evaluations, the pastor will need to be patient with himself. He may need a couple of older pastors to listen to his findings to help him sort out a plan for change. Throughout, he needs to pay heed to godly counsel.

Having received counsel, the pastor then needs to move toward a long-term plan for instituting healthy changes to the church. What is needed?

A Plan for Change

Pastoral ministry should *major* on shepherding the flock and *minor* on creating changes. Yet we're always changing (*semper reformandi*, always reforming) until we stand complete before God's throne. But we want changes to follow a biblical pattern toward the church's health. How do we do that?

1. Develop Good Listeners and Interpreters of Scripture through Faithful Biblical Preaching and Teaching

Good exposition not only opens the text of Scripture but also demonstrates how to properly interpret God's Word (2 Tim. 2:15). Is the pastor more interested in Christ being formed (Gal. 4:19) in his congregation or changing their structure or ministry? Priority on the Word will demonstrate where the focus rests. Concentrate on preaching and teaching with clarity. Be available and open for questions and discussions to further the congregation's grasp of the Word. Interact with the body about the sermons and teaching sessions. Healthy changes follow faithful preaching.

2. Aim to Develop Reading as a Priority for the Congregation

A reading congregation adapts to change far quicker than one simply waiting for someone else to predigest everything for them. Those who begin to read sermons, Bible studies, theology, ecclesiology, mission works, Christian biographies, and history will have an appetite to listen more attentively to the teaching and move more readily to changes, and will do so without complaint. They've been exposed to a world far larger than the perimeter of their church property. They will realize the pastor's leadership follows biblical patterns and needs to be faithfully heeded.

3. Disciple and Train the Men of the Church

Train up men to be leaders in their home and the church (2 Tim. 2:2). By investing in teaching men how to think and live biblically, how to serve humbly, and how to walk faithfully with Christ, the pastor will actually spend less time thinking about how to make change happen. It will happen with men walking with Christ under the pastor's leadership, with these men often initiating it. Provide discipling opportunities for women as well (Titus 2:3–5), who will reinforce the biblically renewed direction of the church.

4. Allow Changes to Arise Naturally from Your Pulpit Ministry

What I mean is not to manipulate changes under the guise of preaching. Rather, through the natural process of preaching expositionally, the Word *exposes* changes in leadership, polity, structure, mission, ministry, and service. Can a pastor expound 1 Peter 5:1–5 without addressing the New Testament pattern for church leadership? Can a pastor preach Matthew 28:18–20, Acts 1:8, Acts 13:1–3, and so on, without setting forth a new trajectory for mission? H. B. Charles Jr. is right: "True spiritual change does not happen by 'casting vision.' It happens by faithfully teaching doctrinal truth. This is an essential but neglected key to faithful and effective pastoral ministry."[5] A pastor may teach a text with every implication aiming toward change without

---

5. Charles, *On Preaching*, 90.

immediately calling for change. Let the church see the changes in the biblical text, then gradually work toward recommending changes.

5. Move Slowly in Years 1–2

Before a pastor makes good changes that will help the church, he needs to know the congregation. He needs to prove himself as a shepherd to them, caring for their spiritual needs. When the church begins to see the pastor *as the shepherd of the flock*, they will more readily follow change. The first couple of years, though, should just be spent in preaching, teaching, visiting, counseling, shepherding, and getting to know the congregation.[6]

6. Make Gradual Changes in Year 3

It may happen sooner or later, but this gives a benchmark for some of the less drastic changes. If one is changing the church's polity structure from a deacon-led structure to plural elder leadership, then I'd suggest it will take longer—maybe five to seven years, perhaps even longer in some settings—before a church will be ready for this kind of lasting, necessary change.

The pastor might develop an *instinctive triage* as he starts his ministry: (1) What vital signs are present in the church? Give attention to strengthening them, for example, culling hymns/songs with unbiblical content and adding songs from the same genre with good content, removing manipulation from services, which plays upon emotions without making disciples, strengthening biblical preaching, and reinforcing biblical qualifications for its officers. (2) What unbiblical practices must change immediately for the church to stay alive and to remain a church grounded in the New Testament? Evaluate *basic* content in the worship and the practice of the ordinances, and regenerate teachers and workers. This leads to year 1–2 priorities and starts to set a trajectory toward more significant changes. (3) What will need to happen to help the church to be consistently healthy? Identify key practices (e.g., church discipline, proper view of baptism and Lord's Supper, elder plurality, deacons focused on service role, etc.). This establishes an aim for the next years. (4) What missing biblical practices need a foundation laid to move toward consistent health? Consider church discipline, qualified spiritual leaders, elder and deacon plurality, and so on. This helps to establish the pastor's preaching, teaching, leadership, small group, and discipling plans to build the foundation.

7. Start Major Changes for Which the Foundation Has Been Laid in the First Three to Four Years

Think of the first few years as the layering process toward the major changes. Intentional preaching, small group discussion, group teaching,

---

6. Make only minimal changes in this time (e.g., a new worship bulletin format, a new time to do pastoral Q&A, a new ministry to shut-ins, a new mission offering, etc.).

conferences, seminars, group book reading, men's and women's discipleship, student discipleship, and worship gatherings all provide the biblical content enabling a congregation that has lived with unhealthy practices to long for and pursue conformity to the teaching of God's Word. Doing these things takes time but produces good fruit. As the foundation strengthens, start implementing changes.

Summary

Patience in laboring through Word, prayer, training men, leadership development, and teaching the church to think biblically will achieve far more in the long term than instituting quick changes. The health of the church for years to come as a people that grow together in grace, truth, service, and mission should steady the pastor's hand in making sudden changes. Long-term commitment by the pastor reassures the church that changes are for their good rather than the pastor's ego. Again, Charles offers an appropriate exhortation for pastors leading toward change: "But nurturing a healthy church that makes disciples of Christ requires a long-term commitment to preach the Word in and out of season with complete patience and teaching."[7] Patience and teaching provide the pathway toward change.

REFLECTION QUESTIONS

1. What is meant by the statement "Healthy and faithful pastoral work rides on the heels of patience and teaching"?

2. What part does pastoral tenure play in making significant changes?

3. How does a pastor discern the health of the church where he serves?

4. How do developing good listeners and interpreters of Scripture aid change?

5. How should a pastor address biblical texts that seem to hit squarely on issues of change needed in the church?

---

7. Charles, *On Preaching*, 91.

How Should a Pastor Lead the Congregation in Practicing Church Discipline?

In our church's early years, I discovered one of our members engaged in behavior contrary to that of a Christ follower. I immediately confronted him over his sin, called him to repentance, and established accountability through initiating church discipline. That was the first occasion our church leadership practiced biblical church discipline. Only the elders and I were privy to what had happened. We established boundaries for him, set up a plan for attacking and uprooting the sin, and had points to meet for accountability. He responded well, so the matter did not need to be reported to the congregation. However, a year later he fell back into the same sin pattern. After failing to respond to our exhortations, we reported his failure to the church. The congregation voted to remove him from membership. Our church broke through the invisible barrier to practice church discipline.

Admittedly, we had no patterns to follow for practicing discipline other than the outline given by Christ in Matthew 18:15–20. Church discipline seemed to have fallen out of sight among area churches. But we realized the nature of his sin, and his refusal to respond in repentance left us no choice. We had to exercise corrective discipline.

Since then, we've addressed others in matters of discipline. Some have responded to initial appeals to repent so that the congregation never knew of any problem, and the member continued in faithfulness. With others, sadly, we walked the solemn path toward removing someone from membership. We've also had the joy of seeing some removed brought to restoration of fellowship. "The motive for discipline," as Tom Schreiner rightly notes, "is invariably love, and the goal is the restoration of the one who has fallen."[1] Since the church, as the body of Christ, is to reflect her head in purity and holiness (Eph. 5:25–27), then when this does not happen, the practice of church discipline must be exercised.

What Is Church Discipline?

The word *discipline* has different connotations. We discipline ourselves for the purpose of godliness (1 Tim. 4:7).[2] We're to lead disciplined lives in keeping with the apostolic gospel and practice (2 Thess. 3:6–13).[3] Bodily discipline, on the other hand, "is only of little profit" when compared to disciplining ourselves for godliness (1 Tim. 4:8). Each use conveys the idea of *training* for a purpose. When discipline is used for correction, the training concept remains. One disciplined by an earthly parent is being trained toward a life of order and respect, even though it may involve a measure of corrective action (Heb. 12:7–9).[4] Discipline, then, conveys the idea of training whether by instruction, setting an example, or correcting when one errs.

In the several *church discipline* passages, that phrase is not used to introduce or discuss the subject. But the term correctly expresses that the church regularly engages in disciplining its members. That is, the church trains, teaches, instructs, and sets an example as *formative discipline*, and on occasion, the church corrects when a member continues to err in behavior or engages in doctrinal heresy as *corrective (formal) discipline*. The church has responsibility for both. "Formative discipline takes place in the ongoing ministry of the church, in the regular discipleship and care of every member," writes Schreiner. "All members are disciplined or discipled through teaching, encouragement, correction, exhortations, and reproof, which are given through the loving care of fellow believers."[5] Corrective discipline takes place "when radical surgery or radical repentance is needed."[6]

---

1. Thomas Schreiner, "The Biblical Basis for Church Discipline," in *Those Who Must Give an Account: A Study of Church Membership and Church Discipline*, eds. John S. Hammett and Benjamin L. Merkle (Nashville: B&H Academic, 2012), 105.
2. The term "discipline" (NASB) is translated from the Greek γυμνάζω and is taken from the ancient athletic literature meaning "to train, undergo discipline" (BDAG, 208). The idea of *training* for a particular purpose, in this case godliness, best expresses discipline. Hebrews 5:14 and 12:11 (NASB) translate it as "trained."
3. The antonym for "discipline" translated, in adjectival form, as "undisciplined" (NASB) in 2 Thessalonians 3:7, 11 is ἀτάκτως, which means "in defiance of good order, *disorderly* . . . without respect for established custom or received instruction" (BDAG, 148). Discipline, on the other hand, follows good order, respects instruction, and lives in an orderly manner.
4. Here the word "discipline" (παιδεία) expresses "the act of providing guidance for responsible living, upbringing, training, instruction," and in biblical literature, "chiefly as it is attained by discipline, correction" (BDAG, 748–49).
5. Schreiner, "Church Discipline," 105–6.
6. Schreiner, "Church Discipline," 106.

Church discipline, then, is the loving and faithful action of the body of Christ to disciple its members, and as part of discipleship, when a member persists in unrepentant sin or doctrinal heresy, the church seeks to bring correction aiming toward repentance. The church aims for immediate repentance in the initial stages of church discipline. If a member refuses the exhortations of a single member, followed by two or more members, the situation falls to the congregation assembled in the name of Jesus (1 Cor. 5:4) to first pursue, then remove the erring member (Matt. 18:15–20).

When Is Church Discipline Necessary?

Perhaps the greatest fear of a church beginning to practice church discipline focuses on knowing when discipline will be necessary. I've been told of churches, generally led by an autocratic pastor rather than elder plurality, using discipline to remove people against whom someone held a grudge or who did not toe the line on some nondisciplinary issues. While wanting to show grace and humility in disciplinary matters, a church must concern itself with its public testimony of the gospel rather than balking due to a few misuses of discipline. What are the matters that should concern the church to practice discipline?

- When a member persists in sin—whether public or private—to the degree that it affects his or her Christian testimony, threatens the purity of the church, and potentially mars the corporate testimony (1 Cor. 6:9–11; Eph. 5:3–5; 2 Tim. 3:1–9; 1 Peter 1:13–16; 2:11–12)[7]

- When a member is involved in scandalous public behavior that even the unbelieving community finds offensive (1 Cor. 5:1–13)

- When a member persists in behavior destructive to the unity and fellowship of the church (1 Cor. 3:16–17; Eph. 4:1–3; 2 Thess. 3:11–15; Titus 1:9–11; 3:10–11)

- When a member persists in doctrinal deviations or heresies, refusing the correction of the elders (1 Tim. 1:18–20; 2 Tim. 2:16–18; Titus 1:9; 2 Peter 2:1–3; 2:17–22; 2 John 9–11)[8]

---

7. "The greatest moral danger to the church is the toleration of sin, public or private," states R. Albert Mohler, "Church Discipline: The Missing Mark," in *Polity: Biblical Arguments on How to Conduct Church Life*, ed. Mark E. Dever (Washington, DC: Center for Church Reform, 2001), 55.

8. "One cannot explain the explosive dynamite, the *dunamis*, of the early church apart from the fact that they practiced two things simultaneously: orthodoxy of doctrine and orthodoxy of community in the midst of the visible church, a community which the world can see. By the grace of God, therefore, the church must be known simultaneously for its purity

How Is Church Discipline to Be Exercised?

Jesus introduced the foundational instruction for church discipline. After the first mention of the church in the NT, with the promise that Jesus will build his church so "the gates of Hades will not overpower it," he announces "the keys of the kingdom" given to his disciples for power to bind and loose (Matt. 16:18). The same binding and loosing is presented in the context of the church at work in disciplining its members (Matt. 18:18). *"The power of the keys (binding and losing) speaks to both entering into the new community and maintaining its life,"* writes Jonathan Leeman.[9] The church's power to declare a repentant member forgiven upon determining true repentance, as well as the power to exclude from the fellowship of the church one that refuses repentance—and thus continuing in unforgiveness—belongs to the corporate body and not to individual members. The word *keys* "emphasizes that the church can have the assurance that what it does on earth represents the will of God," explains Tom Schreiner.[10]

Jesus gave a clear model for churches to follow in cases that might involve discipline. First, "if your brother sins, go and show him his fault in private; if he listens to you, you have won your brother" (Matt. 18:15).[11] There's no intention of spreading details about the brother's sinful action. With utmost care, the concerned brother in the spirit of Galatians 6:1–2 quietly, humbly, and lovingly approaches his brother concerning the sin. It may have been sin against him or sin the concerned brother observes. He shows him his sin, calls for repentance, and when that happens, he rejoices while maintaining the confidentiality of the matter with the brother that has repented.

Second, "if he does not listen to you, take one or two more with you, so that by the mouth of two or three witnesses every fact may be confirmed." Following the pattern in Deuteronomy 19:15, he takes one or two more to strengthen the call to repentance and holiness. The others may or may not have observed the sin in the erring brother but have been convinced it has happened. In similar humility, love, and graciousness, the two or three approach the brother to add to the weightiness of the need for repentance. It may be the other two listen to the erring brother and decide he is not at fault. In such a case, the first brother

---

of doctrine and the reality of its community," wrote Francis Schaeffer, "The Church Before the Watching World," in *The Church at the End of the Twentieth Century* (Wheaton, IL: Crossway, 1970), 144, quoted by Mohler, "Church Discipline," 54.

9. Jonathan Leeman, *The Church and the Surprising Offense of God's Love: Reintroducing the Doctrines of Church Membership and Discipline*, 9Marks (Wheaton, IL: Crossway, 2010), 190 (emphasis original); see 169–227 for Leeman's careful explanation on the church's authority given to it by Christ.

10. Schreiner, "Church Discipline," 110; my comments follow Schreiner's careful explanation. There is the possibility of a church or church leader misguided in discipline (e.g., Diotrephes in John 10–11). Schreiner adds, "Nevertheless, Matthew 18 does not concentrate on such abuses but promises the church divine guidance."

11. The language in this translation uses the generic masculine, but the sinning person could be male or female.

that approached the erring one should humbly submit to their judgment, unless there is just cause to reject it. Or the gravity of two or three calling for repentance melts the erring brother's heart in humble repentance.

Third, "if he refuses to listen to them, tell it to the church." The third stage of discipline introduces the accusation and evidence against the erring brother to the congregation. That's the congregation's call to action in prayer, contacting the brother with exhortations, and using the corporate testimony as a call to repentance. The pressure felt by the unrepentant person from the congregation with which he has entered into covenant may awaken the slumbering one to see his sin and repent. But if not, the church continues with its ultimate responsibility.

Fourth, "if he refuses to listen even to the church, let him be to you as a Gentile and a tax collector"; in other words, remove him from the fellowship of the saints and treat him as an unbeliever. This corporate action by the vote of the church exercises the church's ultimate authority—to bind or to loose. For an erring member to refuse the pleas and exhortations of the church is the last straw before excommunication from membership in which the removed member has no privileges at the Lord's Table or membership responsibilities.[12]

While this fourfold procedure should be the normal way to practice church discipline, Paul took a different approach in 1 Corinthians 5:1–13. A member's sin was so egregious and so scandalous that he called for the church to assemble in the name of Jesus Christ and remove him immediately. Schreiner observes, "The public and gross character of the sin demanded a public and immediate response by the church."[13] But consistent with what Jesus taught in Matthew 18, the final authority for removing someone from membership is not with the elders but with the assembled church taking action.[14]

What Steps Should a Pastor Take to Prepare to Lead His Church to Practice Church Discipline?

First, lay biblical groundwork toward church discipline. This doesn't begin by immediately plunging into Matthew 18 or 1 Corinthians 5. Rather, it begins by laying a gospel foundation in the church. As a gospel issue, church discipline has to do with the purity of the gathered body of those redeemed by Christ through the gospel. If a congregation's grasp of the gospel is weak, then do not expect them to understand the necessity of discipline. Sow the gospel seed so they begin to understand the nature of the gospel, its effect upon us in genuine conversion, and how faulty testimonies imperil the gospel witness of the church.

---

12. Other passages alluding to matters of discipline include Gal. 6:1–2; 2 Thess. 3:6–15; 1 Tim. 1:19–20; 1 Tim. 5:17–21; Titus 3:9–11; James 5:19–20.
13. Schreiner, "Church Discipline," 114. He adds, "Apparently the man was determined and resolute to continue the [immoral] relationship with his stepmother."
14. See Schreiner, "Church Discipline," 113–27, for a more detailed look at 1 Corinthians 5.

Second, seek the Lord concerning the church's grasp of the gospel. Only the Lord can bring about true conversions (Acts 11:18). Only the Lord can soften hearts that have grown hardened by a lack of biblical application. Preach and pray (Acts 6:4).

Third, lay a biblical foundation for the nature of the church. This will include teaching on regenerate church membership and the attending responsibilities of members toward one another. Unless the church sees the importance of membership, they will prefer to fire the pastor than to discipline an erring member.

Fourth, work on marshaling support for following biblical practices. Here's the work of ongoing discipleship. Invest in some men, teaching them the gospel and the nature of the church, including polity, church membership, discipline, and so on.

Fifth, seek to build a discipling relationship with the erring member that has brought on this concern for discipline. Perhaps in a discipling relationship, you will be able to press the nature of the gospel and its effects upon this member. Essentially, you're engaged in a lengthy version of the first step Jesus set forth in practicing discipline (Matt. 18:15). Let's suppose the sin is immorality. What lies behind that but pride, unbelief, arrogance toward God's law, ignorance of the Word, and other sins? Aim for these sins in the patient process of trying to discipline the erring brother, in order to lay the groundwork for calling him to repentance. If he's repenting of the other sins, he will likely be concerned about his immorality.

Sixth, keep steadily teaching your church. As the church shows signs of believing and receiving God's Word, you're moving toward that time of implementing church discipline following Jesus's pattern. The two or more brothers who partner with you in the second step of discipline will stand with you to help reinforce to the congregation the need for church discipline. As I told one young pastor, "You may have to hold your nose on some things until the church's health increases enough to apply discipline." But keep in mind that discipline is a weekly practice by the church through the ministry of the Word, exhortation, encouragement, accountability, and the regular call to live repentant, faithful lives as followers of Christ. Corrective discipline flows naturally out of a healthy practice of formative discipline. In this way, build a climate of formative discipline so that when the time comes to practice corrective discipline, it's natural to the body.

Summary

"It has been remarked," wrote J. L. Dagg, "that when discipline leaves a church, Christ goes with it."[15] Building an ethos within the congregation so that the church's regular gathering demonstrates a (formatively) disciplined

---

15. J. L. Dagg, *Manual of Church Order* (1858; Harrisonburg, VA: Gano Books, 1990), 274.

people will provide the way toward the body maintaining purity in life and doctrine. When a member strays, the others will more naturally seek to call him or her back to repentance. If that fails, the foundation for discipline has been laid by faithful preaching and teaching through God's Word, on the nature of the gospel and the church. Humility, grace, and patience should mark the slow but deliberate process of church discipline.

REFLECTION QUESTIONS

1. What is church discipline?

2. What areas of ongoing sin call for church discipline?

3. What is the pattern for church discipline established by Jesus Christ in Matthew 18?

4. How did Paul's practice of church discipline in 1 Corinthians 5 differ from Matthew 18?

5. What are the key concerns when laying groundwork toward a church practicing discipline?

How Should a Pastor Lead in Changing Polity and Leadership Structure?

Any transition in a local church can likely upset the congregation's equilibrium. Familiar practices feel like a well-worn pair of jeans—they're just too comfortable to change into something new. So why bother? One reason suffices: we want to follow the teaching of God's inerrant Word. If he has given us the authoritative Word that we confess is sufficient for life and practice, then we must take that seriously. Everything we are and do as a church should be regularly evaluated in light of Holy Scripture.

However, evaluating a church's polity and leadership structure in light of the Word, and then moving toward change, will likely meet with resistance. Many churches revolt at the thought of change. Change battles our pride because we must acknowledge deficiency in belief and practice. It unsettles our comforts because we face a new structure redefining who we are and what we're about. It challenges our complacency because it exposes our neglect of regular examination in light of Scripture. But if we're to be faithful as churches of the Lord Jesus Christ, we must seek to follow the teaching of Holy Scripture.

Most people don't pay attention to church polity. They may not even know that it exists. Yet a church's polity—its governing structure—affects membership, discipleship, evangelism, member care, doctrine, leadership, ordinances, and worship. Jonathan Leeman explains that the church without "a palpable and public presence" based on and determined by its polity, "remains an abstract idea."[1] So polity cannot be comfortably laid aside as though the visible church exists without it. As Leeman puts it, "The universal church is united

---

1. Jonathan Leeman, introduction to *Baptist Foundations: Church Government for an Anti-Institutional Age*, eds. Mark Dever and Jonathan Leeman (Nashville: B&H Academic, 2015), 4–5.

in faith. The local church is united in faith and order."[2] The latter, "order," constitutes the church's polity. It's what distinguishes the local church from a conglomeration of Christians that happen to be together but have nothing specific uniting them. Polity shaped by the gospel identifies what a group of Christians believe about the gospel, what constitutes membership in the church, who is admitted to baptism and the Lord's Table, how a member can be removed, who exercises spiritual authority over the church, and what constitutes the church's ministries and mission.

If this seems overstated, consider what Leeman asserts: "Polity is important because it guards the *what* and the *who* of the gospel—what the gospel message is and who the gospel believers are. . . . It separates, distinguishes, and identifies the church before the nations, thereby protecting and preserving the gospel *what* and *who* from one generation to the next."[3] A church's polity gives clarity to its beliefs and practice so that with every generation, the centrality of the gospel continues to shape the congregation's members, leadership, and mission.

A church's polity document (constitution and bylaws, book of order, church manual, church polity—whatever a church decides to call it) should be (1) clearly written, (2) grounded in the gospel, (3) based on an orthodox doctrinal confession, (4) simple and straightforward, (5) approved by the church, and (5) thoroughly usable. It should be detailed enough to help a church understand its doctrine, ordinances, admission to membership, membership practices and constraints, discipline, officers and leadership structure, and mission. It cannot and need not attempt to cover every possible contingency a church faces—that's why we have elders to lead and congregations to be the final arbiter in matters of question and dispute. In other words, I'm advocating for an understandable, readable polity document that will help the church, not encumber it; one that encourages and instructs, not one that puts the reader to sleep.[4]

---

2. Leeman, introduction to *Baptist Foundations*, 5.

3. Leeman, introduction to *Baptist Foundations*, 6–7.

4. The purpose of this chapter is not to give details on what a church should include in its polity documents. Rather, we consider how to lead a church in changing its polity regarding leadership structures. For details on necessary subjects to include, see Dever and Leeman, *Baptist Foundations*; John S. Hammett, *Biblical Foundations for Baptist Churches: A Contemporary Ecclesiology*, 2nd ed. (Grand Rapids: Kregel Academic, 2019); Bobby Jamieson, *Going Public: Why Baptism Is Required for Church Membership* (Nashville: B&H Academic, 2015); Jonathan Leeman, *The Church and the Surprising Offence of God's Love: Re-introducing the Doctrines of Church Membership and Discipline* (Wheaton, IL: Crossway, 2010); J. L. Dagg, *Manual of Church Order* (1858; Harrisonburg, VA: Gano Books, 1990); Phil A. Newton and Matt Schmucker, *Elders in the Life of the Church: Rediscovering the Biblical Model for Church Leadership* (Grand Rapids: Kregel Ministry, 2014).

Having noted the importance of polity in general, in this question I want to give special attention to changing the pastoral structure of a local church.[5] As earlier advocated, unless a church moves to a plural pastoral structure (pastors/elders), it will hinder its health and maturity, as well as the longevity of the shepherds leading the church.[6] Perhaps you're convinced plural elder/ pastor leadership has its roots firmly planted in New Testament practice. But that doesn't mean everyone in your congregation holds the same view. So can a church transition from the more typical deacon-led or committee-led structure to plural elder/pastor leadership?[7] Let's consider five observations to remember for this transition.

Never Take Transitions Lightly

Old wineskins, to use Jesus's analogy about the transitions to his kingdom practices from Jewish traditionalism, are not easily parted from (Mark 2:21–22). Patterns get firmly set in a congregation's thinking. The people morph into a comfort zone that has lulled them into the least effort in exercising thought and making changes. Then suddenly a pastor calls for a completely different polity. Not only have they given no consideration to such a change but the fact that a pastor suggests it calls into question previous, long-standing decisions. Pride raises its head. Tempers flare. Standards and ideas considered firmly set in concrete feel threatened by replacement. People holding offices and positions clamor to hold their titles.

So, don't take this lightly. Keep in mind three things:

1. Be Convinced Scripture Teaches What You're Proposing

In other words, don't just read a book on polity or elder plurality or see another church transitioning and jump into action. Understand what Scripture teaches before you move. This lays biblical foundation for your actions. A church that truly cares about the authority of Scripture will be much more likely to follow your leadership in change *if* they know you're thoroughly convinced by God's Word of the direction you're leading.

2. Be Sensitive to the Spirit's Timing and Leadership

Not every idea of transition is immediately ready for daylight. Lay a strong biblical foundation before starting the structure. To press polity issues without first making sure the congregation sees how everything in the church has its foundation in the gospel will prove counterproductive. For instance, if a church holds a low view of regenerate church membership,

---

5. We will look at reforming a church's membership practices in Question 35.
6. See Question 5.
7. For a more detailed look at the transition process, see Newton and Schmucker, *Elders*, 165–219.

gospel work needs to be done before attempting to transition to elder/pastor plurality. Otherwise, members will see little need for elder/pastoral leadership in shepherding, discipling, and correction if they lack an understanding of regenerate membership. If many of the present leaders give no evidence of genuine faithfulness to Christ, then teaching through the Gospels should precede teaching through the Pastoral Epistles. A pastor should more than likely serve his church for several years before he attempts to change the leadership structure. There are exceptions, such as when a church realizes before a new pastor arrives that they have an unbiblical leadership polity. The church needs to trust the pastor as he leads in this transition, so he needs to build capital with them by faithful shepherding for several years. Plus, he needs to be committed to see the transition through rather than skip out to another church.[8]

3. Be Steadfast in Prayer

You not only face an educational challenge but also a spiritual battle when transitioning to elder plurality. The enemy loves nothing more than to divide a church over biblical teaching. Bathe the process in prayer. Depend upon the Holy Spirit to open minds to receive the teaching that leads to a healthy transition.

Show Love and Respect for Those in the Current Leadership Structure

If you're leading the church and the current leadership into transition, then show honor where honor is due (Rom. 12:10; 13:7). Others have gone before you in establishing the leadership structures of the church. While you may disagree with their interpretation of Scripture, you need to guard against challenging their commitment to Christ. You don't want to come across as one engaging in guerilla warfare to get your way. Honor the office of deacon while laying biblical groundwork toward transitioning the roles of deacons and establishing elder leadership.

Certainly, this is no small task. I'm recommending that you begin the transition by gently but firmly training the deacons to see their biblical roles as the elevated servants of the church. Many see themselves as *de facto* elders without the title, and far too often, they lack the biblical qualifications (1 Tim. 3:1–7; Titus 1:5–9). Others see themselves as a *board* holding the power of the church in their monthly meetings. Yet, the reason they have arrived at an unscriptural position may be due to a longstanding polity not of their making.

While all Christians are called to serve, deacons set the standard—or should. *Help them to see this biblical practice so they relish the opportunity*

---

8. See Question 12.

to serve the congregation.[9] In doing so, you seek to avoid an us-versus-them mindset. They are brothers in Christ who may not have been exposed to teaching on biblical church leadership. They need your patient guidance, not pounding, ultimatums, and demands.

Start Small, Then Spread to Broader Circles

When our church transitioned to elder plurality, we began with a long process of taking key leaders and working through the Scripture. For about fifteen months (not every week!) we slowly walked through every passage in the Bible that dealt with decision-making, leadership, church polity, and biblical offices. I highly recommend this kind of biblical research to lay a foundation with your key leaders. Only after that process did we include the congregation.

Likewise, Mark Dever, when leading Capitol Hill Baptist Church in Washington, DC, toward elder plurality, started with a small group and then gradually worked out with concentric circles of leadership before presenting it to the congregation.[10]

What you're modeling in the process of slowly working through God's Word is reliance upon the sufficiency of Scripture. You're discipling the small circle in how to faithfully interpret Scripture. You're showing through the repetition of walking through the Word the consistency of how biblical polity works and plural elder leadership functions in a congregation. I suggest you not even begin to introduce church history into the equation until you've worked through the Word.[11] I remember one man in the group of seven involved in our discussion saying, when we concluded, "Well, I don't like it but it's biblical." That's enough for me.

Move Patiently toward the Transition Rather Than Acting as a Steamroller

Sometimes we're so enthused about things we've studied we presume a few sermons or lessons on the subject will have everyone convinced. I've watched several pastors attempt to move to elder plurality without this patient teaching and layering, only to meet with division and strife. In such haste we may find the church showing us the door. Maybe that's why Paul told Timothy to preach the Word but to do so "with great patience and instruction" (2 Tim. 4:2). Yes, you want to see the transition happen. It will improve

---

9. See Benjamin L. Merkle, *40 Questions About Elders and Deacons* (Grand Rapids: Kregel Academic, 2008), 227–62; Thabiti M. Anyabwile, *Finding Faithful Elders and Deacons* (Wheaton, IL: Crossway, 2012), 19–43; Hammett, *Biblical Foundations*, 22–247; Dever and Leeman, *Baptist Foundations*, 311–29.
10. See Matt Schmucker's helpful chapters that describe this process in Newton and Schmucker, *Elders*, chapters 2, 4, 6, 8.
11. See Newton and Schmucker, *Elders*, chap. 1, for a historical view of elders in Baptist life.

your shepherding of the congregation. It will intensify the church's ministry. Wiser decisions will be made. But that's still no excuse for impatiently pounding away. Give the congregation time to trust you and your leadership before rushing into polity change.

You will likely have a few setbacks—someone disagrees, another complains, and a few even leave the church. That's just part of any transition in a typical church, particularly unhealthy ones. Better to work on the church's health than to change its polity in hope that it will change its health. Lay a good biblical foundation in sound doctrine before pressing the biblical teaching on polity. Prioritize the gospel before polity.

You're not parting the Red Sea in transitioning to elder plurality, but you are journeying into biblical territory that may be unfamiliar to the church. There may be negative associations with elders (e.g., another denomination's elder rule without a congregational framework). You must work through those things patiently.

Give Attention to the Deacons' Service-Oriented Ministry While Adopting Elder Plurality Leadership

In other words, reinforce you're *not* getting rid of deacons as the church transitions its polity but seeing them as vital to the church's total ministry. Some will likely think deacons will become nonexistent with elders. Instead, explain and illustrate both the congregation's voice under elder plurality and the deacons' role as servants. Show how more ministry will happen—better shepherding, more attentive widow care, efficiency in church responsibilities, accountability for the pastoral staff, and so on. Don't be afraid to admit that you don't have every answer for every potential issue that might arise when you transition. In the same way, you don't have every answer in the current polity either. Show you are committed to serving and shepherding them while leading them in grounding the church's life and leadership in God's Word.

Plural elder leadership strengthens churches, but make sure, as much as possible, the process toward it doesn't divide but unites the congregation in affirming the teaching of God's Word.

Summary

The leadership structure in a church's polity may be only one area needing transition in a church. Deciding the timing on changing polity takes wisdom and sensitivity to the Spirit's leadership. Establish biblical polity to continue the church's healthy growth, as members take seriously their commitment to one another in the body of Christ. Transitioning to plural elder/pastor leadership sets the stage for consistent faithfulness in shepherding a congregation, while deacon plurality assists the elders by serving the congregation in physical areas. Transition needs to show love and respect for those in leadership, while patiently training the church in biblical polity.

REFLECTION QUESTIONS

1. What is church polity?

2. Why do we need to concern ourselves with making sure that we have a healthy, biblical church polity?

3. What three considerations are offered to ensure that the process of transitioning church polity will not be taken lightly?

4. What recommendations are given for training the church in understanding biblical polity?

5. How can the strain between the way elders and deacons are viewed in polity be avoided?

Why Should Pastors Lead in Reforming a Church's Membership Practices?

A strange phenomenon occurred in the early church. A group of 120 men and women met for prayer, biblical discussion, and intense fellowship for a little over a week after Jesus Christ's ascension. Their heads reeled with what they had seen and experienced with Jesus, and what he had taught them (Acts 1:12–26). His last command, to stay in Jerusalem until they were clothed with the Spirit's power for witness, left them with anticipation of their mission (Luke 24:48–49). They would make disciples, baptize them, and keep on teaching them the commands of Christ (Matt. 28:19–20). Through their witness, people would be gathered as *learners* of Christ and his gospel, living life together and growing into a mature people that would visibly display the power of the gospel.[1] The term *disciples* not only characterized the teaching/learning relationship but also became a synonym for *church*.[2] Bound together and accountable to each other in a teaching, learning, maturing, serving, and mission-focused relationship, these gathered disciples were the churches in the various cities, towns, and villages where the gospel took root.

How serious were those in the early church about the accountability of life together as Jesus's disciples? Some sold their property in order to help those among them with needs (Acts 4:32–37). When one couple's deceitfulness threatened the purity and unity of that group, they fell dead at Peter's word

---

1. The word for disciple, *mathētēs* (μαθητής) means "learner," indicating "attachment to someone in discipleship" (*NIDNTTE*, 3:224). This implies relationships of ongoing learning centered in life together in Christ.
2. See Acts 6:2, "the congregation of the disciples"; Acts 9:19, "the disciples who were at Damascus"; Acts 9:38, "disciples" in Lydda; Acts 11:26, "And for an entire year they met with the church and taught considerable numbers; and the disciples were first called Christians in Antioch"; and Acts 14:28, "And they spent a long time with the disciples," referring to the church at Antioch that sent out Paul and Barnabas.

(Acts 5:1–11). At a time when Hellenistic widows received scant attention and support from the group, "the whole congregation" affirmed the apostles' proposal for establishing seven deacon prototypes to serve their needs (Acts 6:1–6). When news about new believers in Antioch "reached the ears of the church at Jerusalem," the church sent Barnabas to help this new congregation continue their discipleship (Acts 11:21–22). The New Testament epistles addressed specific local churches, correcting practice, reproving erring members, reinforcing apostolic doctrine, and calling for unity and purity among them.

If belonging to a specific body of local believers held such importance in the early church, then this same *belonging*—membership, as we typically call it—should hold priority in the focus of pastoral ministry. Yet belonging meant far more than a name on a list. It meant *life together* in Christ.[3] Healthy membership practices reinforce life together in Christ. When membership practices need reforming, pastors must lead the way. How can that be done?

Biblical Responsibility

One does not find "membership" in the New Testament. Yet when we consider the word expressing *belonging* or *being part of a group or people* or *a commitment to others centered in common cause*, then we see "membership" throughout the NT. The church emerging at Pentecost reinforces the idea of belonging. They were baptized together, "devoted themselves to the apostles' teaching and to fellowship, to the breaking of bread and to prayer." They "were together and had all things in common," even selling property and possessions to give to those in need. They continued "with one mind in the temple, and breaking bread from house to house, they were taking their meals together with gladness and sincerity of heart, praising God and having favor with all the people" (Acts 2:41–47). Belonging may not have included a membership roll, but it displayed a clear sense of membership with one another.[4]

---

3. Dietrich Bonhoeffer used the phrase "life together" to describe the church (*Life Together/ Prayer Book of the Bible*, Dietrich Bonhoeffer Works, vol. 5, ed. Geffrey B. Kelly, trans. Daniel W. Bloesch and James M. Burtness [Minneapolis: Fortress, 2005]). Since engaged in training seminarians, he wanted them to understand the church as a body instead of a cold, sterile institution. The editor explains, "The seminarians were to live *with* one another, but only in the spirit of being *for* one another. His community was a gathering of theological students whose 'togetherness' was to be characterized by an unselfish love for one another expressed in the willingness to serve each other, even to be inconvenienced by one another, to intercede for one another in prayer, to extend forgiveness in the name of the Lord, and to share the bread of the Lord's Supper" (8, emphasis original). That describes the practice of the church in the book of Acts.

4. Benjamin L. Merkle observes, "Although there is no proof from the New Testament that the names of new converts were written on a list, such a list would be consistent with the multitude of lists recorded in the Old Testament" ("The Biblical Basis for Church Membership," in *Those Who Must Give an Account: A Study of Church Membership and Church Discipline*, eds. John S. Hammett and Benjamin L. Merkle [Nashville: B&H Academic, 2012], 32).

Paul told the Ephesian church to live with one another in such a way—with humility, gentleness, patience, and "showing tolerance for one another in love"—that they might be "diligent to preserve the unity of the Spirit in the bond of peace" (Eph. 4:2–3). As a Spirit indwelled corporate body, they preserved the unity of the Spirit *among them as members of one another* (Eph. 4:21–22). When Paul commended the Philippian church for their generosity toward him, he narrowed his thanks to the members of that fellowship united in concern for him through supplying his needs (Phil. 4:10–20).

Peter showed the connection or belonging the churches he addressed had experienced as "living stones" that "are being built up as a spiritual house for a holy priesthood" (1 Peter 2:5). John wrote to particular congregations, one addressed cryptically as "the chosen lady and her children" and the other under the leadership of "the beloved Gaius" (2 John 1; 3 John 1). He considered issues demonstrating a personal knowledge of a group united together in Christ. The identity of the seven churches of Asia Minor (Rev. 1–3) shows clearly defined members of congregations with responsibilities to one another for the church's testimony in the community and accountability to the Lord.

Church membership, by whatever name a local church might call it, has strong biblical precedent that gives members responsibility for one another. As Jonathan Leeman notes, "A church *is* its membership."[5]

Pastoral Concern

The various exhortations for pastoral labors point to particular elders/pastors of particular local congregations, serving their particular pastoral needs (Eph. 4:11–16; 1 Thess. 5:12–13; 1 Tim. 5:17; Titus 1:9; Heb. 13:17; 1 Peter 5:1–4). With church membership, elders recognize boundaries within which to exercise their God-designed ministries. They would live in frustration if held accountable for *everyone* living in their town instead of those people who, by reason of covenanting together in membership in a particular church, God calls to obey and submit to their leadership (Heb. 13:17).

Membership is a *local* identification.[6] Reforming the church's membership often involves the tedious process of locating members that have moved away or no longer attend in order to remove their membership to narrow the responsibility for pastoral ministry.

---

5. Jonathan Leeman, *Church Membership: How the World Knows Who Represents Jesus,* 9Marks Building Healthy Churches (Wheaton, IL: Crossway, 2012), 46.
6. Exceptions are members in the military, in mission service, at the university, or similar circumstances that temporarily remove them from local participation. The church should continue serving them as warranted.

Leeman offers what he calls a "clunky definition" of church membership, but one that proves helpful in understanding the pastoral concern in church membership: "*Church membership is a formal relationship between a church and a Christian characterized by the church's affirmation and oversight of a Christian's discipleship and the Christian's submission to living out his or her discipleship in the care of the church.*"[7] While the entire church works together to help one another as members to live as disciples of Jesus, pastors/elders serve as the primary teachers and models for the church (1 Tim. 3:2; 5:17; Titus 1:9; Heb. 13:7). As shepherds, they guard the flock from false teaching and destructive heresy. As elders, they model the Christian life and wisely direct the church toward faithfully following the teaching of God's Word. As overseers, they take the lead in helping the church to fulfill its God-given responsibilities. That cannot be done effectively for those not regularly attending (apart from physical reasons). Pastors need to know for whom they're responsible. An accurate membership of those following the church's membership requirements makes this possible. Otherwise, the church needs to engage in a process of refining membership requirements and taking steps to remove those unwilling to continue in covenant with one another.

Since pastors hold this kind of responsibility and give accountability to Christ for how they've shepherded his people, they cannot be casual about church membership (Acts 20:25–31; Heb. 13:17). As church leaders, they must seek to cultivate an atmosphere where members care for and encourage one another (Heb. 10:24–25). That happens best when the church's membership practices mirror early church precedent.

Life Together

Church membership should be limited to regenerate people[8] committed to helping one another live out the Christian life together.[9] The New Testament's forty-plus "one another" passages can only be practiced when people regularly gather together and participate in one another's lives. How do we love one another (John 13:34), be subject to one another (Eph. 5:21), encourage and build up one another (1 Thess. 5:11), be devoted to one another in brotherly love (Rom. 12:10), be hospitable with one another (1 Peter 4:11), give preference to one another in honor (Rom. 12:10), admonish one another (Rom. 15:14), and be tenderhearted toward one another (Eph. 4:32) when continually absent? It cannot happen. That calls for a church's membership to reflect those who *identify* with Christ and his body, and those who

---

7. Leeman, *Church Membership*, 64 (emphasis original).
8. Members failing to demonstrate regenerate life may be subject to church discipline (Matt. 18:15–20).
9. The exceptions to living life together would be for those members shut-in or with illnesses that prevents participation. Even with shut-ins, some continue ministry in the body by making phone calls, sending notes, and even inviting others to their homes for fellowship.

join in *practicing community* with the local body of Christ.[10] Outside of this identity and community, New Testament church membership does not exist. Therefore, if church practice shows otherwise, pastors must lead in reforming the church's membership practices. How should this reforming take place?

Refining Membership

Most churches have some type of membership requirement and expectation stated in a church constitution or polity document. Consider the following:

1. If those approved documents provide a good foundation for membership, then implementation may be all that's necessary to get started in refining membership.

2. But the polity needs to be changed if the membership requirements lack (a) the need for clear evidence of regeneration, (b) membership classes to discuss the church's doctrinal statement and church covenant, (c) an interview with some of the pastors/elders to discern understanding of the gospel and Christian testimony, (d) regular participation in the life of the church, and (e) accountability to live faithfully as Christians.

3. If the biblical practice of church discipline for erring members is not included (and practiced when needed), then it must also be changed (Matt. 18:15–20; 1 Cor. 5).

4. If these documents need to be changed, then a pastor must lead the way by laying biblical groundwork for understanding the nature of the church, its members, life together, and what the early church valued in its members. This process could take several years to bring to fruition, but it should be done carefully and as soon as possible.[11] Until a church's membership process follows biblical patterns, it will be difficult to improve the church's health.

Mark Dever outlines twelve practical steps to developing meaningful church membership.[12]

---

10. James G. Samra, *Being Conformed to Christ in Community: A Study of Maturity, Maturation and the Local Church in the Undisputed Pauline Epistles*, T&T Clark Biblical Studies (London: T&T Clark, 2006), 134.
11. See Hammett and Merkle, *Those Who Must Give an Account*, for a helpful study of membership and church discipline. See also in the present book, Questions 32, 33, 34, and 36.
12. Mark E. Dever, "The Practical Issues of Church Membership," in Hammett and Merkle, *Those Who Must Give an Account*, 96–101.

1. Regularly proclaim the gospel in your preaching.

2. Have and use a congregationally agreed-upon statement of faith and a church covenant.

3. Require attendance at membership classes before admitting individuals into membership in a congregation.[13]

4. Require an interview after individuals have been brought through the membership classes but before they have been recommended to the congregation for membership.

5. Do not baptize babies, and be careful about baptizing young children into formal local church membership.

6. Realize that admission into church membership is an act of the congregation.

7. Publish a membership directory in which the members of the church are represented by name, picture, physical address, email, and work and home phone numbers.

8. Give active pastoral oversight to the members.

9. Work to create a culture of discipleship in the church.

10. Limit some activities, events, and areas of service to members.

11. After membership is reinstituted in the church, revive the practice of corrective church discipline (including excommunication or exclusion).

12. Finally, recover something of the grandness of God's plan. Remind the congregation that the story we are involved in is greater than our local congregation.

Summary

Churches must be convinced of the biblical foundation and practice of church membership. Their pastors will know whom they serve in shepherding and teaching by understanding the framework and limits of membership.

---

13. See Mark Dever and Paul Alexander, *The Deliberate Church: Building Your Ministry on the Gospel* (Wheaton, IL: Crossway, 2005), 59–64.

Churches covenanting together in membership will encourage and spur one another forward, promoting growth in its health and witness. Refining membership practices may take time but must be a priority for pastors and church leadership.

REFLECTION QUESTIONS

1. What are some of the evidences of membership in the early church?

2. What is meant by Bonhoeffer's phrase "life together"?

3. How do the NT epistles give striking evidence of church membership?

4. How might a church begin to refine its membership practices?

5. Why are membership classes needed for the membership process?

How Can Pastors Recognize the Right Pace of Church Revitalization?

Have you ever had to revitalize the church that you planted? I have. Five years into the plant, it became painfully obvious we needed revitalization. During that period my poor theological understanding began to change. Through expounding the Scripture, I came face to face with theological truths I had never worked through. My heart flooded with joy and delight at what God was teaching me. As I learned, with fervor I also taught my congregation. Some responded with the same kind of joy I had experienced, others with skepticism. I kept preaching, teaching, and dialoguing as I shepherded the congregation to embrace the teaching of God's Word.

This theological shift naturally affected our methodology and worship. At that point, the need for revitalization began to surface. Despite numerical growth (and unfortunately, not healthy growth), the church had serious fault-lines when it came to understanding the authority of Scripture, the gospel and its implications, ecclesiology, and the church's mission. As I rejected my earlier pragmatism, some of the key leaders in the church disagreed. They did not want a church driven by the teaching of Scripture and centered on the gospel. I naively did not think these "friends" would go so far as to oppose the new direction but would listen to the teaching of the Word and follow.

At first, they quietly disagreed, then they grumbled among themselves, and finally their complaints spread throughout the church. At the same time, people that had helped me start the church began to concoct a plan to have me fired. It came to a head when the teachers of the two largest Sunday school classes asked to meet with a man who was a rising leader in the church. They wanted him to partner with them to oust me. Over breakfast, he stood up to them and confronted them biblically. At that moment, because he took a stand, their plan began to unravel. But before leaving, they infected enough of the church that, over a three-year period, about sixty-five percent of the congregation left.

We were then at about the eight-year mark of our church. Most of those pledging to pay for the new building we were in had left. Our finances dwindled with the congregation. But the Lord of the church held us in his hands, sustained us through difficult days, and began to transform the congregation week by week. The sense of unity in the church astounded us. We treasured it as a gift from God. We realized this unity centered in Jesus Christ and his gospel. Every aspect of the church—preaching, teaching, training, children, students, preschool, music, and church officers—were heading in the same direction, loving the same gospel, worshiping the same Lord Jesus, depending upon the same Holy Spirit, and delighting in studying the same Bible. Revitalization took place on the wings of the Word of God, prayer, and loving one another in the body.

Every church I have served needed revitalization. By my observation, most of the churches my friends have served have had the same need. But revitalization does not happen quickly or by short pastorates. It demands a pastor's willingness to suffer hardship, to endure opposition, to exercise patience in teaching and preaching, to keep on shepherding even those hard to shepherd, and to wait on the Lord to do the transforming and revitalizing work in the church that only he can do. What's the pace of appropriate church revitalization? We'll think about it under two categories.

Evaluate the Issues Causing the Need for Revitalization

Some assume a new pastorate with plans and programs galore. Churches generally don't mind new plans and programs as long as they do not disrupt the status quo or call for radical obedience to Jesus Christ. They associate new pastors with new programs, and a few wrinkles the church will adjust to. But plans and programs don't make disciples. Only the Word of God faithfully proclaimed in the power of the Holy Spirit can change a congregation into faithful followers of Jesus Christ (1 Cor. 2:1–5).

So, expect that most churches will react to a pastor faithfully expounding the Scripture. Calling for repentance and faith in Christ, pressing the gospel and its implications for all of life, and ordering the life of the church around the gospel exposes unbelief. Unless a church has been reordered by the gospel then reactions will eventually take place—sometimes immediately or at least within six months to a year. Therefore, pastors need to carefully evaluate the issues causing the need for revitalization in their congregation so that they might regularly address them through preaching, teaching, and discipling.

1. View of Scripture

My denomination (SBC) fought a historic battle over the authority of Scripture for many years, finally declaring victory—that we're a people of the

Book. Yet the biggest issue is still being faced: What does this inerrant Bible you say that you believe *teach*? A congregation *saying* they believe the Bible means very little until it works out in their daily lives. Is the Bible authoritative for salvation, life, doctrine, polity, and ministry? Some think church membership or baptism suffices for salvation rather than the Spirit's regenerating work (John 3:1–8; Acts 11:18; 1 Cor. 1:26–31; Titus 3:5–7; 1 Peter 1:17–25). When those holding such views rise to leadership in the congregation, that church faces perilous times. They ignore the Bible's doctrinal instruction and its design for ministry and mission. Rather than the Bible regulating the church's worship through the public reading of Scripture, praying Scripture, singing Scripture, confessing Scripture together, and preaching Scripture, they want worship services that make them feel better about their lifestyles, beliefs, and choices.[1] When you see that, the church needs revitalization.

2. View of the Gospel

What a church believes about the gospel of Jesus Christ will reveal a redeemed people passionate about serving Christ or a people masquerading as Christians. Questions must be asked. Is the church clear on the gospel? Is the gospel central to the church's life and worship? Is there the ongoing, joyful, grateful conversation about the gospel working among the members? Does the church so believe the gospel that it insists on regenerate church membership? Is there recognition and deep conviction that only through faith in Jesus Christ revealed in the gospel a sinner will be forgiven and transformed into a new creation? Does the church want the pastor to continue to preach and apply the gospel as he expounds the Scripture?

3. View of a New Testament Church

Part and parcel with holding to the authority of the Scripture and believing the biblical gospel is a congregation's view of what the New Testament calls a church. Does Scripture or the culture clarify what the church is and how it must conduct itself? Is there the humbling recognition that Jesus died for the church (Acts 20:28) so that the church might be his body and bride (Eph. 1:22–23; 5:23–32)? Is the church or the individual viewed as the focus of Jesus and his redemptive work (Eph. 1:3–14)? Is there an understanding of the necessity of regeneration to truly be part of the body of Christ (Eph. 2:4–10)? Is there the desire for the church to be pure and holy (Eph. 5:27)? Is there recognition that the way the church is organized and governed must not be left to culture or tradition but to the revelation of Holy Scripture (1 Tim. 3:1–13; Titus 1:5–9)? Is there desire for unity in the Spirit in the bond of peace (Eph. 4:3)? Is there the understanding that sound doctrine is foundational to

---

1. Brian Croft, *Biblical Church Revitalization: Solutions for Dying and Divided Churches* (Fearn, Ross-shire, UK: Christian Focus, 2016), 91–97.

a healthy church (Eph. 4:11–16; Titus 2:1)? The congregation may not fully grasp everything the Bible teaches about the church. But is the church moving in a biblical direction? Does the congregation and its leaders desire to follow what Scripture teaches about the church?

4. View of the Church's Mission

Do the members see the church as the body of Christ, and therefore engaged in Christ's mission in the world (1 Cor. 12; Eph. 3:4–13)? Do they believe the church *alone* constitutes the people of God and God's redeemed family (John 1:12–13; Eph. 2:19–22; 5:1–2; 1 Pet 2:9–10; Rev. 1:5–6; 21:9–11)? Do they believe the church is to live in contrast to the world as a testimony to the power of the gospel (1 Peter 1:13–16; 2:11–12)? Do they believe the church is to be an embassy of heaven and its members ambassadors for Christ (2 Cor. 5:16–21; Phil. 3:20–21)?[2] Do they believe the church has been entrusted to live out a gospel testimony and to proclaim the gospel locally and internationally with a view to disciple-making (Matt. 28:18–20; Rom. 1:16–17; 1 Peter 2:11–12)? Do they believe the church's members are to love and serve one another as evidence of Christ dwelling in them, and as a testimony to the watching world (Rom. 12:3–13; 15:1–7; Eph. 4:1–3; 4:14–5:2)?

Why all these questions? They serve to help the pastor to think through as he studies his Sunday texts and prepares to apply the Word to the congregation. Opportunities arise most Sundays to make firm application in one if not all of these critical areas that reveal the true heart of the church. As Andy Davis wisely puts it, "If you want to see a church reformed, put all your eggs in this one basket, the faithful teaching and preaching of the Word of God."[3] By having a clear picture of the issues that cause the need for revitalization, the pastor's preaching will help the church to see what God has spoken concerning his church.

Establish a Forward Pace toward Revitalization

Consider five important aspects of the pace toward revitalization.

1. Pastor the Church

A pastor can become so obsessed with the problems causing the need for revitalization he forgets the most basic need: shepherd the flock. The church may need revitalization due to a "progression of neglectful, unfaithful shepherds."[4] The pastor burdened to see Christ formed in the church (Gal.

---

2. Jonathan Leeman, *Political Church: The Local Assembly as Embassy of Christ's Rule* (Downers Grove, IL: IVP Academic, 2016), 22.

3. Andy Davis, "The Reform of First Baptist Church of Durham," *9Marks*, October 27, 2011, https://www.9marks.org/article/journalreform-first-baptist-church-durham.

4. Croft, *Revitalization*, 57.

4:19) must not neglect shepherding the wounded, hurting sheep. Take the time to visit members, eat meals with them, listen to their concerns without reaction, watch their response to your gentle care, gauge their listening to the Word expounded, and discuss sermons with them. Start a simple Bible study or discipleship group. Focus on discipling the church rather than trying to make changes during that first year (or maybe longer).

2. Preach Expositionally through Books of the Bible

Let the Word of God do the work of revitalization. Martin Luther famously said about the Reformation in Germany, "I simply taught, preached, wrote God's Word; otherwise I did nothing. And then, while I slept, or drank Wittenberg beer with my Philip and my Amsdorf, the Word so greatly weakened the papacy that never a prince or emperor did such damage to it. I did nothing. The Word did it all."[5]

Major on the gospel, genuine conversion, evidence of regeneration, and gospel applications in your preaching.[6] Highlight applications in the sermons. The pastor need not introduce changes he hopes to make. Just apply the Word. Let the Word do the work on the hearts of the church. Take the time to discuss with congregants what they're learning from the Word. Maybe schedule Sunday evening or midweek discussions on the sermon where the pastor further explains difficult doctrines. Do not be cowed by gruff voices or threats since as a pastor you will give an account to God for the way you shepherd the flock (Heb. 13:17). Demonstrate love and care for the body, as well as a commitment to stay long term—a minimum of ten years—to shepherd them through changes.[7]

3. Don't Be Surprised by Pushback

Someone will likely object to biblical preaching and emphasis on the gospel of Jesus Christ. They will certainly object to the biblical model for a NT church. When that happens, stand firm. *Unless a pastor is willing to stand firmly and to continue the work of biblical revitalization, that church will likely stay in bondage to spiritual apathy, coldness, and lifelessness.* Revitalization calls for courageous pastors, dependent upon Christ for the sake of his church. Standing in the presence of church bullies is never easy, but Christ has not called us to a life of ease. As Paul told Timothy, "But join with me in suffering for the gospel according to the power of God. . . . Suffer hardship with me, as a good soldier of Christ Jesus" (2 Tim. 1:8; 2:3).

---

5. Martin Luther, quoted by Davis, "Reform," 10.
6. See Question 25 for recommendations on a preaching plan.
7. Brian Croft, *Revitalization*, 103. I agree with ten years as minimum, but longer is better.

4. Be Sensitive to the Holy Spirit

Be a man of prayer. Jesus Christ has promised that the gates of Hades will not overpower his church (Matt. 16:18). So, seek his face. Trust his promises. Call upon his name to work among his people, even if that means he removes some who do not genuinely follow him. Live and walk in the Spirit so that you remain sensitive to promptings of when to speak and when to be silent, whom to challenge and train, and whom to confront and call to repentance. Throughout, walk humbly with Christ and boldly in the truth.

5. Be Decisive When Time to Act

Be willing to face loss.[8] Be willing to suffer intense opposition. Be willing, if need be, to even take a pay cut in order to see this work of revitalization through.[9] If it is a matter of changing polity and moving to elder plurality or establishing membership classes as prerequisite for membership or requiring signing a church covenant that expresses a member's commitment to the body or changing the church's governing documents or changing the worship to reflect gospel-centeredness, then do it decisively, boldly, and humbly in dependence upon the Lord. The first attempt may not pass. So, keep shepherding the flock, expounding the Word, majoring on the gospel, praying for the Lord to work, and being sensitive to the Spirit. The second or third time to move toward major changes may be the point where those opposing biblical ministry give up. When that happens, the church begins to change in significant ways to the glory of God.

Summary

Most churches that call a man to serve as pastor will be in need of revitalization. Before seeking to make appropriate changes toward revitalization, pastors need to determine they will stay long enough to see it through. They need to willingly face the hardships required for this faithful work of shepherding a congregation until the Word does its work through the power of the Holy Spirit. Then, the difficulty and effort will be worth it all to see a church growing in health, unity, and faithfulness to the gospel.

---

8. Andy Davis's testimony about biblical reformation at First Baptist Church, Durham, showed his willingness to lose some battles in order to win the war; *Reform*, 1–8. See the *9Marks* journal November–December 2011 for more articles on revitalization: https://www.9marks.org/journal/revitalize-why-we-must-reclaim-dying-churches-and-how. For a lively discussion on revitalization, see Mike McKinley, *Church Planting Is for Wimps: How God Uses Messed-Up People to Plan Ordinary Churches That Do Extraordinary Things* (Wheaton, IL: Crossway, 2010).

9. I'm not counseling you to neglect your family's needs. Do everything possible to take care of your family, especially nurturing your wife through the difficult time of revitalization. I took a pay cut and worked outside the church to supplement income for a while. The loss was soon recovered as the church turned around.

REFLECTION QUESTIONS

1. What issues reveal the need for a church's revitalization?

2. How is the gospel central to understanding a church's spiritual vitality?

3. What is the most important focus that a pastor can have in leading a church toward biblical reformation?

4. How should a pastor handle objections to revitalization?

5. When does the pastor know that it's time to take decisive action toward revitalization?

How Should Pastors Help Their Congregations Face Suffering?

Every book of the Bible explicitly or implicitly considers suffering. Genesis shows the beginning of suffering in the fall (Gen. 3). Judges reveals national suffering with disobedience that led to oppression. Esther narrates the threat to annihilate the Jews. Malachi challenges the postexilic people experiencing loss through spiritual neglect. The Old Testament looks at every angle of suffering in a fallen world.

The New Testament does the same. John warns of tribulation in the world (John 16:33). Acts shows the church facing persecution (Acts 3–28). Romans ties glory to suffering (Rom. 8). First Timothy identifies suffering through false teaching (1 Tim. 1:3–7; 4:1–5; 6:3–5). Third John exposes suffering through an authoritarian leader (3 John 9–10). Revelation pictures suffering as prelude to Christ's return.

Throughout Scripture, hope in Christ shines brightly against this backdrop of suffering.

Suffering accompanies humanity. Previous generations, where dismal life expectancy and infant mortality confronted them daily, understood the normalcy of suffering.[1] Our generation—at least in the West, with so many perceived entitlements—often seems surprised at suffering. Yet the majority world lives with poverty, oppression rampant sickness and disease, civil conflict, spiraling inflation, limited healthcare, natural disasters, cruel dictators, inequitable laws, persecution against Christians, and a host of other forms of suffering.

Suffering knows no boundaries. It may take different shapes in the West, but its effects prove just as harsh and devastating as what others face. Debilitating disease, a young spouse's death, inability to conceive, workplace

---

1. Matthew McCullough, *Remember Death: The Surprising Path to Living Hope* (Wheaton, IL: Crossway, 2018), 31–56.

inequalities, suicide, racism, sexual abuse, poverty, job loss, rejection, way-ward children, addictions, terminal illnesses, church disunity, false teaching, sinful habits, mental illness, social oppression, and much more happen in the lives of those God calls us to shepherd. The gospel, though, changes the way that we face suffering. Pastors live in the challenge of walking alongside their members when they suffer. But before it happens in its many facets, pastors must help their congregations to face suffering with confidence in God's faith-fulness to his children. How can pastors through their ongoing ministries prepare their people to face suffering? Let's consider five ways that we prepare our congregations for suffering.

1. Live Life with Your Flock

Shepherding requires close contact with the sheep. Likewise, effective pas-toral ministry means involvement with our people. We preach and teach God's Word, while applying truth in our ongoing interactions. We live among each other, share meals, pray for one another, and laugh and weep together. Out of these relationships we learn to love each other with a depth of care, compas-sion, interest, and service that spills over from relationship with Christ. Loving one another, we join hands and hearts when suffering comes (1 Cor. 12:26). At that point, how we've loved, served, and listened over a period of years comes to fruition when walking alongside brothers and sisters in suffering. We seek to bear the load with them in our prayers, tears, and acts of support and care.

If pastors neglect living life and building relationships with the body, their pastoral voice will be weakened when suffering hits their members. Pastoral ministry in the day-in and day-out life of the congregation sets the stage for serving in the hard times.

2. Reflect upon the Bible's Teaching on Suffering

It astounded me to see that every book of the Bible presents some notion of suffering. Even in the romantic Song of Solomon, the bride indicates she experienced harsh treatment at the hands of her brothers (Song 1:6). Often the realities of sin bring on suffering through guilt, despondency, broken-ness, family destruction, and national calamities (e.g., 2 Sam. 11–20; Judg. 6). Many of the prophets reveal suffering of divine judgment due to sin (e.g., Amos, Nahum). Yet others suffer due to despair (Ps. 42) or death of a child (Luke 8:40–42, 49–56) or death of a spouse (Ruth 1:1–21) or persecution for proclaiming truth (Jer. 32) or debilitating illness (Luke 8:43–48) or national calamity (Lamentations) or unnamed infirmity (2 Cor. 12:7). The Psalms, Lamentations, Job, and Revelation, in particular, teach us how to lament when encountering suffering.[2]

---

2. See Mark Vroegop, *Dark Clouds, Deep Mercy: Discovering the Grace of Lament* (Wheaton, IL: Crossway, 2019), who clearly demonstrates the place of lament in Christian life and worship.

We expose our congregations to the realities of suffering when we regularly expound God's Word. We show that it comes in all shapes and dimensions, with none excluded from suffering. They need to see and hear Scripture's description of suffering's blunt force in order to prepare them to face suffering in the present. But more, we show them how to live in suffering when those same expositions make clear the power and effect of the gospel of Christ. Here we teach them to live with radiant hope in the gospel. Christ's death, resurrection, and gospel promises support for his people in the hardest times. We show them how suffering detaches us from clinging to the world as ultimate so that we rest in the hands of the Ultimate One.

3. Build a Theological Framework for Teaching on Suffering

Good theology lashes us to truth that works out in the crucible of life. Doctrinally rich exposition couches theology from its roots in the biblical text, so that members learn to apply the Word they're reading and hearing. Aside from salvation, there may be no realm of life that more desperately needs a theological framework than journeying through suffering. Believers weighed down with suffering's bitter force need to see God's design for them to continue persevering through the suffering.

During two sabbatical periods, I spent time studying the biblical teaching on hope. Then in July 2018, I received a diagnosis of a rare non-Hodgkins lymphoma that sent me clinging to what I had studied. The theological framework that considered the nature of God, soteriology, anthropology, providence, eschatology, and Christology buoyed me in the heaviness that I faced. Having taught on these theological truths in my regular expositional ministry not only readied me to walk through this ongoing physical and mental suffering, but also served my wife, children, and congregation. I experienced firsthand that a sturdy theological framework gives suffering members a strong tower of refuge in the Lord's faithfulness to his people.[3]

4. Walk with Your Members through Suffering

Not long after a year of treatment for mantle cell lymphoma, my wife and I reflected one night on how difficult the past months had been, especially when the treatment intensified and required hospital stays. I felt weakness like I'd never imagined. In the darkness of the night, tethered to an IV pole with poisonous chemicals dripping into my veins, I felt like death had enveloped me. Yet the body of Christ prayed. Family and friends visited, texted, emailed, and called. At just the right moment, someone offered a word of encouragement, a card that lifted my spirits, or the sturdiness of bearing my burden. On that

---

3. As an example of how this works out in a very personal way, consider the following talk that I gave to my congregation in 2019, just two months after my last chemo treatment: http://www.southwoodsbc.org/sermons/reflections-on-romans-8-and-r-hyper-cvad.

night, I started uncontrollably weeping. My wife kept asking what was wrong. But I couldn't stop weeping long enough to tell her. Finally, when I gathered my emotions, I told her that I suddenly realized what I had been doing hundreds of times through forty-plus years of pastoral ministry. I had been coming alongside church members in suffering, seeking to shoulder their burden, reading God's Word, explaining truth about his faithfulness, and praying for them in their need. Now, on the receiving end with others ministering to me, I realized how vital pastoral ministry to those suffering really is.[4]

I visited with a man that recently had surgery and is struggling to recover. I read Psalm 121 and kept showing how the psalmist emphasized the keeping power of the Lord. That's his faithfulness! Then I quoted 1 Peter 1:5: we "are protected by the power of God through faith for a salvation ready to be revealed in the last time." I prayed for him and applied the text in prayer. When we finished, I looked up to see tears in his eyes. I knew that while he suffered, the Lord had allowed me to bear a little of his burden by speaking God's Word into his life.

By visits, pastoral prayers, handwritten notes, calls, and text messages, join in burden bearing for those enduring suffering. Point them to the sufficiency of Christ in all things and in all times.

5. Help Your Members See God's Purpose in Suffering

The visceral struggle with suffering doesn't disappear in the pages of Scripture. David prayed, "How long, O Lord? Will you forget me forever? How long will You hide Your face from me?" (Ps. 13:1). "O God, You have rejected us. You have broken us; You have been angry; O, restore us. You have made the land quake, You have split it open; heal its breaches, for it totters. You have made Your people experience hardship; You have given us wine to drink that makes us stagger" (Ps. 60:1–2). David prayed with the consciousness that God's providence brought on suffering to bring him low, so that he might find rest in God's presence, promises, and power at work in his need. He understood, as Elisabeth Elliot wrote, "Suffering is never for nothing."[5]

A few reflections on God's purpose in suffering will help pastors to gently, faithfully speak into the lives of their people as they teach them how to live as Christians in suffering.

- Suffering is normal in a fallen world (2 Tim. 2:3).

- Suffering is assured due to opposition to Christ and the gospel (2 Tim. 3:12).

---

4. For an example of how to serve the terminally ill, see my article "Seven Ways to Shepherd the Terminally Ill," *Gospel Coalition*, June 11, 2019, https://www.thegospelcoalition.org/article/7-ways-shepherd-terminally-ill.

5. Elisabeth Elliot, *Suffering Is Never for Nothing* (Nashville: B&H, 2019).

- Suffering builds hope in the believer for seeing Christ (2 Cor. 4:16–5:5).

- Suffering is an instrument for maturity, purity, and glory (1 Peter 1:6–9).

- Suffering strips away the extraneous and unimportant (2 Cor. 12:7–10).

- Suffering sharpens our senses and intensifies our focus on eternal things (Ps. 42).

- Suffering makes us aware of our sinfulness and weakness (Ps. 38).

- Suffering teaches us the importance of lament (Ps. 13).

- Suffering increases our prayer life (Ps. 55).

- Suffering opens new insights into God's Word (Ps. 119:71).

- Suffering detaches us from the world (Phil. 1:12–26).

- Suffering unites the church in dependence upon Christ (Acts 4:1–32).

- Suffering reminds us of life's brevity and future glory (Rom. 8:18–39).

- Suffering brings us into Christ's afflictions (Col. 1:24).

A good theological foundation laid in regular ministry brings these truths into focus during members' suffering. They serve the church to persevere in confidence that "suffering is never for nothing."

Summary
Relationships between pastors and congregations built around the gospel lay groundwork for serving one another in times of suffering. Steeped in the biblical richness of how God works in suffering, pastors can come alongside their people to help them walk in hope and joy. Pastors serve the flock while ministering the Word, making personal contact, and giving ongoing support through difficult times. As pastors reflect on suffering, they can better serve their congregations as they travel through dark days.[6]

---

6. Consider the following resources: Sinclair B. Ferguson, *Deserted by God? Understanding the Ways of God through the Experience of the Psalmists* (Edinburgh: Banner of Truth Trust,

REFLECTION QUESTIONS

1. How pervasive in the Scripture is the subject of suffering?

2. What kind of theological themes help build a framework for facing suffering?

3. What are some biblical examples of suffering that reveal God's faithfulness behind the suffering?

4. What tangible ways can pastors serve their members during times of suffering?

5. How does understanding the varied purposes of God in suffering help pastors to serve church members in difficult days?

1993); John Flavel, *The Mystery of Providence* (1678; Edinburgh: Banner of Truth Trust, 1963); David Powlison, *God's Grace in Your Suffering* (Wheaton, IL: Crossway, 2018).

How Should Pastors Lead the Church to Engage in International Missions?

A few years ago, with my congregation's support, I traveled to a country with no welcome mat out for Christian workers. My mission was to serve national pastors and elders by teaching, answering ministry questions, engaging in dialogue, and seeing firsthand local church ministry in a persecution setting. Knowing that the local government spied on church gatherings left me wondering about the safety of these believers. Yet they seemed oblivious to the threat, focusing instead on learning how to lead their congregations with greater faithfulness. They taught me to trust the Lord and press on. My joy increased throughout the week as I witnessed the grace of God at work among them through the power of the gospel.

In its over thirty-three years of existence, the church I serve has sent out dozens of mission teams to do evangelism, pastoral training, children's work, field workers' support, construction, retreats, teaching, and preaching. An ethos of missions developed over the years so that being engaged in praying, giving, going, and sending has become normal for our church. But it did not happen immediately. Our pastors developed practices that helped us toward international mission engagement. What follows are some things we've learned about leading a church to engage in international missions.

Nurture Missions Thinking

The Antioch church under the leadership of Paul and Barnabas began to think beyond their congregation regarding the need for gospel work. When the Holy Spirit instructed the church leaders to set apart these two men for a mission call, the church responded without hesitation and continued their involvement with them throughout their missionary journeys (Acts 13:1–3; 14:26–28; 15:36–41; 18:22–23). They modeled what every church can do by praying, giving, going, and sending for the sake of missions. Two thousand years later, how do we nurture that kind of mission spirit in the local church?

1. Include Unreached People Groups in the Church's Life

An Unreached People Group (UPG) is a distinct ethno-linguistic people residing in one or more countries with less than 0.1 percent following Jesus Christ. Out of the 17,070 people groups in the world, according to the Joshua Project, 7,098 (3.15 billion people) remain unreached with the gospel.[1] The UPGs have little to no gospel witness among them. Some UPGs live among other people groups, for example, Afghan people living in Memphis. Others live in hard to reach or inaccessible places, for example, Dagestan people in the North Caucasus region of Russia or the Sivandi in Iran. Attention to UPGs through praying, giving, supporting workers among them, and sending short-term teams refocuses the church's mission aims.

2. Pray Weekly for UPGs and International Workers

To alert our congregation to the thousands of UPGs, we highlight one or two every week in our Sunday worship folder and include them in the pastoral prayer. The goal is to call the congregation's attention to the unique people that can only be reached by intentionally crossing the ethnic and linguistic barriers preventing them from hearing the gospel. Weekly, we corporately pray for missionaries or national workers with whom we're involved. That keeps both UPGs and international Christian workers before our congregation. We do try to be security-conscious in any public prayers or discussions about those serving in persecution areas.

3. Build Relationships with Missionaries and National Workers

A few years ago, I put a pastor friend in contact with a missionary working with a UPG. They continued corresponding and talking. That relationship developed with the pastor leading his congregation to send teams to this UPG. Relationships can start by a visit, correspondence, attending a missions conference, getting to know visiting national workers, and asking missionary personnel to put you into contact with other missionaries or national workers. These relationships develop into a strong support network for mission involvement.

4. Welcome Mission Testimonies

Welcome people to give testimonies in your church, whether members of your congregation serving internationally or other workers. I often do

---

1. See the homepage of the Joshua Project, https://joshuaproject.net. This site provides the most updated research on UPGs; plus, it provides daily prayer alerts for different UPGs that one may subscribe to.

interviews with visiting missionaries so that I can tailor their experiences to better help our congregation know how to serve them.

5. Train and Lead Short-Term Mission Exposure Trips

Short-term trips do not replace national or missionary workers, but they help the local church know how to better serve them; plus, they help clarify a mission's call among your members. Our members serving internationally first participated in a short-term trip before publicly expressing their call to serve long term in missions.

6. Promote Missions Giving

We support our denomination's international mission fund. But we also identify a different missionary or mission organization to highlight and give special gifts to each month, in order to help with their work. That has increased our mission giving and has increased the congregation's exposure to different mission work.

Engage in *Local* International Missions

During one visit to a "closed country,"[2] I had dinner with a wonderful Christian couple. Both were professionals and highly educated in their country. Their government sent them to a large Western city for more education and to participate in a fellowship in their field of study. While there, *local* believers took an interest in them. They had meals with them, did activities together, and helped them to get around the metropolitan area. They also invited them to attend their church. Although both were atheists, they decided to attend the services. They witnessed the corporate body loving and serving one another. They heard the gospel proclaimed and saw the gospel in action. Both came to faith in Christ. *Local* international missions proved fruitful.

When they returned to their home country after a two-year "discipling" during their work fellowship, they boldly witnessed to their families. They sought out a Christian congregation in their city and began to worship and fellowship with this "underground" church. I participated in this man being set apart as an elder by the same congregation.

Missions is not monolithic. It doesn't always involve a flight and visa or even another language. Cross-cultural missions has come to the doorstep of our communities through international students at our universities, businessmen joining local companies, technical workers receiving training in the United States, and a stream of tourists.

I sat next to a young man from Saudi Arabia on an international flight. He had spent several years attending an American university. While I could

---

2. One missionary friend reminded me that there are no "closed countries," just some a little harder to access.

not go to his country with missionary intent, he came to my country. I had the opportunity to engage him in gospel discussion and to give him a gospel e-book. His desire to continue to learn English would likely motivate him to read this e-book. Perhaps the Lord brought him to our country for the purpose of downloading a gospel book on his phone, reading it, and learning the good news while the Holy Spirit opened his heart.

Where do we find these internationals that might be here for one or more years? Visit local universities. Invite internationals to join your family for Christmas or Thanksgiving holiday. Be alert to major companies in your community that have multiple internationals. Look for opportunities to invite them for a meal or a visit in the city. Get involved with refugees, especially those coming from the hard-to-reach parts of the world. They welcome anyone who shows them care, helps them navigate the city, recommends medical and dental care, or helps them get their children involved in a local school. A refugee family that members of our church have reached out to attended our Good Friday service, where they heard the gospel proclaimed. Look for small stores or restaurants operated by those from UPGs trying to be part of the community. Visit with them and get to know them. For instance, a large Kurdish community lives in Nashville, Tennessee. Several local churches have taken on the challenge of reaching out to serve them, love them, and take the good news to them. No expense for international travel or hotel was needed, just time to visit and engage internationals.

Cultivate Missionaries through the Local Church

The mission call is twofold. First, there's an internal call, when the believer has the growing sense and desire to proclaim Christ and be engaged cross-culturally in gospel work. His or her consciousness of humanity's lost condition and the growing burden for a particular people intensifies this internal call. Second, there's an external call, when the local church where he or she is in covenant recognizes this burden for international missions and cross-cultural gifts for evangelism. That generally happens when the church has observed both the believer's faithfulness in engaging people locally with the gospel and a true love for internationals. It may be spurred by the way the believer has responded to an international mission trip with a passion for continuing the work as a calling.

How does the pastor lead the church to cultivate church members for international gospel work?

1. Pray for the Lord of the Harvest to Send Out Laborers into the Harvest (Matt. 9:36–38)

Instead of praying generically in corporate worship, pray for UPGs by name, as mentioned previously. Pray for new workers to take the gospel to them. Some mission organizations provide details on UPGs that can be incorporated in the church's regular praying.[3]

2. Preach on Mission Texts throughout the Scripture
I've found through the normal exposition through books that I regularly encounter mission texts, as well as texts with mission application. Help the congregation understand missions as the normal work of local churches rather than a task belonging to parachurch groups.

3. Invite Missionaries to Speak to Your Church
Ask local families to host them for a meal or as overnight guests. Conduct interviews with the missionaries or open the floor for a question and answer time. Aim toward your church becoming familiar enough with missionaries that they not only recognize their names when mentioned but they also seek to communicate with them as prayer partners.

4. Utilize Mission Stories for Illustrations in Preaching and Teaching
Mission biographies, stories on mission websites, and personal correspondence and conversation provide great sources for increasing missions consciousness. Maintain anonymity for any stories of those serving in high-security areas.

5. Keep the Church Regularly Involved in Mission Giving
A significant portion of the church's budget should go toward missions, as well as gifts given to support special needs or projects.

6. Lead Members of the Congregation on Short-Term Mission Exposure Trips
The pastor's lead and involvement on short-term mission trips will help members willingly travel outside their comfort zones. Participation allows members to see firsthand what takes place in global settings as missionaries build relationships, teach the gospel, and plant churches. Plus, it allows the pastor an opportunity to observe members with cross-cultural gifts.

7. Recognize Potential Missionaries in the Congregation
When the elders recognize someone's interest in missions, then continue the conversation: read mission books together, pray together for missionaries and UPGs, watch for cross-cultural inclinations, visit local internationals, enlist the person to help lead a study on missions, and encourage him or her to visit a mission setting with the church supporting the effort. Pray for the Lord

---

3. For instance, see the Southern Baptist Convention's International Mission Board webpage at www.imb.org, or YWAM's page on UPGs in South Asia at www.ywamfrontiermissions.com.

to give the congregation discernment about that person serving internationally. The local church that lives with a global missions consciousness will be keen to recognize when the Lord's hand appears to be on a member for missionary service. Then the church affirms the internal call by their external affirmation.

Summary

Local churches have the responsibility to engage the nations with the good news of Jesus Christ. The pastor must lead the way by nurturing missions thinking in his congregation. He may further this nurturing by leading the church to engage *local* internationals. This helps with crossing language and cultural barriers to take the good news to those the Lord has brought near. An atmosphere that welcomes mission work may lead to new volunteers from the congregation to be sent out by the church for Christian service.

REFLECTION QUESTIONS

1. What are some ways the pastor can nurture his church with missions thinking?

2. What is an Unreached People Group?

3. Why should there be an emphasis congregationally on Unreached People Groups?

4. What are the potential effects of short-term mission trips?

5. How might a pastor cultivate missionaries in his local church?

How Does a Pastor Know When to End Ministry and Transition to Another?

When we think about ministry transition, no scriptural pattern fits our scenario. The ancient church did not operate with résumés, pastoral candidating, and church calls. The Jerusalem church sent representatives to help other churches (Acts 8:14; 11:22). The first missionary journey established elder plurality in new congregations (Acts 14:23). Paul left Silas and Timothy in Berea (Acts 17:15) and, quite possibly, Luke in Philippi.[1] He assigned trainees to serve as apostolic delegates in Ephesus (Timothy and Tychicus) and Crete (Titus and Artemas). Those churches operated under the wisdom and authority of the apostles.

Overall, the early church functioned in a smaller geographical region—with missionary journeys expanding that range. They developed leaders from within or by apostolic appointment. We live in a different era, with varied circumstances in local ministries and far more churches to be served. Yet we still have men called by the Spirit and affirmed to gospel ministry by local churches. With training and mentoring, as in the early church, they desire to serve Christ's churches. These circumstances call for churches to connect with pastoral candidates for consideration as their shepherds. Once called, a pastor might spend his life with one congregation, but probably most don't. So how does a pastor work through the possibility of transitioning to another pastorate?[2] Working from the assumption that a pastor presently serves a congregation and senses the possibility of transitioning to another pastorate,

---

1. The so-called "we passages" in Acts 16 (e.g., vv. 10, 13, 16) change to "they" after Philippi (Acts 17:1), and resume in Acts 20:6, indicating that Paul may have left Luke to continue pastoral work in Philippi.
2. Harry L. Reeder, "When to Accept a Call or Leave My Church," in *Fifteen Things Seminary Couldn't Teach Me*, eds. Collin Hansen and Jeff Robinson (Wheaton, IL: Crossway, 2018), 85–92.

church plant, or mission work, let's consider some questions that will help to work through this major challenge in pastoral ministry.

Questions to Consider *before* Pursuing Pastoral Transition

Consider these questions before you start a process to transition. Let them assist your thinking and discussions with your wife and/or confidants about the wisdom in transitioning to another pastoral ministry.

1. *Do you need a good vacation or sabbatical instead of pastoral transition?*

A pastor can reach a point where he thinks he can survive ministry only by a new pastorate. However, time away may invigorate him in his present ministry. Be sure to schedule a weekly day off and yearly vacations. Work to build a sabbatical into pastoral rhythm. A month sabbatical every five to seven years will renew a pastor's ministry. Prayerfully discern whether you just need a good break instead of a new pastorate.

2. *Are you focused on your pastoral responsibilities?*

We can become so engrossed in issues and problem people that we lose sight of preaching, discipling, and shepherding. Check out your spiritual disciplines. Are you faithfully walking with the Lord? A new pulpit won't change you when you're failing to nurture your spiritual life. Consider ways that you might improve your walk to refocus on your pastoral work before pursuing transition.

3. *Is your motivation to leave in order to avoid some people in your church?*

If you've been unwilling to deal with bitterness, anger, and resentment toward some members, do not think transitioning will clear your responsibility as a Christian (Eph. 4:32; Luke 17:1–4). Sin patterns tend to follow us wherever we go. Leaving to avoid gospel application is not a legitimate reason for transition.

4. *Has the church neglected caring for you and your family?*

A humble discussion with church leaders may be the first step instead of updating your résumé. Do they demonstrate care for your family's spiritual needs? Sometimes church leadership fails to notice how the compensation package has not kept up with your needs. If they're able to do something but unwilling to properly care for your needs, then that might be a signal that a move should happen (1 Thess. 5:12–13; 1 Tim. 5:17). Not every church can adequately compensate a pastor as his family grows. If the pastor and his family wisely steward their resources yet continue to come up short, and the church has no willingness to help, then he either needs to find a part-time job to assist with the needs or earnestly seek the Lord about transitioning. It may be that a little time and belt-tightening will suffice; otherwise evidence to transition will be clear.

5. Is opposition to your ministry the motivation to pursue transitioning?

If opposition is motivating you, then realize that the next pastorate will likely be no different. Every pastor serving for a few years in ministry faces opposition. The nature of gospel preaching brings opponents to the surface. Failures in our pastoral care and work can produce opponents, too. Instead of transitioning, consider whether staying and working through opposition would be best for you and for the church.

6. Have you hit a wall in ministry so that you secretly want an easier path?

Sometimes we think we can bear no more, so we must leave. We decide that we'll recycle old sermons to get us through a few years and then move on to another church. But those thoughts expose an unwillingness to "suffer hardship . . . as a good soldier of Christ Jesus" (2 Tim. 2:3). Check your motives. They may be good and right; or they may be skewed by laziness and indiscipline. Discern the difference.

7. Is your motivation to transition for a larger or better-known church?

There's nothing wrong with pastoring a larger church. Yet in doing so, the pastor will answer to God for shepherding more of his flock. Guard against rashly thinking you deserve a larger flock. That may be the Lord's plan, but before moving in this direction, make sure you're faithfully shepherding those presently under your charge.

8. Are you convinced transitioning makes for a better ministry?

While your present ministry may be difficult, you do not know what you will face in a new pastorate. I remember thinking, as I transitioned to another pastorate, that all would be much better. My thinking proved totally wrong. Guard your motives. A change of ministry does not guarantee a better pastorate.

9. Have you taken the church as far as they are willing to go, so that you think you serve to no effect?

You may have reached a point where your gifts and abilities no longer fit that particular church. In such a case, they show no more interest in biblical preaching and teaching, no desire to mature, no willingness for Scripture to shape polity, and no concern for gospel outreach and mission. If you've given several years in patiently shepherding yet they still show no interest, it may be time to transition. The years you've spent with them could be divine preparation for another pastorate.

Questions to Consider When Pursuing Pastoral Transition

If the previous questions confirm transitioning to another church, use these questions to help you sort through the decision.

1. Have you prayed through until God's peace fills your heart about transitioning?

Paul, Silas, and their missionary team sought to go to Asia Minor and then to Bithynia, but being prayerful and sensitive to the Spirit, they had no peace about those intentions (Acts 16:6–7). This example instructs us. Rather than feeling anxiety about a move, we're to seek the Lord until God's peace guards our hearts (Phil. 4:6–7).

2. Do you sense that God has released you from your present pastorate?

Obviously, the subjective nature of this question calls for much prayer, soul searching, evaluation of motives, and sensitivity to the Holy Spirit's leading. I had served one church for four-and-a-half years when I sensed a burden to plant a church in a metropolitan area. We had made a lot of progress in the church, with room to continue. Yet I could not shake the church-planting burden. I did not move immediately, but gave time to pray, study church planting, investigate a possible field, and discuss the idea with my wife and close friends. After months of working through this process, I sensed release from my pastorate, and so moved forward. That didn't mean I faced no fears or uncertainties, since I had never planted a church, but resolute peace filled my heart about the transition.

3. Is there another church pursuing you, or are you simply testing the waters?

During one period, a church sent their pastoral search committee at different times to listen to me preaching where I served. Many things about the church attracted my attention. But they never formally contacted me. Their visits piqued my interest, but without any official contact, I realized that I had to quell my thoughts. They went a different direction, and looking back, I saw God's providence at work to strengthen me where I served. Without pursuit by a particular church, a pastor may utilize contacts to test for opportunities, yet while doing so, he should keep his focus on shepherding the flock *still* entrusted to him.

4. If you are married, does your wife totally concur with transitioning to another pastorate?

Unity between each other in such a decision will be essential. Building resentment in a hasty, little-discussed decision of this importance can unravel a marriage and unsettle a ministry. Do you and your wife see your family settling into a ministry rhythm in the new church? Are you willing to patiently work through adjustments together?

5. Do your closest confidants concur with the decision to transition?

Sometimes close friends may discern motives that we cannot see. Their frankness may temper the idea of moving, or it may give encouragement to move forward. In a healthy church, your fellow elders who best know you and the church can offer wise counsel.

6. Do you sense a burden to shepherd the church that pursues you?

The question is not, Are you looking for a new pulpit or better facilities or improved salary or more staff; rather, do you sense love and desire to shepherd them through the Word, pastoral care, counsel, and leadership?

7. Have you discussed doctrinal, ecclesiological, and pastoral beliefs and convictions with the new church?

It may be that you do not cross every *t* and dot every *i* with the new church, but there should be enough agreement or openness to your teaching that you will not begin the work in a theological quandary. That doesn't mean you will not face questions or even challenges to your doctrinal positions as you work through Scripture. What you want to discern, then, will be the teachable spirit of the church, what they've been taught by former pastors, and the desire to be shaped by God's Word.[3]

Summary

These questions serve to help you to seek God's will with understanding when considering a pastoral move. Ultimately, after weighing your answers to these questions, the peace of God will need to direct you in the final decision. If you transition, seek to do so with graciousness toward the church you leave and faithfulness to the new one you serve. If you stay, then learn from the probing and questioning that you've done to help you be a more effective pastor. Never look back and wonder, "What if I had gone?" You didn't, so focus on serving your congregation. God will take care of that other church's needs without you dreaming about *what if!*

REFLECTION QUESTIONS

1. How does our current process of pastoral transition differ from the early church?

2. Why should a pastor question and reflect before considering a transition?

---

3. On the importance of standing by your convictions, see H. B. Charles, *On Pastoring: A Short Guide to Living, Leading, and Ministering as a Pastor* (Chicago: Moody, 2016), 59–63.

3. What misplaced motives might give a false reading on transition?

4. How might a pastor discern if God has released him from his current pastorate?

5. Why should the pastor discuss doctrinal, ecclesiological, and pastoral convictions when considering another church?

Why Should Pastors Aim for Long Pastorates?[1]

My generation learned a lot about ladders but little about roots. Talk among my college ministerial association and seminary community had little to say about putting down roots in a church and staying for the duration. We talked leaps, not longevity.

Twenty-five years after those academic days and fifteen years into my present pastorate, someone asked, "How long do you plan on staying at South Woods?" I'd not given that much thought. I blurted, "I guess the rest of my ministry." My mind churned with that hurried comment. Staying for the duration went against youthful naivety. But by that stage I found it deeply satisfying. Yet I knew staying until the reins need to be turned over to another would not happen automatically but demanded prayer-saturated labor. The process since then, and the horizon ahead, has given me immeasurable joy in the thirty-plus years I've served my congregation. Throughout the time, I've been learning a few lessons about the joy of putting down lasting roots.

A Case for Roots

Accepting a church's call to pastor doesn't guarantee longevity. Some churches and congregations mesh well. Others don't. It might be due to the pastor's lack of maturity, particular gifts, family dynamics, personality, cultural background, or other distinctions. Or it could be due to the congregation's mentality, impatience with the pastor's weaknesses, financial neglect, poor view of the local church, lack of concern for growth in grace, or other

---

1. This chapter is adapted from Phil A. Newton, "The Joy I Can Know over a Long Tenure," in *Fifteen Things Seminary Couldn't Teach Me*, eds. Collin Hansen and Jeff Robinson (Wheaton, IL: Crossway, 2018), 129–37 (used by permission).

matters. Yet in such a setting where the young pastor has little chance of longevity, he may struggle with guilt over the thought of leaving.

Once, a gifted young pastor needed to move where he could put down
deep roots. Guilt froze him in pastoral idealism. But guilt doesn't cultivate joy.
It stymies pastoral roots and offers a poor rationale for a long tenure. I nudged
him to consider another ministry where he might best use his gifts. His move
has proven fruitful as his roots keep digging deeper.

Yet that doesn't mean moving is always best. A healthy pause to survey
the field of ministry may slow down the greener-pasture syndrome. Short
pastorates keep looking across the fence to find a little better pasture. They
pay scant attention to the potential of sustained ministry that endures the
seasons and strains that ultimately lead to joy.

I went through such a season around years six through eight in my current pastorate. Sundays were difficult. Murmuring and dissension challenged
my focus. But the Lord sustained me and worked in the congregation in this
time of strife and weakness. The congregation and I needed to learn together
about grace, perseverance, pastoral ministry, and true joy that could only be
discovered in the fire of struggles.

People left, finances dipped, but the gift of unity in the body unexpectedly
grew. I would have missed the unbridled joy of unity in Christ that the fire re-
fines and polishes had I peered too long over the fence and bolted to another
pasture. Some joys can only be experienced in the grace of perseverance.

Bumps in the Journey

Pastoral longevity will meet with bumps in the journey. The seminary
dream of smooth pastoral sailing was just a mirage. Shepherding involves
dealing with sheep. Sheep are messy. And the shepherd is not the sweetest
smelling fellow on the hillside either. The clash of personalities, spiritual
warfare, unregenerate church members, turf lords, power grabbing, communication failures, misunderstandings, leadership changes, expositional
preaching, theological clarity, immaturity, and inexperience all combine to
create bumps—sometimes big bumps. However, that's the pastoral journey.
If a pastor would do more than the typical three- to four-year stop-off on the
way to bigger and better things, he will need to learn to persevere through
the bumps.

Only in a persevering ministry that presses through the difficulties will a
pastor know the joys of triumph in spiritual warfare, the unity of once con-
flicting personalities, and the reordering of polity structures to practice servant leadership. On two occasions, six to eight years after removing members
in church discipline, I've had the joy of asking the congregation to restore
them to fellowship. A *journeyman* pastor would likely have missed out on the
experience of seeing redemptive church discipline work.

Realistically, the soil of a particular church may not fit a pastor's roots. Yet he must test the soil by faithfulness in life, devotion to Christ, humble shepherding, and dogged perseverance to see if the church he serves is precisely where the Lord is pleased to plant him. What does it take for this kind of endurance?

1. Passion for the Congregation

A pastor can look at his duties as just a means of compensation, continuing until something better comes along. However, the Lord of the church calls us to humbly shepherd and serve a portion of his flock, preach the Word, comfort in need, correct when erring, encourage toward perseverance, and exemplify faithfulness to Christ (see Acts 20:28; 1 Peter 5:1–4; 1 Tim. 4:11–16; 6:17–21; 2 Tim. 2:1–26; 3:10–4:5; Heb. 13:17). The fruit in that kind of ministry may be long in coming, but it's more certain when the pastor stays with the flock.

Passion for the flock grows when we spend time with them, listening, serving, and praying for them. I didn't grasp that well in early pastorates. I liked serving, and even spending time with *some* of them, but regularly praying for them and listening to them didn't quite fit my busy routine. I had years to go before I developed the passion for a congregation with whom I might spend my life in ministry.

2. Willingness to Persevere

Perseverance taxes us. Without perseverance, a testy elders meeting, the brunt end of a rumor, disagreement with staff, or a run-in with ornery members leads to updating the résumé. Long pastorates are *always* tested pastorates. Perseverance becomes the grace-laden tracks on which long pastorates last.

3. Discipline for the Long Haul

Long tenures require developing sustainable patterns for study, counseling, leadership development, prayer, administration, and communication. They don't happen automatically. Pastors nurture them toward greater effectiveness by disciplines shaped through longevity.

Longevity requires setting boundaries on your schedule. You cannot do everything, so conquer the Superman complex. Be willing to delegate to others while you give attention to what you do best. This doesn't mean there's never any crossover or refusal to dirty your hands with a clogged toilet or other mundane issue. You're a servant, so willingly serve. But you're also a servant ministering the Word and shepherding the flock, so prioritize your schedule while doing so with grace and gentleness toward others (Acts 6).

4. Development of Lay and Staff Elders (Leaders)

You are not a one-man show. You're *the leader* of the team serving a congregation. Study Paul's ministry. He exceeded the normal person's abilities, yet he worked with a team around him. He trained others to serve with him and in the churches that he planted.[2]

As he told Timothy, "What you have heard from me in the presence of many witnesses entrust to faithful men, who will be able to teach others also" (2 Tim. 2:2 ESV). Timothy was evidence that Paul did what he told Timothy to do. You cannot sustain the demands of a lengthy ministry with healthy mind and heart apart from developing leaders around you who join in the work. Plus, you cannot develop the next generation of spiritual leaders by hopping from one church to another. One of my greatest joys has been the *slow process* of training future elders, pastors, missionaries, and leaders. That doesn't happen in a short pastorate.

Relationships Make for Longevity

You won't shepherd those you're unwilling to get close to. You certainly won't persevere in pastoral ministry if you keep the congregation at arm's length. You need close relationships that endure the years to help shape you, too. How is it done?

1. Invest

A fellow elder and I rode with a missionary in his community when he told us he needed to stop at a house and *invest* in someone. We wondered what he meant. As we thought about the financial term, we realized it fittingly described pastoral relationships. You invest in what is valuable to you to expand its value. As pastors we invest time, thought, energy, love, and service in those we desire to live in faithfulness to Christ. Long tenures allow you the joy of seeing returns on your *investment*.

2. Pray

As a young pastor, I heard another pastor tell how he prayed each week for every member of his church. His comment rebuked me. It changed my pastoral relationships. You will build long relationships with those you regularly take before the throne of grace. As you labor in prayer for them, you grow in love, passion, and longing for the flock. You find that despite their many idiosyncrasies, you want to stay with them. Calling them *family* is no longer ministerial bravado. The years prove you gladly feel it.

3. Listen

Relationships involve communication. The biggest side of communication is listening. As those accustomed to speaking, we sometimes find it difficult to listen. We want to dish out nicely framed speeches, then hurry

---

2. See Phil A. Newton, *The Mentoring Church: How Pastors and Congregations Cultivate Leaders* (Grand Rapids: Kregel Ministry, 2017), 163–82.

to the next thing on our list. But relationships call for patience, gentleness, and tenderness. When you spend time listening, you find satisfaction in serving a brother or sister. In the process, your roots dig deeper into the congregation's soil. The joy of life together in the body rewards the years of faithful ministry.

4. Participate

Participate in the joys and sorrows of your congregation. As the pastor you will likely be called on if there's a death or tragedy. Be there with heart and soul. But join in knowing and rejoicing in their joys too.

After spending more than thirty years with the same congregation, I've listened to problems, rejoiced at successes, shared burdens, wept at losses, and laughed at joys. That builds relationships that endure difficult days, makes room for accepting my faults and weaknesses, and builds trust that allows others to listen to my teaching and counsel.

5. Shepherd

Shepherd the flock rather than preaching *at* them. Visualize the congregation as you prepare to stand before them with God's Word. Pray through your sermon with them on your heart. Look at them while you preach. Feel their heart cries, burdens, and needs as you apply the Word. With all their faults (and yours), the Lord of the church entrusted the flock to you. So, let the roots dig deeply into their lives. The long journey with them enriches your preaching with tender compassion, careful application, and confident hope in Christ. Your preaching will become more transparent as you, with all your weaknesses, trust in Christ to shepherd your flock.

6. Cherish

Cherish the diversity of the church as it displays the beauty and power of the gospel. If everyone were like you or me, the congregation would be entirely boring. Be grateful the Lord has put different backgrounds, ethnicities, personalities, and interests in the flock you're called to serve. Instead of complaining about their tics, give thanks that Christ finds pleasure in showing forth his glory among the people you serve. The pastoral transformation that results from cherishing the flock leaves you with untold joy in your calling.

Summary

Ladders work well to climb immoveable structures, but they lose their passengers when winds blow and structures shake. Strong roots, on the other hand, withstand the wind and storms, leaving firmness and steadfastness. Pastoral ministry traffics in the storms. By God's grace, only with strong roots in the congregation can pastors experience the immeasurable joy found in long ministry.

REFLECTION QUESTIONS

1. What circumstances and dynamics challenge pastoral longevity?

2. What kind of fruit does perseverance in pastoral ministry produce?

3. What is needed for pastoral longevity?

4. How do relationships endure in a lengthy pastorate?

5. What does "investing" in the congregation mean?

Selected Bibliography

Alexander, J. W. *Thoughts on Preaching*. 1864. Edinburgh: Banner of Truth Trust, 1988.

Allen, Lewis. *The Preacher's Catechism*. Wheaton, IL: Crossway, 2018.

Avis, Paul D. L. *The Church in the Theology of the Reformers*. Eugene, OR: Wipf & Stock, 2002.

Bridges, Charles. *The Christian Ministry with an Inquiry into the Causes of its Inefficiency*. 1830. Edinburgh: Banner of Truth Trust, 1967.

Brooks, Thomas. *Precious Remedies against Satan's Devices*. 1652. Puritan Paperbacks. Edinburgh: Banner of Truth Trust, 1968.

Bucer, Martin. *Concerning the True Care of Souls*. 1538. Translated by Peter Beale. Edinburgh: Banner of Truth Trust, 2009.

Calvin, John. *The Necessity of Reforming the Church*. 1844. Translated by Henry Beveridge. Dallas: Protestant Heritage Press, 1995.

Charles, H. B., Jr. *On Pastoring: A Short Guide to Living, Leading, and Ministering as a Pastor*. Chicago: Moody, 2016.

Dever, Mark. *Nine Marks of a Healthy Church*. Expanded edition. Wheaton, IL: Crossway, 2004.

Dever, Mark and Paul Alexander. *The Deliberate Church: Building Your Ministry on the Gospel*. Wheaton, IL: Crossway, 2005.

Greidanus, Sidney. *The Modern Preacher and the Ancient Text: Interpreting and Preaching Biblical Literature*. Grand Rapids: Eerdmans, 1988.

Hammett, John S. and Benjamin L. Merkle, eds. *Those Who Must Give an Account: A Study of Church Membership and Church Discipline*. Nashville: B&H Academic, 2012.

Hansen, Collin and Jeff Robinson, eds. *Fifteen Things Seminary Couldn't Teach Me*. The Gospel Coalition. Wheaton, IL: Crossway, 2018.

Hellerman, Joseph E. *When the Church Was a Family: Recapturing Jesus' Vision for Authentic Community*. Nashville: B&H Academic, 2009.

Helm, David. *Expositional Preaching: How We Speak God's Word Today*. 9Marks Building Healthy Churches. Wheaton, IL: Crossway, 2014.

Johnson, Dennis E. *Him We Proclaim: Preaching Christ from All the Scripture*. Phillipsburg, NJ: P&R, 2007.

Kimble, Jeremy M. *40 Questions About Church Membership and Discipline*. Grand Rapids: Kregel Academic, 2017.

Laniak, Timothy. *Shepherds after My Own Heart: Pastoral Traditions and Leadership in the Bible*. New Studies in Biblical Theology 20. Edited by D. A. Carson. Downers Grove, IL: IVP Academic, 2006.

Leeman, Jonathan. *Church Discipline: How the Church Protects the Name of Jesus*. 9Marks Building Healthy Churches. Wheaton, IL: Crossway, 2012.

Lloyd-Jones, D. Martyn. *Preaching and Preachers*. 40th anniversary edition. Grand Rapids: Zondervan, 2011.

Merkle, Benjamin L. *40 Questions About Elders and Deacons*. Grand Rapids: Kregel Academic, 2008.

Newton, Phil A. *The Mentoring Church: How Pastors and Congregations Cultivate Leaders*. Grand Rapids: Kregel Ministry, 2017.

Newton, Phil A. and Matt Schmucker. *Elders in the Life of the Church: A Guide to Ministry*. Grand Rapids: Kregel, 2014.

Piper, John. *Expository Exultation: Christian Preaching as Worship*. Wheaton, IL: Crossway, 2018.

———. *The Supremacy of God in Preaching*. Grand Rapids: Baker, 1990.

Ryken, Philip Graham, Derek W. H. Thomas, and J. Ligon Duncan III, eds. *Give Praise to God: A Vision for Reforming Worship*. Phillipsburg, NJ: P&R, 2003.

Sibbes, Richard. *The Bruised Reed*. 1630. Puritan Paperbacks. Edinburgh: Banner of Truth Trust, 1998.

Spurgeon, Charles H. *Lectures to My Students*. 1881. Pasadena, TX: Pilgrim, 1990.

Tidball, Derek. *Ministry by the Book: New Testament Patterns for Pastoral Leadership*. Downers Grove, IL: IVP Academic, 2008.

Watson, Thomas. *The Godly Man's Picture*. 1666. Puritan Paperbacks. Edinburgh: Banner of Truth Trust, 1992.

Scripture Index